TAKING THE JESUS ROAD

THE HISTORICAL SERIES OF THE REFORMED CHURCH IN AMERICA,
NO. 50

TAKING THE JESUS ROAD

**The Ministry of the Reformed Church in America
Among Native Americans**

LeRoy Koopman

WILLIAM B. EERDMANS PUBLISHING COMPANY
Grand Rapids, MI / Cambridge, U. K.

Wm. B. Eerdmans Publishing Co.
255 Jefferson Ave. S. E., Grand Rapids, Michigan 49503/
P.O. Box 163, Cambridge, CB3 9PU U.K.
www.eerdmans.com

Printed in the United States of America

Library of Congress Cataloguing-in-Publication Data

For four wonderful grandchildren,
Chelsea and Taylor Duda
and
Patrick and Megan Koopman

The Historical Series of the Reformed Church in America

The series was inaugurated in 1968 by the General Synod of the Reformed Church in America acting through the Commission on History to communicate the church's heritage and collective memory and to reflect on our identity and mission, encouraging historical scholarship which informs both church and academy.

General Editor,
    The Rev. Donald J. Bruggink, Ph.D, D.D.
    Western Theological Seminary
    Van Raalte Institute, Hope College

    Laurie Baron, copy editor
    Russell L. Gasero, production editor

Commission on History
    James Hart Brumm, M.Div., Blooming Grove, New York
    Lynn Japinga, Ph.D., Hope College, Holland, Michigan
    Mary L. Kansfield, M.A., New Brunswick, New Jersey
    Scott M. Manetsch, Ph.D., Trinity Seminary, Deerfield, Illinois
    Melody Meeter, M.Div., Brooklyn, New York
    Jesus Serrano, B.A., Norwalk, California

Contents

Preface

In the course of my years as a writer and editor for the Reformed Church in America I have had several opportunities to visit the American Indian congregations of the Reformed Church, to write articles, take photos, and write the scripts for two audiovisual presentations, *Moving Toward Self-Reliance* and *The Columbus Five Hundredth: A Time for Reflection.* When the opportunity presented itself to take a three-month sabbatical, my wife, Marge, and I spent a week visiting each of the Reformed Church's six Indian congregations. That was the beginning of a six-year endeavor to tell a story that until this time has emerged only in bits and pieces. It's a story of dedication and patience by missionaries and a story of commitment on the part of Native American Indian Christians. Unfortunately, it's also a story that sometimes reflects all too well the sad record of the United States in its dealing with America's first inhabitants. But it's a story that needs to be told, both for its inspiration and for its sobering instruction.

Why is this book called *Taking the Jesus Road*? Because that was the term most often used by the early missionaries of the Dutch Reformed Church when they invited native people to become Christians, and it was the term the Indian Christians used when they gave testimonies at camp meetings. The old road, said the missionaries, was a road of paganism, superstition, and despair. The new road, the Jesus Road, was the road that would lead them to a better life on earth and a life in heaven when they died. At the mission schools, at the annual camp meetings, and at church services, the invitation was always given to forsake the old path and to choose the Jesus Road.

Writing this account has not always been easy, and one of the challenges has been getting the real story. Over the years the Reformed Church in America has produced most of its printed sources to stimulate interest in the work and to encourage financial and prayer support. I should know; that was my job for twenty-one years. This does not mean that these reports are untrue, but it does mean that when missionaries, mission executives, and denominational writers choose what details to use, they are more likely to report the positive than the negative.

Then, too, mission work—and most church work, for that matter—is fueled by faith and hope. Even in the face of difficulty, pastors and missionaries press on with the conviction that their efforts will in the end be blessed in some way by the Holy Spirit. In recent years, the letters written by missionaries, processed by the denomination, and sent to supporting churches, have often displayed remarkable candor about the difficulties and discouragements of the work. Yet these letters inevitably conclude with a vignette that breathes hope, be it only a story about a fifth grader who is "showing interest" in the Christian faith following vacation Bible school. That attitude is a powerful motivator for ministry, but it doesn't necessarily produce balanced accounts for historical documents. As you read this book, please keep in mind my struggle to read between the lines. I've tried my best to figure out what actually happened, but I can't always be 100 percent sure.

I would rather not have written some of the chapters; they record some very unpleasant details of our journey together as saints and sinners. But to gloss over or ignore them would untruthful and would defeat one of the purposes of this book, which is to learn today from the lessons of yesterday.

A second challenge was to determine what should be my point of view. In the early days of this project I was urged by an Indian leader to "write this history, as much as possible, from the Indian's point of view." After considerable thought, I have concluded that this is neither advisable nor possible.

For one thing, almost all of the written sources are non-Indian sources. The Indian people are people of the oral tradition, not of the written word. In the early days of Reformed church mission very few Indians knew English at all, and in most cases even their own tongues had not been reduced to written languages. I have, however, interviewed

a number of Indian Christians, and they have been very helpful with
personal remembrances and impressions.

For another thing, there is no such thing as an "Indian point of
view," any more than there is a "white point of view" or an "Asian point
of view" on any subject. Indians, like people of any race, have a wide
variety of perspectives and viewpoints. Some Christian Indians, for
instance, believe that their Indian legends should be accepted as having
as much validity as such biblical stories as Noah and the ark, while
others blanche at the idea. Some believe that customs such as cedaring
can be incorporated into Christian worship, while others believe that
Indian Christians must make a clean break with their ceremonial past.
In other words, it is impossible to write from "the Indian point of view"
simply because one such point of view does not exist.

Even if one, and only one, Indian viewpoint would exist, it would
be arrogant for a white person to claim to represent it adequately.
Vine Deloria, Jr., in his classic, *Custer Died for Your Sins*, describes both
humorously and contemptuously the hoards of anthropologists who
each summer "emerge, as if responding to some primeval fertility rite,
and flock to the reservations" to make scholarly studies—studies which
accomplish only to secure financial backing for next year's safari.[1]
Deloria's chapter, "The Problem of Indian Leadership," helps show why
the Indian psyche is largely opaque to most Anglo minds, even those
who have spent years in ministry with them. The Reverend Reuben
Ten Haken, after having served seven years in Mescalero, New Mexico,
wrote, "It would seem that in that perfect unit of time we ought to
know perfectly. The perfect truth of the matter is that we really know
very little of the people we love. But we do try to "sit where they sit."[2]

In 1967 the Reverend Jonah Washington, a Native American pastor
in the Reformed Church in America, advised Beth Marcus, executive
secretary of the Board of North American Missions, "Don't make the
mistake others have made in the past, and that is, don't presume to
be an authority on Indian Americans just because you worked among
them for about eight or ten years. Remember, the Federal Government
has worked or dealt with the Indians for almost 250 years and has yet to
find the right solutions to their problems."[3]

1. Vine Deloria, Jr., *Custer Died for Your Sins: An Indian Manifesto* (Norman,
   Okla.: Univ. of Oklahoma Press, 1988, 78.
2. Reuben Ten Haken, "I Sat Where They Sat," *Church Herald*, Nov. 9, 1951, 5.
3. Jonah Washington, letter to Beth Marcus, May 29, 1967.

A wealth of information was available for the preparation of the early history. The denomination as a whole was very interested in missions; this was an exciting new venture, and several publications were devoted almost exclusively to publicizing missions. The *Christian Intelligencer*, the official weekly publication of the Reformed Church, included mission articles in nearly every issue. The *Mission Field*, a monthly publication, covered all aspects of denominational work, including foreign missions, domestic missions, education, and youth work. The monthly *Day Star* promoted mission work to children. The annual reports of the General Synod contained detailed reports from every field, and Elizabeth Page's *In Camp and Tepee* (1915) is a detailed and sometimes rambling account of those heady early days of mission to America's native people. All of this, of course, was written from the perspective of the missionaries and mission boards, and very little written material is available from the Indians themselves.

I am admittedly writing as a member of the dominant culture. Having said that, I have attempted to be as fair and objective as possible, and I have invited feedback from interested Indians and non-Indians alike. Some readers may consider this book to be too candid; others may think it is not candid enough. I do not pretend to be a missiologist, anthropologist, or expert in intercultural studies. I have simply done my best to relate the facts as I have come to know them.

Still another decision involved terminology. What names should a white author use when writing about America's indigenous peoples? Where are the thin lines between historical accuracy, cultural sensitivity, and political correctness?

Over the years, authors have used several names for America's first inhabitants—some of them pejorative, some of them reflective of the times, and some of them displaying a conscious attempt to be culturally sensitive. Originally the most common term was simply "Indian," and then the word "American" was added. For a period of about ten years beginning in 1958 the acceptable term in Reformed Church literature was a reversal of the two words, as in "Indian American." Then it went back to "American Indian," thence to "Native American," and in 1998, with the adoption of a new council constitution, "Native American Indian." For the most part, the Indians themselves stood by and watched as white people debated what to call them.

It is obvious that any attempt to be completely and consistently culturally sensitive and politically correct would be doomed to failure. In the interest of simplicity, and to avoid a disjuncture between the text and quoted sources, this book will for the most part use the terms "Indian" and "American Indian" for early history and "Native American" for later history.

I wish to acknowledge those many people who have been helpful in the preparation of this manuscript. Reformed Church missionaries, mission executives, and individual Indian Christians have shared their resources and their memories. Russell Gasero, director of the Reformed Church Archives in New Brunswick, New Jersey, has been proactive in finding illustrations and incorporating them into the text. Gasero, the authors, and the Reverend Dr. Donald Bruggink, general editor of the Historical Series, all donate their time and talents in the production of these publications. The staffs of the *Church Herald* and the Joint Archives of Holland, Michigan, have been helpful in giving access to their resources. A word of thanks is due the Reverend Carl Gearhart and Steven Boint, who were generous in sharing the lists of mission personnel that appear in this book, as well as their research on the mission work in Oklahoma and New Mexico. Gladys Narcomey of the Comanche Reformed Church in Lawton, Oklahoma, has made a special effort to track down elusive information. Thanks, also, to the many folks who were generous in sharing their photos for this volume, with special appreciation to Audrey Keuning Mondeel.

I also wish to thank Dr. Sidney Heersma, who generously provided funds for the publication of this book in a cloth cover format. Dr. Heersma's aunt, Anna Heersma, served in the early 1900s as a missionary in Lawton, Oklahoma; and a good friend of the late Mrs. Ellen Heersma, Bertha Bruining, taught for a time at the Cook school in Tempe, Arizona.

And I must not ignore my debt to my wife, Marge, who never complained (well, maybe a little) about the notes, papers, notebooks, and miscellaneous paraphernalia that cluttered our home for six years.

LeRoy Koopman

CHAPTER 1

Seven 'New Days' for the American Indian: An Overview of Policies and Attitudes

The relationship between Indian mission work of the Reformed Church in America and the government of the United States of America has often been a symbiotic one. For that reason, the church's mission cannot be understood in isolation from government policies. Especially in the late 1800s and the early 1900s, the U.S. government relied heavily on churches to carry out its policy of "civilizing" the Indians—especially, but not exclusively, by educating their children in Indian boarding schools.

It was a mutually beneficial arrangement. The Reformed Church, like other religious groups, was offered an open door to evangelize the Indian people, unfettered by the niceties of the separation of church and state. Reformed Church missions received property, encouragement, cooperation, and, often, financial support from the local government agency. On the positive side, this relationship of church and state allowed the church to bring the message of Christ to the Indian people without restriction. On the negative side, it identified the Christian faith with the unrelenting subterfuge of the white oppressor. The church has ever since that time struggled to overcome the stereotype of Christianity as the "white man's religion."

Another result of the close association between church and state is the fact that the Reformed Church has seldom criticized U.S. policy toward Native Americans. Articles in denominational publications and reports of the mission agencies sometimes blamed individual white people for offering a poor example to Indians, but seldom did these

1

reports reprimand the government itself for deceit, misguided policies, thievery, or even violence. On several occasions, in fact, the problems between the races were attributed to "misunderstandings." In 1938, for instance, the Annual Report of the Women's Board of Domestic Missions stated that "continuous misunderstandings" have punctuated the years since the coming of the white man to America.[1]

Reformed missionaries did, however, sometimes lobby authorities in Washington D.C. as well as local agencies to secure justice for the native people they were serving. Prior to 1913, the Reverend Walter Roe made repeated trips to Washington in an effort to secure the release of the Chiricahua Apaches being held as prisoners of war at Fort Sill in Oklahoma. The strain of this effort was likely a contributing factor to his death a few months before the prisoners were released to Mescalero, New Mexico. Pioneer missionary J. Denton Simms, for all of his opposition to Indian culture, repeatedly sought medical and economic help for the Jicarilla Apaches in Dulce, New Mexico. Similar stories can be told of other missionaries.

Changing Policies of Church and State

Since their more-or-less accidental discovery by Christopher Columbus in 1492, the indigenous peoples of North America have been subjected to five hundred years of policy changes by the immigrant peoples and their governments. Again and again the native peoples have endured what was often heralded as "a new day for the American Indian."

As one examines U.S. and denominational policy and attitudes toward American Indians, the parallels become obvious. It would be easy to conclude that when the government announced a change in policy, as it frequently did, the Reformed Church would quickly respond by saying, "Me too." That, however, would be an oversimplification. It is probably more accurate to say that the church and the government both reflected changing public opinion, and that the shifts and turns were more or less simultaneous—much as a school of fish changes direction.

Native historian C. L. Sonnichsen summarized the Indians' dilemma with only slight exaggeration:

The main trouble was lack of comprehension. The Indians,

1. *Annual Report of the Women's Board of Domestic Missions*, 1938, 38.

not knowing about politics, expediency, and instructions from Washington, could not understand how a white man could say one thing on Sunday and reverse himself on Monday....[The Indian] saw no point in trying to remodel himself according to the white man's suggestions, especially where the white man seemed unable to inform him what he was supposed to be like when the remodeling was finished.[2]

Historians have suggested various summaries of the different policy eras, these "solutions to the Indian problem," these "new days for the American Indian," but we suggest the following as being reasonably accurate:

Policy	Dates	The "Ideal Indian"	Implementation
1. Extermination	1492-	Corpse	Warfare and disease
2. Segregation	1787-	Far-away pensioner	Removal by treaty and/or force
3. Civilization through education and evangelism	1819-	Civilized Christian	Education and evangelism
4. Civilization through agriculture	1887-	Farmer	Allotment and citizenship
5. Restoration	1934-	Tribal member	Revived Indian heritage
6. Urbanization	1953-	City dweller	Termination of government responsibility and removal to cities
7. Self-determination	1960-	Self-supporting citizen	Community development

These dates are approximate and sometimes even arbitrary. Only opening dates are listed, because in most instances the policies of the

2. C. L. Sonnichsen, *The Mescalero Apaches* (Norman, Okla.: Univ. of Oklahoma Press, 1958), 5-6, 8.

past era continued to some extent even after a new policy was put into place. The practice of extermination, for instance, did not stop in 1787. In some instances these dates denote movements, and in others (such as 1887 and 1934) they represent specific governmental legislation.

Most of these proposed solutions to what was often referred to as the "Indian problem" grew out of a realization that the previous approach was not working. It should also be pointed out that most of these proposals for a new direction were made without significant consultation with the people most affected—the native people themselves. Elected officials, for the most part, did the bidding of those who voted—and Indians were either not allowed to vote or were a minuscule segment of the voting population.

First Policy: Extermination

The period of extermination began shortly after the arrival of Columbus in North America and continued intermittently for the next three hundred years, although killing continued well beyond the time when extermination was the policy. Violence against Indians actually began with Columbus himself. On the island of Hispaniola in the West Indies Columbus required each Arawak to meet a three-month quota of gold and ordered their hands cut off if they did not meet it. Unfortunately for the Indians, no gold was to be found on the island.

Up north, along the Atlantic Coast, Indian/European relations began with a degree of civility, with the native peoples tolerating and sometimes even welcoming the white-skinned strangers. Initially the newcomers built their small settlements on land obtained from the natives by treaty or purchase—the legendary purchase of Manhattan Island for $24 in miscellaneous items being a case in point. But as more and more Europeans arrived in big boats, their settlements proliferated with alarming rapidity. If the Indians did not back-peddle peacefully—and sometimes even if they did—hostilities ensued. The artwork of the time is replete with nearly naked warriors wielding tomahawks over the heads of terrified white damsels. Within a generation after the colonists landed, brutal wars had decimated the indigenous tribes along the eastern seaboard.

Historian Sonnechson writes:

It became the mission of the white invaders to convince this free and proud people that the country did not belong to them after all—to assure them, in effect, that the Maker of All had turned his face from his red children and that the white man had a divine right to whatever he could lay his hands on. It was now the duty of the Indian to submit, no matter what cruelties and injustices were visited upon him.[3]

Throughout this period the English, Spanish, French, and (to a lesser extent) the Dutch vied against the indigenous population as well as against each other for squatting rights in the new world. These included the founding of the first permanent settlement on the North American mainland (St. Augustine, by the Spanish, in 1565); Drake's exploration of the California coast in 1578; the founding of Jamestown by the English in 1606; the arrival of the Pilgrims at Plymouth in 1620; the founding of New Amsterdam by the Dutch in 1628; and the settlement of the Massachusetts Bay Colony in 1630. Conflicts included those involving various alliances among the French, English, and Indian tribes. Interspersed were bloody confrontations between Indians and colonists on the East Coast and between Indians and Spanish troops in the Southwest. The Dutch were not free from Indian violence (see chapter two), and for a brief time the Dutch in New Amsterdam offered bounty payments for Indian scalps.

The effort to exterminate Indians continued well into the other eras of U.S. Indian policy. Following the California gold rush, which began in 1848, Indian killing became, in the words of Fergus M. Bordewich in his fascinating book, *Killing the White Man's Indian: Reinventing Native Americans at the End of the Twentieth Century*, "a way of life, a form of reliable, state-subsidized off-season work for rangers and unemployed miners; between 1850 and 1859, the federal government reimbursed the State of California $924,259 for what was basically freelance murder."[4] The Apache wars occupied U.S. troops for more than forty years in the American West. In December of 1890 United States troops killed 146 Sioux—44 women, 18 children, and 84 men and boys of fighting age—at Wounded Knee Creek on the Pine Ridge Reservation in South Dakota.

Even more dangerous than the newcomers' guns were their diseases, against which the native population had no immunity. Smallpox, tuberculosis, and influenza were especially deadly. A smallpox epidemic in 1633, for instance, killed ten thousand Hurons in New England, and in other incidents several tribal groups were completely

3. Sonnechson, *Mescalero Apaches*, 4.
4. New York: Doubleday, 1996, 50-51.

wiped out. These plagues were most often introduced accidentally, but stories abound of germ-infested blankets being distributed deliberately to native tribes (one such incident is described in chapter five).

All in all, the policy of extermination—whether official or unofficial—was eminently successful. Estimates of the original indigenous population of North America in 1500 range from two million to sixty million, depending, it seems, on the predisposition of the one making the estimate. Many scholars have arrived at the figure of fifteen million as a reasonable figure.[5] By 1900, according to the U.S. census estimate, the Native American population in the U.S. portion of North America had been reduced by disease, warfare, and outright genocide to less than 250,000.

Second Policy: Segregation

In order to acquire Indian land without the messiness of violent confrontation, the U.S. Government turned to the art of writing treaties. Treaties before 1787 had been made locally or by the foreign powers that were contending for dominance in the new world. When the Second Continental Congress agreed to the Articles of Confederation in 1777, treaty-making was placed in the hands of the federal government. Among the powers given to the government were making war and peace, coining and borrowing money, and regulating Indian affairs. Significantly, Indian affairs were placed under the jurisdiction of the War Department, where they were to remain for more than a hundred years.

Removal by Treaty

The federal government lost little time in exercising its prerogatives with indigenous peoples, who now were to be treated as sovereign nations. In 1778 the government signed a treaty with the Delaware tribe, the first of some six hundred treaties and agreements with the tribes of North America—almost all of which were broken by the government within six months to two years of their signing.

Treaty documents were always written in English, and their contents were not always explained accurately to the Indians who signed them. Sometimes the treaties were amended after being signed, and the amended versions were brought to a different group of tribal

5. Ward Churchill, *A Little Matter of Genocide* (San Francisco: City Light Books, 1997), 135.

representatives for final signing. Sometimes the Indians who signed the treaty did not rightfully represent the people, and sometimes the Indian leaders were first plied with alcohol. Then, too, having lived freely on land they believed was given by the Creator for the good of all, Indians found it difficult to grasp the concept of private land ownership and were often dismayed to learn of the finality of their losses.

In any case, most treaties were written as stop-gap measures to bring a semblance of calm until the pressure of new settlers forced further removal. A common tactic was for the government to encourage white settlers to move into Indian lands, then to tell the Indians that the government was no longer able to assure their security. The Great Father in Washington, said the treaty negotiators, was their friend and was prepared to give them a new and secure territory of their own, farther west, to be theirs forever.

When Thomas Jefferson was elected president in 1800, he adopted a federal policy of land acquisition and encouraged all territorial governors to do everything they could to secure Indian land. In 1803 Jefferson negotiated the Louisiana Purchase, paying France $15 million, or three cents an acre, for all the land from the Gulf Coast to Canada and from the Mississippi River to the Rocky Mountains, doubling the territory of the United States. There was one problem, however; this was not vacant land begging to be filled. It was occupied by the original inhabitants, whose ancestors had lived there for hundreds of years and who questioned anyone's right either to buy or to sell it. Thus began a new round of treaty making and breaking. The stories of several of these treaties are told in the chapters that follow on the individual mission sites of the Reformed Church in America in Nebraska, New Mexico, and Oklahoma.

Removal by Force

President Jefferson had suggested in 1803 that if Indians did not leave their homelands voluntarily, they be removed by force, but no subsequent president had felt comfortable using the military force of the United States to do so. Not so with president Andrew Jackson, who was well known for his animosity against the Indian people. After pledging to support westward expansion during his presidential campaign, Jackson proposed in his first message to Congress that Indians voluntarily remove themselves westward for the protection of both themselves and the settlers. When no evacuation was forthcoming, Congress passed the Indian Removal Act on May 28, 1830.

The Indian Removal Act required the removal of all Indians east of the Mississippi to a "permanent home" in Indian Territory, now Oklahoma, Arkansas, and Kansas. Little was known of what was called the "great American desert," and it was assumed that white people would not want to live there. Thus began some of the most onerous of United States operations against American Indians, the best known of which is the removal of the Cherokee nation from its ancestral home in southern Appalachia, an event commonly known as the Trail of Tears.

The removal of the Cherokees was the more heinous because, more than any other tribe, they had complied with attempts to "civilize" them. The Cherokees had succeeded at farming, were earning their own living, had built homes, were living peacefully with their neighbors, had even purchased slaves, and had adapted remarkably to white culture.

Of the sixteen thousand Cherokees who rode and walked the trail of tears, more than four thousand died of hunger, exposure, and disease. Of thirteen thousand Choctaws who left huge tracts of land in Mississippi and Alabama, nearly the same number suffered a similar fate. By 1840, more than one hundred thousand Indians had been forced to leave their homes east of the Mississippi. These new residents of Indian Territory, having once been self-supporting residents, were now pensioners, wards of the state.

John Schermerhorn and the Indian Removal Act

The man most active in the removal of these one hundred thousand people, beside President Jackson himself, was an ordained clergyman of the Reformed Church in America, the Reverend John F. Schermerhorn (1786-1851). Schermerhorn's complex and even strange career has been meticulously traced by Reformed Church pastor and professor the Reverend James Van Hoeven in a doctoral dissertation, "Salvation and Indian Removal: the Career Biography of Rev. John Freeman Schermerhorn, Indian Commissioner."[6]

John Schermerhorn was baptized and confirmed at "Old First" Dutch Reformed Church in Schenectady, New York. Feeling a call to the ministry, he graduated from Andover Seminary. He was drawn into Indian affairs by involvement in a missionary movement at Andover, a survey of the frontier, and appointment as an Indian agent. In 1832 he was appointed by president Andrew Jackson as one of three Indian commissioners and given the task of negotiating the treaties for Indian

6. Vanderbilt University, 1971.

removal. Over a five-year period, from 1832 to 1837, Schermerhorn participated in treaty negotiations with twenty tribes, paving the way for the removal of thousands of Indians.

Although Schermerhorn has been described as "the sanctimonious glove concealing the fist of that uncompromising hater of Indians, Andrew Jackson,"[7] Van Hoeven believes that Schermerhorn was "fundamentally a minister of the gospel who believed that the Indians' racial and eternal salvation required their removal west of the Mississippi River."[8] Schermerhorn assumed that eventually the Indians would organize themselves into a state and be admitted to the union—and, oddly enough, that he might himself become its governor.

Schermerhorn was relieved of his duties in 1837 by president Martin Van Buren (also a member of the Reformed Church), who wished to disassociate himself from some of the more distasteful appointments of the Jackson Administration. According to the current Schermerhorn web site, Schermerhorn left his position as the owner of 400,000 acres of land in Virginia.

One of the chief opponents of the Indian Removal Act was the American Board of Commissioners for Foreign Missions, a powerful interdenominational organization headquartered in Boston. This board had sponsored many of the mission stations then in operation and had marshaled strong support for the Indians. To counter this influence, Jackson sought support among other church groups, and he found that support among the leaders of the Missionary Society of the Reformed Dutch Church, headquartered in New York City. On July 22, 1829, several Reformed Dutch clergymen formally organized the Indian Board for the Emigration, Preservation, and Improvement of the Aborigines of America, with the "exclusive object" of promoting the Administration's Indian removal policy.[9]

In February of 1839 the Classis of Cayuga directed Schermerhorn to appear before it to answer charges that he made treaties fraudulently with carefully chosen and unqualified members of the Cherokee nation. The classis records were later destroyed by fire, but apparently Schermerhorn was not prosecuted, because in 1841 he was appointed as a missionary to the Indian Territory.

7. Ralph Gabriel, *Elias Boudinot, Cherokee, and His America* (Norman: Univ. of Oklahoma Press, 1941), 145.
8. Van Hoeven, "Salvation and Indian Removal," 3.
9. Ibid., 13.

The banishment of Indians across the Mississippi postponed the "Indian problem" but did not solve it. The building of railroads, the discovery of gold in California, and the expansion of agriculture and industry to the West made the presence of Indians increasingly inconvenient. The "five civilized tribes" had been promised new homes in perpetuity, "for as long as the grass grows and water runs," but in 1889 president Benjamin Harrison issued a proclamation opening the "unassigned" lands of Indian Territory for white settlement. The process began immediately and reached its peak at noon of September 16, 1893, when more than one hundred thousand whites raced to stake their claims in what had originally been promised as "Indian Territory."

The Women's Executive Committee of the Board of Domestic Missions, in its report of 1902, brought up the matter of new settlements in Oklahoma. The report points out that Kiowa and Comanche lands had been opened, that thousands of people were pouring into the area to find home sites, and that there was a splendid opportunity for the Reformed Church to establish congregations there. The report makes no comment, however, on the ethics of Indian removal and broken treaties.

The Reformed Church did, in fact, establish white congregations in Oklahoma—twenty of them—and in 1906 the denomination founded the Classis of Oklahoma. But the effort faltered. Most of the Dutch, finding Oklahoma too hot and dry, returned to their former neighborhoods. Five years later the classis was dissolved and the congregations were either disbanded or transferred to the Southern Presbyterian Church. Some of these churches exist to this day.

Grant's 'Peace Policy' Involves Churches

After the Civil War, president Ulysses Grant brought churches into the process of supervising the Indians who had been herded onto reservations. Violence between Indians and whites had continued, and the government's Indian agencies had become notoriously corrupt. Many agents were able to retire after only four years on the job, and one agent is recorded to have saved $50,000 in three years on an annual salary of $1,500. In 1870 Congress voted to prohibit army officers from holding the position of Indian agent, and President Grant invited Christian denominations to place people in charge of Indian agencies. Congress also appropriated $100,000 for Indian education, much of it contracted through Christian churches. Promoted as a quick, easy, and inexpensive way to bring an end to hostilities, Grant's "peace policy," as it was called, was designed to segregate all Indians to reservations, teach them farming and Christianity, and prepare them for eventual citizenship.

Mission brochures of the time made vague references to the Reformed Church's involvement in Grant's "peace policy," and the Reverend Richard Harper, an early missionary in Oklahoma, says in his history of Reformed Church Indian missions that the church participated by sending agents for the Pima/Maricopa Agency and the Colorado River Agency.[10] One prominent agent was John Clum, a member of the Dutch Reformed Church who grew up in the Hudson Valley of New York. Clum attended Rutgers College as a divinity student (where he played in the first intercollegiate football game) and went west with his friends. In 1873 Clum was appointed as the agent at the arid San Carlos Reservation in Arizona, where he gained the respect of the Apaches, allowed them to police their own affairs, and kept them busy with farming and construction work. He also, by trickery, engineered the first capture of Geronimo. Clum resigned in 1877 after four years of contention with the military over authority issues. A short time later, Geronimo escaped the hated reservation. Grant's peace policy continued officially for about twenty years, during which time the bloodiest Indian wars took place and agency corruption continued. The Reformed Church's participation lasted ten years, from 1870 to 1880. By 1882 all denominations had discontinued their involvement.

Removal by Buffalo Slaughter

The fate of the plains Indians was sealed in the late nineteenth century by two events: the completion of the transcontinental railroad and the destruction of the buffalo. The completion of the railroad in 1869 opened the door to an even greater invasion of settlers and left the Indians completely surrounded by white people. The government then came to realize that the only remaining resources of the Indian tribes were the vast herds of buffalo that still roamed the plains. Without buffalo to supply food as well as the materials for clothing and shelter, Indian tribes would have no choice but to accept government rations, thus making them wards of the state.

10. Richard H. Harper, "The Missionary Work of the Reformed (Dutch) Church in America in Oklahoma," Part I, *The Chronicles of Oklahoma*, vol. 18, no. 3 (September 1940), 252-53.

Jicarilla Apaches on their way to the agency on rations day

In the early 1870s hunters began killing buffalo in earnest, shipping the hides east and leaving the carcasses to rot on the ground. Within twenty years some thirty million animals had been slaughtered. The buffalo became a truly endangered species, with a total population of less than a thousand animals. General Phillip Sheridan, in addressing the Texas legislature, said that the hunters "have done...more to settle the vexed Indian question than the entire regular army."[11]

Third Policy: Civilization through Education and Evangelism

As violent confrontations continued in the wake of white expansion and broken treaties, U.S. national leaders struggled to craft a policy that was more humane (and economical) than extermination and that would calm the Indians' alleged violent nature. The solution, they said, was to "civilize" the Indian, to help him shed his barbarism, embrace what was now called American culture, and become a loyal citizen of the United States. After the segregation policy transformed the Indians into pensioners and wards of the state, the civilization policy was intended to return them to the status of self-sufficient people who would eventually fit in with the people who had displaced them. "Indians must conform to the 'white man's ways,' peacefully if they will, forcibly if they must." Thus did Thomas Morgan, commissioner

11. Judith Nies, *Native American History* (New York: Ballentine Books, 1996), 281.

of Indian affairs, summarize U.S. policy in the first year of his tenure, 1889.[12] This era would officially last until 1934, with the passage of the Indian Reorganization Act, which rescinded the assimilation policy and said in effect, "It's o.k. to be an Indian."

The effort to civilize Indians and thereby assimilate them into American culture took place through three interconnected means: evangelism, education, and allotment. Through evangelism, Indians were urged to take the "Jesus Road," a new trail that left the old customs behind. Through education, Indians were to forsake their Indian identity by going to schools specifically designed to wean them from their native culture. Through allotment, Indians were to receive a family plot of land, take up farming, become weaned away from their tribal mentality, and thus become self-supporting units in a more-or-less integrated society.

Even though the policies of evangelism, education, and allotment were carried on more or less simultaneously, this book will deal with them separately. Mission agencies held evangelism as their highest priority and were active in education through schools and churches, but they were involved in allotment only by supporting its theory and effort.

Evangelism's Emphasis: Cut All Ties with the Past

As the government granted permission for mission agencies to evangelize and educate at Indian boarding schools, it expected these schools to "civilize" Indians by "Christianizing" them. It expected the church to include a powerful cultural component in its teaching. Seldom did anyone make a distinction between the white man's religion and the white man's culture.

It would be unfair to say that the primary purpose of early Reformed mission work was to "civilize" Indians. The first and foremost goal was to bring them to a saving knowledge of Jesus Christ. Evangelism was the priority. But the church also believed that the "Jesus Road" must necessarily exclude the ancient customs, culture, legends, beliefs, and dances. Missionaries not only sought sincerely to lead Indians to Jesus Christ, but also to persuade them to cast off all evidences of their former lives. Missionaries believed that nearly all aspects of Indian culture were inexorably intertwined with the native

12. Wilcomb Washburn, ed., *The American Indian and the United States: A Documentary History*, vol. I (New York: Random House, 1973), 424.

religion, so converts had to make a clean break with the past. Mission staffs also believed that they were called by God to prepare Indians to become solid and productive American citizens, happily accepting their new status and blending into the mainstream of American life. In other words, missionaries believed they were simultaneously seeking the Indians' spiritual and temporal welfare.

As a result, pastors and teachers waged war on tribal dances and festivals, forbade children in mission schools to speak their own language or wear native clothing, sometimes urged adult converts to adopt the white people's style of clothing as a sign of their new faith, and introduced "wholesome" games such as baseball and basketball as an alternative to Indian sports.

The Reverend J. Leighton Read, serving the Comanche mission in Lawton, Oklahoma, reflected the thinking of most, if not all, of his fellow missionaries when he wrote in 1926, "When it comes to a matter of religion and the daily walk of the Christian, we insist on the complete 'cutting off' of the old, and yet at the same time seeking to adapt the teachings of Jesus to the peculiar Indian temperament and need."[13]

How effectively the missionaries adapted the teaching of Jesus to the "Indian temperament and need" is difficult to tell, because few sermons of that time remain. The few that are available, however, contain few references to Indian life. There is abundant evidence that missionaries did indeed call for a complete break from the culture and beliefs of the past.

The 1928 report of the Women's Board of Domestic Missions speaks with hope concerning the older Indians who are "willing to break with the old tribal customs and ceremonies and accept the new trail."[14] The following year an article about Winnebago rejoiced that the season of powwows was past but voiced concerns about the new openness of the government to Indian ceremonies: "It is unfortunate that the Federal Government, pouring its millions into the Indian service, should countenance such revelries on Federal ground for weeks at a time, thus undoing much of the work of the church and state."[15]

13. J. Leighton Read, "Passing of the 'Old Time Indian,'" *Christian Intelligencer and Mission Field* (Dec. 29, 1926), 833.
14. *Annual Report of the Women's Board of Domestic Missions*, 1928, 17.
15. "Notes from the Winnebago Mission," *Christian Intelligencer and Mission Field*" (Oct. 9, 1929), 644.

Clothing and Houses as Signs of the Faith

Indian boarding schools required that Indian children discard their traditional clothing for suits, ties, dresses, and short hair. But clothing style was more than a sign of civilization; it was also regarded as a sign of the Christian faith. Early converts were sometimes encouraged to identify themselves as followers of Christ by cutting their hair and dressing like white people. A spring reception of the Women's Board of Domestic Missions, held April 11, 1912, at the Collegiate Church of St. Nicholas in New York City, featured a dramatic presentation about the work in Oklahoma and New Mexico. The "missionary" spoke in sign language to "Indian maidens" (white women in Indian dress) while Christian Indians were portrayed by "three Indian women in the gay calico dress of the Christian Indians."[16]

An undated brochure, *The Call of the Trail*, published by the Women's Board of Domestic Missions (at that time located at 25 E. 22nd St. in New York City), asked "Which Trail Next?" One arrow pointed to a picture of a powwow, with the caption, "Indian Social Dance." The other arrow pointed to a photo of a couple with a baby, with the caption, "Young Indian couple with their baby who has just been baptized." All three are dressed in Anglo clothing—the man in a much-too-tight suit and tie, the woman in a dress and hat, and the baby in a white dress and bonnet.

Indian tepees also came in for their share of criticism, with missionaries regularly describing them as "filthy." Indian agents and missionaries alike were convinced of the importance of moving Indians out of their tepees and into rectangular wooden homes. The government, in fact, sometimes required Indians to build log houses, but when agents came back later they found that the Indians had moved back into their tepees and were using their wooden houses for storage. The Oglala Sioux medicine man, Black Elk, in his famous *Black Elk Speaks*, asserted, "Everything the Power of the World does is done in a circle," pointing out the seasons, bird nests, and the world itself. He concluded that log houses were "a bad way to live, for there can be no power in a square."[17]

16. L.L.B., "Spring Reception Women's Board of Domestic Mission," *Christian Intelligencer* (April 17, 1912), 249-50.
17. As told to John G. Neihardt, *Black Elk Speaks: Being the Life Story of a Holy Man of the Oglala Sioux* (Lincoln, Neb.: Univ. of Nebraska Press, 1932, 1959, 1972), 194-95.

Criticisms of Indian Ceremonies and Dances

While traditional Indian clothing and tepees took their share of criticism, the most aggressive campaign was waged against Indian dances. An undated brochure, *Some Facts about the Mescalero Apache Indians*, describes the coming of age ceremonies for girls, saying that "these and similar ceremonies lead to drunken brawls and immorality, and the missionaries must constantly try to keep the Christians from attending them."[18]

A 1923 description of the fiesta in Dulce, New Mexico, was typical. The fiesta, says the article in the *Christian Intelligencer and Mission Field*, is "a call to all the heathen and barbaric in their natures and retarding to all that stands for the better civilization, but it also means the neglect of sheep and crops and a great loss in many ways." The article goes on to say that the government representative and the mission are in "close cooperation in their work for the abolishment of such festivals and in their effort to give the younger Indians a taste for a far less barbarous recreation."[19]

In 1923, Edith Allen, corresponding secretary of the Women's Board of Domestic Missions, painted this melodramatic contrast between the "old" Indian and the "new" Indian:

> Dark faces, huddled blanketed forms, tepees, the circle of the pagan Indian dance, the sound of the beating tom-toms. Over-against this the newer picture. Indian children clean, neatly dressed, healthy, playing and working joyously because of the teaching of the mission schools.
>
> Church services, men and women earnest, kindly, decently dressed, singing, praying, listening—getting the better life in Christ Jesus, then working on their farms—living the "Jesus Way."[20]

"Civilization" through Indian Boarding Schools

The partnership of church and state in teaching Indian people began officially in 1819 when Congress established the Civilization Fund to pay mission groups to teach the "habits and arts of civilization"

18. Board of Domestic Missions, Reformed Church in America, n.d., 3.
19. E.H.A., "An Indian Dance: A Personal Experience," *Christian Intelligencer and Mission Field* (May 23, 1923), 325.
20. *Annual Report of the Women's Board of Domestic Missions*, 1923, 23.

to Indians.[21] Between 1819 and 1842 the government funneled $214,500 through missionary societies to educate Indian children, and these missionary societies raised an additional $180,000 for this purpose.

The lynchpin of the effort to "civilize" Indian people was the creation of the Indian boarding school, the first and best known of which was the government's Carlisle Indian Industrial School in Carlisle, Pennsylvania. Captain Richard Pratt founded the school in 1879 and was its first headmaster. Opened in an abandoned military barracks, the purpose of the school was to "kill the Indian and save the man," to eradicate "Indianness" and to instill white values and white civilization. Instead of being "pagan wanderers," Indian youth would become proficient in English and would be trained to become farmers, lawyers, mechanics, tradesmen, and efficient housewives. The only way to do this, it was reasoned, was to remove the brightest of Indian youth hundreds and even thousands of miles from their homelands and to isolate them from their Indian heritage. After the transition was complete, Indians could choose to return to their own people to serve them or (preferably) to stay in the eastern states and become absorbed into "civilized" society.

Upon arrival at Carlisle, an Indian child received a bath, a haircut, a new set of clothing, and an "Americanized" name. "Before and after" photographs showed boys now dressed in suits or military uniforms, and girls in frilly dresses, their soft moccasins replaced by hard shoes. Students were forbidden to speak anything but English, with noncompliance triggering a soapy mouthwash. The school was run according to a military model. Discipline was strict, and runaways faced severe punishment. The first half of the day was spent on academic subjects, and the second half was devoted to vocational skills such as farming, woodworking, and dressmaking. Student labor provided most of the cooking, cleaning, sewing, laundering, farming, and maintenance. Indian flutes and tom-toms were replaced by clarinets and tubas. The Carlisle band marched at every presidential inaugural parade while the school was open.

Haskell Institute was founded three years later in Lawrence, Kansas, and about twenty-five additional schools were opened in succeeding years, most of them offering a high school education not available locally. Local elementary schools were also founded as

21. Arlene Hirschfelder, *Native Americans* (New York: Dorling Kindersley, 2000), 49.

boarding schools, following the pattern of Carlisle. Transportation to and from school each day was not practical, and even students who lived nearby were boarded at the school in order to remove them from their home environment. This meant that children as young as five were separated from their families for at least nine months of the year. Boarding schools received full support from the local Indian agency. If parents refused to allow their children to attend or tried to hide them, agents sometimes threatened to withhold food rations.

By 1887, some ten thousand Indian children were enrolled in 227 institutions, both boarding and day schools. Of these, 163 were operated by the Indian service and sixty-four were run by private agencies, mostly mission societies, under government contract. Even the schools operated by the government, however, included explicitly Christian instruction in their curricula. It was a perfect symbiotic relationship: the government had an enthusiastic and cost-efficient ally in educating, civilizing, and pacifying the Indians; and the Christian church had full access to Indian children—to teach them academic and religious subjects in school, to require attendance at church and Sunday school, and to provide nurturing care in the school dormitories.

An 1891 article in the *Christian Intelligencer* not only approved the effort but sought to quell apparent doubts that the Indian could indeed be educated:

> During the last twelve years, ever since Captain Pratt established his famous school at Carlisle, it has been proved that the Indian is in most instances as capable of education as the white man, and in many cases more desirous of it....Can any one who has interested himself in the fate of the once despised and degraded Indian continue to believe that the only good Indian is a dead Indian? Has not the power of Christian philanthropy proved that he is not an abnormal monstrosity, but a man fashioned like ourselves and endowed with the same reason, feelings, emotions, and passions?...That he is not born cruel and savage we must acknowledge when we see how soon his nature is changed when surrounded by a Christian environment, and it is a Christian environment which is destined to transform the character of the whole race.[22]

---

22. Claude Fay, "The Progress of the Indian," *Christian Intelligencer* (Dec. 9, 1891), 6.

"Having thus disposed these people, often by fraud and violence, what can we offer them?" asked an article in the *Mission Field* in 1904. Not their old conditions, their old homes, or their "old-time freedom and lawlessness of life":

> What we can still give them is a *Christian* (italics mine) civilization. Let them replace their tepees by the house of the settler, the bow and rifle by the axe and the plough, the ignorance of the savage by the culture of the new century, the incantations of the "Medicine man" by the Gospel story of the Christian teacher, and though they can never be what they once were, they may become, what is far better, a useful and contented element in this great nation.[23]

The Reformed Church Adopts the Carlisle Pattern

The Reformed Church admired the Carlisle pattern, and, with the government's blessing and support, established elementary schools and/or dormitories in Colony and Lawton, Oklahoma; Mescalero and Dulce, New Mexico; and Winnebago, Nebraska. From time to time the missionaries announced proudly that some of their graduates had moved on to one of the high schools such as Haskell.

Early moving pictures taken by a mission assistant at Dulce show girls sobbing as their hair is being shorn, students marching to church dressed in suits and white dresses, and runaways being released from their punishment in the basement. Yet, mission personnel expressed genuine concern for the dilemma of the Indian children. Helen Brickman, an officer of the Council of Women for Home Missions, presented this view of what a typical seven-year-old experienced when taken from home to a boarding school:

> Who can picture the heartache of the older Indians as they see their children leave the tepee or hogan....Who can picture [little Johnny Walking Stick's] loneliness and desolation as he bumps along in the government truck or stares out of the window of the fast moving train, the like of which he quite probably has never seen before?
>
> Every misgiving and doubt seems justified when he finally arrives at the big school. Instead of his father's tepee this seven-year-old finds his home in the white man's land to be one of the many large houses which surround him on every side. Instead of

23. A. DeW (sic) Mason, *Mission Field* (June 1904), 76-77.

Dormitories, Dulce, New Mexico

a sack on the floor with his family around him, he and perhaps fifty other small boys sleep in beds with sheets, blankets and pillows that seem a very unnecessary burden to him. He discovers the thing called TIME—which plays such an important role here. He must get up by it, go to school and to work by it, eat meals according to it, and finally at the end of the long, bewildering day, go to bed by it. His new clothes feel awkward, but he is quite proud of them. His short cut hair must be kept neatly brushed....The language of his fathers is not used. He must learn and himself use the white man's tongue. He finds the food different and it seems strange that he is not allowed to carry away in his pocket that which is uneaten.[24]

Reports of these early schools often included descriptions of patriotic ceremonies, including Columbus Day—apparently oblivious to what seems to be a self-evident irony. John Gebhard, staff member for the Board of Education of the Reformed Church, visited the school in Colony, Oklahoma, in 1904 and reported proudly that the Cheyenne and Arapahoe scholars were "accompanied by patriotic music as they waved the United States flag and sang 'My Country, 'Tis of Thee.'"[25]

Was the effort to Christianize/civilize the Indian successful?

24. Helen Brickman, "American Indians Today," *Christian Intelligencer and Mission Field* (Oct. 9, 1929), 652-53.
25. "Education at Fort Sill," *Mission Field* (Aug. 1904), 149-50.

Setting aside any considerations of sincere faith, the government's preliminary answer was a resounding, "Yes, it certainly paid off," the operative word being "paid." Consider the address by the Reverend William Carter, pastor of the Madison Avenue Reformed Church in New York City on the occasion of the twenty-fifth anniversary of the Women's Executive Committee of the Board of Domestic Missions, November 13, 1907. "Our theory as a nation, up until a few years ago," Carter said, "seemed to be that the only good Indian was a dead Indian. Therefore we made war on him and apparently were trying to exterminate him." Carter then went on to explain the benefits of the new government policy:

> The Government found, after a careful compilation of the statistics of the Indian wars, that it cost $1,000,000 and twenty-five lives to kill one Indian! They then decided that this was altogether too extravagant, so they changed their tactics and turned the Home Missionaries loose on him. The result was [that] it cost only $200 to save him, making a savings of $999,800 and twenty-five lives; nay, twenty-six, counting the poor Indian. Does it pay? In statistics kept for seven years of 2,200 Dakota Indians, it was found that while savages it cost the Government $120 a year for each Indian just to police him and keep him in subjection. After this tribe was Christianized, however, it was found that the cost per year for each Indian was just $8![26]

The Problem of 'Going Back to the Blanket'

Despite the economic considerations, it was found that the Christian education of Indian youth did not solve all problems. A continuing difficulty was the return of Indian youth to their old environment. A study of Carlisle graduates by the War Department revealed a high rate of recidivism, of well-scrubbed students who, when they returned home, let their hair grow long again, threw away their school clothing, and refused to speak English. Elizabeth Page, long-time president of the Women's Board of Domestic Missions, in her significant history, *In Camp and Tepee: An Indian Mission Story*, says that the missionaries came to understand that "the most tragic figure of the Indian camps" was "the tame wolf gone wild again, the returned

26. "Home Missions and the Great West," published by the Women's Executive Committee, circa 1908, 13.

student reverted to the blanket." Students came back from the schools, she said, "full of high ideals of service, often eager to lead and help, to be met in the tepees by suspicion and ridicule." The students "struggle, often heroically, to keep the faith and ideals the school has given them, but they are so alone, so terribly alone." After a time, she said, the school experience fades, the longing for the fellowship of their own kind overpowers them, and "they go down before it...with a hardened recklessness."[27] Various remedies were tried. To prevent students from returning to "the blanket" during the summer months, some were assigned to live with white families during the school's vacation time.

In 1930 the Women's Board of Domestic Missions related the "true story" of a girl on the Mescalero reservation who had graduated with honors and had "become aware of the beauty and inspiration of good literature" and "could appreciate the niceties of life" but who must now return to the reservation:

> The first night at home was one of bitter unhappiness; "home" was a tepee with absolutely nothing inside except a pile of dirty rags and goat-skins flung in a corner to sleep on, and as she pulled one of these over her, she thought of the clean white sheets of her bed at the dormitory and the clean blankets that had covered her. The first meal with her mother and father had been eaten squatting in front of the fire outside the tent, the old battered coffee-pot boiling over into the flames, and all three of them dipping with their fingers into the one pan of stew. And into her mind flashed the picture of the dining-room at school, the table set daintily, the food served graciously, surrounded by the smiling faces of friends. And then came days when she was torn between the strong family loyalty, which is the heritage of the Indian, and the feeling that she could not go back to the old way of living and fall so far below the standards that had been taught her for years.[28]

The dilemma of educated and Anglicized Indian students was that they often were unable to find employment in their own culture, but neither were they ready to face the loneliness of living outside the reservation while struggling with low-paying jobs in the cities. The

27. New York, Chicago, and Toronto: Fleming Revell, 1915, 67-68.
28. "The Tragedy of the Present Indian Generation," *Christian Intelligencer* (Dec. 10, 1930), 804.

problem of the young lady mentioned above was happily solved, says the article, when she was given a position as a maid "in the home of kind Christian people in Phoenix"—apparently one of the few options for Indian girls with high school diplomas.

The Boarding Schools Had Some Successes

In fairness it ought to be noted that all six Reformed Church Native American pastors graduated from these schools, as did the interpreters for the various missions. Many tribal leaders, whether or not they stayed with the church, were graduates of the mission schools. The Reverend Henry Roe Cloud, a national leader whose story is told in chapter eight, attended the Indian boarding school in Genoa, Nebraska, and then went on to Yale University. Jim Thorpe, 1912 Olympic pentathlon and decathlon champion and the first American to play professional football and baseball simultaneously, graduated from Carlisle. The Reverend Wendell Chino, tribal chairman in Mescalero for thirty-four years and two-term president of the National Congress of American Indians, graduated from the Indian boarding school in Santa Fe, New Mexico.

In an ironic twist, some boarding school graduates used their newly learned skills to campaign for the restoration of native rights and culture. Chino was a national leader in the struggle for Indian rights. Francis La Flesche, son of Joseph La Flesche, chief of the Omahas, wrote outstanding studies of the Omaha and the Osage tribes and accompanied his sister, Susette, a medical doctor (also a graduate), on a lecture tour of eastern cities to support the Ponca's case for a return to their homeland. But of the 10,669 students who attended Carlisle until it closed in 1918, and the tens of thousands of Indian children who attended the other boarding schools, very few fulfilled the promise of assimilation into "civilized" society. Of Reformed Church members who went through the boarding school experience, many look back with appreciation for the education and for the kindness shown by the teachers and housemothers, but they are still resentful of the attempt to destroy their heritage.

Fourth Policy: Civilization through Agriculture

Despite the economic advantages of Christianizing and educating Indians rather than killing them, it became apparent as the nineteenth century drew to a close that the "Indian problem" hadn't gone away. Moving Indians out of the way of westward-charging settlers—by force, by broken treaties, and by the destruction of buffalo herds—had been largely successful. The native peoples had been largely removed to reservations where they were no longer a threat to the dominant society. But now the Indians were pensioners, having no source of livelihood. They were still living in close-knit tribal groups, isolated from the mainstream of society and under the jurisdiction of a huge, unmanageable, and expensive network of government agencies. It became apparent that the government had created a vast and permanent welfare state. Many Indian children attended boarding schools in the hopes of making them "civilized," but the projected payback was still in question.

The General Allotment (Dawes) Act of 1887

Enter Henry Dawes, United States senator from Massachusetts, widely regarded by government and church officials as a friend of the Indians, who introduced the General Allotment Act of 1887, generally known as the Dawes Act. Briefly, the Dawes Act called for the head of each Indian family to receive an allotment of 160 acres of Indian land and each single person over eighteen years of age to receive eighty acres. The United States would hold this allotted land for twenty-five years in trust, for the sole benefit of the Indian, and after that time would transfer the title. Meanwhile, agricultural skills would be taught at Indian boarding schools.

The perceived relationship among agriculture, civilization, and Christianity was not a new one. As early as 1802 president Thomas Jefferson urged the Miamis, Potawatomis, and Weas "to cultivate the earth, to raise herds of useful animals and to spin and weave," saying that hunting will only "expose your women and children to the miseries of hunger and cold."[29] It was the recommendation of David Zeisberger, a Christian missionary among the Delawares, that "those who come to Christ and join the church turn to agriculture and raising stock, keeping cattle, hogs, and fowls."[30]

The General Allotment Act had several goals: (1) To encourage Indian people to become self-supporting farmers; (2) to teach the concept of private property and capitalism to people who from time immemorial had held a communal view of property; and (3) to break up the closely knit tribal structure by physically separating Indians from

29. Bordewich, *Killing the White Man's Indian*, 38.
30. Ibid, 39.

other tribal members. Especially appealing (although said quietly) was the provision that after allotments were made, the "surplus" land would be made available to white settlers.

Indians were not asked for their opinion, but the Dawes Act received wide support from such organizations as the Indian Rights Association, the Board of Indian Commissioners, various Christian mission boards (including that of the Reformed Church) and the Lake Mohonk Indian Conference. Since the latter group played such an important role in government policy, a word ought to be said about that organization.

The Lake Mohonk Indian Conference

In the late 1800s the *Christian Intelligencer* reported with regularity and enthusiasm about the Lake Mohonk Indian Conference. The Reverend Denis Wortman, a Reformed Church pastor in Saugerties, New York, called it "the most important undenominational annual Christian gathering in the country" after the National Evangelical Alliance.[31]

The annual event, begun in 1883 and held at Lake Mohonk, New York, was a gathering of 150 to 200 "acknowledgedly wise friends of the Indian."[32] These included clergy, editors, judges, missionaries, military personnel, politicians, and even a few Indian converts. Church representatives consisted of both conservatives and liberals, including Baptists, Unitarians, Congregationalists, Episcopalians, Friends, Methodists, Presbyterians, and Reformed. The purpose of the gathering, according to the article by Wortman quoted above, was to "assist the Government in the education and naturalization of the Indian, to help him in due preparation for his coming privileges, and so far as possible, to make his civilization sound, permanent, and useful to the nation by endowing it with practical Christian belief."[33]

In support of the purpose of breaking up the tribal relationship, the *Christian Intelligencer* reported:

> The uncivilized tribe enforces no law. The tribal relation dwarfs family life and weakens family ties. The reservation shuts off the

31. "The Indians at the Late Conference at Lake Mohonk" (*Christian Intelligencer*, Oct. 22, 1890), 3.
32. Ibid.
33. Ibid.

Indians from civilization, and rations distributed unearned tend to pauperize them. Therefore we are convinced that the sooner family ties and family households replace tribal relations and unsettled herding upon the reservation, the better."[34]

"The bill is a wise one," said the unnamed author of a *Christian Intelligencer* article in January of 1886. Although acknowledging that one-half of the Indians are not prepared to cultivate farms with profit, "They are savages and must be taught." The author then goes on to justify the breaking of treaties with Indians: "Frankly, the time is rapidly coming when we will no longer be able to perform the engagements of these treaties to the letter....Selling the remainder of Indian land and putting the money in the treasury to pay for schools and improvements virtually fulfills the treaties."[35]

In 1890 the members of the eighth annual Lake Mohonk Conference, with Senator Dawes, his wife, and his daughter present as special guests, adopted a platform that included approval of abandoning the "pernicious reservation system," the allotment of lands, the improvement of justice, and the gradual discontinuation of the policy of "feeding the Indian and making him a mendicant." The Mohonk platform concluded with a ringing affirmation that all of this should be done

in anticipation of and in preparation for the time when the Indian races of this country will be absorbed into the body of our citizens, and the specific Indian problem will be merged into that great problem of building up a human brotherhood which the providence of God has laid upon the American people.[36]

The General Allotment Act Brings Disaster

As it turned out, the Dawes Act, so highly touted by "friends of the Indians," was later called by John Collier, commissioner of Indian Affairs, "the greatest single practical evil to be committed against the American Indian."[37]

---

34. "The Mohonk Conference," *Christian Intelligencer* (Nov. 3, 1886), 3.
35. "The Indian Question," *Christian Intelligencer* (Jan. 20, 1996), 2.
36. "The Mohonk Indian Platform," *Christian Intelligencer* (Oct. 20, 1890), 31.
37. Bordewich, *Killing the White Man's Indian*, 123.

Former agricultural facilities—a barn and home
for an instructor—in Winnebago, Nebraska

Often the most fertile land was declared "surplus" and transferred to whites, while Indians received acreages that were practically worthless. Even if the land was tillable, most Indians had neither the financial resources nor the experience to begin farming—much less the inclination to do so. Historically, some tribes had indeed raised vegetables, but this was done by women in small garden plots while the men hunted. Many allotments were suitable only for grazing, in which case 160 acres was not nearly enough for a decent living. Very few Indians actually farmed their allotments, and in 1891 the government made provisions for leasing them.

It was even easier for white people to take land from individual Indians than from a tribe, so Indians, unschooled in the finer points of capitalism, were easily swindled out of their holdings. Fraudulent wills were drafted for dead Indians, and whites were appointed as guardians for Indian children poised to inherit land. Good farmland sold for a bottle of liquor, and even when a fair price was paid the proceeds were quickly squandered. Soon the Indians were as poor as before but with no government rations and with no homes (they moved in with relatives). Before the Dawes Act, Indian tribes collectively owned 140 million acres of land. In 1934, when the allotment policy was abandoned, 90 million acres had disappeared from Indian ownership. Dawes had hoped that allotment would destroy tribal life once and for all, and in this he nearly succeeded.

Elizabeth Page acknowledged in 1915 that the allotment process had imposed social hardships on the Indian people. "The Indian allotments," she said, "are scattered and lonely, while Indians are above all else a social people. The old camps existed not only for defense, but even more for the enjoyment of companionship."[38]

In 1924, more than four hundred years after being "discovered," the first inhabitants of North America became official citizens of the land they had originally occupied. The Indian Citizenship Act of 1924, initiated by Charles H. Burke, commissioner of the Bureau of Indian Affairs, and signed by president Calvin Coolidge, awarded citizenship to every Indian born in the territorial limits of the United States. This process had taken several years, as tribes were one by one declared "competent." Some two hundred thousand Native Americans had already been made citizens by previous acts of Congress, and the 1924 legislation granted that privilege to the remaining 12,500. After having been first enemies, then wards, they had become citizens. Yet fourteen years later, several states still denied Indians the right to vote. It was not until 1948 and 1962, and then only as a result of lawsuits, that Indians in Arizona and New Mexico, respectively, were granted the right to go to the polls.

It was also in 1924, just ten years before the historic Indian Reorganization Act (explored in the next section), that the Reverend G. A. Watermulder, writing in the annual report of the Women's Board of Domestic Missions, declared that the "new day" of assimilation was about to dawn:

> The inevitable new order is upon us. Assimilation into our general civilization must continue until the solution of this problem will be complete....The new day for the whole Indian race to hear the Gospel and "be set free" has come.[39]

Fifth Policy: Restoration

By the 1920s it became clear that neither the Indian boarding schools nor the allotments were working. The Carlisle Indian School had closed in 1918. Indians hadn't accepted their role as farmers. They had sold or had been defrauded of millions of acres of land and were as

---

38. Page, *In Camp and Tepee*, 66.
39. *Annual Report of the Women's Board of Domestic Missions*, 1924, 32.

poor as before. Nor had they become honorary white people; they were still holding tenaciously to their tribal loyalties and ancient customs.

The Meriam Report

The Indians' plight was brought to the attention of the public by the publication of a study, *The Problem of Indian Administration*, edited by Lewis Meriam and widely referred to as the Meriam Report. One of the members of the study commission was the Reverend Henry Roe Cloud, a Winnebago who had been brought to Christ through the Presbyterian mission in Winnebago, Nebraska, and later "adopted" as a young man and supported by Reformed Church missionaries Walter and Mary Roe. (Cloud's story is told in chapter eight.) The study, commissioned by the Department of the Interior (which had taken over Indian affairs from the War Department in 1848), documented the plight of the Indian people and revealed the inadequacies of the Bureau of Indian Affairs. Grave problems were cited in all areas—health, education, housing, economics, and family and community life. In response to the Meriam Report, commissioner John Collier and others formulated the Indian Reorganization Act of 1934, also called the Wheeler-Howard Bill. The legislation was often called the "Indian New Deal," in reference to president Franklin Roosevelt's contemporary New Deal designed to pull the nation out of the Great Depression.

The Indian Reorganization Act of 1934

The Indian Reorganization Act in effect called for a reversal of the policies that had been in place for the last fifty years. It repealed allotment and took steps to rebuild the rapidly disappearing land base. Forsaking the idea of separating Indians from each other, it encouraged tribes to establish their own governments and manage their own affairs. Giving up on the goal of transforming Indians into white people, it lifted restrictions on the practice of Indian ceremonies. Abandoning the idea that all Indians were destined to be farmers, it introduced federal programs supporting Indian vocational education, a student loan program, economic development, individual employment preferences, and Indian arts and crafts. Soft-pedaling the policy of Christianizing the Indians, the Reorganization Act guaranteed religious freedom, limited Christian instruction in Bureau of Indian Affairs schools, and continued transferring children from Indian boarding schools to community day schools, a process that had begun six years earlier. One of the first of these day schools was in Winnebago, Nebraska, which in 1928 began phasing in the public school on a grade-by-grade basis.

For the Reformed Church, as well as other denominations, this meant that the church could no longer sponsor Indian boarding schools. School transportation was limited on many reservations, however, so dormitories were still needed, especially for high school students. At several locations the Reformed Church continued to maintain dormitories, at which Bible classes continued, and from which students were transported on Sunday mornings to church services and Sunday school. Even after the dormitories were no longer needed, permission was granted to transport children to the churches on Wednesday afternoons and evenings for released-time religion classes.

When the word first got out that major changes could take place in Indian policy, especially regarding the free expression of native religion, most missionaries and mission boards saw the movement as a frightening step backward. The Reverend Richard Harper in Oklahoma voiced concern that "many white people, among them professing Christians, are doing all in their power to perpetuate Indian ceremonies."[40] J. Denton Simms, founding missionary in Dulce, went so far as to criticize the artists from the East who portrayed Indian costumes and customs, calling such artwork "propaganda" for the ancient dances and ceremonies.[41]

The 1925 report of the Women's Board of Domestic Missions, with the theme of "America for Christ," had this to say:

> First we fought him—then we fed him through the ration system—then we fathered him—he became a ward of the nation—now we are making him an archaeological specimen, asking him to please keep his paint, befeathered naked body, tom-tom, and war club that through his ceremonies we may get the flavor of his ancient savage culture....Obviously he cannot remain half primitive savage and have in his inner life the qualities that will fit him for a worthy place in this nation and day.[42]

---

40. Richard Harper, "The Government and the Indian," *Christian Intelligencer and Mission Field* (July 29, 1925), 468-69.
41. J. Denton Simms, "What 'Artists' Do for Indians," *Christian Intelligencer and Mission Field* (Oct. 22, 1924), 676.
42. *Annual Report of the Women's Board of Domestic Missions*, 1925, 17.

Changing Attitudes in the Church

Within a few years, however, attitudes changed—largely, it seems, through the influence of one man, the Reverend Henry Roe Cloud. In late 1928 Ada Quinby Knox, chair of the Indian Committee of the Women's Board of Domestic Missions, attended the Friends of Indians Conference in Atlantic City, New Jersey, under the auspices of the Indian Rights Association. The purpose of the meeting was to study the Meriam Report. With Knox was Mary Roe, serving as "missionary at large" for the Reformed Church since her husband's death in 1913. Also attending was Cloud, who had taken "Roe" as his middle name to honor his benefactors. Knox, in her board report the following year, reflected a major reversal of opinion by quoting Mary Roe as saying, "If the recommendations in the survey are carried out, great good will accrue the Indians."[43]

"It seems that surely a new day has dawned for the red man," said the 1931 report of the Women's Board of Domestic Missions. "There is a new spirit manifest in the government Bureau of Indian Affairs and for the first time in years the general public is aroused to an awareness of the Indian problem." The report spoke with approval of sending Indian youth to public schools and educating Indians away from the "old paternalistic system of the past."[44]

A *Christian Intelligencer* article in 1933 quotes with approval Collier's view that "those Indians whose culture, civic tradition, and inherited institutions are still strong and virile should be encouraged and helped to develop their life in their own patterns, not as segregated minorities, but as noble elements in our common life." It goes on to commend Collier's ideas that individual Indians ought to be entitled to the same educational privileges as others, "not in sequestered institutions but in the schools and colleges that serve us all."[45]

The Christian Reformed Church, incidentally, was not as sympathetic to the proposed provisions of the Wheeler-Howard Bill, especially those having to do with Indian religion. Carl Mapes, Republican representative from the Fifth District in Michigan, testified in a congressional debate that he had received "innumerable petitions" from the Christian Reformed churches in his district, "definitely and

43. Annual Report of the Women's Board of Domestic Missions, 1929, 28.
44. Annual Report of the Women's Board of Domestic Missions, 1931, 13, 24.
45. "Changes in the Indian Bureau," *Christian Intelligencer* (Aug. 1, 1933), 439.

positively opposing" this legislation. These constituents, he said, believe that "this legislation will have a tendency to de-Christianize and paganize the Indians rather than to help them. It will undo the work which it has taken the Christian missionaries years to do."[46]

Although most Reformed Church pastors working among American Indians continued to oppose the use of peyote as a religious ceremony, none of them except J. Denton Simms of the mission in Dulce, New Mexico, openly opposed the new legislation. Simms, in fact, resigned his position in 1936 rather than live with a new regime that encouraged Indians to "reinstate customs and religious ceremonies which we thought we had discouraged" and was "shutting me out of the discussion of Indian matters."[47]

Thus, Reformed Church missions among Indian people during the 1920s and 1930s made several adjustments to changing sentiments concerning Native Americans. They took the closing of Indian boarding schools in stride and even with some enthusiasm, even though this meant that they no longer had the exclusive right to teach the Christian faith to a captive audience. They had misgivings about the revival of Indian customs and rituals but largely accepted it as part of the package that emphasized Indian rights.

Renewed Emphasis on Indian Leadership

Two mission emphases began to emerge at this time: indigenous Christian leadership and community development.

From time to time, over the years, mention had been made of emphasizing Indian self-determination. The 1921 report of the board's Committee on Indian Work announced that all five missions were now fully supporting their interpreters and that some of the missions had assumed the running expenses of the church. The report of the following year announced that all of the Indian missions now had a "definite and determined policy to throw Indians on their own responsibility" and are endeavoring to "discover boys of promise...whom the Lord can use in His work." The doors of our denominational schools are open to them, said the report, and friends are ready to support them.[48] A few years later, in 1928, Ada Quinby Knox, chairperson of the Indian Committee,

46. Wilcomb E. Washburn, *The American Indian and the United States: A Documentary History*, vol. III. (New York: Random House, 1973), 1976-77.
47. J. Denton Simms, *Cowboys, Indians, and Pulpits* (Roy, N. Mex.: Floersheim Printing, 1982), 126.
48. *Annual Report of the Women's Board of Domestic Missions*, 1922, 29.

stated the purpose of Indian mission work as three-fold:

> The great purpose of our Reformed Church Missions to the Indians is primarily to bring them into fellowship with Jesus Christ, and secondarily to train them in Christian service, and lead them to become useful citizens.[49]

Results of these efforts appear to be slim, however. Stewardship was indeed stressed from the very beginning, but most special offerings were for such causes as mission schools in China and Alabama rather than for their own work. Mission staffs were large, including pastors, community workers, teachers, dormitory matrons, maintenance workers, and office workers, all of whom were white. Some efforts were made to hire local people for maintenance work, but often with disappointing results. Only the translators and a few Sunday school teachers were Indians. Pastor Watermulder of Winnebago, in an address to the Home Missions Council in 1936, admitted that on some reservations no real attempt had ever been made to train and use Indians in church work. "We do not render our full service and perform our full duty by sending some white man or woman to do the work," he said. "No mission can claim to have achieved any permanent success until the Indians, themselves, manage their churches, sacrifice for its operation, and propagate their faith."[50]

New Emphasis on Community Development

Although the Women's Board and individual missionaries still believed that the Indian's eventual adoption of the dominant culture was the only realistic solution to the "Indian problem," rhetoric against traditional Indian life slowly declined, and missionaries began to feel a new responsibility to the Indian community as a whole.

In 1930 the Women's Board acknowledged the importance of Indian culture, stressed Christian education, and emphasized serving the entire tribal community—the latter being a goal not previously emphasized. The board spelled out four objectives for the year. "Evangelistic" headed the list as it always had. In second place, surprisingly, was "Social," with the explanation that the Indian "cannot understand a Christian religion that is not related to his home and

49. Ada Quinby Knox, "Evangelism Among the Indians," *Christian Intelligencer and Mission Field* (May 2, 1928), 281.
50. "Rev. G. A. Watermulder Addresses," *Intelligencer-Leader* (Mar. 18, 1936), 12.

Six missionaries of the Women's Board of Domestic Missions
attended the National Fellowship of Indian Workers in 1941.
Left to right: John Keuning, Dulce; Robert Chaat, Lawton; G. A.
Watermulder, Winnebago; Peter Van Es, Jr., Mescalero; James
Ottipoby, Mescalero; and George Laug, Macy.

community life" and that the church must not only serve the individual but also the social group of which he is a part. The third objective was "Younger Generation," helping young people find employment when they move to towns and cities. The fourth objective was "Native Leadership," because Indians understand the thinking of their own people.[51]

Watermulder, in the 1936 speech already alluded to, encouraged his fellow Christian workers to stand behind Indians in the management of their own affairs and resources. "In our community," he said, "we must not fail to help render every possible service in the right direction to bring some kind of economic security."[52]

The Reformed Church's relationship to the Indian community changed not only because the church's attitude changed, but also because the Indian community changed. Shortly after the passage of the Indian Reorganization Act, Indian communities began to organize as tribal governments, something they had not been allowed to do previously. Among the first to do so were the Mescalero Apaches in southern New Mexico in 1936 and the Jicarilla Apaches in northern New Mexico in 1937, both Reformed Church mission sites. Now the

51. *Annual Report of the Women's Board of Domestic Missions*, 1930, 18-23.
52. "Watermulder Addresses," 12.

missions could relate not just to scattered Indian communities but to organized tribal governments.

The Beginning of Intertribal Organizations

With new empowerment, Indian peoples began to organize not only as tribal units but also as intertribal organizations. In 1944 tribal leaders from one hundred reservations formed the National Congress of American Indians for the purpose of advancing Indian rights, preserving native culture, and safeguarding tribal lands. The Reverend Wendell Chino, trained as a pastor in the Reformed Church and for thirty-four years the chairman of the Mescalero Apaches in New Mexico, served for several years as chairman of the National Congress of American Indians.

Two years after its founding, the organization successfully lobbied for the creation of the Indian Claims Commission, a federal tribunal that provided the machinery to claim compensation for loss of land through fraud and neglect. Despite the fact that compensation could be given only in money (as opposed to land) and was based on the value of land when it was taken (not its current value), over $800 million was awarded to 832 claims before the commission went out of business in 1978.

Native Americans and World War II

All Native American men were required to register for the draft for World War II, even though in some states they were still not allowed to vote. Nearly 25,000 served in the war, many from Reformed congregations and the tribes served by the Reformed Church. Ira Hayes, a Pima from Arizona, was one of the five soldiers photographed raising the flag at Iwo Jima.

Key players in the war were Indian "code-talkers"—Navajos, Comanches, and others who developed a code that the Japanese and Germans were unable to break. The code used native words and added expressions when no words were available. The code word for "dive bomber," for instance, was the Navajo word for "chicken hawk." Thus the native languages that the government had tried so hard to squelch became a significant factor in allied victories.

The internment of Japanese Americans during the war affected not only the ethnic Japanese but American Indians as well, for most of the Japanese relocation camps were set up on Indian lands. Approximately nine hundred thousand acres of Indian land were commandeered for military purposes.

Sixth Policy: Urbanization

In 1949 the Hoover Commission recommended that the federal government terminate its responsibilities for Indian affairs and that Indians be integrated economically, politically, and culturally into mainstream American society, thus launching yet another "new day" for the American Indian. Simultaneously, Indian people were to be encouraged to leave their reservations and to relocate to urban areas. In other words, reservations—which were "in" from 1830 to 1887, "out" from 1887 to 1934, and "in" from 1934 to 1949—were "out" again in 1949. The "ideal Indian" was now an urban dweller instead of a tribal resident. Termination became official four years later, in 1953, under the Eisenhower Administration. This policy would remain in place until negated by the Kennedy Administration.

As the government moved forward to "get out of the Indian business," it made a study of various tribes to determine if they were ready for the discontinuation of federal support. A 1954 report included the Jicarilla Apaches (no), the Mescalero Apaches (no), the Kiowas/Comanches/Apaches of Oklahoma (no), the Omahas (yes), and the Winnebagos (yes).

Over the next several years the government enacted several bills designed to divest the federal government's involvement in Indian affairs. These included ending the prohibition against the sale of liquor to Indians off the reservations, transfer of criminal and civil jurisdiction from the federal government to the states, and the transfer of health programs from the Bureau of Indian Affairs to the U.S. Public Health Service.

Termination was accompanied by urbanization—a massive effort to take Indians away from reservations and relocate them in urban centers. In 1948 the U.S. government offered job placement services for Navahos in such cities as Denver and Los Angeles, and two years later the service was extended to other Indians. By 1952 employment assistance was offered in eight cities—Chicago, Cleveland, Dallas, Denver, Los Angeles, Oakland, San Jose, and Washington, D.C.

The Response of the Reformed Church to Termination

Whereas the response of the Reformed Church to earlier policy changes had usually been enthusiastic, the response to the policy of termination and urbanization was more guarded. In 1955 the Board of Domestic Missions reported in the *Church Herald* that it had approved a statement on Indian affairs prepared by the National Council of Churches. The statement stopped short of condemning the termination policy but cautioned against moving too quickly, stating that many tribes are not prepared to accept the responsibilities. The statement deplores "the haste with which the recent termination bills have been drawn up" and said that "careful social planning is necessary to make the transition a just and equitable one, so that the termination of federal services does not become a program of abandonment."[53] The 1954 report of the Board of Domestic Missions said that the government was closing Indian schools and hospitals, and that it "therefore becomes all the more imperative that our Board assist the Indian in accepting the privileges and responsibilities of full citizenship status."[54]

The Church Becomes Involved in Urban Indian Ministries

The Reformed Church tried to be of some assistance to Indians as they moved to the cities. Having previously served the Mescalero church, the Reverend Reuben Ten Haken directed the urban Indian ministry in Los Angeles from 1957 to 1960 under the auspices of the Southern California Council of Churches, an effort to help Indians with housing, jobs, and social services as well as provide spiritual direction. Ten Haken reported that the church was speaking out on the "evils that lurked" in the relocation program. These included "too rapid an exodus for proper assimilation, inadequate screening of applicants, and overselling of what the city had to offer."[55] Feeling that the work could be done better through other agencies, the Reformed Church withdrew from the Los Angeles relocation program in 1960.

The Reverend Gradus Aalberts made a similar move in 1958, leaving Winnebago for Minneapolis to direct the urban Indian ministry under the sponsorship of the Minnesota Council of Churches. Both pastors found the experience to be frustrating, however, and after a few years returned to the pastoral ministry, Ten Haken to Macy and Aalberts back to Winnebago.

53. "The Welfare of the American Indian," *Church Herald* (July 22, 1955), 4-5.
54. Reformed Church in America, *Minutes of the General Synod*, 1954, 70.
55. Reuben Ten Haken, "The Church's Responsibility in the Relocation of the Indian American," *Church Herald*, (Nov. 20, 1959), 112-13.

Not only the pastors, but most of the Indians themselves returned eventually to their reservations. Since that time, Indian people have been free to relocate, but few have done so, at least permanently. Despite the rampant poverty and depressing living conditions on the reservations, relatively few have become urban dwellers. The Reverend Harvey Calsbeek, who spent twenty-three years in Indian ministry, explained it in this way:

What makes the Indian people stay on the reservation? One reason is much like the importance of Israel to the Jewish people. This is their homeland. It is "holy ground." They say, "We have been born here and we want to die and be buried here." Cities may have employment, but they are threatening. Many of the people have tried city life and have returned to the reservation. They hope to get a HUD house at a reasonable rent, or they move in with some relatives. Here there are available to them medical care, schooling, and relatives. Here they can have hand games, feasts, gourd and war dances, and be a part of the powwows. Here they can bury their dead, celebrate a birthday or an anniversary in the more traditional way. Here they can feel good about being what they are—Indians. In spite of poverty, here is a sense of security and here are their loved ones. This is home![56]

Shift in Emphasis to Church Extension

With World War II behind it, the nation experienced a new sense of hope and optimism. This was also true of the denomination, which placed a major emphasis on evangelism and church growth. The number of active communicants, 176,244 in 1945, increased to an all-time high of 232,978 in 1967. During the decade of the 1950s, the Reformed Church organized an average of 14 churches per year (compared to 9.9 in the 1960s, 5.5 in the 1970s, 8.7 in the 1980s, and 5.1 in the 1990s).

Although the ministries continued at all six Indian congregations and the emphasis on Indian leadership increased, much less attention was given to Indian missions in annual reports and mission promotion. In a 1951 review article, "Domestic Board Meeting Highlights," the

56. Harvey Calsbeek, typewritten report to Gregg Mast and Richard Vander Voet, circa 1987.

Church Herald emphasized church extension, city work, and ministry to immigrants, but made no mention of Indian work except that Gertrude Van Roekel, a missionary in Dulce, New Mexico, spoke on "Indians I Have Known." The Reverend James Benes, commenting on his first meeting as a member of the Board of North American Missions (as it was now called) in 1957, reported that while the Reformed Church remained committed to the "tremendously important" work among Indians, and in Kentucky, Alabama, Mexico, and Canada, "the endeavor which will demand the whole consecrated heart of the Reformed Church lies in the area of church extension."[57]

Reformed Church Takes Active Role in Cook Christian Training School

At mid-century the Reformed Church in America began to play a very active role in the work of Cook Christian Training School, now in Tempe, Arizona. Since that time the denomination has not only supported many staff members at the school but has sent countless volunteers.

The school had begun in 1911 through the efforts of the Reverend Charles Cook, a Presbyterian missionary to the Pimas. The school was first located in Tucson and moved three years later to Phoenix. For its first thirty years it remained a Presbyterian institution, but in 1940 it was restructured as an interdenominational school with a board of trustees drawn from many denominations, including the Reformed Church. Reformed Church involvement was accompanied by a five-year news blitz in the pages of the *Church Herald*. After World War II the campus was graced with buildings scavenged from a former Japanese relocation camp on a Pima reservation.

The first Reformed Church staff member at Cook was the Reverend G. A. Watermulder, who came as dean and teacher in 1943 after three decades of service in Winnebago, Nebraska. He died four years later, but his wife, Hattie (Hospers), a former missionary at Fort Sill, in Oklahoma, stayed on to teach Bible and English to Indian women. Anna Berkenpas, who had also worked for more than thirty years at the Winnebago mission, also came to Cook at that time as an office manager and later as a women's counselor.

Watermulder was followed as dean by the Reverend Cornelius Bode, who served from 1949 until his death in 1957. His widow,

57. James W. Benes, "The Reformed Church Mission in North America," *Church Herald* (April 26, 1957), 9.

The campus of Cook College and Theological School, Tempe, Arizona

Frances, also stayed on as a teacher for an additional ten years. The longest tenures at the Cook school were those of the Reverend Harry and Luella Van't Kerkhoff and of William and Marion Hocking. The Van't Kerkhoffs served from 1949 to 1969. Harry Van't Kerkhoff taught theology and Bible, and Luella Van't Kerkhoff taught church music. The Hockings, who had previously worked in Dulce, served at Cook from 1968 to 1981. William Hocking worked as maintenance supervisor, and Marion Hocking served in a number of ways, including promoting the school through writing and speaking. William and Peggy De Boer served on Cook's staff from 1971 to 1982, initially as

William and Marion
Hocking

Harry and Luella Van't Kerkhoff

dorm parents and later as leaders in the Theological Education by Extension (TEE) and residence programs. The De Boers then went as missionaries to Chiapas, Mexico, and, after Bill's ordination in 1994, they accepted a call to the Jicarilla Apache Reformed Church in Dulce, New Mexico, where, as of this writing, they still serve.

Cook School moved from Phoenix to Tempe in 1965, where it occupies a twenty-acre campus adjacent to Arizona State University. A prominent feature of the campus chapel is the "Indian Christ," a striking, life-sized painting by Native American artist Michael Paul. The school has undergone several name changes: Cook Bible School (1911), Cook Christian Training School (1914), Charles Cook Theological School (1986), and Cook College and Theological School (1992). White people administered the school until the late 1960s, but since then most of the leadership, as well as the teaching staff, has been Native American.

Enrollment has varied widely over the years, from more than sixty students in the 1950s to about twenty resident students at the time of this writing. A major change was made in 1975, when the TEE program was added, enabling students from across the continent to take classes by correspondence. The school directs its energies not only to Indian students preparing for lay and pastoral leadership, but also to white workers and pastors who seek orientation for work among Native Americans. Almost all of the Reformed Native American pastors studied at the school, as have several lay leaders, such as Thurman Cook, who served his own church in Macy, Nebraska.

An Era of American Indian Pastors

Beth Marcus was appointed in 1953 as executive secretary for the Board of Domestic Missions (soon to be called the Board of

The "Indian Christ" painting
at Cook School

North American Missions), a position she held for fifteen years. The overarching emphasis of Marcus during her tenure on the mission board was training leaders. "Right or wrong," she said in retrospect, "we kept on emphasizing education, education, education."[58] Four of the Reformed Church's six Native American pastors were ordained during this era.

The Reverend Robert Chaat, a Comanche, had been ordained many years earlier (1934) and had served first as assistant, then as pastor, and finally as moderator at the Comanche Reformed Church in Lawton, Oklahoma, a period of service that covered more than forty years.

The Reverend James Ottipoby, a Comanche, had been ordained in 1938, served as an assistant in Winnebago, Nebraska (1938-40), and Mescalero, New Mexico (1940-43), then became a military chaplain. He later was dismissed to the Presbyterian Church and served churches on the Laguna reservation in New Mexico.

The Reverend Wendell Chino of Mescalero was ordained in 1951 and went on to serve as assistant and then pastor of the Mescalero Reformed Church from 1951 to 1955, at which time he was elected tribal chairman—a position he held until his death in 1998. He demitted (voluntarily relinquished) his ordination in the Reformed Church in 1972.

58. Interview with the author, March 27, 1977.

Robert and Elsie
Chaat

Wilbur and Lupita
DeCora

James and Lucille
Ottipoby

Wendell and Patricia
Chino

Frank and
Pat Love

Jonah and Edith
Washington

The Reverend Wilbur De Cora, a Winnebago, was ordained in 1958 after serving two years as an assistant in Mescalero. He was pastor at the Winnebago church from 1958 to 1962, resigned from that position, and, although he had not demitted or been deposed, was reordained in 1970 and served in Winnebago for five more years until his death in 1975.

The Reverend Jonah Washington, a Pima, was also ordained in 1958 after working as an assistant in Mescalero from 1946 to 1951. After ordination he served briefly as the pastor in Apache, Oklahoma (1958-59), worked as chaplain at the Chilocco Indian School in Chilocco, Oklahoma, from 1959 to 1968, then returned for a pastorate in Dulce, New Mexico (1968-72).

The Reverend Frank Love, an Omaha from Macy, Nebraska, was ordained by the Classis of California in 1965 and served as assistant and pastor in Mescalero from 1965 to 1969. He was pastor at the Macy church for two years, 1969-71, and then left the employ of the Reformed Church and worked for a series of Indian agencies in several parts of the country.

Of these six Native American men ordained in the Reformed Church in America, three graduated from theological seminaries—Chino and Love from Western Theological Seminary and Washington from Austin (Presbyterian) Seminary. The other three—Chaat, De Cora, and Ottipoby—were given dispensations based largely on experience under the supervision of Reformed pastors. Four (Chino, Chaat, De Cora, and Love) studied at Cook Christian Training School. Three (Love, Washington, and Ottipoby) graduated from an accredited four-year college. All received financial assistance from the denomination.

Indian Churches Transferred to Contiguous Classes

Throughout the nineteenth century, Native American congregations (all in Nebraska, New Mexico, and Oklahoma) had remained members of the Classis of New York—probably because of the proximity of the classis to the board offices. Finally, in 1957, the Synod of New York transferred the native churches to classes in their own area. All were transferred to the Particular Synod of Iowa, which at that time covered the entire United States west of the Mississippi River. Classis assignments were as follows:

Apache, Oklahoma: West Central
Comanche, Lawton, Oklahoma: West Central
Jicarilla Apache, Dulce, New Mexico: West Central
Mescalero, New Mexico: California
First, Macy, Nebraska (newly organized): East Sioux
Winnebago, Nebraska: West Sioux

These congregations were no longer called mission stations or mission churches; instead, they had the status of "board-aided churches." The Nebraska churches, eight miles apart, were transferred to different classes, presumably to promote diversity in both classes.

Ministry at Phoenix Indian School

In 1961, long after most of the Indian boarding schools had closed, the Reverend John Lucius began a ministry at the Phoenix Indian High School in Arizona, a tenure that continued for twenty-two years. Previously, John and Helga Lucius had served the Native American congregations in Macy, Nebraska, and Dulce, New Mexico.

The government's Phoenix Indian School had opened in 1891 and had been patterned after the Carlisle Indian School in Pennsylvania. Like Carlisle, it originally tried to stamp out Indian languages and traditions, but changing public sentiment gradually modified the focus. By 1935 it offered regular junior and senior high school classes as well as vocational classes. When the Luciuses arrived, the school was reaching its zenith of nine hundred students, all of whom were required to attend church services on campus. This policy was soon

John Lucius   Helga Lucius

changed, and Lucius began encouraging local churches to minister to Indian youths while he continued the campus religious and counseling program. It was a daunting task, as Indian youths were dealing with intertribal rivalries; special educational, social, and psychological needs; and the dynamics of being uprooted from tribal and family life. By the time John Lucius retired in 1983, the enrollment of the Phoenix Indian School had declined to about five hundred students, and the school closed in 1990. In all, John and Helga Lucius spent thirty years in Indian ministry.

Ministry at Chilocco Indian School

Another of the surviving boarding schools was in Chilocco, Oklahoma. Its religious and chaplaincy program was directed for ten years (1958-68) by the Reverend Jonah Washington. Washington's service at Chilocco was sandwiched between pastorates in Apache, Oklahoma, and Dulce, New Mexico.

The Chilocco school was founded in 1884 to educate the children of the tribes of western Oklahoma. The school expanded gradually to include others as well, and by 1907 the campus included thirty-five buildings. The school, like others of the time, offered academic subjects and training for farming and homemaking, but in later years it also included a wide variety of vocational training courses. Early students included Richard Imach and Amy White, children of the Fort Sill Apaches. Chilocco was one of the more popular Indian schools, drawing as many as twelve hundred students from throughout North America, and it remained open until 1980.

Washington's responsibilities included conducting worship services, planning the annual Religious Emphasis Week, and counseling students. Harriette Washington served as a guidance counselor.

Seventh Policy: Self-Determination

On December 1, 1955, Rosa Parks refused to take the back seat of a bus in Montgomery, Alabama, triggering the Civil Rights movement. The struggle for minority rights eventually spread to the Native American population, where its more assertive branch was called the Red Power movement.

Campaign for Indian Rights

The National Congress of American Indians, which had been founded in 1944, was reinvigorated, and its 1961 gathering in Chicago was the largest multitribal gathering in decades. But college-age Indians were dissatisfied with what they considered the nonconfrontational approach of their elders, and they founded the National Indian Youth Council in the summer of that year. Sit-ins, marches, and demonstrations followed, including a "fish-in" at a river in Washington State to support treaty rights. The founding of the American Indian Movement (AIM) in 1968 was followed by such demonstrations as the occupation of Alcatraz and the "reclaiming" of Mt. Rushmore. In 1969 Vine Deloria published his classic, *Custer Died for Your Sins: An Indian Manifesto*. In 1972 AIM mobilized a "Trail of Broken Treaties" march from San Francisco to Washington, D.C., which culminated in the occupation of the Bureau of Indian Affairs building. In February of the following year, AIM took over the town of Wounded Knee on the Pine Ridge Sioux Reservation in South Dakota, an incident that resulted in the death of two Indians, the wounding of a federal marshal, and the indictment of three hundred Indians.

Most Indians, however, distanced themselves from public tactics, to the chagrin of black leaders who had tried to draw them into the more activist aspects of the Civil Rights movement. Even when the tactics of the two racial movements were similar, the goals were quite different. Blacks were seeking integration into mainstream America, while Indians—who for years had resisted such integration—were seeking the right to preserve their own culture while retaining the land that was still theirs and collecting reparations for land that had been taken from them.

Wendell Chino, president of the National Congress of American

Indians, tribal chairman of the Mescaleros, and former pastor of the Mescalero Reformed Church, was pictured in the December 7, 1969, issue of the *New York Times Magazine*, flanked by vice president Spiro Agnew and secretary of the interior Walter Hickel. The accompanying story, "The War Between the Redskins and the Feds," told of Chino's testimony in Washington D.C. on behalf of Indian rights and welfare. Chino and others believed that it was indeed possible for native peoples to use the United States' legal and legislative systems in the struggle to retain their remaining tribal homelands, protect their sacred sites and burial grounds, and preserve their traditions from outside interference.

Positive Political Response

These efforts began to show fruit. A task force appointed by president John F. Kennedy recommended that the termination policy be discontinued. In 1964, for the first time, tribal governments gained access to federal antipoverty funds through the Office of Economic Opportunity rather than the Bureau of Indian Affairs. The Bureau of Indian Affairs established a Division of Economic Development, and by 1965 forty tribes had received technical assistance in the development of natural resources, businesses, industries, home construction, and public works.

Three years later, president Lyndon Johnson proposed in a speech to Congress ("The Forgotten American") that termination talk be replaced by a positive emphasis on self-determination. He proposed (1) a standard of living for Indians equal to that of the country as a whole; (2) freedom to choose whether to remain in their homelands or to move to towns and cities of America; and (3) full participation in the life of America while retaining their identity as Indians.

Richard Nixon campaigned with promises that largely reflected Johnson's policies. Indians were skeptical at first, but under Nixon the relocation strategy was reversed, traditional Indian religious practices were protected, and increased spending was approved for Indian schools, health care, and tribal businesses. In a radical break from the past, Nixon staffed the Bureau of Indian Affairs almost exclusively with Indians.

'Red Power' and the Founding of the American Indian Council

The Reformed Church in America heard echoes of the Red Power

movement in December of 1969 when tribal chairmen Edwin Cline of
Macy and Gordon Beaver of Winnebago, both elders in their churches,
published an article, "Is a Show of Red Power Next? An Open Letter
to the Reformed Church in America," in the *Church Herald*. In June of
that year James Forman and other members of a group that called
themselves the Black Economic Development Conference had occupied
the denominational offices at the Interchurch Center in New York
City. Forman handed the Reformed Church a "Black Manifesto" that
cited racial injustices and demanded, among other things, $30 million
and the establishment of four black publishing houses. In response,
the General Synod formulated a "Response to the Black Manifesto,"
disagreeing with Forman's ideology and tactics but allocating $100,000
in anticipation of the formation of a Reformed Church Black Council.

Citing the Forman occupation and the church's response, Cline
and Beaver asked, "Is this the only way the church will listen to the
requests of minority groups?" Citing the denomination's commitment
to self-determination in its "Response to the Black Manifesto," the
letter asked, "Over the years, what self-determination has the red man
been allowed to exercise?" The authors brought up the perceived lack of
Indian involvement in the closing of the Winnebago Children's Home,
the three-year vacancy in the Macy church, and the reduction of funds.
"Too long," they wrote, "have we been silent and allowed great white
fathers and mothers to determine our future and destiny. All we ask is
that we be treated as human beings rather than puppets dangling on a
string." Referring to the Black Power movement, they said, "If you want
'Red Power,' we can furnish it. At least give us a chance."[59]

This letter came as a surprise to mission administrators and
personnel. From their viewpoint, the Winnebago tribe had been very
much involved in the decision to close the Winnebago Children's
Home. In 1967 the Reverend Albert Van Dyke, newly commissioned
as the Reformed Church's director of Indian work, had written, "Our
witness for Christ in the Indian communities has had as its goal the
development of a self-propagating, self-governing, self-supporting
church."[60]

The Reverend Isaac Rottenberg, secretary for program
interpretation and resource development, wrote a response published

59. Gordon C. Beaver and Edward L. Cline, "Is a Show of Red Power Next? An
    Open Letter to the Reformed Church in America," *Church Herald* (Dec. 26,
    1969), 12.
60. Albert Van Dyke, "You Are Too Late," *Church Herald* (Aug. 11, 1967), 11.

alongside the Beaver and Cline letter. Rottenberg stated that although the message "contains assertions and emphases which we would be tempted to challenge...we should above all else listen, and let our consciences be pricked by the cries of our suffering brothers and sisters. In view of our own burden of guilt with respect to the plight of the Indian people in America, repentance and constructive action are needed more urgently than polemics."[61]

Three years later, in 1972, the American Indian Council became the second racial/ethnic council of the Reformed Church, the first being the Black Council in 1971. The Hispanic Council followed in 1974, and the Council for Pacific and Asian American Ministries was organized in 1980. Although there was early pressure within the American Indian Council to the contrary, the council quickly adopted a nonconfrontational stance with regard to the white majority of the Reformed Church. (See chapter 10, "The American Indian Council.")

Indian Culture Romanticized

Alongside this new sensitivity to the plight of the Indian came a movement to idealize all things Indian. The former Blood-thirsty Savage suddenly became the Noble Red Man. "Most contemporary literature," wrote the Indian activist Vine Deloria, "is a thinly disguised romanticism that looks at Indians as the last and best spiritual hope for a society disheartened and disorganized."[62] Said C. L. Sonnichsen,

> Now the pendulum swung to the other extreme and the "Indianists" took charge. Indian religion suddenly became nobly spiritual. Indian life and customs seemed admirable, especially to people who had never been on a reservation. Indian arts and crafts embodied all beauty and originality.[63]

As part of this romantic revision, it was alleged that the practice of scalping originated not with Indians but with white people. There is no evidence, however, that Europeans practiced scalping before coming to the western hemisphere, and there is plenty of evidence that scalping took place in the western hemisphere long before the arrival of white people.

61. Isaac Rottenberg, sidebar to "Is a Show of Red Power Next?" *Church Herald* (Dec. 26, 1969), 12.
62. Vine Deloria, Jr., *Custer Died for Your Sins: An Indian Manifesto* (Norman, Okla.: University Press, 1988), ix.
63. Sonnichsen, *Mescalero Apaches,* 8-9.

The Reformed Church in America also began to issue positive statements about Indian culture. The 1961 report of the Board of North American Missions quoted with approval an unidentified writer who gave Indians credit not only for corn, potatoes, tobacco, cotton, peanuts, pumpkins, quinine, cocaine, and witch hazel, but also for the love of nature (institutionalized in athletics, the Boy Scouts, and family vacations), and roads that follow Indian paths. Indians were given credit for inspiring Thomas Jefferson to advocate local self-government in the Declaration of Independence. In fact, says the article, "Indian America helped to civilize Europe when early international law was written," and "the Indian's passion for liberty was a thing that nourished the flame and caused the bursting forth of the American Revolution."[64] In other words, the American Indian (now called an Indian American) had suddenly become a savior instead of a savage and had become a civilizer instead of a civilizee.

Limited Publicity

During this time the printed record of American Indian mission became much less detailed. The mission emphasis of the *Church Herald* was limited mostly to "Mission of the Month" articles assigned by the denominational communications office and occasional news items sent by the churches. This meant that each of the five Indian mission congregations was highlighted only once every five years. (Comanche Reformed Church in Lawton, Oklahoma, was self-supporting and therefore not included in the "Mission of the Month" program.) Later, the *Church Herald* eliminated the regular "Mission of the Month" feature and printed only special mission features and occasional news items. Simultaneously, reports to and by the General Program Council and the General Synod were considerably streamlined, and reports on Indian American ministries often included no more than a sentence or two about staff comings and goings, plus a statement about "an increase" in something—whether it be "attendance," "membership," "commitment," or "sense of mission."

Pastoral Calling Reverts to the Mission Board

In 1957 the Indian American churches had been released from their more-or-less pretend membership in the Classis of New York to

64. *Minutes of the General Synod, 1961,* 20-21.

become members of classes near them geographically. This move had obvious advantages, but it caused problems as well. One problem was assessments. The Reverend Albert Van Dyke, chairman of the Indian Committee of the Board of North American Missions (1961-67) and then director of Indian Work (1967-70), reported to this author that when Indians came to classis meetings and stayed in some rather fancy homes, they couldn't understand why the white man wanted their money. Van Dyke urged the Indian churches to reduce assessments by placing inactive members on the "absent or inactive" list, but the churches felt that this would be counterproductive in their culture. Despite pleas by Van Dyke, the classes refused to make allowances. In recent years, financial realities have overcome cultural resistance, and most Indian American congregations regularly report inactive members.

The 1950s and early 1960s were difficult for several of the Indian American churches, who experienced many short and unhappy pastorates involving both white and Indian clergy—including one white pastor whose wife required Indian visitors to use the back door lest they get the carpet dirty. The mission board and its administrators, chiefly Marcus and Van Dyke, spent a great deal of time and energy doing damage control and making suggestions as to who might be shifted from one place to another.

The new classis arrangement also meant that the Indian congregations had authority to call their own pastors in consultation with mission executives. But the Board of North American Missions believed it was time to regain authority over its troubled churches, and in October of 1962 it adopted a policy statement that soft-peddled its earlier emphasis on self-determination. The new policy said that the board would confer with the consistory and/or congregation and the classis, but made it clear that "until such a church is able to meet all its operating expenses, and gives sufficient evidence of responsibility and leadership, and demonstrates its ability to reduce its financial requests for the pastor's salary, the Board shall appoint the personnel to serve in these fields." The policy also made it clear that the recruitment and training of pastors would be directed both to Indian and non-Indian pastors, and that "a fully trained, ordained, and sustained ministry is the goal of the churches."[65]

65. *Which Way Tomorrow? Ministries in Indian American Communities/A Statement of Policy and Philosophy* (Reformed Church in America, Board of North American Missions, 1965).

The issue of mission board authority was raised in the fall of 2002 when the mission staff terminated the employment of the Reverend Darrell Dalman, pastor of the Winnebago church, as an employee of the General Synod Council. The consistory retained Dalman, however, and the Classis of Central Plains submitted two overtures to the General Synod concerning the matter, with the result that the synod voted "to instruct the General Synod Council, in consultation with the Commission on Church Order, to address the structural arrangement between a mission pastor of a Native American church, Mission Services, the classis, and the consistory of the local church in which the missionary pastor serves."[66] As of this writing, the results of that study have not been published. (See chapter 8 for further details.)

1968 Statement Emphasizes Development

A 1968 statement, *Philosophy and Policy for Indian Ministries*, closely followed goals adopted by the National Council of Churches and placed a strong emphasis on social and economic development. "The church and its leaders must understand and respect the philosophy, psychology, and culture of Indian people," it said, but "the church must aid them in refining, enriching, and adapting their culture so they may share more abundantly in the American way of life." The ten goals of this policy statement were:

1. Strong Christian witness through Indian participation and interchurch planning.
2. An effective Christian witness in the local church.
3. Fullest opportunities for Indian self-determination.
4. Maximum opportunity for Indian youth in self-realization and training for any society.
5. Involvement of the church in economic development.
6. Involvement of the church in securing better housing and sanitation.
7. Achievement of health levels comparable to prevailing standards.
8. Recognition of movement of Indians to metropolitan and non-metropolitan centers as a challenge to extend friendly understanding and Christian presence.

66. *Minutes of the General Synod*, 2004, 189-90.

9. Recognition of the church's responsibility to see that legislation, appropriations, and administrative actions are acceptable to Indian people and meet their needs as they see them.

10. Authentic, non-condescending public information.[67]

End of the Era of Indian Pastors

With the death of Wilbur De Cora in 1975 during his second tenure as pastor in Winnebago, Nebraska, the era of Native American Reformed Church pastors came to an end. At one time as many as four Native American pastors had been serving Reformed pulpits simultaneously, most of them the products of Reformed mission work and educated for at least a year at denominational colleges and seminaries. With the exception of Chaat, who served for forty years in Lawton, Indian clergy had averaged just eight years of total ministry and less than four years per pastorate. The pastorates of De Cora, Love, and Washington were fraught with discord and controversy. All in all, the effort to train and ordain native pastors for Native American congregations of the Reformed Church in America has produced limited results. The Reformed Church has not ordained a full-blooded Native American pastor since 1965.

One might legitimately ask why these Native American pastorates were often so difficult. At least two factors were involved:

1. Being an Indian leader in an Indian congregation does not ensure acceptance, and in many cases makes acceptance more difficult. This rejection is seldom articulated in the manner of non-Indians—as, for instance, church members of Dutch extraction might have roast preacher on Sunday noon—but it lurks beneath the surface. If the pastor is from the same tribe, there may be the sentiment that "we knew him when he was young; who does he think he is now?" If the pastor is from a different tribe, feelings of ancient tribal rivalry may come into play. In either case, Indian culture emphasizes social leveling and cooperation rather than individual achievement, which is often interpreted as self-aggrandizement.

2. Most Indian clergy in the Reformed Church were educated in white colleges and seminaries, with a strong dose of European-based culture and theological training. Reformed theology tends to be academic and comes from a background of the theological debates of

67. *Philosophy and Policy for Indian Ministries,* typewritten document (Reformed Church in America, May 1968), 21-23.

the Reformation. For the most part, Indian pastors did their best to reflect their academic training in their preaching and teaching, seldom contextualizing the gospel in Indian culture and customs. When it came to record keeping and report making, most native pastors found it difficult—if not onerous—to meet the expectations of the denominational structure.

If they stayed long enough, most white pastors of Indian congregations, despite their deficiencies of culture and language and their identification with the dominant society, have over time gained the trust and even affection of the Indian people. White pastors have the distinct advantage of being able to stand apart from tribal politics, which can be bitter and divisive. Most Indian people are used to working with white professionals such as doctors, teachers, and business people. The white pastors generally have made a conscious attempt to relate the gospel to Indian culture, and as long as they don't try to be "pretend Indians," this effort is appreciated.

Other Native American Pastors and Spouses

A number of more recent Reformed pastors and spouses have come from a Native American heritage: Nancy Crump, pastor's spouse in Winnebago, Nebraska (1987-94), part Cherokee; the Reverend Earl Smith, pastor in Macy, Nebraska (1995-), part Oneida; and Dawn Dalman, pastor's spouse in Winnebago, Nebraska (1994-2002), Kiowa.

Meanwhile, the Reverend Nickolas Miles, a registered member of the Pumunky tribe of Virginia, has served the United Reformed Church of Rosendale in Bloomington, New York, since 1973. His father and grandfather, says Miles, never spoke of their Indian heritage as he was growing up in New Jersey, but he made public his lineage during the activism of the 1970s. Miles maintains some contact with his tribe, and his brother was at one time the tribal chairman.

Casino Gambling Enters Tribal Economics, 1988

Tribal economics underwent a major change during the Reagan presidency, when the Indian Gaming Regulatory Act (1988) paved the way for tribal-sponsored casinos. As government funds were gradually terminated, as tribal governments had no viable tax base for support, and as tribal unemployment ran as high as 70 percent, several tribes had opened gaming (as it was euphemistically called) operations as a business enterprise. States moved quickly to stop or severely restrict tribal gambling, even though they often allowed gambling by charitable organizations and by the state itself. The Indian Gaming Regulatory Act declared that tribes have the right to conduct gambling enterprises if that activity is not prohibited by federal or state laws. The act established three classes of games, with escalating levels of outside regulation: (1) traditional Indian games (no nontribal regulation), (2) games of chance such as bingo, and (3) casino-type gambling such as slot machines and blackjack.

In 1992 the Foxwoods Casino opened in northeast Connecticut. Today, Foxwood, with its constellation of five casinos and 6,400 slot machines, is the country's largest gambling establishment, with about forty thousand players on an average day and an annual revenue of $1 billion. In 2003, Indian casinos reported total revenues of $16.7 billion—more than 20 percent of the money spent on legalized gambling each year in the United States. (Americans spend an additional $40 billion annually on state-run lotteries.)

Not all that glitters is gold, however. Federal regulations allow non-Indian casino managers to charge as much as 40 percent of net revenues. Some casinos are poorly managed, many are located at inconvenient distances from potential patrons, the income often has little relationship to the number of people in the tribe, and some tribes spend their proceeds on per capita payouts rather than on tribal infrastructure and industry.

The most successful casino in the areas of Reformed Church mission is the Apache Casino in Mescalero, New Mexico, an operation engineered by the late tribal chairman and former pastor, Wendell Chino. Chino resisted intense pressure to distribute large sums to individual tribal members and insisted that most of the profits be reinvested in tribal facilities and industries that in turn employed hundreds of members of the tribe.

The Jicarilla Apache tribe near the northern border of New Mexico has a small casino located in a motel, but its remote location severely limits white patronage. The Winnebago tribe in Winnebago, Nebraska, operates WinneVegas, and the nearby Omaha tribe owns Casino Omaha, both of which are actually in Iowa, across the Missouri River just off Interstate 29. The tribe has a tradition of allocating some of the income from WinneVegas for the childcare center conducted at the Winnebago Reformed Church. The Comanches have a large and busy casino on the east side of Lawton, Oklahoma, and the Apaches have a smaller casino, also located on the east side of Lawton. While the virtues and vices of casino gambling continue to be debated, it is generally conceded that tribal "gaming," where properly conducted, has provided employment and income for a people who historically have had little of either.

Further Classis Realignment

In 1989 the particular synods of the Reformed Church underwent a major realignment, which also included a number of classis changes. The Macy and Winnebago churches became part of the newly formed Classis of Central Plains in the Particular Synod of the Heartland. The Comanche and Apache churches were placed in the newly formed Classis of Red River in the Particular Synod of the Heartland. The New Mexico Indian congregations were assigned to the Synod of the Far West—the Dulce church to the Classis of Rocky Mountains and the Mescalero church to the Classis of the Southwest. Two years later, in 1991, the synods became known as "regional" rather than "particular." Then in 2004 the Synod of the Heartland dissolved the Classis of Red River and transferred its four Texas churches to the Classis of Central Iowa and the three Oklahoma churches (including those at Lawton and Apache) to the Classis of Central Plains. The congregations in Macy and Winnebago, Nebraska, were already in that classis, so four of the six Native American churches are now in one classis.

Omaha and Lincoln, Nebraska

Eventually most native people who had moved to the city returned to their homes on the reservations. For the most part, they had secured only menial jobs, found it difficult to adjust to city life, and were homesick for family and friends. Still, some stayed in the cities, and the Reformed Church became involved cooperatively in a number of urban ministries. These have included the Native American Urban Transition Program in Denver, Colorado, and ecumenical ministries in Omaha and Lincoln, Nebraska, under the auspices of Interchurch Ministries of Nebraska. The Reformed pastors in Winnebago and Macy, Nebraska, as well as lay pastor Thurman Cook, were involved in planning the Omaha and Lincoln work, which got underway in 1990 with the Reverend Reaves Nahwooks, a Baptist minister from Oklahoma and a Native American, as pastor. The Reformed Church in America joined seven other Protestant denominations in contributing financial support to these Nebraska ministries but phased out its support in 2002.

Indian Ministries in Canada and Alaska

In 1991 the Reformed Church committed itself to limited financial support of LAMP, the Lutheran Association of Missionaries and Pilots. LAMP is an independent mission society that supports clergy/pilots who bring pastoral, educational, social, and occasional medical services to scattered and isolated Inuit villages in northern Canada.

Since 1993 the denomination has supported Brian and Elizabeth Bruxvoort, who work in Soldotna, Alaska, under the auspices of Mission Aviation Repair Center (MARC). Brian pilots a small plane that flies pastors and others to remote Alaskan villages, and Elizabeth conducts children's ministries in Soldotna. As with LAMP, most of the people served by MARC are indigenous peoples.

The Reformed Church Responds to the Columbus Quincentennial, 1992

As the church looked ahead to the nation's observance of the five hundredth anniversary of Columbus's arrival in the western hemisphere, the General Synod of 1990 proclaimed 1992 as a "year of reflection and repentance, standing in solidarity with the peoples of the Americas who have suffered the onslaught of colonialism, neocolonialism, and cultural imperialism."[68] A new video, *The Columbus 500th: A Time for Reflection*, was produced by the Reformed Church's Office of Promotion and Communication; the spring 1992 issue of the *City Gate*, produced by the Office of Social Witness, included several related articles; a list of audiovisual and print resources was sent to the churches; and a collection of prayers, litanies, and other worship resources was made available.

In June of 1992 the American Indian Council (which kept a relatively low profile during observances) held its annual meeting in Albany, New York, in conjunction with the General Synod. The Reverend Reaves Nahwooks, pastor of urban Indian ministries in Omaha and Lincoln, Nebraska, led one of the worship services. That synod also passed several recommendations regarding American Indian issues: (1) to designate a Native American Awareness Sunday; (2) to request Reformed Church seminaries to provide courses and seminars to help non-native American pastors become aware of Native American culture, history, and language; (3) to support legislation promoting the

68. *Minutes of the General Synod*, 1990, 122-23.

self-determination of Native Americans; and (4) to explore investments in development projects in partnership with tribal peoples.[69] At best, the results of the above actions were minimal. The following year a study resource, "Breaking Down the Walls: Responding to the Racism That Divides Us," which dealt in part with derogatory names and images of Native Americans, was included in the 1993 peace packet of the Office of Social Witness.

One Hundredth Anniversary of Indian Ministry

In 1997 the Reformed Church celebrated the one hundredth anniversary of the beginning of board-initiated Indian mission. (Actually, mission work began in 1895, but somehow that date was overlooked.) The event took place at the 1997 General Synod, held at the Milwaukee campus of the University of Wisconsin. The occasion included a historical display, a tribute to Mildred Cleghorn of Apache, a plaque presentation to Kenneth Mallory, past executive of the American Indian Council, and the presence of several Native American Reformed Church members as well as present and former missionaries.

Raymond Nauni, Jr., an elder at the Comanche Reformed Church in Lawton, Oklahoma, addressed the synod on behalf of the council. He quoted at length a 1867 speech by Parra-Wa-Semen (Ten Bears) of the Yamparika Comanches, outlining the abuse of Indians by whites. Nauni then gave a short history of the denomination's work among Indian people and concluded with a word of thanks to the Reformed Church for "leading us to God through examples, words, deeds, love, and tolerance." Although we are in various stages of growth, he said, "We are all one in the Spirit and all striving for the same goal to follow the Jesus road and be with our Lord and God in heaven."

Mission Staff Administrators

During the last half-century, eight administrators have supervised American Indian ministries on behalf of the Board of Domestic/North American Missions, the General Program Council, and the General Synod Council: Beth Marcus (1953-68); the Reverend Albert Van Dyke (1967-70); the Reverend John Hiemstra (1969-72); the Reverend Harold Brown (1972-79); the Reverend Richard Vander Voet (1980-92); the Reverend Robert Terwilliger (1993-1996); Nola Aalberts (1996-2001) and the Reverend Roger De Young (2001-present). Their

69. *Minutes of the General Synod*, 1992, 119, 149, 150.

duties have included supervising the mission budgets, raising funds from churches and individuals, counseling pastors and churches, and consulting on mission policies and procedures. Almost to a person, these administrators have said that their greatest challenge has been encouraging Native American self-determination, self-sufficiency, and leadership development.

The Continuing Struggle with U. S. Political Systems

For the past quarter century, federal policy has largely reflected principles laid down during the Nixon Administration (1969-74). From another viewpoint, it may be fair to say that government interest in Indian affairs has been minimal since that time. The Native Americans' relatively small numbers and scattered demographics mean that they are not a major force at the polls. *Newsweek* magazine, in reporting on President Clinton's visit to the Pine Ridge Reservation in South Dakota in the summer of 1999, said, "It's hard to believe, but Clinton is the first American president since Franklin Roosevelt to visit an Indian reservation."[70] The article, incidentally, reported that unemployment at Pine Ridge was 73 percent.

In the 1960s and '70s Native Americans learned how to use the American legal system to gain reparations for their massive losses during the previous century and to retain the limited property they still held. The struggle involves more than property, however; it also involves the preservation of archaeological sites, the repatriation of Indian remains, the development of reservation resources, the right to worship as they choose, and the preservation of mineral, water, timber, and fossil fuel rights.

The battle is still uphill. Among the efforts to revive and retain Native rights was the filing, in 1996, of a class action suit against interior secretary Bruce Babbit and treasury secretary Robert Rubin for mismanagement of tribal trust funds. In an audit, the Bureau of Indian Affairs couldn't account for $2.5 billion in Indian trust funds going back to the 1887 Dawes Act. In 1999 it was revealed that the Treasury Department had covered up the shredding of 162 boxes of government records that could have helped in tracing the funds, and in 2001 the total of unaccounted funds was estimated to be $3 billion.

Reformed Church mission administrators, pastors, and the American Indian Council (now the Native American Indian Ministries Council) have continued to stress self-determination and self-

70. Jonathan Alter, "Trade Mission to Misery, USA," *Newsweek*, July 19, 1999, 34.

sufficiency. Progress has been made, as all of the Native American congregations underwrite most of their ongoing expenses and subscribe to one or more mission shares in their pastor's support. The Comanche Reformed Church in Lawton, Oklahoma, however, is the only Native congregation that wholly supports its part-time pastor. Volunteer work crews still make their summer safaris, both because they can benefit from a cross-cultural mission experience and because they are needed. The goal of self-sufficiency is still far from being reached. The "new day" for the Native American is still only a glow on the horizon.

CHAPTER 2

Mission to Indians in New Netherland

The two hundredth anniversary booklet of the First Reformed Protestant Dutch Church in Schenectady, New York (1880), pointed out that the whole world has heard of John Eliot, missionary to Indians in Massachusetts. But, said the author, "the Dutch domines of Albany began preaching to the Indians three years before Eliot held his first service." With a flair for the dramatic, the booklet describes the Indians who worshiped with the Dutch in Schenectady:

> There the Indian papooses were held in the arms of their dusky mothers, who stood in beads and blankets, before the same baptismal font...at which waited the white lady and her infant in christening-quilt of silk and embroidery. There, too, the Indian lover stood with his Indian bride, and in the name of the Father, and of the Son, and of the Holy Ghost, in the words of the Christian ritual, vowed to love and cherish one wife in his wigwam; and when our fathers came annually to pay their pew rent or subscriptions in beaver skins, the Christian Indians came also with like gifts for the sanctuary. When the domine died, the Mohawks out of sympathy presented peltries and strings of wampum as tokens of condolence.[1]

No history of the mission work of the Reformed Church in America

---

1. *Two Hundredth Anniversary of the First Reformed Protestant Dutch Church of Schenectady, New York,* (June 20-21, 1880), 38.

among Native Americans would be complete without the story of how several of the pastors of New Netherland, freshly commissioned to the "new world" by the Classis of Amsterdam, preached to the Indians they found in and around Rensselaerwyck (now Albany) and Schenectady, but had less inclination to evangelize in New Amsterdam.[2]

Tensions with Indians in New Amsterdam

The Dutch West Indies Company sent colonists to New Netherland for the primary purpose of financial gain, but the ecclesiastical authorities in Holland stipulated in 1624 that the settlers should "by their Christian life and conduct seek to draw the Indians and other blind people to the Knowledge of God and His Word."[3]

Given the tensions between the Dutch and the Indians in and around New Amsterdam, this was a formidable task. Relations between the two peoples began amicably enough, when Peter Minuit, the first director of New Netherland, purchased Manhattan Island rather than capturing it, paying with a box of trade goods (presumably such things as hatchets, metal pots, cloth, and beads) worth sixty Dutch guilders. At the time this was worth 2,400 English cents, hence the legendary $24. It must be remembered, however, that the European concept of purchase was quite different from that of American Indians, who simply could not understand the concept of human ownership of land. If anything, Indians understood the transaction as a kind of lease that gave rights for a limited amount of time, not an irrevocable agreement that took away their land forever.

Jonas Michaelius Describes Indians as 'Savage and Wild'

It is not certain whether Bastian Krol, the colony's first "comforter of the sick," attempted to evangelize the Indians. However, there is evidence that he may have possessed some knowledge of the Indian language—which implies prolonged contact with them.

With the Reverend Jonas Michaelius, New Amsterdam's first ordained minister, who arrived from the Netherlands in 1628, the

2. Those who wish a more detailed history of this era should read the excellent work by Gerald F. De Jong, *The Dutch Reformed Church in the American Colonies,* Historical Series of the Reformed Church in America (Grand Rapids: Eerdmans, 1978); and Robert S. Alexander, *Albany's First Church,* (published by the First Church in Albany, New York, 1988).
3. A. J. F. Van Laer, ed., *Documents Relating to New Netherland, 1924-26* (San Marino, Calif.: Henry E. Huntington Library and Art Gallery, 1964), 2-5.

't Fort nieuw Amsterdam op de Manhatans

An early depiction of New Amsterdam harbor

evidence is more clear: he despised the Indians. "As to the natives of this country," he wrote, "I find them entirely savage and wild, strangers to all decency, yea, uncivil and stupid as garden poles, proficient in all wickedness and godlessness." Their language, he said, is "entirely peculiar," and he suspected that "they rather design to conceal their language from us than to properly communicate it."[4]

Michaelius believed that any effort to evangelize adult Indians was doomed to failure. In an eerie prophecy of the Carlisle-type boarding school that would come 250 years later, he suggested that the only way to evangelize these people was to first civilize them, and to civilize them it would be necessary to separate the children from their parents. "Without this," he said, "they would forthwith be as much accustomed as their elders to heathenish tricks and deviltries." The children, he said, should be placed "under the godly instruction of some experienced and godly schoolmaster...[to be] instructed not only to speak, read, and write our language, but especially in the fundamentals of our Christian religion, and where, besides, they will see nothing but good examples of virtuous living."[5] He acknowledged, however, that his proposal posed two difficulties: (1) Indian parents are likely to have affection for their

4. A. Eekhof, *Jonas Michaelius: Founder of the Church in New Netherland* (Leyden: A. W. Sijthoff, 1926), 132.
5. Ibid., 133-34.

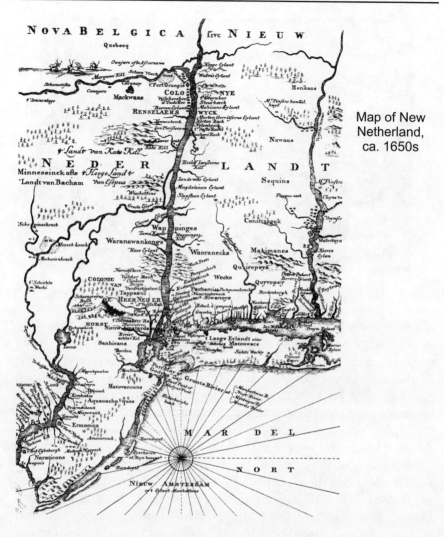

Map of New
Netherland,
ca. 1650s

children and to object to parting with them, and (2) antagonizing the
Indians might jeopardize the fur trade.

Escalating Hostilities in New Amsterdam

Michaelius left New Amsterdam in 1632 and was succeeded the
following year by the Reverend Everardus Bogardus, who arrived a year
after his ordination in Amsterdam. Bogardus's fourteen-year ministry
was punctuated by contentious relationships with the governors of
New Amsterdam—first with Wouter Van Twiller and then with Willem
Kieft.

Kieft arrived in 1639 during a time of relative peace with the Indians and immediately levied a tax on them for their "protection." The chiefs ignored his demand, and it soon became apparent that Kieft's ultimate goal was to remove all Indians, preferably by force. His rationale for war included the alleged stealing of several hogs belonging to David De Vries (the thieves apparently were really Dutchmen) and the murder of an elderly gentleman, Claes Swits, by a young Indian acting alone. When the settlement's governing council of twelve (including De Vries) tried to dissuade Kieft from violence, Kieft dissolved the council. On February 25, 1643, at the governor's orders, the Dutch surrounded the Indian village of Pavonia by night, burned it to the ground, and massacred everyone who tried to escape, including women and children.

By the time hostilities ended several years later, nearly a thousand Indians and Dutch settlers had been killed. It was not an environment conducive to evangelism among the Indians, and none was attempted. Ironically, Kieft and pastor Bogardus were on the same ship, the *Princess,* when it sank on its way to Holland in 1647, killing all aboard.

Indian Evangelism in Albany and Schenectady

Henry Hudson sailed as far as present-day Albany in 1609, and Dutch traders built Fort Nassau in 1614, which was later replaced by Fort Orange. Here in upstate New York the story of mission among the Indians was quite different from New Amsterdam in almost every respect—in context, effort, and result. Eventually more than three hundred Indian names were recorded in the church rolls of Albany and Schenectady.

Johannes Megapolensis Has a Heart for Indian Evangelism

Whereas relations with the Indians were for the most part hostile in New Amsterdam, they were generally friendly in Albany and Schenectady—at least with the Mohawks, otherwise known as the Iroquois.

Fort Orange had been founded as a trading post, with Dutch traders receiving a broad assortment of furs from the Mohawks, and the Indians receiving, among other things, firearms and liquor. In fact, the Indians sometimes received the liquor free, since it was found that they were more amenable to negotiation after a bit of priming with the white man's intriguing beverage.

Dutch involvement in upstate New York was limited to trading until the 1630s, at which time a movement began to establish a more permanent presence in the new world through agricultural colonies. A plan was put in place involving "patroons" (patrons), who were granted permission to purchase land. These patroons in turn solicited colonists from the Netherlands who would agree to come to the new world and work as tenants, in a system much like the European feudalism of medieval times. One such patroon was Kiliaen Van Rensselaer, an Amsterdam pearl and diamond merchant. Not surprisingly, he named his territory, which included Fort Orange, Rensselaerwyck—later renamed Albany.

Van Rensselaer wished to include among his colonists an ordained clergyman, whom he found in the person of the Reverend Johannes Megapolensis, a young man who, after a few years of ministry in the Netherlands, become excited about the possibility of ministry among trading companies in the new world. (Megapolensis's family name was Grootstadt, but after the clergy custom of the day, he had adopted its Latin equivalent.) Megapolensis began his work at Rensselaerwyck in 1642, having been commissioned not only to meet the spiritual needs of the Dutch colonists but also to seek "the edification of the inhabitants and Indians."[6]

Two years after his arrival, Megapolensis wrote a lengthy description of Indian customs, religion, marriage, family life, dress, government, and language, a document that was published as a brochure in the Netherlands. He found the Indians' language to be difficult and their customs generally unsavory, but he spent considerable time with them, traveling in canoes and visiting them in the woods. He opened his house to them, and several Indians sometimes spent the night sleeping on the floor, their preferred place of rest. He was impressed by the fact that, although the Indians had no laws or prescribed punishments, there were not half so many murders among them as in the Netherlands, which had severe laws and heavy penalties.

Occasionally ten or twelve Indians attended church services, standing in the back. Their incisive questions and observations about the white man's worship and conduct reveal a few reasons why the progress of the Christian gospel has been so torturously slow among their people, both then and later. Wrote Megapolensis:

6. J. F. Van Laer, ed., *Van Rensselaer Bowier Manuscripts, Being the Letters of Kiliaen Van Rensselaer, 1630-1643* (Albany: Univ. of the State of New York, 1908), 607.

[They] will stand awhile and look, and afterwards ask me what I am doing and what I want, that I stand there alone and make so many words, while none of the rest may speak. I tell them that I am admonishing the Christians that they must not steal, nor commit lewdness, nor get drunk, nor commit murder, and that they too ought not do these things; and that I intend in process of time to preach the same to them in their own country...when I am acquainted with their language. Then they say I do well to teach the Christians; but immediately add... "Why do so many Christians do these things?"[7]

Megapolensis served for seven years in Rensselaerwyck, where he fostered positive attitudes among both the Indians and the Dutch, paving the way for more fruitful evangelism in the future. He then moved on to New Amsterdam, where he served until 1670. In New Amsterdam, of course, he faced a history of extremely bad relationships with the native population. Despite his best efforts to learn the language, his concern for evangelism, and his positive relationship with Indians, he gained few, if any, converts.

Meanwhile, French Jesuit missionaries apparently enjoyed greater success among the Indians, especially in the St. Lawrence valley. This may have been because the ceremonies and rituals of the Roman Catholic faith were more appealing, or because the Catholic missionaries baptized everyone who requested it. Even more significant, perhaps, was the fact that the Roman Catholics sent many full-time Jesuits whose sole vocation was evangelizing the Indians, whereas the Dutch Reformed Church afforded only the part-time service of pastors whose primary calling was shepherding the Christian community. The Netherlands sent few pastors to carry on any of the Christian work, and most clergy were assigned to several churches and preaching stations, leaving little time for evangelizing Indian people. The Anglicans also conducted mission work in the Albany area with some success, establishing an Indian chapel on the Mohawk.

Godfriedus Dellius, Evangelist and Translator

While Megapolensis had been the first Protestant minister in North America to make a serious attempt to evangelize the Indians,

---

7. J. Franklin Jameson, *Narratives of New Netherland, 1609-1664* (New York: Barnes and Noble, 1959),177-78.

it was the Reverend Godfriedus Dellius (christened Godfrey Dell) who made the greatest strides in this endeavor. Soon after Dellius arrived in Albany (as it was now called) from the Netherlands in 1683, he began making brief visits to Indian villages. He found that he was expected to make a gift as evidence of his friendship, to make a contribution to the Indians' material welfare before speaking to them of their spiritual welfare. He did so at first out of his own meager income but found that as his ministry expanded he could no longer continue this practice. He requested additional funds from the Netherlands but was turned down. Dellius then turned for help to the English, who by this time had defeated the Dutch, and they were more amenable. Their motives were not entirely spiritual, however. Enmeshed in an ongoing struggle with the French for superiority in the region, the English governor reasoned that Indians who were both Christian and Protestant were more likely to be their allies. Therefore Dellius and several Albany ministers who followed him received modest financial subsidies from the English crown.

It took six years before the Albany church recorded its first Indian baptism, a Mohawk renamed Paulus. It was recorded on December 27, 1689, that "after a previous public confession [there] was baptized a certain heathen who became blind a number of years ago, and whose name among his nation had been Ock-Kweese. He was about 40 years old."[8]

Indians who followed in baptism were likewise given "Christian" names. Kanarongwe ("drawer of arrows"), for instance, became Pieter. Thowariage ("one whose fence has broken down") became Brant. Sakkoherriho ("one who re-enters the bushes") became Dorcas. Biblical names were popular, and new names given to twelve converts in 1690 included Seth, Rachel, Adam, Sara, Jacob, Lydia, Isaac, Rebecca, and David.

The minutes of the Albany church include the baptism of 125 Indians, aged four weeks to eighty years, during the last ten years of the Dellius pastorate. His contributions, with the help of an interpreter, included the translation of the Ten Commandments, the Apostles Creed, the liturgies for baptism and Communion, and several prayers and psalms. For these, Dellius and his translator used English letters with Mohawk phonetics. All this was done in the midst of conflict, as

8. "Albany Records: Names of Members, Marriages, and Baptisms," *Yearbook of the Holland Society of New York, 1904* (New York: Knickerbocker Press, 1904), 49.

Street scene of colonial New Amsterdam

Indians who were allied with the French frequently attacked both the Dutch community and the Mohawks who had befriended the white settlers.

Dellius's tenure in Albany came to an end in 1699 after he became involved in a political dispute with Governor Bellomont and made a questionable purchase of several hundred square miles of Indian land. The governor annulled Dellius's land purchase and suspended his ministerial charter (the provincial government was paying part of his salary), and Dellius returned to the Netherlands, never to come back to the colonies.

Johannas Lydius and Peter Van Driessen Continue the Work

There followed one of the strangest tales of Dutch Reformed pastoral history: two pastors arriving from the Netherlands in 1700 on the same ship, both expecting to fill the pulpit at Albany. Space does not allow us to go into the details of this debacle, except to say that it was resolved when one of the domines, the Reverend Johannas Lydius, took the pulpit in Albany, and the other, the Reverend Bernardus Freeman, agreed to go to Schenectady, which had been without a pastor for ten years following a devastating massacre.

Lydius served for nine years until his death in 1709 and was both loved and respected by the Indians. Records show that "the converts from the heathen had resumed praying and singing exercises at his house."[9] On one occasion, Lydius was defended publicly by a group of "praying Indians" (as Christian converts were called), who attested that

9. Edwin T. Corwin, ed., *Ecclesiastical Records of the State of New York*, vol. III (Albany: James B. Lyon, 1901), 1477.

because of his efforts they no longer lived "in envy and malice...but in peace and concord."[10]

The Reverend Peter Van Driessen, the next regularly installed pastor in Albany—and the first to retain his Dutch name—continued Indian mission work during twenty-six years of service (1712-38). In 1731 he wrote the Classis of Amsterdam that the tribes near Albany had been "altogether Christianized"[11] and suggested to some friends in Holland that a chain of Indian churches be organized. This was never done, but it attests to the number of Christian Indians living in the area.

As later missionaries in the western United States were to discover, numerous baptisms do not necessarily ensure continuing and stable communicant membership. Despite Dellius's count of over one hundred converts, his report of 1694 mentioned only sixteen Indian communicant members. At the time of Lydius's death in 1709, the church listed thirty Indians as members, with no mention of their attendance.

Van Driessen was apparently the last Albany pastor to take an active interest in the conversion of the Indians. A few Dutch Reformed laywomen worked among Indians who lived on the outskirts of Albany during the summer months, and some of these converts in turn witnessed to their own people when they moved away during the winter. Gerald De Jong reports burial record evidence that some Indians continued their membership and even that an Indian man may have served on the consistory in 1769.[12] Robert Alexander, author of the history of the Albany church, reports 332 Indian names in the church records from 1685 to 1770.

Bernardus Freeman, in Schenectady, Learns the Indian Language

Meanwhile in Schenectady, twenty miles to the northwest, relations with the local Indians ranged from massacre to evangelism. The massacre took place February 8, 1690, when French troops and their Indian allies swooped down from Canada and decimated the settlement, killing sixty, carrying away twenty-seven, and burning almost all the houses to the ground. Among the dead was the Reverend Petrus Tassemaker (spelled Peter Tesschenmaeker in the *Historical*

10. Ibid, 1867.
11. Ibid., 2548-49.
12. De Jong, *The Dutch Reformed Church*, 160.

Directory of the Reformed Church in America[12]), the church's first pastor, whose head was carried away on a pike.

Schenectady was a dangerous place to live after the devastation of 1690, and no one ventured outside without a musket. Peace was finally declared in 1697, and in 1700 the church and community were stable enough to call a second pastor. As has been noted, the church received a pastor by default when two domines arrived for the Albany parish at the same time, and one of them, the Reverend Bernardus Freeman, agreed to go to Schenectady instead. Freeman served the Schenectady church with distinction from 1700 to 1705. The Classis of Amsterdam had rejected him, considering his academic credentials to be weak, and he had appealed to another classis for ordination, but Freeman gained a reputation as a hard worker and an excellent preacher. It is also likely that he had a better grasp of the Indian language than any other Dutch Reformed preacher before or since. Like Dellius, he did translation work, including translating parts of the Old and New Testaments and the *Book of Common Prayer* into the Mohawk language.

Between 1702 and 1717 the Schenectady church recorded 39 Indian marriages, 101 baptisms, and 14 communicants received into membership. Most of these were recorded before Freeman left in 1705 for Long Island. After his departure only 19 Indians were baptized and one received as a communicant member. During this time a group of Indians petitioned for Freeman's return, this time to live among them instead of in Schenectady, but he declined the invitation because of his wife's objection to living in an Indian village.

Other Indian Evangelism in the East

Records indicate that missionary work among Indians was also conducted in other regions of New York. In 1741 the Reverend Michael Weiss wrote the Classis of Amsterdam that he had baptized several Indians in the upper Mohawk Valley. The records of the Schoharie church show that several Indian adults and children were brought into the church and that some Indian and mixed-race couples were married according to the rites of the Dutch Reformed Church.

Then interest in Indian evangelism waned. A number of issues may have been contributed to the change: increasing hostility between settlers and Indians as white encroachment on Indian land continued

---

12. Russell L. Gasero, The Historical Series of the Reformed Church in America, No. 37 (Grand Rapids: Eerdmans, 2001), 392.

its relentless course; white disappointment at the lack of long-term commitment on the part of Indian converts; the dissonance of Indian and Dutch culture in the churches; the failure to organize distinctly Indian churches; and the absence of pastors who made Indian evangelism a priority. The final blow to Indian evangelism came with the American Revolution—an event that mystified the Indians. For generations they had been told that the French were their enemies and the English were their friends, and they were utterly confused when the colonies went to war with England. In retrospect, the wonder is not that mission work among American Indians faded in time, but that it had existed at all, and with considerable success.

It would be a hundred fifty years before Indians would again be included in the mission efforts of the Reformed Church in America. This time the initiative would be taken, not by Dutch dominies from the Netherlands but by the women of the Reformed Church in America, through the Women's Executive Committee of the Board of Domestic Missions. Significantly, the women of the Albany church were among the most ardent supporters of mission work among the Indians of the West.

CHAPTER 3

The Beginnings of Indian Mission in the West: Columbian Memorial Church in Colony, Oklahoma

Before the Civil War the Reformed Church in America, then commonly referred to as the "Dutch Reformed Church," had virtually no machinery in place to conduct mission work in North America on a denominational level. When the first efforts were made, they were made by the women of the church.

A pioneer of the "domestic" mission effort of Reformed women was Sarah (Mrs. Thomas) Doremus, possibly the most remarkable laywoman in Reformed Church history. In 1861 Doremus helped found the Women's Union Missionary Society for Heathen Lands to support women as missionaries. She was the organization's first president, a position she held until her death in 1877.

This mission union, the first of its kind in the United States, gave birth to the Reformed Church's Woman's (sic) Board of Foreign Missions in 1875 and the Woman's Executive Committee of Domestic Missions in 1883. In 1896 the latter changed its name to the Women's Executive Committee of the Board of Domestic Missions. (In the interest of simplicity, we will often simply refer to it as "the Women's Board" or "the board").

Although the aim of the Woman's Board of Foreign Missions was to aid the denomination's Board of Foreign Missions in its work, the Women's Executive Committee of the Board of Domestic Missions chose the specific task of providing funds for the building of parsonages for the new churches being established in the West. But the board members soon grew restless and appointed an Indian Committee to explore new avenues of ministry.

The 'Paper Mission'

For some years the women's board had conducted a "paper mission" by requesting individuals and eastern churches to send their used magazines and Sunday school materials to the parsonages of newly established western churches. Then, in response to inquiries from Indian missions (not established by the Reformed Church in America), the board began an Indian branch of the paper mission, providing names and addresses to those who were willing to recycle their used reading materials to Indian people who were beginning to read English. The board especially asked for reading materials with illustrations: "As they are children in intellect, Sunday school papers are often sent to them, and they learn the 'old, old story' in the simplest words."[1]

The response was enthusiastic, and the annual reports almost always included testimonials from happy beneficiaries. The paper mission continued for nearly thirty years, until the early 1920s. The board then suggested that it might be cheaper to subscribe for others than to personally send old copies.

A Historic Mission Tea

In 1889 the Reverend Stephen John Harmeling, pastor of the Sandham Memorial Reformed Church in Marion Junction, South Dakota (later moved to nearby Monroe), wrote an article published in the *Christian Intelligencer* that advocated mission work among American Indians. Harmeling took a generally sympathetic view of Indians, who he said, because of land grabbing and misguided government policies, had little to do except "eat, sleep, and for exercise go on the war path occasionally."[2]

1. *Annual Report of the Woman's Executive Committee of Domestic Missions,* 1890, 80.
2. S. J. H., "What Apology Will the Reformed Church Offer?" *Christian Intelligencer,* July 3, 1889, 3. This is the same author who two years later published in the *Christian Intelligencer* one of the most scurrilous attacks on Indians ever printed in a Reformed Church publication, comparing Indians to their nasty broncos and saying that "the tribes of the west, including the Sioux, are the ugliest and meanest of all the tribes." S. J. Harmeling, "The Indian and His Broncho," *Christian Intelligencer,* April 29, 1891, 6.

It was not Harmeling, but a Presbyterian minister from Omaha, Nebraska, the Reverend William Justice Harsha, who motivated the women of the Reformed Church to begin an Indian mission. Harsha, outraged by the plight of Indians in America, went on a speaking tour that included New York City. Among those who heard him was a group of women of the Women's Executive Committee of Domestic Missions, who resolved to do something to help.

About this time, nationwide attention was being turned to the 1893 World's Fair in Chicago, Illinois, called the Columbian Exposition in commemoration of the four hundredth anniversary of the discovery of America by Christopher Columbus. The Women's Board hit on the idea of establishing a "Columbian Memorial" for American Indian work, since the arrival of Columbus had not only caused great distress for the Indian people but had placed them in a position to hear the gospel.

In a fascinating illustration of how things were done in those days, the Indian Committee sponsored a Columbian Tea February 24, 1894, at the Reformed Church headquarters at 25 East Twenty-second Street in New York City. The tea produced gifts totaling $3,093.96—an amazing amount, considering that a loaf of bread sold for three cents and the average annual income was $644. The fund soon mushroomed to more than $4,000, but still no specific plan was in place. So the Indian Committee of seven, headed by Louise (Mrs. Charles) Runk, set out to find a missionary for the Columbian Mission.

Women's Board Chooses Frank Hall Wright

The search took them no farther west than New York City. Pastor Harsha, who had inspired the women in the first place, had by that time transferred to the Reformed Church and was serving the Harlem Collegiate Church in New York City. (He served from 1892 to 1899, after which he returned to the Presbyterian Church.) Harsha met with the Indian Committee and suggested that they talk to an evangelist of Choctaw/white descent presently living in New York, the Reverend Frank Hall Wright. "He is splendidly fitted for the work," said Harsha. "Himself an Indian, he would not be likely to fall into the mistakes that would be inevitable to a white man. He has a glorious voice, a magnetic personality, and unbounded enthusiasm."[3]

---

3. "Indian Missions," *Golden Years in Miniature: A History of the Women's Board of Domestic Mission of the Reformed Church in America*, 1932, 50.

Frank Hall Wright

Wright, thirty-two, had been born in Old Boggy Depot in Indian Territory (now Oklahoma), the son of the Reverend Allen Wright, a Choctaw minister, and Harriet Mitchell Wright (a descendent of William Brewster of the *Mayflower*), who was serving as a missionary teacher among the Choctaws. The elder Wright, whose Choctaw name was Kiliahote, graduated from Spencer Academy in the Choctaw Nation; from Union College in Schenectady, New York; and from Union Seminary in New York City. He then returned to his tribe as a missionary, where he met and married Harriet Mitchell.

The younger Wright had graduated from the same three institutions as his father. He married a white woman, Addie Lilienthal, from Saratoga, New York, and began work among his people in Indian Territory. After a few years he and his wife moved east to undertake itinerant evangelistic work among white people, but after one and a half years he contracted pulmonary tuberculosis, which almost cost him his life.

Emily Bussing, president of the Women's Board, and Louise Runk, chair of the board's Indian Committee, visited Wright in New

York. The initial call did not seem promising. Elizabeth Page, who subsequently became the long-time chair of the Indian Committee, later dramatically described the meeting in her significant chronicle, *In Camp and Tepee: An Indian Mission Story:*

> They saw a man, emaciated and weak, whose thin frame was even then shaken with the paroxysm of coughing which the excitement of their coming had caused. Yet they laid the stupendous task of founding their new work in the hands of this apparently dying man.[4]

Despite his illness, the warnings of his doctor and friends, and despite the fact that he had once left his work among Indian people, Wright accepted the invitation of the Women's Board to begin a new work in Oklahoma.

The Harlem Collegiate Church, of which Harsha was pastor, agreed to provide Wright's salary. At the commissioning service just before Wright's departure, the new missionary spoke briefly on the text, "This is the victory that overcometh the world, even our faith" (1 John 5:4). Wright said, in part, "I go...and I know not that I shall be permitted to live and bring the gospel to these poor Indians, or whether God will call me to the higher service, but whichever it is, it will be victory."[5]

The Church in Colony, Oklahoma, Becomes the 'Mother Church'

In May 1895 Wright started with his family for the West and settled his wife and children in Dallas, Texas. It is not clear when, if ever, they joined him on a permanent basis, and Addie Wright was rarely mentioned in Reformed Church publications.

Wright procured a camping outfit and a helper (never named) and set out for Indian territory. He went, as agreed, to the Fort Sill military installation adjacent to the present city of Lawton, Oklahoma, with the intention of evangelizing the Indians encamped there. He went first to the Comanches, who after years of struggle with the white invaders, had laid down their arms and set up camp near the army outpost. But Wright was turned away both by government agencies and by the Indians themselves, so he turned to Geronimo's band of Chiricahua

---

4. Elizabeth Page, *In Camp and Tepee: An Indian Mission Story* (New York, Chicago, and Toronto: Revell, 1915), 22.
5. "Death of Rev. Frank Hall Wright, D. D.," *Christian Intelligencer and Mission Field,* Aug. 2, 1922, 493.

Apaches, who had been returned recently from Florida and Alabama and were being held as prisoners of war at Fort Sill. (A more complete history of the Chiricahua imprisonment can be found in chapter four.) Again, Wright was rebuffed.

The Mission Is Diverted

Feeling obligated to fulfill the mandate of the Women's Board to begin a mission to Indian people, Wright looked for other possibilities. Hearing of an encampment at Red Moon, 150 miles to the north, he and his companion again set out. But on the way, about seventy miles from Fort Sill, Wright came upon a cluster of red buildings. Here, at a place called Colony, the government had built a school for the Cheyennes and Arapahoes and had established an agency to which the Indians came regularly for rations.

The agent in Colony was John Seger, a devout Christian who had proposed an "Indian colony" (hence the name) where Indians would be taught to become self-supporting through education and farming. Believing that Christian teaching was the missing factor in his plan, Seger invited Wright to speak to the children on a Sunday morning. Impressed with Wright's earnestness, and learning that he was a man in search of a mission, Seger invited Wright to stay in Colony and establish his mission there. A council of Indian leaders agreed, Seger made the necessary arrangements for a tract of land, and the Columbian Mission of the Women's Board of Domestic Missions was established.

Visiting Elusive Indians

Most of the Indians did not live in a colony, as Seger had envisioned, but instead gathered in scattered camps. To these camps Wright pursued them, with great persistence and patience, but with little immediate tangible success. Elizabeth Page described Wright's visits to the less-than-enthusiastic objects of evangelism:

> Every week after the services at the school were over the missionary would harness his team and set out over the hard roads to the distant camps. Sometimes they knew in advance of his coming and would pack up their belongings and get away... Occasionally he surprised them when he pulled in at night, tired and dusty, but happy in finding them. Then would follow an evening of going from group to group and from tepee to tepee. Often when he entered with his interpreter by his side all laughter

Columbian Memorial Church, Colony, Oklahoma

and talk would cease, each task would be instantly laid down and the whole family would sit as if frozen into stony immobility. He knew they could hear, although they strove to seem as deaf, and he talked on....In the morning he would perhaps find they had all slipped out while he slept and had escaped him. At such times he never gave up, but followed their trail across the prairie, pulling in at night, gay, friendly, and determined to help [with such things as carrying wood for an old lady or giving a dose of quinine, or sharing drinking water]....So October passed and part of November, and little by little he won his place. The Indians grew to know that here was one man who was persistently following them, not for what he could get, but for what he could give.[6]

Although Wright's health was slowly improving, he was still frail and thought it best to leave Colony during the coldest months. He went to Dallas, where his wife and children lived, and while there was asked to preach at a Presbyterian church at which the Reverend Walter C. Roe was the minister. Wright's invitation to preach was no

6. Page, *In Camp and Tepee*, 32-33.

doubt engineered by Roe's wife, Mary, a sister of Elizabeth Page, who happened to be visiting at the time. Wright and the Roes got along well and determined to keep in touch.

Wright returned to Colony in the spring, and work soon began on a small stone building with a red roof and pointed spire. On November 15, 1896, the funds raised less than three years earlier by the ladies' Columbian Tea in New York City culminated in the dedication of the Columbian Memorial Church in Colony, Oklahoma. Among those present were Walter and Mary Roe.

Twenty-two people were received by confession of faith or transfer, and eleven more were received in the months following. The records do not indicate how many of these were Indians, but given the icy response to Wright's early ministry and the fact that Colony was the site of a government school, it can be assumed that the majority were students of the school and white members of the school and agency staff. More than one hundred children attended the Sunday school (attendance required), staffed by a superintendent and teachers from the government school.

Meanwhile, Wright went back to Fort Sill from time to time, preaching to reluctant Comanches and seeking to find an open door to the Chiricahua prisoners of war. He also went on evangelistic forays to other Indian encampments and sometimes conducted evangelistic rallies at white churches. The annals of the First Presbyterian Church (later Covenant Presbyterian Church) in Amarillo, Texas, record that Wright conducted several revivals there. The church described him as a "highly educated, fascinating, dynamic man who not only moved his audience by his preaching but touched their hearts by his singing of such gospel hymns as 'The Ninety and Nine.'"[7]

Walter and Mary Roe Come to Colony

Wright, stronger, but still in ill health, and—perhaps more importantly—intent on pursuing his first love, itinerant evangelism, sought additional help. Meanwhile, Walter Roe's health had deteriorated in Dallas, and his doctor had suggested an assignment that would offer more open air. Wright felt that no one was better qualified to assist him than Roe. Elizabeth Page, Mary Roe's sister and now chair of the Indian

7. Selvin Allen, "A History of Covenant Presbyterian Church of Amarillo, Texas," website of St. Luke Presbyterian Church, Amarillo, Texas, July 2002.

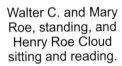

Walter C. and Mary Roe, standing, and Henry Roe Cloud sitting and reading.

Committee, saw no problem with that. The Roes began their work in Colony in 1897.

Walter Roe stayed in Colony for sixteen years until his death in 1913, becoming a highly respected father figure among the Reformed Church's missionaries to American Indians. He established policies and practices that became standard for the Indian work and generated wide denominational interest and financial support through personal speaking appearances and the pages of the *Christian Intelligencer.*

Roe, a bespectacled little man who parted his hair in the middle and plastered it down, had been born in 1860 and had graduated from Williams College in Williamstown, Massachusetts. Although listed as a minister in the Reformed Church's *Historical Directory*, there seems to be no record of his ordination. He briefly served Presbyterian congregations in Fort Worth (1892-95) and Dallas (1895-97) before beginning his work with the Reformed Church. It would seem that the Roes were people of some financial means. Although the source of the wealth is not clear, it likely came from Mary Roe's side, since it is apparent that her sister, Elizabeth Page, also had significant resources.

Another Indian Tea and a New Parsonage

Wright lived in a tepee, but with the Roes expected to arrive, the Women's Board established a parsonage fund. The Albany Missionary Union of five churches contributed $100, but the real fundraiser was the tried-and-true Indian Tea, held April 6, 1897, at the Reformed Church headquarters:

> The Assembly Room was beautifully decorated with Indian relics, loaned by interested friends, and guests were entertained by music and recitations. A miniature tepee at the entrance reminded all who came of the object of the gathering....At the tea-table, Falling Star, a Christian Indian woman, helped in serving the guests....All the afternoon the rooms were thronged with friends.[8]

The results were "beyond expectation," and $1,025 was raised, including contributions from the western societies. A parsonage was built that fall, a home that Page described in a flair of whimsy as "hunching its red roof on its stone shoulders and staring unwinkingly down the whole length of the mission compound to the church."[9]

Rapid Growth in Colony

An entry of the Minutes of the Colony church, dated January 10, 1897, states:

> Evangelist Wright examined and received on profession of faith the following persons: Vernon Purde, Harold Little Medicine, Lula Little Medicine, Nellie Little Wolf, Mary Little Wolf, Cora Prairie Chief, Agnes Black Wolf, Heap-O-Birds, Sioux Little Calf. By Letter: Peter Ratz and his wife.[10]

Similar entries were recorded almost weekly, with an extraordinary number of converts, apparently with little or no special instruction. Louise Runk, chair of the Committee on Indian Work, reported in the *Mission Field* in May 1898 that membership had grown rapidly and now stood at sixty-four—a figure different from the board's official report of

8. *Annual Report of the Women's Executive Committee of the Board of Domestic Missions*, 1897, 68.
9. Page, *In Camp and Tepee*, 40.
10. *Minutes of the Reformed Church of Colony, Oklahoma*, now in the possession of the Presbyterian Church of Cordell, Oklahoma, January 10, 1897.

seventy-three members—of whom fifty-three were Indians. Membership consisted mainly of the older pupils of the government school, the employees of the school, a few white people, and some camp Indians. The annual report for the year ending April 30, 1899, indicated thirty-five Indians and two whites admitted by profession of faith. Reported attendance was 140 in church, 130 in Sunday school, 100 at prayer meeting, 20 in the parsonage on Sunday evening, 28 in Senior Christian Endeavor, and 27 in Junior Christian Endeavor.

Some new converts were raised quickly to positions of spiritual leadership. William Little Chief, a Cheyenne chief who professed faith at the first camp meeting in 1898, was ordained as an elder less than a year later. Some adult Indians who quickly became candidates for membership also quickly became candidates for church discipline. Weekly consistory meetings in 1898 and 1899, for instance, charged several members with such offenses as drunkenness, gambling, immorality, absence from church, and marrying according to the Indian custom.

Roe soon became the resident pastor of the Colony church, while Wright, ever the evangelist, resumed his tours of the surrounding territory, Fort Sill, and beyond. The Roes sometimes accompanied him, even though Walter Roe continued to suffer from typhoid fever.

Colony Establishes Patterns of Indian Mission

Although the church in Colony was closed as a mission of the Reformed Church in 1932, it has great historical significance. Colony was the "mother church" for some thirty years, and as such it established the policies and practices that were used at almost every Reformed mission site that related to American Indians. These included: (1) use of interpreters, (2) close cooperation with government agencies and schools, (3) open parsonages, (4) camp meetings, (5) community centers, (6) full range of church activities, (7) Christmas gifts, and (8) "giving Sunday."

1. *Use of Interpreters.* While missionaries who were assigned to serve in foreign countries were usually required to spend two or more years in language study, those who served on Indian reservations didn't spend even a month or two in a crash course. Interpreters were key personnel in all mission locations, and in fact were used as late as the 1950s in some areas. Several considerations were involved.

In the early years, one of the objectives of both the government and the church was to "civilize" the Indians by weaning them away from their native customs and languages. In the Indian boarding schools the children were usually forbidden to speak their own languages and were punished if they did. It would, in fact, have seemed counterproductive for white missionaries to speak in an Indian language, because this would undercut one of their primary goals—preparing Indian people to live in the white world.

Despite this point of view, some missionaries did make an attempt to learn the native languages, only to encounter allegations of favoritism. When Walter and Mary Roe joined Frank Hall Wright in 1897, the missionaries decided that Wright would study Cheyenne with the assistance of his interpreter, and that the Roes would undertake the study of Arapaho. The plan was thwarted, however, by what Elizabeth Page called "the strange and indomitable jealousy that existed between the tribes."[11] These dynamics mystified the missionaries because the two tribes, although having quite different languages, had always been closely allied in hunting, feasting, and fighting common enemies. But, according to Page, the missionaries "wisely fell back on interpreters and sign language,"[12] the latter being a system highly developed and used among most whites and tribes west of the Mississippi. Since most Reformed mission sites included more than one tribal group, this problem would have existed elsewhere as well.

It should also be pointed out that the mission board did not (and does not) require long-term commitments from pastors of American Indian congregations. The choice to become a foreign missionary was assumed to be life-long, so a two-year commitment to language study was considered reasonable. On the other hand, many clergy who accepted calls to serve American Indian congregations assumed that after a few years they could move on to other pastorates, much as their contemporaries who were serving white churches.

These reasons (or contributing factors, or excuses) having been given, it should also be pointed out that in the summer of 1966 the Reverend Harold "Shorty" Brown served as a seminary intern in Mescalero, New Mexico, and at the end of the summer gave his farewell speech in the Apaches' native tongue. Older people from Mescalero still mention Brown's speech with deep appreciation. Whatever the reasons for the English-only policy of missionary preachers and teachers, there can be little doubt that this practice contributed to the image of

11. Page, *In Camp and Tepee*, 41.
12. Ibid., 42.

Christianity as the white man's religion.

   2. *Close Cooperation with Government Agencies and Schools.* It was a given that early American Indian ministries would work hand-in-hand with government agencies and government schools. The U.S. Government expected religious organizations to play an integral role in "civilizing" the Indians. Government permission was necessary for the ministry to take place, and the mission compound was almost always a grant from the government. Missionaries and missionary teachers had virtually unlimited access to the government Indian schools, and the government frequently paid the teachers' salaries. Pupils who attended boarding schools were required to attend church services and Sunday schools, and sometimes weekday catechism classes as well.

   3. *Open Parsonages.* The Roes opened their home to Indian people at any time of the day or night for meals, conversation, training, and general help. This included Sunday afternoons, when Indian children were invited to come and play with toys sent by "eastern friends" and then to carefully put everything away, "thus learning the lesson of neatness and order so sorely needed by these people who have no true homes."[13]

   4. *Camp Meetings.* Wright and Roe introduced another major innovation that was to become a lynchpin of Reformed Church Indian ministry: the camp meeting. Reflecting on the success of Indian dances in bringing together families who were widely scattered in camps, the missionaries devised a Christian version of the same. The first such gathering was held in 1897, but it was not until 1901, when a great feast was added and an arbor was built, that the camp meeting became a popular and integral part of the mission.

   Not only did the Indians eat well during the four-day series of meetings, but they also received generous rations of coffee, sugar, flour, lard, and—the most valued of all—beef, all financed by the eastern churches. Evangelist Wright preached the sermons, translated simultaneously into Cheyenne, Arapahoe, and other languages as well. At the end of the week, usually on Sunday, new converts were baptized immediately. Down through the years the camp meeting served the dual purpose of seeking new converts and (perhaps as important) calling Christian wanderers back to the "Jesus Road."

   Attendance at the 1905 camp meeting was reported to be 427, not counting school children and babies. This appears to be about average

---

13. *Annual Report of the Women's Executive Committee of the Board of Domestic Missions,* 1898, 76.

Frank Hall Wright at a camp meeting in Colony, Oklahoma

for those years. The Reverend Richard Harper, who came a few years later, gave this description of a typical camp meeting:

> Here they come! Over the hill, into the large Government pasture southeast of Colony, on Cobb Creek; Indians in wagons, in hacks, or buggies (today, some in autos), boys on horseback—they follow each other through the gate, and put up their tepees and tents. "What's doing?" someone asks. "Camp Meeting" is the reply. Soon the tents are pitched and the horses are turned loose to graze.
>
> What an attractive sight! A short distance from the creek stands the large Camp Meeting tent, which holds hundreds of people. Near the trees are the tents of the missionaries. Not far from the creek and meeting tent are the Cheyennes, Arapahoes, and visiting Comanches, Apaches, and Kiowas. The camp is in a quiet spot, far enough removed from the main road to avoid traffic noises. From Wednesday night through the following Sunday the meetings are held. Not only Indians, but many whites and Negroes come, especially on the last day.
>
> Each morning begins with a prayer meeting, before breakfast. At about ten o'clock a second service is held, with Rev. Frank Hall Wright preaching one of his earnest, appealing sermons. At

half past two a testimony meeting is held, when the Indians have opportunity to tell what the Saviour has done for them. There is not time enough for all who are eager to tell their story. At dark comes the last service of the day when Mr. Wright preaches again.

Will you sit on the front seat, please; and, along with the ministers and church officers—most of the latter being Indians—face the audience. The congregation is distinctively Indian. The shawls worn by the women and girls are attractive—bright with red and pink. The men, you notice, wear citizens' clothing. Some of the older men wear the customary Indian sheet over their suits. Here and there will be seen a pair of prettily beaded moccasins, the handwork of one of the many industrious women. The decorated cradles, made to be carried on the backs of the mothers, catch your attention. The bright eyes looking out from them win you. During the meeting the cradles are held in the mothers' arms, or stood upon the ground, leaning against their knees.

How captivating are the faces of the listeners! They reveal happy hearts of many who, for months, have been looking forward to the Camp Meeting. Some faces are solemn, showing a consciousness of sins committed. Others are sad, as thoughts pass through their minds of friends who have attended previous gatherings of those who now have gone out on the "long trail." Some faces are defiant, for Satan is here, and is helping his followers to wage a strong fight against Christ and His Gospel.

The hymns are inspiring. "When the Roll Is Called Up Yonder" is started. While the Indians sing it in the Cheyenne tongue, we who speak English join them in our language. The Indian hymn is a translation of that of the same title in our hymn books, and is sung to the same tune....

Each tribe represented must have its own interpreter. From the lips of the preacher, sentence by sentence, or thought by thought, each of these faithful men takes the message of the Lord and passes it on to his own tribal group. All the interpreters talk at once, and none seems to interfere with the speech of the others. Cheyennes, Arapahoes, Comanches, Apaches, Kiowas sit, each in the tribal group to which he belongs. Every Indian listener catches the words of his own interpreter, apparently being able, by concentration of mind, to eliminate from his hearing the voices of the other speakers.

At the close of the sermon the preacher gives an invitation for those desiring to become Christians to come forward, and to shake hands with the ministers and the church officers; also inviting Christians who wish to reconsecrate themselves to more earnest Christian living to do the same. An Indian hymn is sung, and those who wish to respond to the invitation given come forward, sometimes many, sometimes few. A prayer is offered; the meeting closes; those who have come forward are now talked with; and then all go to tents and tepees for meals, or for a night's rest.

On the last Sunday of the Camp Meeting the new converts, after careful examination and instruction, are received into the Church. The results of such meetings cannot easily be overestimated.[14]

5. Community Centers. A fifth major mission component was added in 1899—the community center, which for many years was called the lodge. This, too, would become a prototype for nearly all the Reformed Church's Indian mission compounds. Always a proactive missionary, Mary Roe presented the concept at the 1898 Mohonk Conference for Indian Workers, held annually at Lake Mohonk in New York State. A collection of $1,200 was received on the spot, and the building was constructed the following spring. It was named the Mohonk Lodge, after the conferences that had played such an integral role in Indian ministry.

The lodge was to serve a dual purpose: to provide a social gathering place and to introduce Indians to the niceties of domestic white culture. The lodge's main feature was a large room with a fireplace, easy chairs, books, and games. The floor was also available for those seeking refuge from the cold and storms. The other large room was equipped with a cook stove, washing tubs with wringers, tables, cupboards, and sewing machines. Other small rooms provided space for medical treatment and a refuge for returning boarding school students who were urged not to go back to their family tepees.

The construction of the lodge led to the employ of Reese Kincaide (whose wife was a sister of Walter Roe) as supervisor of the lodge and its industrial work. Other lodge supervisors and field workers of those early years included Johanna Meengs, Marie De Keyser, and Anna

14. Richard H. Harper, "The Missionary Work of the Reformed (Dutch) Church in America in Oklahoma," *Chronicles of Oklahoma*, vol. 18, 1940, 259-61.

Berkenpas. The role of the lodge became more important in 1902 when the government discontinued its ration system, leaving Indians without support. Mary Jenson, one of the workers, encouraged the dying art of Indian beadwork, and soon a new industry was underway.

Yet the lodge was not without its problems. Mary Roe had envisioned that the Indian women would keep it clean, but when this did not happen, the missionaries took over this task. A greater problem was what the missionaries called the Indians' "strange unconquerable jealousy."[15] The lodge had been built on land where Cheyennes had always camped. Therefore the Arapahoes considered this to be a Cheyenne institution and viewed it with cold hostility until an old and very ill Arapahoe was cared for at the lodge and gave the building his blessing before he died.

6. *Full Range of Church Activities.* Although camp meetings, school-based evangelism, and community buildings were specific to Indian ministry, most of the remaining church activities followed the pattern of typical white churches of the day. These included morning and evening worship services, Sunday schools, choirs, women's missionary societies, men's fellowships, Christian Endeavor meetings for youth, visitation in the homes, and help for the needy.

7. *Christmas Gifts.* Still another major component of the Indian ministry first became a tradition at Colony—the annual Christmas celebration and gift distribution. Early every December the mail wagon from Weatherford, fourteen miles away, brought boxes and barrels from churches out east. The mission staff sorted and wrapped the gifts, designating them for adults as well as for children. The children received toys, games, candy, dolls, and mittens; the women received blankets and clothing; and the men received tools and clothing. The gifts not only brought positive feelings for the mission but also ensured spectacular crowds at Christmas services—all of which were reported with great enthusiasm in the various publications of the Reformed Church. The Christmas programs always included pageants and carols presented by the school children. The missionaries, who so zealously guarded against "pagan" Indian traditions, also introduced Christmas trees and Santa Claus.

8. *"Giving Sunday."* Each year, the Sunday before Christmas was designated as "Giving Sunday," on which special offerings were received for benevolent causes. These were most often designated for

15. Page, *In Tent and Tepee,* 77.

some project of the Reformed Church's Board of Foreign Missions or Board of Domestic Missions, including mission schools in China and the Middle East. Parents often brought their children for baptism at this time, and sometimes the two observances were combined. Harper told of one such incident:

> There were times when some of the Christians had no money to give. On one such Giving Sunday Frank Hamilton, the mission interpreter, and his wife, Enosta, came forward in the church service at the time of the offering. They brought their little boy to the missionary, saying that they would "put him into the basket" as a gift to the Lord. They asked that Dr. Roe would look after his education, and would see that the little son should be so trained that his life would be lived for Jesus.[16]

A few years later at the Comanche mission near Lawton, the parents of Robert Chaat, who would become the first American Indian pastor ordained by the Reformed Church, dedicated their son in a similar scenario on a Giving Sunday.

Pastoral Assistants Needed

In 1903 Roe was accompanied to the Reformed Church General Synod by Wautan, who was chief of the Arapahoes and also an elder of the Columbian Memorial Church. Wautan addressed the synod in sign language, telling the story of his life and of his hopes for his people.

Roe's health, never robust, finally gave way entirely, and the Women's Board gave the Roes a year's leave of absence, which they spent in Europe. Elizabeth Page came to assist for the summer, and Wright interrupted his evangelistic travels occasionally to conduct Sunday services.

His strength renewed, Roe was appointed in 1905 as superintendent of all the Oklahoma church work, both white and Indian. At that time the Reformed Church had organized nine white churches, following the settlers who staked claims on what had earlier been promised as "Indian Territory." The Classis of Oklahoma was organized with twenty-two churches by the Particular Synod of New York in 1906, only to be disbanded five years later when Dutch settlers found Oklahoma too hot and dry for their liking. Roe's duties for Indian

16. Harper, "Missionary Work," 261.

work included organizing conferences of Indian workers, attending camp meetings, exploring the possibilities of new fields, writing annual reports for the Women's Board, and responding to emergencies. In the fall and winter of 1909-10, for instance, various crises called him to Lawton, Winnebago, and Mescalero.

To relieve Roe of his additional workload, the board sent the Reverend Arthur Brokaw, a recent graduate of Rutgers College and New Brunswick Theological Seminary (1904). Brokaw was enthusiastic and well received by both Indians and whites, and in short order he organized a Boys Club. But about a year later he died suddenly, stricken with typhoid fever and spinal meningitis. His death, openly mourned by the Indians, seemed to spark a revival, and many of the prominent men began to take the "Jesus Road." A chapel was erected in Brokaw's honor in 1908, on land west of Colony donated by the Roes.

After Brokaw's death, the Reverend L. L. Legters, a graduate of Hope College (1900) and New Brunswick Theological Seminary (1903), served briefly (1906-07) as an assistant to Roe. He then moved on to the Comanche mission, which by then had been established near Fort Sill. The Reverend James A. Hoffman, a recent graduate of Union Theological Seminary, also worked briefly in Colony before turning to Oklahoma's white churches.

The 1906 Colony report to General Synod indicated that thirty-three members had been received the previous year, making a total of 203 communicants. Weekly meetings included Sunday school, a Women's Missionary Society (including Indians and whites), a prayer meeting for camp Indians, a parsonage training meeting for Sunday school teachers, and no fewer than five Christian Endeavor societies. The following year fifty-five persons were received into the church, bringing the total to 231. Of these, 190 were Indians. "The pioneer days were over," wrote Elizabeth Page in her account, "and instead there was a future of less vivid fascination perhaps but more permanent results."[17]

Richard Harper Enters Indian Ministry

It was at this point that the Reverend Richard Harper, one of the legendary pastors in Indian mission, entered the ministry of the Reformed Church in America. He served only briefly in Colony (1907-09), then moved on to Mescalero (1910-15) and Lawton (1915-23).

17. Page, *In Camp and Tepee*, 126.

Harper, like all of the pioneer pastors of the Reformed Church's work among American Indians, came from outside the denomination. Harper was a Congregationalist, born in Plymouth, England, the oldest of three sons who followed their father into the ministry. A graduate of Chicago Theological Seminary, he was ordained in 1891. He began his ministry in Oklahoma in 1895, serving with the Congregational Church, and came to the Reformed Church twelve years later. His wife, Ella Mae Boggs, was a descendent of Paul Revere.

In his history of the Reformed Church's work in Oklahoma, Harper lists a number of prominent Indian church officers, interpreters, and workers. Among the Arapahoes were Wautan, Washee, Hartley Ridgebear, Joel Little Bird, and Kendall Sore Thumb. Among the Cheyennes were Frank Hamilton, Paul Goodbear, Wolf Chief, William Fletcher, and Stacy Riggs. "Many earnest Christian women," he wrote, "also might be named."[18]

Wautan, an elder, was later highlighted in the *Christian Intelligencer and Mission Field* (those two publications having merged), taking his place with such better-known leaders as Nahwats (Comanche), John Smith (Winnebago), and Robert Chaat (Comanche). Wautan was pictured with dark pants, coat, and hat, and with long braids over his shoulders. "When but few stood by Rev. Frank Hall Wright and Rev. and Mrs. Walter C. Roe to give courage and assistance," said the article, "this man was among them."[19]

It was the custom during those years for the Indians to give Indian names to the white workers. Walter Roe was "Iron Eyes," Mary Roe was "Happy Woman," Elizabeth Page was "Our New Sister," Mary Jenson was "Fast Walker," Richard Harper was "Black Beard," and Ella Mae Harper was "Walking Around" because of her visits to Indian camps.[20]

Two Short Pastorates

Harper was followed by the Reverend William Wauchope, who had confessed his faith at the Columbian Church, studied for the ministry, and returned as associate pastor "among the Indians whom he knew as a boy,"[21] implying, perhaps, that he was not an Indian. He left Colony in 1910 and was dismissed to the Presbyterian Church.

18. Harper, "Missionary Work," 263.
19. Richard Harper, "Some Indian Leaders, Past and Present," *Christian Intelligencer and Mission Field*, Sept. 30, 1925, 616.
20. Harper, *Chronicles*, 259.
21. *Annual Report of the Women's Executive Committee of the Board of Domestic Missions*, 1909, 20.

Then came the Reverend John Baxter as associate pastor, also from the Presbyterian Church, having served two short pastorates in Colorado before coming to Colony in 1910. Baxter stayed just three years before moving on, returning to work in the Presbyterian Church.

The church building was renovated in 1909, and the stoves were replaced by a furnace in the basement and a large central register to defuse the heat. The Indians shied away from walking on the register, says an article in the *Christian Intelligencer*, "until one woman weighing well over 300 pounds inadvertently walked over it and established confidence."[22]

Meanwhile, despite the rapid turnover of associate pastors, the church under Roe continued to grow, and by 1911 the membership had reached 282. Despite the fact that these pastors had not come out of the Reformed Church, they placed a strong emphasis on denominational mission causes. The 1910 report, for instance, showed that the Colony church had given $568.81 for denominational causes, over against $433.20 for church purposes.

Clouds on the Horizon

Under the leadership of the Roes and a passing parade of associate pastors, the congregation had shown unprecedented growth, but in 1912 two clouds appeared on the horizon. The annual report of the Women's Board of Domestic Missions of that year indicated that the government had proposed the closing of the school in Colony, but "thank God, that danger is past."[23] The second emerging problem was the increasing popularity of "mescal worship," the use of peyote as a religious ceremony, especially by young men. That threat, too, was dismissed: "It stands like a dragon in the way but will yield, as have so many other dragons, to the onset of the Prince of Peace."[24]

Walter Roe Dies

Walter Roe's health, always marginal, began to deteriorate—exacerbated, no doubt, by his strenuous efforts to secure the release of the Chiricahua Apaches, who had been held for twenty-seven years as prisoners of war in Florida, Alabama, and at Fort Sill. While in Colony, Roe had made frequent trips, not only to Lawton, but also to

22. "Another Christmas at Colony," *Christian Intelligencer*, Jan. 20, 1909, 41.
23. *Annual Report of the Women's Board of Domestic Missions*, 1912, 19.
24. Ibid, 20.

Washington, D.C. He went to Nassau in the Bahamas in order to regain his strength, but he died there March 12, 1913, six days after his fifty-third birthday. A leaflet produced by the Women's Board, published in June of that year, described him as "sincere, straightforward, and uncompromising in what he conceived to be the truth, and whenever righteousness was at stake, he was a lion! He frankly pointed out wrong whenever he found it in any individual." Despite the fact that for more than twenty years he was little more than an invalid, said the leaflet, "He was miraculously upheld by an unseen Hand for a special task."[25] After her husband's death, Mary Roe was appointed immediately by the Women's Board as missionary-at-large, a title she did not take lightly.

Henry Roe Cloud, Adopted Son

One of the enduring legacies of Walter and Mary Roe was their virtual adoption of a young Winnebago, Henry Roe Cloud. Converted through the ministry of the Presbyterian mission in Winnebago, Nebraska (predecessor to the Reformed mission there), Cloud completed his high school education and entered Yale University in 1906. He met Mary Roe when she addressed an assembly there, accepted her invitation to spend a summer at Fort Sill, and began a life-long friendship. The Roes supported him financially through Yale, where Cloud excelled and became its first Indian graduate.

Cloud went on to become an ordained Presbyterian minister, earn a master's degree in anthropology, and fulfill a dream of his adopted father by establishing the Roe Indian Institute in Wichita, Kansas, for the purpose of training Indian Christian leaders. Cloud served on a number of government committees and agencies, the most important of which was the panel that authored the Meriam Report of 1928, which laid the foundation for the historic Indian Reorganization Act of 1934. Cloud showed his appreciation by taking Roe as his middle name, and he maintained a close relationship with his benefactors as long as they lived.

Vruwink: First Colony Pastor from the Reformed Church

The Reverend Henry Vruwink, the first minister in Colony to come from the ranks of the Reformed Church in America, became the senior pastor after Roe. A Michigan native who came to Colony immediately

25. *Rev. Walter C. Roe, D. D., March 12, 1913*, leaflet produced by Women's Board of Domestic Missions, June 1913, 1.

after graduating from New Brunswick Theological Seminary in 1913, Vruwink stayed just a little longer than his predecessors, four years. In 1917 he moved to Grand Haven, Michigan.

Vruwink reported in 1916 that during the twenty years of the mission, 479 people had become members. But at the same time he implied discomfort with the ease that new converts had been accepted. "Now," he said, "an applicant for membership must give reasonable assurance by life as well as by confession that he really believes in Jesus Christ as Savior and Lord. In most cases this policy necessitates a period of systematic instruction and probation with real sacrifices on the part of the applicant."[26] The next year the church received only eight people on confession of faith. Vruwink also discontinued the practice of issuing beef at camp meetings. That decision resulted in lower attendance, he acknowledged, "but those who were present listened respectfully."[27]

Peyote Causes Alarm

The year 1917 marked the entrance into Reformed missionary work of yet another Presbyterian minister, the Reverend John Leighton Read. Read had been born in Paris, Texas, in 1879 and was educated at Austin College and Austin Theological Seminary. He served three Presbyterian churches in Arizona before coming to Colony. Read served at Colony for six years.

For several years, uneasy references to the increasing popularity of peyote had crept regularly into Colony reports. In 1918 Read took a strong stand:

> It is evident that the peyote (or mescal) habit has a strong hold on these people, being used by 75 percent to 90 percent, and it is by far the greatest obstacle in the way of the progress of Christianity. Mrs. Roe and others have made heroic efforts to get Congress to suppress it as a very injurious drug but the latest report is not encouraging. The very fact that it is used as a kind of worship makes it the more insidious as an instrument of evil against the truth. The time is not far distant when the line must be drawn between those who profess to be Christian and still use peyote and those who do not.[28]

26. *Annual Report of the Women's Board of Domestic Missions*, 1916, 35.
27. Ibid, 37.
28. Report of the Committee on Indian Work, *Annual Report of the Women's Board of Domestic Missions*, 1918, 35.

The Colony Mission Closes, 1932

Gradually the demographics of Colony changed. It was no longer the center of population for the Cheyenne and Araphoe tribes, and by 1921 only about twenty Indian families lived in or near the village. The only way the pastor could contact the Indian population was by visiting them in their camps, an arduous and slow process. Most of the confessions of faith, about twenty each year, were made by students of the government school. By 1922 Read was holding meetings in various homes some distance from Colony. Meanwhile, camp meetings continued, with men like Wright, former pastor Baxter, and Winnebago's missionary, the Reverend G.A. Watermulder, bringing the messages.

Frank Hall Wright Dies

Nine years after the passing of Roe, evangelist Wright, the founder of the mission, also died. Despite his fragile health when he arrived in Oklahoma, Wright had been invigorated by his new challenge and lived to be sixty-two years old. He had continued to be active, not only in Colony, but also as a frequent speaker at the camp meetings of other Indian missions and at white revival settings. His death in Muskoka Lakes, Ontario, Canada, was unexpected. He had gone there for a visit and died there July 16, 1922, after a very short illness.

Calling his home going an "irreparable loss," the 1923 report of the Women's Board of Domestic Missions recalled his "messages in sermon and song" and his "unique and Christ-exalting ministry, his warnings and his persuasive power in winning back into the 'Jesus Road.'"[29]

Peyote an Increasing Problem

In 1923 Read reported that "because of the strength of the peyote cult, very few of the older Indians can be reached by the regular services of the church."[30] Worship services, he said, are attended mainly by the children of the Indian school, government employees, and white people from the community. He reported 190 communicants, but of these, 117 were on the absent list. Sunday school enrollment, he reported, was 180. In the fall of that year, after six years in Colony, Read left for the

29. *Annual Report of the Women's Board of Domestic Missions, 1923*, 29.
30. Ibid, 20.

Comanche Indian mission in Lawton, Oklahoma, where he was to stay for eight years. Then the Reverend John Baxter, who had served Colony from 1910 to 1913, was called back.

'The First Volume Is Closed'

In the 1924 report of the Women's Board of Domestic Missions, the Committee on Indian Work reported regarding the Colony mission, "The first volume is closed. The Book of the Acts of the Apostles is written. We are now in the Epistolary stage. The tribes have been as thoroughly evangelized as people ever get to be and more thoroughly than most."[31]

Johanna Meengs, a veteran worker at Colony, reflected on the changes over the eighteen years of her service there:

> Tents and tepees have given way to two, three and four room houses, and tents are used only as temporary homes, and a tepee only upon special occasions, such as a wedding feast, a Christmas encampment, or an Indian fair. The old time dress, moccasins, and blanket are gradually giving place to simple house dresses, shoes and sweaters, and once in a great while a hat or a sunbonnet to keep a woman from being tanned. Books, papers and magazines are eagerly accepted and often bought....the "old-time Indian" is slowly but surely passing away.[32]

The mission faced a time of transition and confusion. The Indian agency was removed from Colony. Many of the Indian people had already left, and the families who remained were extremely poor, having sold their land allotments and spent the proceeds. Since Indians were unable to find work, the Mohonk Lodge played an even greater role by offering employment making beadwork and other crafts.

Baxter left for the second time, accepting a call to the Calvary Presbyterian Church in Wichita, Kansas, this time also having served but three years. Johanna Meengs became critically ill, and Mary Roe came back to help out for several months. Richard Harper, who had served briefly from 1907 to 1909, also returned, but his health failed and he was able to serve only two years, from 1927 to 1929. He was

31. *Annual Report of the Women's Board of Domestic Missions, 1924*, 29.
32. Johanna Meengs, "Facing Forward in Colony," *Christian Intelligencer and Mission Field*, April 2, 1924, 219.

sixty-three at the time and retired from active ministry. He did, however, continue to go on speaking tours for the Women's Board.

But there were some brief bright spots as well. The government's Indian school was enlarged to include children from several tribes, and the officials continued to send the students to church and Sunday school. The latter grew to about 175. The Christian Endeavor Societies also got a boost, increasing to four, and daily vacation Bible school was held for the first time in 1929.

The Sunday school reached a record attendance of 235 on Easter Sunday of 1932. The celebration was short-lived, however. In June of that year the school suddenly closed, giving way to the government's new (and more humane) policy of placing Indian children either in local public schools or Indian day schools adjacent to their homes.

Thus ended thirty-seven years of Reformed Church ministry to the children of the government school in Colony. It was still called the Seger School, after its founder, John Seger, who in 1895 had convinced Wright to establish a mission in his Indian "colony." With the closing of the school, the few Indians who had remained in Colony to work at the school began to leave.

The Colony Mission Closes

The Reverend Peter Van Es, Jr., who had just graduated from Western Theological Seminary, came in 1930 and began reaching out to the white community that was growing up around the church. He and his wife, Henrietta, organized a white Ladies Aid, for instance, as well as an Indian one.

When it was determined that its members were to be primarily white, the church decided to affiliate with a denomination that had more presence in Oklahoma. The Classis of Oklahoma had dissolved in 1911 after only five years, and all of the other white Reformed churches had either disbanded or joined with Presbyterian denominations.

Negotiations took place with the El Reno-Hobart Presbytery of the Presbyterian Church in the U.S., the "Southern Presbyterian Church." On November 13, 1932, the Reformed Church in Colony, Oklahoma, was formally disbanded. Its seventy-seven members were dismissed to the presbytery for the purpose of organizing a community church for Indians and white people. The consistory minutes show two lists, one apparently white and the other Indian, with about two-thirds of the names on the white list.

The church continues to this day as the Columbian Memorial

The historical marker in Colony, Oklahoma, mentions Reformed church missionaries Wright and Roe

Presbyterian Church, affiliated with the Presbyterian Church (U.S.A). The congregation has a total membership of about fifty and an average worship attendance of about thirty. None of its members are full-blooded Indians, but several Indian families return to the church every Christmas Eve—a tradition that mystifies the present pastor but no doubt dates back to the mammoth Christmas celebrations of the Colony mission. The Colony church is yoked with a somewhat larger Presbyterian church in Cordell, twenty-two miles to the west—the Cordell church also having been founded by the Reformed Church. Colony remains a very small settlement, with about 160 citizens. The Colony church building was destroyed by fire in 1968, but the records were saved and are now held by the Cordell church.

The Van Eses devoted twenty more years to Indian mission work, serving in Mescalero, New Mexico (1932-44), and Macy, Nebraska (1944-52). The Kincades also left Colony at this point, having served as lodge staff for twenty-eight years.

Mary Roe outlived her husband by twenty-eight years. In her role as missionary-at-large, she continued to be deeply involved in Indian ministry. She assisted at camp meetings, visited all mission sites regularly, and traveled widely across the country promoting the cause of Indian missions. In a tour of the Midwest in the spring of 1936, for instance, she made twenty-five presentations within a month in Iowa, Illinois, Wisconsin, Michigan, and Minnesota. Her husband had been a long-time advocate of initiating mission work in Mexico, Central America, and South America, and Mary Roe continued this emphasis.

A boarded up building of the former Indian school
in Colony, Oklahoma

She visited these areas several times and promoted interest not only across the United States but also in Indian churches. In 1925, for instance, the Colony church received an Easter offering of $64.07 for a proposed work in Chiapas, Mexico.

Mary Roe lost her life in an automobile accident June 16, 1941, shortly after leaving a meeting of the National Fellowship of Indian Workers in Farmington, New Mexico. A tribute to her in the *Intelligencer-Leader* said, "At the meeting in Farmington, it seemed that her life work had received its crown of glory. All present eagerly sought her advice, and her long and rich experience impressed those present at the conference with a deep feeling of reverence. Her messages to them during the devotional hour will never be forgotten. They were like a valedictory."[33]

33. Women's Board of Domestic Missions, "Tribute to Mrs. Walter C. Roe," *Intelligencer-Leader*, Sept. 19, 1941, 22.

CHAPTER 4

The Apache Mission at Fort Sill and the Apache Reformed Church in Apache, Oklahoma

To understand the mission among the Fort Sill Apaches,[1] we must first revisit some of the history of the Apache people in general and of the Chiricahua band in particular—that group of which Geronimo was the most colorful and well-known leader.

The Apaches

The Apaches likely came to the American Southwest from western Canada as early as 850 A.D., and their many dialects are related to a language system known as Athapascan. The Apaches are identified by dialects into several groups, including Kiowa, Mescalero, Lipan, Jicarilla, Chiricahua, Western Apache, and Iowa Apache. The Apaches were primarily nomadic hunters and gatherers, but throughout much of their history they also raided other tribes for much of their food

---

1. In the interest of clarity, this chapter will cover only the mission as it related to the Chiricahua Apache prisoners at Fort Sill, commonly called the Fort Sill Apaches. It will also tell the story of the Apaches who elected to remain in Oklahoma after their release as prisoners of war, continuing as the Apache Reformed Church in Apache, Oklahoma.

    However, many of the same missionaries were working simultaneously among the Comanches at Fort Sill. The story of that work, which resulted in the Comanche Reformed Church in Lawton, Oklahoma, will be told in chapter five. Chapter six will tell the story of the mission in Mescalero, New Mexico, which served not only the Mescalero Apaches, but also the Fort Sill Apaches who chose to go to New Mexico after their release.

and possessions. It was the Zunis who gave them the name Apache, meaning "enemy."

The Apaches were probably the first Indians in the United States to acquire horses, which they did about 1600. Says historian Gordon Baldwin, "Between the 1630s and 1660s most Apaches and Navajos had stolen or traded enough horses to put everyone in the tribes on horseback. More mobile now, they were able to strike fast and get away equally fast. They took everything that wasn't nailed down—food, clothing, blankets, jewelry, weapons, horses, mules, cattle, sheep, and women and small children."[2]

The American Southwest, traditional home of the Apache people, became part of the United States through the Mexican-American War in 1848 and the Gadsden Purchase from Mexico in 1853. For some two hundred years the Spanish had tried in vain to subdue the Apaches, and the Mexicans could do no better during their quarter-century rule. Now American troops, settlers, and gold-seekers descended on Apache territory, and the Apaches fought back.

The Apache wars raged off and on for twenty-five years, punctuated by periods of peace, promises, broken promises, false charges, rumors, imprisonments, escapes, massacres, treachery, attacks, and counter-attacks. During this time, the U.S. Government spent some $38 million and lost more than one thousand soldiers and civilians in its attempt to subdue the Apaches but managed to kill less than one hundred Apaches, including women and children.

The Saga of Geronimo

The best known of the Chiricahua Apaches was Geronimo, a legend in his own time. Geronimo, whose Apache name was *Goyathlay* ("one who yawns"), had served in his youth under leaders Cochise and Mangas Coloradas. He was not a chief as is commonly thought, but rather a respected medicine man, brilliant strategist, and a brave (and sometimes brutal) warrior. He had become embittered against non-Indians in general and Mexicans in particular when in his absence Mexicans killed his wife, mother, and three children. For nearly twenty years he and his band of warriors engaged both Mexicans and Americans in a cycle of attacks, raids, surrenders, and escapes. He became legendary for his cunning, his cruelty, and his ability to escape capture and conduct lightning raids on the U.S. military.

2. Gordon Baldwin, *The Apache Indians: Raiders of the Southwest* (New York: Four Winds Press, 1978), 40.

Perico, Geronimo, Naiche, and Isisnah

By 1876 the government had placed all Apaches on reservations or in prison, bringing an end to the Apache wars. These included the Chiricahua Apaches, who with other Apache groups were relegated to the San Carlos reservation in Arizona, located on searing desert land about 130 miles east of Phoenix. (The agent at San Carlos, incidentally, was John Clum, Reformed Church member and one-time Rutgers divinity student from rural New York.) But Geronimo and his band broke out of the hated reservation and fled, and for ten years they were hunted throughout Mexico and the American Southwest.

Finally, facing extermination or starvation, pursued by five thousand troops, and reduced to sixteen warriors, twelve women, and six children, Geronimo surrendered voluntarily in September 1886 to General Nelson Miles at Skeleton Canyon in Arizona. Geronimo's words are famous: "Once I moved about like the wind. Now I surrender to you and that is all."

Chiricahuas Sent to Florida

Shortly before Geronimo's surrender, several hundred tribal members, including women, children, and Apache scouts who had helped the government, had been shipped from San Carlos to Fort Marion in St. Augustine, Florida, where they were kept as prisoners.

During their time in Florida, 112 children were sent to the Indian boarding school at Carlisle, Pennsylvania, and nearly one-third of them died there.

Now the government, realizing the futility of returning Geronimo once more to San Carlos, sent him and his small band by train to Florida. But instead of sending them to be with their people at St. Augustine, as had been promised, President Grover Cleveland sent them to Fort Pickens on Santa Rosa Island, outside Pensacola. (The next month, in October 1886, Cleveland officially accepted from France the Statue of Liberty, a symbol of welcome to European immigrants.)

The San Carlos reservation had been hot and dry, but the Florida weather, hot and damp, proved to be even worse for the Chiricahuas' health. Many contracted tuberculosis and were transferred to the barracks at Mt. Vernon, Alabama. In May of 1888 the former warriors at Fort Pickens were reunited with their families in Alabama, but lung disorders continued to take their toll, and more Apaches died during imprisonment than during the Apache wars.

General Miles (who had received Geronimo's surrender) and George Wratten (a white interpreter and advocate who had accompanied the Apaches to Florida) lobbied that the Apaches be kept together and relocated to the military installation at Fort Sill, in Indian Territory (now Oklahoma). Approval was finally given, and the Comanches, who were already living near Fort Sill, agreed to give up some of their land to the Apaches.

Lawton and Fort Sill: A Short History

Fort Sill, on the north edge of the present city of Lawton, was founded as Camp Wichita in 1869, after the nearby Wichita Mountains, and later named Fort Sill in memory of Brigadier General Joshua Sill, who had been killed in a Civil War battle. Fort Sill has, since 1911, been the home of the U.S. Army Field Artillery School, with about twenty thousand military personnel. The museum at Fort Sill is rich in lore about Geronimo and his band, including a model of the Apache village on the outskirts of the military post.

The city of Lawton was not founded until 1901, when the last of the Kiowa-Comanche-Apache Indian lands of the Indian Territory were opened for white settlement. Unlike the earlier helter-skelter land rushes, would-be settlers registered for 160-acre land allotments. Of the 29,000 registrations at Fort Sill, 6,500 names were drawn. Lawton sprang up almost overnight, with an estimated 25,000 living in tents.

The present population of the city, not including the military base, is about 70,000.

The settlement of Lawton was celebrated in an article in the *Mission Field*, a Reformed Church publication, in 1901. Reprinted from the *Saturday Evening Post*, the story was exuberant about the new people arriving from all over the United States and said that in time "the desert shall blossom; the harvest shall be garnered. The English-speaking race has let no land conquer it."[3] Neither the *Post* article nor the *Mission Field's* introduction to it makes any mention of the Indian people who were being displaced and who had no homeland left except tents pitched around the military post.

The Chiricahua Apaches Arrive at Fort Sill

Finally, October 2, 1894, a train left Mobile, Alabama, with 346 Apaches bound for Oklahoma. At each stop along the way, crowds gathered to catch a glimpse of the "savages" and especially of Geronimo, who obliged them by smiling and waving.

The Chiricahua Apaches were kept at Fort Sill as prisoners of war until 1913. Although not imprisoned in a jail, the Indians were prisoners nevertheless, since anyone who left the compound without permission would be hunted down and brought back. They were limited in potential marriage partners, because outsiders did not want to submit themselves to their situation. Yet largely through the insistence of their friend George Wratten, they were treated humanely and allowed to maintain some semblance of community life. Captain Hugh Lenox Scott, in charge of Fort Sill, proved to be both wise and humane in his treatment of the Indians.

Wratten helped divide the Chiricahuas into twelve small villages following the leadership structure of the tribe. The leaders of these groups were Geronimo, Loco, Naiche, Alfred Chatto, Roger Toclanny, Jacob Kaahteney, Carl Mangus, Tom Chiricahua, George Noche, Leon Perico, and Martin Kayihtah (later succeeded by Charles Martine).[4]

The Apaches, after instruction in carpentry, were put to work building their homes. All the homes were designed in the then-familiar frontier style of "two pens and a passage"—two rooms separated by a roofed passageway that could be used for storage. The Apaches were

---

3. "Our Newest Town," *Mission Field* (November 1901), reprinted from the *Saturday Evening Post*, n.d.
4. Various sources spell some of these names differently.

The "Geronimo"
Guardhouse at Fort Sill

assigned plots of land, on which they grew Kaffir corn, melons, and various vegetables. Later they raised cattle.

A word ought to be said here about George Wratten, whose life was intertwined with those of the Indians, and ultimately with members of the Reformed Church. Wratten, who traveled as interpreter with the Apaches to Florida and back, constantly advocated for their rights and was one of the few white men trusted by the Indians. He took an Apache wife, Annie White, with whom he had two children—Amy (born 1890) and Blossom (born 1893), both of whom were educated in Reformed Church schools and became faithful members of the church. Several of Wratten's grandchildren, including Mildred Cleghorn, also became active leaders in the tribe and the Reformed Church.

Previous Missionaries

Missionaries of the Reformed Church in America were neither the first nor the only missionaries sent to this area of Oklahoma. The first missionary to the Kiowa and Comanches was the Reverend Harrison Sterling Rice Ashby, sent in 1881 by the Methodist Episcopal Church. He abandoned the work four years later and became a politician. The Presbyterians came to the area in 1889 when the Reverend W.W. Carrithers set up a mission and constructed a stone church in the country five miles west of the present town of Apache. That ministry, called the Cache Creek Mission, continued until 1974, when some of its members transferred to the Apache Reformed Church. In 1893 the Reverend Deyo of Rochester, New York, set up a mission west of the present-day Lawton, a ministry that continues to this day.

The Mission Begins at Fort Sill

The Reverend Frank Hall Wright had been turned away by

the authorities when he first requested permission to evangelize the Apaches; he then went northward to Colony and established the work there. Having installed the Reverend Walter Roe as the pastor at Colony, Wright returned often to the Fort Sill area to preach to the Comanches and to renew his request to be given access to the Apaches.

Fort Sill Gives Permission to Wright

Finally, with the arrival of a new administrator, Lieutenant Beach, Wright received permission to begin work among the prisoners of war. In fact, according to Wright, it was Beach who approached Wright and said "Preach to my people."[5]

Elizabeth Page told it somewhat differently. According to her, Wright had arrived by wagon and met a military man on horseback who asked, "Stranger, that's a queer looking outfit you have there; might I ask what your business is in this country?"

"I am a missionary to the Indians," replied Wright, "and I am looking for a place to begin work."

"Well, if it's your business, why don't you do something for these Indians? God knows they need it badly enough."

Wright explained that he had been trying to do so for three years but could not get permission; whereupon Lieutenant Beach introduced himself as the new man in charge and invited Wright to see him the next day at Fort Sill.[6]

Beach called a council of the Indian leaders, including Geronimo; and Wright immediately played his trump card. He planned, he said, to build a school for the Apaches at Fort Sill, where children would learn to read and write and also learn about the Jesus Road. The government already had a school near Fort Sill for the Comanches. There was no room for the Apaches, so plans had been made to send the Apache children to an Indian boarding school in Anadarko, forty miles to the north, and Indian mothers were reluctant to give up their small children for long periods of time. At last, according to Page, Geronimo got up and made an astonishing speech:

> I, Geronimo, and these others are now too old to travel your Jesus Road. But our children are young and I and my brothers will be

5. *Annual Report of the Women's Executive Committee of the Board of Domestic Missions,* 1900, 28.
6. Elizabeth Page, *In Camp and Tepee: An Indian Mission Story* (New York, Chicago, and Toronto: Fleming Revell, 1915), 67-68.

School and orphanage at Fort Sill

glad to have the children taught about the white man's God.[7]

Beach secured permission from Washington, the government granted land, and the Reverend Walter and Mary Roe of Colony headed east to raise money. Junior Christian Endeavor groups throughout the Reformed Church, better known then as the Dutch Reformed Church, donated desks, maps, lamps, and school supplies.

A School Is Built

In the fall of 1899 the facilities were ready: a cottage with one large room for thirty-five students and religious services, plus an apartment for workers. Two unmarried women joined the mission team: F. A. Mosely as the teacher and Maud Adkisson as a mission worker. Mosely was supported by missionary unions in the east, and Adkisson by unions in the Midwest.

But as the school year opened, news came that twenty-three kindergarten children had somehow been overlooked and would be sent away to school in Anadarko. Mothers again objected, and Wright headed east on a fund-raising tour. The Reformed Church of Brighton Heights, Staten Island, New York, pledged to pay the salary of a teacher, and Anna Baty was hired, soon to be succeeded by Mary Ewing of New Albany, Indiana. Ewing remained with the school until 1913, when most of the Apaches left for Mescalero and the school was closed.

Another house was soon added to the mission compound, containing a kindergarten room, large dining room, and kitchen. Teachers discovered that children frequently had no lunch, so they began serving a noon meal at the mission, with the government supplying the rations.

A regular school assignment was writing letters to boys and girls in supporting churches. Many of these letters were printed in the *Day*

7. Ibid, 74.

Apache schoolboys at Fort Sill

Star, the mission publication for children. Some of the letters appear to have been heavily edited, while others had not. Frequently, they told how much they enjoyed coming to school and how much they liked their teachers. These are typical of the unedited or lightly edited letters:

> Dear Friend: I am going to write to you a letter. This school is near the creek. I am a little boy about eleven years old, but I don't know how old you are. We are in Apache Mission School. Thirteen children are in my class—three girls and ten boys. We are all in third grade. We are near the creek. The grass grow green and some trees, too. We all go to Sunday school and to our C. E. Society. The boys are glad to go to school every day, and I am. Miss Mosely read your letter to all of us. I think I close my letter for this time.
>
> Your little friend, Harry Perico[8]

> Dear Friends—I am going to tell you about our school we always have service on every Friday afternoon we read the Bibles. I have a Bible that Miss McMillan gave to me and I like to read it whenever

8. "Our Little Brown Brothers," *Day Star,* June 1900, 2.

I come to school. We have a nice time over here all the time, and the boys always love to play ball. I love to come to Sunday-school to hear the Bible that they read. Some of the men are plowing and some of them planting corn. Some white people always come fishing on Sunday. All the children are well and happy all the time, and some of the girls and boys are staying over here and when ever school is out the boys go fishing. All over the prairies there so many different kinds of sweet flowers and the children when they come to school in the morning they pick flowers on the way to school.

Emma Toclanny, age 15 years [9]

An Orphanage Is Added

In 1902 the missionaries felt the need for an orphanage. After considering the options, they decided to build a new house for the female staff (now four) and to remodel the original cottage to serve as an orphanage for sixteen children. Funds were provided by a legacy, hence the name Ida H. Van Alst Memorial Orphanage. Additional funds were provided by an "Indian Reception" held at the Second Reformed Church in Albany, New York.

Early photos of the orphanage show a large, square, two-story structure with a huge front porch and a long wooden walkway leading to the front door, but entirely devoid of trees, bushes, or other landscaping. Until the mission closed in 1913, the orphanage continuously housed between twenty-three and twenty-nine children. The older boys and girls were taught to cook and clean, and they played a major role in preparing the meals for the house. A 1906 report said that these children were "happy" and "carefully trained." In fact, said the report, the teachers of the day school "wish that all the pupils could live in the Home; they find those thus privileged so much better prepared in every way for the daily instruction."[10]

Among the orphanage's sixteen residents in 1903 was Blossom White, described as "a pretty little half-breed girl who was abandoned by her parents when she was only a few weeks old" but who is "now learning the ways of civilization and has a bright, sweet loving disposition."[11] She was supported and clothed by a Sunday school in

9. "Our Indian Mail Bag," *Day Star*, September 1903, 2.
10. *Annual Report of the Women's Board of Domestic Missions*, 1906, 28.
11. "The Indian Orphanage," *Day Star*, March 1903, 2.

Bronxville, New York. Although the article does not identify her lineage except as "half-breed," her mother was Annie White and her father was George Wratten, the interpreter for the Chiricahuas. Blossom's parents had separated, and her mother was unable to care for her. Blossom eventually married Sam Haozous, and they become long-time faithful members of the Apache church. Blossom died in 1981 at the age of eighty-eight.

Christianity, Christmas, and Baseball

Almost immediately Christmas became a major event at the school, complete with a Christmas tree and Santa Claus. Reformed churches sent huge quantities of Christmas gifts for both children and adults. Maud Adkisson reported that at the Christmas celebration of 1899 girls received hair ribbons, gloves, and a doll; boys received stockings, handkerchiefs, balls, and marbles (which they soon lost to older boys); and adults received candy, apples, and oranges. In a column in the *Day Star* called "The Pow-Wow," Adkisson added a comment that surfaced on several occasions in mission reports: "Everybody had a good time, we <u>know</u> that, but not one person remembered to say so. That is something we will teach them by-and-by."[12]

Other holidays, such as Valentine's Day, Washington's Birthday, Lincoln's Birthday, and Columbus Day, were celebrated at the school and were used as opportunities for teaching "civilized" culture. Very soon the missionaries also introduced white people's sports as a Christian alternative to native customs. Louise Runk, chairwoman of the Committee for Indian Work, reported proudly in 1900 that the children not only enjoy their lessons but also play football and croquet "as heartily as their white brothers and sisters. Very soon now the boys will be made happy by a baseball outfit, which is on the way to them, the exact counterpart of a set used by some boys in New Jersey."[13]

Bible lessons were a regular part of the curriculum, along with reading, writing, and arithmetic. On Sunday mornings the classroom doubled as a Sunday school, with attendance required. The lessons were taught only in English, in keeping with the English-only school policy. The adults who attended, according to Runk, enjoyed "the bright pictures on cards and charts," and the children sang "the beautiful hymns which are familiar to us."[14]

12. Maud Adkisson, "Santa Claus' Visit to Fort Sill," *Day Star*, March 1900, 2.
13. *Annual Report of the Women's Executive Committee of the Board of Domestic Missions,* 1900, 30.
14. Ibid, 29.

The 'Civilization' of Indian Children

The Reverend John G. Gebhard, corresponding secretary for the Reformed Church's Educational Committee, visited the school in 1904 and gave this glowing report of the "civilization" of the Indian children:

> At the head of the table, by the teacups, sat one of the little girls who invited us to tea, with one of the guests on her right, and at the foot of the table sat a little Indian boy, with another guest occupying the place of honor next to him. But was there even a sweeter surprise? This little Indian boy and girl, scarcely in their teens, were the host and hostess, as we clearly discovered as soon as grace had been said. With perfect ease and charm of manner they did the honors of the table....So we found that at Fort Sill the children were receiving an invaluable education in the refinements of Christian social life."[15]

Several years later, mention was made of a school fair in which a number of schools, including Presbyterian, Catholic, and Reformed, showed off their beadwork, farm produce, cooking, sewing, embroidery, and canned fruit.

Following the long-established pattern of Reformed congregations, the missionaries almost immediately organized a Christian Endeavor (C.E.) Society, with Maud Adkisson in charge. The group of about fifteen in their late teens was composed almost entirely of students who had been educated in the eastern boarding schools such as Carlisle and Hampton. A 1902 photo shows the boys in suits and ties and the girls in skirts and white blouses. Benedict Jozhe, one of the early C.E. members, later became a charter member and elder in the Apache Reformed Church. The photo also includes Jason Betzinez, who later married mission worker Anna Heersma and wrote the well-known book, *I Fought with Geronimo*, still in print.

Although Maud Adkisson had frequent contact with the Comanches, especially with Nahwats, Dorothy, and Tocsi (see chapter 5), her primary responsibility was the Apaches. The talents of missionary Wright lay in the realm of evangelism rather than

15. John G. Gebhard, "Education at Fort Sill," *Mission Field*, Aug. 1904, 150.

administration, so most of the ongoing responsibility came to rest on Adkisson's shoulders.

Jason Betzinez reports that an influential Indian with the English name of Harold Dick hindered the work of the mission by his denunciation of the white man's religion. He strongly advocated the continuation of medicine dances, which were adamantly opposed by the missionaries. During the winter of 1899-1900, Betzinez says, worship attendance fell off alarmingly. Sometimes he was the only Indian in attendance. Then, acknowledging the key role of the women missionaries, Betzinez writes, "As the springtime approached, the work of the two women began to bear fruit as more and more Indians began coming to church and Christian Endeavor meetings."[16]

Noche, the First Apache Convert

According to Elizabeth Page, the first Apache to take the "Jesus Road" was Noche, who, although serving as a U.S. scout, was held as a prisoner of war with the other Apaches. The story of his conversion illustrates how many Indians struggled in their decision to follow the "white man's God."

Maude Adkisson had decided Noche was ready for baptism and asked pastor Roe to administer the sacrament when he came from Colony to conduct Easter services. Suddenly, on Saturday night, Noche's only child, a baby, died. The next day an angry Noche strode into the service and announced, "I was a foolish old woman to listen to you white people. The justice of your God is like the justice of your government. I fought for your government, and I am a prisoner. I served your God and my baby is dead. But Noche is not a woman. I know your road. I shall not serve you again. I shall not serve your God. I have spoken."

After he sat down, Roe responded through an interpreter. He pointed out that when Noche went out to find wood for a bow, he tested it by twisting and bending it to be sure that there was no hidden weakness that might show up in time of battle. Roe went on to say that there are two kinds of trouble in the world—one kind that we bring on by ourselves, and another kind that God uses to test us. "He bends you and twists you to see if there is any hidden weak spot in your heart," said Roe. "God is very careful with his war-bows." Then, according to Page,

---

16. Jason Betzinez with Wilbur Sturtevant Nye, *I Fought with Geronimo* (Lincoln: Univ. of Nebraska Press, 1987, 172).

the Indian rose and the two men shook hands. "I shall not break in his hand," said Noche, "He can trust me."[17] When the Apache Reformed Church was formally organized in 1907, Noche was elected as one of the elders, the other being Benedict Jozhe.

Christian Naiche

Noche was followed on the Jesus Road by several other leaders, including Chihuahua, Chatto, and Naiche, the second son of Cochise and the last hereditary chief of the Chiricahuas. Professor J. T. Bergen of Hope College, who later played a key role in the conversion of Geronimo, said of Naiche that he was "tall, strong, handsome, a true man of unsullied integrity, and a warm believer in Jesus. I have heard him open his heart to his people, powerfully persuading them to accept Christ."[18] Naiche adopted the first name of Christian and remained a loyal member of the church until his death in Mescalero, New Mexico, many years later.

In 1904 Naiche visited the General Synod, accompanied by his son-in-law James, a Carlisle student, as interpreter. "They told their story simply to those who came to hear them and all were impressed with their earnestness, the firm desire to follow in the Christian path," said Louise Runk in her annual report of the Committee on Indian Work. "We must remember," she went on to say, "that very few Indians have any idea of the number of Christian white people in this country... and it is equally a privilege for us to learn and know and admire the better and stronger traits of character in a people so far removed in habits, life and surroundings from ourselves."[19]

Camp Meetings Follow the Colony Pattern

It is not surprising that Wright should continue the camp meeting strategy that he and Roe had begun at Colony. As many as three hundred Indians, including Comanche, Apache, and Kiowa, gathered for the feasts, with translators for each language group. Several Reformed congregations paid for the provisions. At these meetings the Comanches outnumbered the Apaches two to one. Comanches attended in their traditional Indian dress; the Apaches, as prisoners of

---

17. Page, *In Camp and Tepee*, 137-40.
18. J. T. Bergen, "How Geronimo Came Out," *Mission Field*, January 1903, 336.
19. *Annual Report of the Women's Executive Committee of the Board of Domestic Missions*, 1905, 20.

war, had already adopted more "civilized" attire. Camp meetings were primary tools not only for evangelistic appeals to walk the Jesus Road but also for exhortations for wanderers to return to that road.

Exactly when the Apache church was organized is a matter of some confusion. In 1901 the Committee on Indian Work reported that Wright toured the Indian camps, "preaching and singing the gospel to them...and finally organizing a church there, on September 30, 1900, with twenty-two members."[20] That's all; no further details, no mention of a consistory or other clergy involved. It can only be assumed that Wright did this entirely on his own and without participation of a classis. Neither Roe nor Wright had been ordained and installed by the Reformed Church, and they apparently were given free rein in those early days. As we shall see, the Apache church was organized again in 1907, this time with classis participation.

The Reformed Church did not begin publishing membership statistics until 1911, and statistical reports of the Apache mission were sporadic in the annual reports of the Women's Board. Membership apparently averaged about eighty. In 1913, when members were transferred to the Mescalero church, eighty-nine Indians carried letters of transfer. Reports of confessions of faith were likewise sporadic, ranging between five and twenty-nine. Sunday school enrollment was reported only once during this time—seventy students in 1909.

The Conversion of Geronimo

The camp meetings of 1902 and 1903 proved to be pivotal in the decision of Geronimo to take the Jesus Road. The Reverend J. Tallmadge Bergen, a professor at Hope College, participated in several of these camp meetings, along with Wright and Roe. In a tract published by the Chicago Tract Society (and borrowed from heavily by Elizabeth Page in her account, or vice-versa), Bergen gave a detailed account of the conversion of Geronimo:

Geronimo, the medicine man, the former hero, had felt his tribal authority gradually slipping away. Several of his fellow warriors, including his close friend chief Naiche, had become Christians, and Geronimo had become more and more bitter against the Jesus Road, the white man's religion. He had retreated, said Page, "in sullen

---

20. *Annual Report of the Women's Executive Committee of the Board of Domestic Missions,* 1901, 19.

Geronimo

acquiescence to his lonely village, contenting himself by showing his hostility now and again in some underhanded scheme."[21]

But in September 1902 Geronimo showed up at the camp on a Sunday noon, the last day of the meetings. The sessions had begun on Thursday, and Bergen had preached seven times on such doctrinal topics as regeneration and God's sovereignty. Rather than go to the meetings, Geronimo went to the tent that his wife had erected.

After the afternoon meeting, Wright and Bergen met with Geronimo in his tent and finally were able to extract from him a promise to attend the evening meeting. The old man kept his promise and even sat near the front. Bergen preached on the doctrine of atonement, and when Wright followed the sermon with an invitation, a "throng" of Indians came forward for prayer. Then Geronimo, according to the account of Bergen and Page, leaped to his feet and began to speak with great passion, the gist of which was, "The Jesus Road is best and I would like my people to travel it." He concluded, "Now we begin to think the Christian white people love us."

21. Page, *In Camp and Tepee*, 142.

After the service Wright and Bergen talked with Geronimo and prayed with him, but the pastors detected a "vein of self-importance, hardly consistent with deep repentance," and they left feeling that the old warrior was "still afar off." During the next year Geronimo wavered, at some times seeming friendly toward Christianity and at other times showing resentment against anything that interfered with tribal dances and other customs.

In July of the next year, 1903, Wright held another camp meeting and again invited Bergen to preach. Geronimo failed to appear at the first meeting, but, while the missionaries were resting in the afternoon, Geronimo rode up and painfully dismounted, explaining that he was late because he had been injured by falling off a horse. Through an interpreter he told the missionaries that he knew he was not on the right road and that he wanted to find Jesus. Thereafter he listened to every sermon. On Saturday afternoon, after hearing Bergen preach on the topic, "Jesus made just like sin for us," the old man stayed and said, "Pray that Jesus will give me a new heart." On Sunday morning, in response to Wright's energized invitation, Geronimo was the first to come forward and to declare his surrender.

A week later, Roe, having come down from Colony, examined him carefully. Geronimo displayed more knowledge than anyone had anticipated, and Roe recommended his baptism, saying, "No consistory of our church could refuse to admit this man into membership." Geronimo and six others were then baptized, amid the happy celebration of whites and Indians alike, including his family and Naiche.[22]

Wright, in his account of Geronimo's conversion, wrote that "it required faith to accept his profession of faith as genuine. But he made a most impressive statement of his earnestness in the step which he took. He professed his faith in Christ and determination to follow him. 'You must help me,' he said. 'Pray for me. You may hear of my doing wrong, but my heart is right.'"[23] In his autobiography, as told to S. M. Barrett, Geronimo said this about his faith:

> Since my life as a prisoner has begun I have heard the teachings of the white man's religion, and in many respects believe it to be

22. "Geronimo's Conversion," tract published by the Chicago Tract Society (no date) and reprinted in *Historical Highlights,* Reformed Church Historical Commission, February 1994.
23. F. H. Wright, "Geronimo at the Camp Meeting," *Mission Field,* October 1903, 213.

better than the religion of my fathers. However, I have always prayed, and I believe that the Almighty has always protected me.

Believing that in a wise way it is good to go to church, and that associating with Christians would improve my character, I have adopted the Christian religion. I believe that the church has helped me much during the short time I have been a member....I have advised all of my people who are not Christians, to study that religion, because it seems to me the best religion in enabling one to live right.[24]

Barrett adds as a footnote that "Geronimo joined the Dutch Reformed church and was baptized in the summer of 1903. He attended the services regularly at the Apache Mission, Ft. Sill Military Reservation. Later Geronimo was expelled from the church for incessant gambling."[25] (The last sentence, as we shall see, is probably incorrect.)

In the years after his conversion, Geronimo achieved a certain celebrity, being a star attraction at the St. Louis World's Fair and at major expositions in Buffalo and Omaha. He also became something of an entrepreneur, selling autographed photos, buttons off his coat for fifty cents, and walking sticks for a dollar.

In March of 1905 Geronimo traveled to Washington, D.C., there to ride in President Theodore Roosevelt's second inaugural parade. Even Geronimo's horse was shipped in for the event. "I wanted to give the people a good show," said Roosevelt when questioned by a reporter.[26]

"He lived for seven years to walk the new road" [actually, it was less than six], wrote Elizabeth Page in her account, "seven years during which the missionaries almost came to question the wisdom of ever taking him in."[27]

Page acknowledged that Geronimo had difficulty breaking with lifelong habits of gambling and drinking. He died of pneumonia February 17, 1909, in his nineties, after falling off his horse and lying out in a cold rain for the night after a drinking spree. "Yet," concluded

24. *Geronimo: His Own Story,* as told to S. M. Barrett, rev. (New York: Penguin Books, 1996), 165-66. Originally published as *Geronimo's Story of His Life* (New York: Duffield, 1906).

25. Ibid, 166.

26. Albert E. Wratten, "George Wratten: Friend of the Apaches," *Journal of Arizona History,* Spring 1986, 119.

27. Page, *In Camp and Tepee,* 146.

Page, "he tried, he honestly tried, and who are we to judge him—we who often make failures of roads far less hard to travel?"[28]

Missionary Hendrina Hospers echoed a similar sentiment, writing several years later, "The old medicine man and warrior never became what you would call a paragon of Christian behavior. The old influences were too great, and his resistance to some forms of vice too weak."[29]

Was Geronimo ever suspended from membership in the Reformed Church? An article in the *Lawton Constitution* on the occasion of his death says that "he returned to his beloved habit of drink and engaging also in gambling and horse racing, practically renounced his religion when lectured by his missionary, Rev. L. L. Legters. Shortly afterward, he was suspended from the church."[30] One of Geronimo's best-known biographers, Angie Debo, says he was suspended from the church, but she quotes the *Lawton Constitution* article as her source. The original article, however, is full of errors, and its accuracy is in question. It identifies the church as the "German Reform Church," calls Geronimo's place of residence a "reservation," misspells "Chiricahua," states that Geronimo had espoused the Christian religion four years before, and displays a cynical and even hostile attitude toward Geronimo himself. There is no evidence, either in the records of the Apache church or in any article published by the Reformed Church, that Geronimo was ever suspended from membership.

Geronimo was buried in the Indian cemetery at Fort Sill, his often-visited grave marked by a pyramid of stones. In 1986 about three hundred members of the Apache tribes from several states gathered at Geronimo's grave to honor the hundredth anniversary of the surrender of the Apache warriors. Wendell Chino, former pastor and president of the Mescalero Apaches, was the principal speaker, saying that the Apaches should be proud of the men who tried to preserve their land and heritage. Mildred Cleghorn, a prominent member of the Apache Reformed Church and chairperson of her tribe, voiced a similar opinion.

28. Ibid., 147.
29. Hendrina Hospers, "I 'Rode' with Geronimo," *Corral Dust*, Summer, 1958, 11-12.
30. "Apache Chief Geronimo Dead," *Lawton Constitution*, Feb. 18, 1909, 1.

Martha Prince (left) and Hendrina Hospers at the Apache mission

The Apache Church Is Organized—Again, 1907

The Apache mission, and subsequently the Apache church, did not have a full-time minister until many years later—1958, to be exact. Wright, always the itinerant evangelist, never settled down to long-term pastoral work at Lawton. It would appear that he spent only summers there, and much of that time was spent conducting camp meetings at various Indian mission sites. Roe made frequent trips from Colony, seventy miles north, but obviously could not devote full time to the work.

The Key Role of Women Mission Workers

It was Maud Adkisson who carried on the bulk of the work after her arrival as a field worker in 1899. A 1903 report said of Adkisson, "With only occasional assistance from some of our ministers, she has taken full charge of the services, in addition to her special work for the women."[31]

Hendrina Hospers, in her early twenties and from Orange City, Iowa, came in 1905 as a teacher but often also preached and

31. *Annual Report of the Women's Board of Domestic Missions*, 1903, 35.

Anna Vos and Indian girls prepare a meal at the Apache mission school.

conducted funerals. Although the current pastor of the Comanche church conducted some Sunday afternoon services and an occasional Wednesday evening meeting with the Apaches, Hospers did almost all of the home visitation and Bible reading.

The mission school and orphanage at Fort Sill were served by a substantial list of unmarried women who came to Indian Territory as missionary teachers, matrons, and field workers. Some stayed only a year or two; others stayed as long as six or seven years. Some received much publicity; others received so little recognition that their first names were never recorded. These teachers included Mary McMillan, Mary Ewing, Miss Weddle, Miss Mosely, Anna Voss, Miss Apsley, Mary Moore, Miss Hawkins, Joan Saunders, Clover Mahan, Martha Prince, Jenny Dubbink, Jennie Pikkart, Hattie Hospers, Hendrina Hospers, and, of course, Maud Adkisson.

Several mission workers married through their contacts at the mission. Hattie Hospers, for instance, married the Reverend Gustavus Watermulder of Winnebago, the ceremony being conducted at a workers' conference in Colony in the spring of 1911. Maud Adkisson, as we shall note, married the Reverend L. L. Legters.

As previously noted, Anna Heersma married Jason Betzinez, a cousin of Geronimo. Betzinez had become a Christian while attending Carlisle and took an exceptionally strong stand against Indian dances. Heersma, who came from the Dutch settlements south of Chicago, came to the mission to take care of the orphanage in 1907 and met Betzinez, a blacksmith at that time. Heersma returned to Chicago in 1912 but returned five years later. She then married Betzinez, who had

Maud Adkisson

remained in Oklahoma as a farmer when most of the Apaches chose to go to Mescalero. They joined a Presbyterian church in Lawton. At the age of ninety-six, Betzinez traveled to New York to participate in the TV show "I've Got a Secret," in which a panel tried to guess a "secret" the guest was harboring.

Maud Adkisson Married

In 1906 Maud Adkisson was united in marriage to L. L. Legters, who had accepted an invitation to undertake the work among the Comanches and Apaches at Fort Sill. Legters had come originally from Clymer, New York, had graduated from Hope College and New Brunswick Theological Seminary, and had served briefly at Colony. Upon coming to Lawton, he and Adkisson quickly struck up a friendship. They were married June 28, 1906, at the Colony church and then moved into the newly constructed parsonage in Lawton. As Mrs. Legters, Maud continued to play a major role in the Oklahoma Indian work until 1910, when she and her husband moved to California to assume an administrative position with an Indian association.

L. L. Legters

Apache and Comanche Churches Organized

On May 1, 1907, there occurred a unique event in the history of Reformed Church mission work—the organization of two sister congregations on the same day. The Comanche congregation was organized in the morning and the Apache congregation was organized that afternoon. Officiating at both services were Walter Roe; Frank Hall Wright; Richard Harper, recently arrived at Colony; Leonard Legters, pastor of the Comanche and Apache congregations; and Edgar Tilton, pastor of the Harlem Collegiate Church in New York City, the church that from the beginning had supported Wright. Interestingly, Wright is identified as "of Dallas," which indicates that Oklahoma was not his primary residence or scene of ministry.

The Apache congregation was organized with fifty-five charter members, and the Comanche church with sixty-three members. The original consistory of the Apache congregation included Benedict Jozhe and Noche (the first Apache convert), elders; and Eugene Chihuaha and Sam Haozous, deacons. Other members included Chatto, John Loco, Nalotsi, Amy Wratten (Mildred Cleghorn's mother), and a number of women identified only as Susie, Lillian, Rachel, and Cora. One woman was given the name of Elizabeth at the meeting, named after Elizabeth Page.

These two congregations were organized as members of the Classis of Oklahoma, which had been founded a year earlier by the Particular Synod of New York. When the classis was dissolved in 1911, the Apache and Comanche congregations reverted to their previous status with the Classis of New York.

The Comanche church was organized with a church building and with an installed pastor, but the Apache church had neither luxury. It is likely that, because negotiations for the release of the prisoners had been ongoing for several years, hiring a full-time missionary pastor and constructing a church and parsonage were not high priorities. Most of the responsibility for the church rested on the young shoulders of Hendrina Hospers, who had arrived two years before, and on the newlyweds Legters, who gave as much time as they could to the Apaches. Pastor Legters preached every Sunday afternoon at the Apache church—the first time in the history of the Apache mission that an ordained minister regularly conducted Sunday services.

In the minds of the missionaries and of the church leaders, convincing the Indians to give up their old ways continued to be a problem. Several consistory actions expressed concern, and in some cases consistory members were assigned to dissuade members from sponsoring dances. Legters, in talking about his work with the Apaches, wrote in 1910:

> The great problem for the workers to solve has been the "coming out dances." They have been the downfall of many of our church members; it is so hard to eradicate the old customs and superstitions. These dances are, as all others, of a religious nature...they seem to believe that the dancing medicine men have peculiar powers at that time. Then, too, there is the ever present immorality, which is as bad as any of the temple worship in India. We have succeeded in getting at least two of our people to give a feast and discard the dancing and everything that goes with it.[32]

A few entries in the consistory minutes of 1911 give interesting insights into church membership:

> September 10: Oliver and Tstai married at the parsonage. If correctly informed, they are the seventh couple among the Apaches married according to the white man's way.

> September 17: Belle, the notorious Apache woman of whom it is said, "she has been married to every man in the Apache tribe," was received into membership....She made a good confession, and our hope and prayers are that she may remain faithful.[33]

---

32. *Annual Report of the Women's Board of Domestic Missions*, 1910, 24-25.
33. Consistory Minutes of the Apache Reformed Church, 1911, 32, 33.

When the Reverend Henry Sluyter took over the pastorate of the Comanche church in 1910, he also assumed responsibility for the Apache work. A report in the fall of 1911 hinted at the uncertainty of the mission: "What may be the future of these Apaches we cannot tell, but surely the seeds sown in our mission, and especially in the lives of the children, cannot die."[34] At that time the orphanage housed twenty-three children and the day school served thirty students. Sluyter stayed until 1913 and accompanied the Apaches to their new home in Mescalero, New Mexico.

Church statistics from 1908 to 1913 were only sporadically included in consistory minutes, but the church reported that membership had nearly doubled (from fifty-five to ninety-four) during the one year following organization. Two years later the communicant membership numbered one hundred. Sunday school enrollment was reported as sixty-nine in 1908 and seventy-five in 1910. Attendance records were even more rare, but on June 11, 1911, fifty-nine people were present for a Communion service.

A Typical Camp Meeting

Joint Comanche-Apache camp meetings continued to be a major source of evangelism and revival. Although the Apache and Comanche consistories usually met separately, they held joint meetings when planning camp meetings. At these meetings the consistories set the dates and appointed committees for such duties as collecting the funds, preparing the grounds, setting up the tent, and cleaning the area afterwards. It may have been at one of these meetings that a remarkable photo was taken of the elders and deacons of the two congregations, published in the February 1913 issue of the *Mission Field*. This photo, together with a thumbnail sketch of each consistory member, can be found on page 171.

The Reverend Henry Willoughby, pastor of the Reformed Church in Fort Plain, New York, gave this 1912 report of the Apache-Comanche camp meeting in which he participated:

> A piece of open prairie beside a quiet stream is suddenly peopled, filled with the bustle of life, made to flare with a multitude of lights, and to resound with songs and other sounds not quite so melodious. Tents and tepees spring from the dry sod as if a magic

34. "Our Indian Mission," *Christian Intelligencer*, Sept. 6, 1911, 576.

Annual tent meetings in Lawton included Apaches,
Comanches, and several other tribes,
each with its own translator.

seed had been sown. While the sun sprints from east to west the
grazing place of cattle is turned into a habitation of man...

In the gray light of morn the call of the Indian crier summons
the men to the sunrise meeting. This is purely an Indian service,
inaugurated and carried on altogether by the Indians themselves.
Only men attend, presumably because the female part of the
camp is busy preparing the food that comes from the earth, while
the male part seeks that which comes from above....Morning after
morning I lay quiet in my cot listening to the songs and prayers
uplifted in spirit by their earnestness and reverence though not a
word was intelligible. The Indian's prayer is peculiarly touching
and uplifting. When an Indian prays he prays as if in the presence
of his creator and saviour....

Morning and evening the tent was filled, often more than filled.
In the heat of the afternoon the attendance was not small.

The audience, divided first into tribes and then into groups
according to sex, was novel to eastern eyes. It was a satisfaction
to see only shining black hair framing the faces in the female
section....The young people among the Indians are rapidly
developing a taste for music. There was never any difficulty in
collecting a large group about the organ to join in singing Gospel
songs. On the second day of the meetings a large and efficient
chorus choir was organized under the musical director, Mr.
Hammond. The Apaches who heretofore have not made much

use of their musical gifts are now beginning to use their talent and for the first time in the history of the camp meetings songs of praise to Christ rang out in the Apache tongue.

To judge from the preaching and the confessions made at testimony meetings, the Indian has a ready consciousness of sin. To this consciousness Rev. Frank Wright, the preacher at these gatherings, constantly and powerfully appealed. The uncompromising holiness of God was honestly declared and all were exhorted to "put aside the old man with his deeds and to put on the new man created in Christ Jesus unto good works." Such incisive preaching was received with a fine spirit of meekness.

Thoroughness seems to be a keynote with the mission workers. Compromise is always discouraged and Jesus' claim to the first and highest place in the individual life is strongly asserted. That this has had a marked effect is shown when the Indians are given opportunity to speak of their experiences. Confession enters largely into their testimony. They seek to hide nothing. Frequently what is said is preferred by the remark, "You all know me and what I have been." Then in the searching light of the people's knowledge of him the witness for Christ goes on to disclose the working of the power of God in his life...

Christian Indians are encouraged in the presence of many friends to assert their faith more strongly...as believers see life-long opponents give way they are more fully confirmed in their faith....

The camp-meeting is a time of ingathering. More than thirty adults received baptism and were welcomed into Christian fellowship on Sunday, the closing day. It was a day of harvest joy for the workers. But the meeting is also a time of plowing and seed sowing. Here first impressions favorable to Christianity are made...the process is started by which many will at last be brought to the measure of the stature of the fullness of Christ.[35]

The Apache Prisoners Are Released, 1913

When the Chiricahua Apaches were brought from Alabama to Fort Sill in 1894, they were told that they would be receiving allotments

35. H. C. Willoughby, "The Apache-Comanche Camp Meeting," *Christian Intelligencer*, Oct. 16, 1912, 668, 674.

and that Oklahoma would be their permanent home. It seemed at the time like a good solution to this segment of the "Indian problem." The Apache's warlike reputation precluded their removal to areas farther west, and Fort Sill's 23,000 acres were scheduled for abandonment.

Within three years of their arrival the Apaches had taken major steps toward self-sufficiency, caring for substantial cattle herds and planting melons, corn, and other vegetables. A famous photo shows Geronimo and his wife and children in a melon patch, proudly displaying their produce. Realizing the need for additional acreage for cattle, the military added another 27,000 acres, taken by agreement from the Kiowas and Comanches. This brought the Apaches' total to 50,000 acres.

A Settlement Plan Aborted

With everything seemingly in place, the War Department asked the Interior Department to take custody of the Apaches. But, feeling pressure from the white constituency to retain all land for themselves, the Interior Department refused in 1897 and again in 1902 to assume its responsibilities. In other words, the Apaches remained prisoners not because somebody wanted to punish them, but because nobody wanted to allot them the land that had been promised and was rightfully theirs.

The following year the War Department, despite its earlier agreement, decided to retain the post for artillery training. It immediately annexed for its own use the 27,000 acres that had been secured from the Kiowas and Comanches—land that was to have become the permanent home of the Apaches. The prisoners of war, who had suffered such hardship and death in Florida and Alabama and who had been led to believe that this area of Oklahoma was to be their permanent home, were dispirited.

The Apaches were not without friends. Despite the official stance of the War Department, Major George Scott at Fort Sill worked actively on their behalf, as did the Bureau of Indian Affairs, the Board of Indian Commissioners, the Indian Rights Association, and the Reformed Church in America.

Finally a solution was proposed: send the Chiricahua Apaches to join their fellow Apaches, the Mescaleros, on their reservation in Mescalero, New Mexico. If any members of the tribe elected to stay in Oklahoma, they would receive an allotment of 160 acres of "unclaimed" Comanche land.

It seemed like a good solution. The Mescaleros were willing to accept the Chiricahuas. The Chiricahuas would have a place to live, and the white settlers in Oklahoma would not feel threatened. But even this solution triggered vigorous opposition from New Mexico. Senator Albert Fall, who wished to preserve the grazing interests of white cattlemen, introduced legislation to turn Mescalero into a national park. Senator Thomas Catron called the band of Chiricahuas "the most desperate, the most bloodthirsty and murdering that has ever existed." What Senator Catron failed to mention was that of the 246 Chiricahuas held at Fort Sill, only six had ever lifted a hand against the United States of America. In the end, the interests of the military establishment prevailed, and the Chiricahuas were given the option of leaving or staying. In either case, they would be free.

Missionaries Play a Key Role in the Release of the Prisoners

John Anthony Turcheneske, Jr., in his doctoral thesis for the University of New Mexico, "The Apache Prisoners of War at Fort Sill, 1894-1914," spoke highly of missionaries Hendrina Hospers and Walter Roe in securing the release of the prisoners.[36] The role of Roe in these negotiations cannot be overestimated. The legislation, as originally proposed, stipulated that the Indians could go free in Mescalero *or remain captive* at Fort Sill. This, of course, would make it unnecessary to give them land. Fortunately, Roe assisted the Indians in reading the fine print. Roe stayed in Washington D.C. throughout the winter and spring, monitoring legislation and stirring up public opinion. One could say it proved to be his last measure of devotion. He died March 12, 1913, one month before the Apaches' release. Always in frail health, he lived to be fifty-three years old.

Of the Apaches being held at Fort Sill, about two-thirds chose to leave for Mescalero and one-third elected to stay in Oklahoma. But as soon as they made the decision to stay, the government tried to eliminate or greatly reduce their promised 160 acres. Hospers, characterized by Turcheneske as an "unsung heroine,"[37] joined the fray, alerting Roe and others to this new challenge. The missionaries' efforts did not entirely succeed, however, as many Indian families received less than half of the promised allotment. Hospers was honored many years

36. John Anthony Turcheneske, Jr., "The Apache Prisoners of War at Fort Sill, 1894-1914," PhD diss. (University of New Mexico, 1978), 219-21.
37. Ibid., 252.

later, in 1966, when a community building adjacent to the Reformed
Church in Apache, Oklahoma, was named Hospers Hall.

In the spring of 1913, 246 Chiricahua Apaches were living in the
environs of Fort Sill, their numbers having been reduced by accident,
disease, and discouragement from the 341 who had come from
Alabama in 1894. Some twenty-seven years after Geronimo and his
tired little band had laid down their arms, the Apaches were poised to
take their place as free citizens of the United States of America.

The Chiricahuas Take the Train to Mescalero

On April 2, 1913, 163 Chiricahua Apaches (according to
Turcheneske; Page says "about 175"), eighty-nine of them carrying
transfers of membership to the Mescalero Reformed Church, boarded
a special train of the Rock Island Railway.[38] They left behind eighty-
three family members and friends, as well as 331 graves in the Fort Sill
cemetery. Having experienced so much deceit, they were filled with
apprehension about their promised homesite.

Accompanying the Indians were a government nurse, several
military men, pastor Henry Sluyter of the Comanche church (who also
spent some time with the Apaches), and missionaries Martha Prince
and Hendrina Hospers. In an interview many years later, Hospers
shared her recollections of the journey:

> Schools were let out all along the train's route, through
> Oklahoma, the Texas Panhandle, and in eastern New Mexico,
> so that the school children might witness this historic event.
> For miles before the train reached a town and after it passed, the
> tracks were lined with people.
>
> The funniest incident happened at the station in Tucumeari,
> where we stopped briefly. I was sitting by the car window with
> an Indian child on my lap. Outside, many people were gathered
> on the platform. Suddenly a man pointed to me and shouted,
> "There! That's one of Geronimo's captive white women and
> that's their child!"[39]

---

38. Their original membership documents are housed in the Archives of the
    Reformed Church in America, in New Brunswick, New Jersey.
39. Amy Passmore Hurt, "Life Among the Apaches," *New Mexico*, March 1962,
    16.

The last cattle roundup at Fort Sill, 1913

Two days later, on April 4, the Mescaleros met the train at Tularosa, New Mexico, with scores of wagons to bring the Chiricahuas to their new home. Major Goode officially transferred their custody to Clarence R. Jefferies, agent at Mescalero, and the Chiricahua's twenty-seven-year status as prisoners of war came to an official end.

The next Sunday, April 6, Easter, the Mescalero church received eighty-nine new members, whom Pastor Sluyter exhorted to "be strong in the Lord and in the power of his might."[40]

Difficult Times for the Apaches Who Remained in Oklahoma

On March 27, 1914, nearly a year after their relatives and friends left by train for Mescalero, the eighty-three Apaches who chose to remain in Oklahoma were finally released from their status as prisoners of war. For those who were twenty-eight years and younger, this was the first time they had experienced the status of free citizens in the land of their ancestors. But if any of them believed that this freedom would bring an end to their troubles, they were sadly mistaken. In fact, for most of them, the new situation was worse than the old.

Their cattle—some seven thousand head—had been sold by the government so the Mescalero-bound contingent could have an economic base, leaving those in Oklahoma without a source of income. (The money from this sale mysteriously disappeared in government

40. *Annual Report of the Women's Board of Domestic Missions,* 1913, 25.

offices, and it wasn't until a year later that the Chiricahuas in Mescalero received enough cash to purchase twelve hundred head of cattle.)

The government had promised 160 acres to every family, but as soon as the train pulled out for Mescalero most of the allotments were reduced to eighty acres. With Hospers on her way to Mescalero and Roe dead, the Apaches were left without a strong advocate. In keeping with the Dawes Act, the land allotments were intentionally scattered throughout the area in order to destroy any sense of tribal solidarity. This intensified the loneliness the Indians already felt following the departure of so many of their friends and family members.

One year's subsistence had been promised but was never delivered, so the Chiricahuas had to spend what little cattle money they had for survival needs rather than for implements, seed, and replacement livestock.

Limited Support from the Denomination

The orphanage was closed immediately. One teacher, Clover Mahan, remained behind to teach the few children left at Fort Sill; Mary Ewing, the long-time kindergarten teacher, left to seek work elsewhere. For the next forty-eight years, from 1914 to 1962, when lay preacher Andy Kamphuis arrived, the Apache congregation would have no full-time pastor. During this time they were served by pastors from the Comanche Reformed Church in Lawton, by lay people from their own congregation, by the brief tenure of the Reverend Jonah Washington in 1958-59, and by an extraordinary Pima lay leader, Leeds Soatikee.

A Church of Their Own

The majority of the allotments were near the town of Apache, twenty miles to the north of Lawton, and at Fletcher, about two miles southeast of Apache. Members of the Reformed church were invited to use the facilities of a Presbyterian church on Sunday afternoons. They benefited from the pastoral services of the Presbyterian church in town and of the Cache Creek Presbyterian Mission, six miles west of Apache. But in 1915 the Reformed Church members decided that they wished to continue having a Reformed church, much like the one the missionaries had maintained at Fort Sill.

Three of the consistory members had remained in Oklahoma—deacon Sam Haozous and elders Benedict Jozhe and James Kawaykla. Many other prominent people remained as well, including Chatto, John Loco, Eugene Chihuaha, and Amy White Wratten, together with their families. These members, about twenty-five in all, pledged twenty-five dollars per family to build their own church.

They did not raise the money immediately, and it became necessary to borrow $350 from the Women's Board of Domestic Missions in order to proceed with the building project. With the loan, which was eventually repaid, and with funds on hand, the congregation built a small wooden church on the outskirts of Apache on land purchased for $150 by the Women's Board of Domestic Missions. That building still exists, although it is hardly recognizable, having been incorporated into the present Apache Reformed Church building when the church was expanded and renovated in 1967. Two years after the original church was completed, in 1920, the Apache church sent $21 to the Women's Board for the new mission school in Dulce, New Mexico. Meanwhile, an outstation was established in Fletcher, where a home for mission worker Jennie Lewis was built. Lewis's health failed, and the station was closed in 1923.

Harper Provides Pastoral Services

When the Reverend Richard Harper arrived at the Comache Reformed Church in 1915, he began conducting worship services at the Apache church on the second Sunday afternoon of every month and at Fletcher on the fourth Sunday afternoon. By 1916 membership at the Apache church had grown to thirty-three. Long-time elder Benedict Jozhe died July 14, 1918, and Sam Haozous was elected to take his place. Two years later Jozhe's son, also named Benedict, entered the Chilicco Indian School; he also become a member of the church but stopped attending many years later when Mildred Cleghorn became the first woman elected to the consistory.

The Reformed Church in America considered the Apache church to be part of the Comanche parish, and Harper usually included news of the Apache church in his Comanche report. In 1920 he said that the Apache church had about twenty families and that the members were faithful in attendance. "As nearly all of them are Christians," he wrote, "there is little opportunity for growth in numbers except as the children become old enough to unite with the church." The church, he went on to say, had no Sunday school, "since no one is competent to lead it," but "every family is supplied with the Reformed Church Home Department Quarterly and urged to make use of it."[41]

41. *Annual Report of the Women's Board of Domestic Missions*, 1920, 23.

The following year Harper reported that the work at Apache was "going along as well as could be expected, considering the small amount of service which the pastor is able to give them."[42] He was proud to say that the congregation had reached its Progress Campaign quota (set as a financial goal by the denomination). The weather was such, said Harper, that he hadn't missed one monthly appointment during the past winter, and that the elders had conducted the worship service on many Sundays when he wasn't there. About this time the church added a small sleeping room to the church so visiting pastors could stay overnight.

In 1923, his last year at Comanche, Harper began visiting twice a month at Apache instead of once, with the elders conducting a prayer and testimony meeting on alternate Sundays. In addition, the Women's Missionary Society met twice a month. Five members had been added by confession of faith, for a total of forty-five communicants and thirty-two baptized noncommunicants. This small group gave 28 percent of their offerings ($15 of $54) for denominational purposes, despite minimal pastoral services from the Reformed Church.

The Reverend John Read, the new pastor at Comanche, continued to serve the Apache group two Sunday afternoons of the month, but the participation of the elders on alternate Sundays waned, and the active congregation slipped to about ten families. The core group at the time included John and Marian Loco, Benedict and Rachel Jozhe, James and Mabel Kawaykla, Sam and Blossom Haozous, Amy Imach, Helen and David Chinney, and Lawrence and Dolly Mithlo. Read reported an "apparent spiritual awakening among the Fort Sill Apaches" in January of 1927, at which time the group decided to try to revive the Sunday afternoon services when the missionary was not scheduled to come. For this task they chose elder James Kayawkla, who "reluctantly consented to try it."[43]

Attendance nearly doubled for a time, and the members soon began having prayer meetings in their own homes and in the homes of nonmembers on Sunday and Wednesday evenings. But the momentum could not be maintained, and attendance and membership again slipped back. From 1928 through 1933 the church reported ten to twelve families and twenty-nine to thirty-nine communicants, about

42. *Annual Report of the Women's Board of Domestic Missions*, 1921, 29.
43. Leighton Read, "Apparent Spiritual Awakening Among the Fort Sill Apaches," *Christian Intelligencer and Mission Field*, May 4, 1927, 275.

half of whom were reported to be absent. In 1929 the church reported that twenty of its thirty members were in the absent category.

Chaat Makes Sunday Afternoon Trips to Apache

Read left Comanche—and, consequently, Apache—in 1931, at which point the Reverend Robert Chaat begin his long ministry in Lawton. Chaat continued the tradition of preaching faithfully at the Apache church two Sunday afternoons of each month, in addition to conducting funerals, weddings, baptisms, and a limited number of pastoral calls.

Chaat wrote in 1936, "For a long time it was very hard to get any of them to lead. They all speak English and have some education but are afraid to take the lead." One Sunday afternoon, Chaat said, he laid squarely before them the challenge of conducting meetings on the Sundays he was not there. Finally one of the women said, "If no one else is willing to try, I will try," and after that a few of the men came forward as well.[44]

When Chaat took over, he began including the Apache statistics with the Comanche statistics, making it impossible to determine the membership of either congregation. This practice continued for more than twenty years, from 1934 to 1957, when the Reverend Jonah Washington became pastor, and the church was transferred from the Classis of New York to the Classis of West Central. Even in 1957 no statistics were given, the church being listed as "recently organized."[45] The 1958 report, the first with statistics in twenty-four years, listed fourteen families and eighteen communicant members, of whom nine were listed as absent or inactive. The Sunday school enrollment was twenty-five, and total contributions (all listed in the "other benevolences" column) were $90. Church member Ben Kawaykla, interviewed by the Reverend Carl Gearhart in 1989, recalled that in the late 1940s and early 1950s only about five people attended regularly.

Soatikee and Cleghorn: Two Outstanding Lay Leaders

Over the years two outstanding lay leaders emerged from the Reformed Church's work among the Apaches in Oklahoma. The first,

44. "Progress Among Fort Sill Apaches," *Intelligencer-Leader*, May 13, 1936, 12.
45. This was the third time the church was reported to have been organized, the other times being in 1902 and 1907.

Leeds Soatikee, is hardly known outside the church, but he played a vital role in keeping the Apache church alive and in founding the American Indian Council. The other, Mildred Cleghorn, became known nationally as both a tribal leader and a church leader.

The Unsung Ministry of Leeds Soatikee

In addition to pastors Read, Harper, and Chaat, the person most responsible for keeping the Apache congregation together for so long was an Indian layperson without any theological training, Leeds Soatikee.

Soatikee, a Pima, was born of Christian parents near Phoenix, Arizona. He spent his elementary and high school years at the Indian boarding school in Phoenix, where he was allowed to see his family only during the summer months. He contracted tuberculosis, and while being treated at the Phoenix sanitarium he attended Sunday school classes led by Robert Chaat, who was attending nearby Cook Christian Training School.

Although Soatikee's medical history prevented him from serving during World War II in the regular army, he came to Fort Sill and served in the National Guard. While there he met and married Ethelene Haozous, daughter of Sam and Blossom Haozous, and he became reacquainted with Robert Chaat, now pastor at the Comanche Reformed Church. It was not until he attended an evangelistic rally in Oklahoma City, however, that he made a commitment to Christ.

Acknowledging that he had no training in the Bible, but saying he could sing and read the Bible, Soatikee offered to help Chaat with the meetings at Apache. Chaat gladly accepted the offer. Soon Soatikee took another step, offering to take charge of the services on the second and fourth Sundays, when Chaat was not there. Soatikee did not preach, but he led singing and Bible studies, having spent countless hours privately studying the Scriptures. John Loco, of the Apache group, contributed by writing Apache hymns. Soatikee and his wife, Ethelene, became members of the Apache church, and Leeds was elected elder. The Apaches accepted Soatikee readily, even though he was Pima, as they had accepted Chaat, a Comanche.

Soatikee continued his volunteer service from about 1945 to 1958, when the Reverend Jonah Washington arrived. When Washington left a year later, Soatikee requested that his membership and that of his wife be transferred to the Comanche Reformed Church. The reasons are not clear, but it can be speculated that he was unhappy that the Reformed

Leeds Soatikee

Church had expressed no commitment to continue the ministry at Apache. It was another three years before a full-time worker arrived in the person of Andy Kamphuis, and it was not until Kamphuis had been there six years that Soatikee returned and again gave leadership as an elder. Although he rejected the spirit of Indian militancy in the 1960s, Soatikee played an active role in organizing the American Indian Council, serving as its first president.[46]

During all of this time, Soatikee had been commuting to the church from various places, sometimes as far as eighty miles away, and he finally moved to the town of Apache in 1990. The feebleness of old age kept him from attending worship regularly after the mid-1990s, but despite his frailty he was able to lead the congregation in singing "The Lord's Prayer" at the funeral of Mildred Cleghorn in 1997. Soatikee died in February of 2004 at the age of ninety-five.

The Broad Influence of Mildred Cleghorn

No history of Reformed Native American congregations would be complete without mention of Mildred Imach Cleghorn (1910-1997), who was born as a prisoner of war at Fort Sill and was four years old when the Apaches who chose to remain in Oklahoma were finally released.

---

46. See chapter ten, "The American Indian Council."

As a long-time member of the Apache Reformed Church, she taught Sunday school, served as its first female elder (which, she said, "caused quite an uproar") and as an elder represented the church on the classical and regional synod level.

Cleghorn was also a charter member of the American Indian Council of the Reformed Church and served as its treasurer during most of her twenty years with that agency. She served for six years as a member of the denomination's General Program Council, first as an at-large member (1973-76) and then as a representative of the American Indian Council (1976-79).

Cleghorn was elected tribal chairperson at age sixty-seven and served for eighteen years in that capacity. During that time she worked with others in her tribe to establish a daycare center, attract new jobs, and instill pride in their Indian heritage. In 1996 she was one of the lead plaintiffs in a class action suit against the U.S. Government, charging mismanagement of Indian funds being held in trust.

She was one of eighty Americans to receive Medals of Honor at Ellis Island on October 27, 1986, a televised event hosted by Tom Brokaw. The recipients, which included Walter Cronkite, Jacqueline Kennedy Onassis, Joe DiMaggio, and Coretta Scott King, were honored as those who "exemplified the ideal of living a life dedicated to the American way while preserving the values or tenets of a particular heritage group." Cleghorn is also one of the Chiricahuas featured in the 1988 PBS film, *Geronimo and the Apache Resistance*, and she was one of the persons asked to read the names of the victims of the 1995 bombing of the Murrah Federal Building in Oklahoma City on the first anniversary of that tragedy.

As chairperson of her tribe and as one of the last surviving prisoners of war, Cleghorn spoke in 1986 at a ceremony held at Geronimo's grave marking the one-hundredth anniversary of his surrender. Geronimo, she said, should be remembered as a man who tried to save his homeland. "We lost our land and most of our heritage," she said. "What we have now, we are trying to retain."[47]

Both Mildred Cleghorn and her mother were born as prisoners of war, her mother at Fort Pickens, Alabama, and Mildred at Fort Sill. Mildred's mother, Amy White Wratten, was a daughter of Annie White and George Wratten, and Mildred's father was Richard Imach. She

---

47. Jack Elliot, "Ceremony Marks Surrender of Geronimo Apaches." *Saturday Oklahoman and Times*, Sept. 27, 1986, 1.

Mildred Cleghorn

was one of the few Indian children who attended the public school in Apache while most of the others were attending Indian boarding schools elsewhere. As a child she heard the sound of the violin on the radio and determined to play it—which she did frequently at worship services and special occasions. She was ridiculed in early years for her intense pursuit of education, but she persisted and came close to receiving a master's degree from the University of Oklahoma. She was employed by the Bureau of Indian Affairs as a home economics teacher, and her assignments took her to various locations throughout the West, including a four-year stint in Mescalero. Her marriage ended in divorce, a victim of her husband's alcoholism, and she never remarried. She returned to Apache in 1965 and lived there until her death. Her hobby of making authentic tribal doll costumes resulted in a display at the Smithsonian Institution in Washington, D.C.

Cleghorn died April 15, 1997, at age eighty-six, in an automobile accident near her home as she was taking her great-grandson to school.

Some 650 people attended her funeral at the tribal complex in Apache. She is buried at the Apache prisoner of war cemetery at Fort Sill, not far from the grave of Geronimo. The Apache Reformed Church has established a memorial fund in her honor.

The Twenty-Three-Year Ministry of Andy and Marjorie Kamphuis, 1962-85

In 1957 the Apache church was organized for the third time—or so it seems. In 1958 (reporting 1957 statistics) the Classis of West Central reported that statistics for Apache were not available because the church had just been organized. In actuality, the Comanche and Apache churches had just been transferred from the Classis of New York, where for many years the statistics for both churches had been lumped in the Comanche report. From this point on they were listed separately.

As soon as the church had again been declared organized, the mission board determined that it was time to close it. Less than a dozen people were attending worship services, and the building needed repair badly. But church members objected, pointing out that since its organization in 1907 the church had never had a full-time pastor. The Apaches still considered it to be "their" church, and they wanted another chance—but this time with their own pastor.

Apache Receives Its First Full-Time Pastor

Meanwhile, the Reverend Jonah Washington, a Pima Indian from Arizona, had graduated from Austin (Presbyterian) Seminary in 1958 after having served from 1946 to 1951 as an assistant at the Mescalero Reformed Church. (At Mescalero he had met and married Edith Sombrero, the daughter of Solon Sombrero, the interpreter there.) Now the mission board was looking for a place for Washington to serve. So Washington was ordained in 1958 by the Classis of West Central and assigned to become the first full-time pastor of the Apache.

Washington began a Sunday school program and a Sunday evening service and was well received by the congregation. But he soon found himself in conflict with the classis because of his failure to submit membership and financial records, and he resigned in 1960. He moved from Apache to the Indian school at Chilocco, Oklahoma, where he served as chaplain for eight years. At that time the Apache consistory reviewed the membership records, dismissed six members,

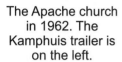
The Apache church in 1962. The Kamphuis trailer is on the left.

dropped eleven, and concluded that only eight families belonged to the church.

Now Robert Chaat resumed his biweekly trips to Apache. The Classis of West Central gave little encouragement for the reinstatement of a full-time pastorate, nor was the mission board inclined to hire a pastor for so few people. But the small group of Apaches who remained asked that the church be given the chance to succeed with a full-time pastor. The board compromised by sending Andy and Marjorie Kamphuis, lay workers from Winnebago, Nebraska. The Kamphuises came to Apache in 1962 for a two-year trial period and stayed twenty-three years.

Natives of Waupun and Brandon, Wisconsin, the Kamphuises had served for six years as maintenance worker and houseparents at the Children's Home in Winnebago. Andy Kamphuis had received training at Moody Bible Institute in Chicago but not at a theological seminary.

A Parsonage Moved from Anadarko

The Kamphuises lived for four months at Apache in their own house trailer. Then, at a cost of $3,000, a house was moved from Fort Cobb at nearby Anadarko, and the church had a parsonage. "They don't have basements in Oklahoma," said Andy Kamphuis later, "but in Wisconsin we all had basements, so this stubborn Dutchman thought we could do that."[48] The basement proved to be useful for Sunday school, ladies' quilting meetings, and rummage sales.

48. Interview with Andy Kamphuis, Oct. 11, 1998.

Andy and Marjorie Kamphuis

Three days after the parsonage was dedicated, the Apaches were further assured of the permanence of the new arrangement by the arrival of church pews from Macy, Nebraska, replacing the seventeen folding chairs. Some of the older people actually wept, because now the building finally looked like "a real church." The next year the Classis of West Central met at the refurbished church, a further encouragement.

Andy Kamphuis built the ministry almost entirely on personal contact. He began by calling on the members who at one time had been faithful but over the years had left for one reason or another. During his pastorate he made a point of making several trips "downtown" every day, always on foot, chatting with everyone along the way. Marjorie Kamphuis always kept the parsonage open to impromptu visitors, as was the practice at all American Indian churches.

Drunks—and Others—in Church

At one point church members raised questions about drunks who were attending church. The consistory minutes of February 14, 1964, include this entry:

> Discussion was held on drunks coming to church services. Some felt that should not be allowed. Mr. Kamphuis said the doors of the church are open to everyone. It should be up to the consistory

members to sit with them or gently take them out if they are a big disturbance.[49]

As people started coming back, Kamphuis "integrated" the church to include non-Apaches—partly out of ignorance, he said. "I didn't know one tribe from the other, so I just invited everybody."[50] One man, a Fort Sill Apache, was offended when Kiowas started attending. "If that's the kind of trash you have in church, I'm not coming," he said. But Kamphuis kept calling on him, and nearly four years later the church member came back. In time the congregation included not only several tribes but also a smattering of whites, blacks, and Mexican-Americans. Partly because of this integration and partly because the older Apaches were dying, the singing of Apache hymns gradually faded away.

Faced with the problem of a nonexistent youth group, Kamphuis enlisted the help of Ted Chaat, son of Robert and Elsie Chaat in Lawton. The younger Chaat, who was in charge of the youth in Lawton, brought his group to Apache on Sunday afternoons until the Apache group was strong enough to function on its own. Gradually other traditional church functions were added—a men's group, a women's sewing group, a junior choir, and a vacation Bible school—all of which were enhanced by a van provided by the denomination.

Hospers Hall Dedicated

Additional space for visiting work groups and social gatherings was secured in 1966 when an old army barracks was shipped from Fort Sill and renovated by volunteer work crews. The building, which included sleeping rooms, a kitchen, and recreational areas, was dedicated January 30, 1966. It was named Hospers Hall, in honor of Hendrina Hospers, who had served the Apache mission at Fort Sill for many years and had accompanied the released prisoners to Mescalero in 1913.

At the dedication service the Reformed Church in America was well represented by Beth Marcus, executive secretary of the Board of North American Missions; the Reverend Albert Van Dyke, chairman of the board's Indian Committee; and the Reverend Harold Colenbrander, president of the Board of World Missions, who gave the sermon. Church

49. Minutes of the Apache Reformed Church, Feb. 14, 1964.
50. Kamphuis interview, Oct. 1998.

members who participated were elder Donald Kawykla (prayer), elder Lane Kawaykla (responsive reading), Elizabeth Anquoe (clarinet solo), deacon Raymond Loco (prayer), Donna and Donise Kawaykla (duet), deacon Benedict Jozhe (responsive reading), and Mildred Cleghorn (violin solo). The director of the museum at Fort Sill gave a history of the Apache Indians, and representatives of the Comanche church and neighboring churches brought greetings. The following year the church was remodeled by adding rooms to the rear and removing partitions to enlarge the sanctuary. Additional pews were purchased from a nearby Lutheran church. The enlarged facility was dedicated April 2, 1967.

A Pastor with a Key to the Jail

Kamphuis was probably the only Reformed Church pastor to carry a key to the local jail. He received permission to conduct services in the jail for the inmates, almost all of whom were there for public intoxication. Kamphuis then went to the town board and asked permission to take the prisoners to church on Sunday mornings and evenings, and on Wednesday evenings as well, promising to take their place if any escaped. The jail keeper was not always there to let them out, so he finally gave Kamphuis the key. He never lost a prisoner, Kamphuis said, but he did panic on one occasion. On a Sunday during the morning service he observed that the prisoners were no longer in church. He excused himself, went on a search, and found them chatting in Hospers Hall. Volunteer work groups often returned home with jail stories. The only place they could take a shower was the jail, and they almost always spent some time talking with the inmates.

Kamphuis Ordained

Andy Kamphuis had come to Apache as a lay pastor, and after several years a movement got underway to request that he be ordained by the Reformed Church despite his lack of training at a theological seminary.

In 1970 the Classis of West Central brought to the General Synod an overture requesting on Kamphuis's behalf a dispensation from both the academic requirements and the professorial certificate. The executive committee of the Board of Theological Education recommended that the request be denied, saying, "The Classis has given no indication as to why Mr. Kamphuis cannot meet the full requirements of the professorial certificate," and, "There is every reason to believe that Mr. Kamphuis is

Andy Kamphuis was ordained in 1970 at
the Apache Reformed Church.

carrying on a successful ministry without benefit of ordination until
now. We commend him for his present endeavors in ministry."[51]

It so happened that the two elder delegates from the Classis
of West Central were Philip Narcomey of the Comanche church and
Leeds Soatikee of the Apache church. Both elders made impassioned
pleas on the floor of the synod, saying how important it was for the
Apache church to have this recognition bestowed on their pastor. The
General Synod responded by voting against the recommendation of
the committee and adopting a resolution that Kamphuis receive the
necessary dispensations, clearing the way for ordination.

Kamphuis was ordained at the Apache Reformed Church July
13, 1970. Participants included Van Dyke, Marcus, and Chaat, with a
sermon by the Reverend Henry Poppen, president of the West Central
Classis. Music included the customary violin solo by Mildred Cleghorn
and the singing of an Apache hymn. Kamphuis was installed as pastor
three months later.

51. *Minutes of the General Synod,* 1970, 33.

The Apache congregation in the new church

A New Church Is Built

Even with the 1967 expansion, the Apache church building seated only forty-five people comfortably, but morning attendance had reached the seventies and eighties. Something had to be done. The denominational mission administration advocated demolishing the original structure and constructing a new church building on the site. The congregation objected, citing the fact that they and their parents had invested personally and financially in that place of worship for so many years.

The Fair Haven Reformed Church in Jenison, Michigan, came forward and volunteered to help. Several builders and the Reverend Leonard Weesies came to look over the situation, and they devised a plan to add on to the north and south sides of the present building. In January of 1975 ten men from the Jenison church arrived in Apache, together with a check for $10,000 collected as a Thanksgiving offering. Each man was skilled in some aspect of the building trade, and most of them had already done volunteer construction work in Taiwan, Kenya, and Mexico. An Indian group worked side by side with the Fair Haven group, and within two weeks the building was completed.

The Board of North American Missions contributed $1,100 for an additional half acre of land. In appreciation for the use of Hospers Hall as the town's community building, a local bank paid for air conditioning. Members of the Apache church purchased new pews, having sold the old ones to the local Methodist church. The remodeled and expanded church was dedicated April 13, 1975, with pastor Weesies of Fair Haven preaching the sermon. Other participants included the Reverend Harold "Shorty" Brown, area secretary for the Reformed Church American Indian Ministries; the Reverend Robert Chaat, for the American Indian Council; Danny Swanda, mayor of Apache; and Apache elders Leeds Soatikee and Raymond Loco.

Another congregation, the First Reformed Church of Sheboygan Falls, Wisconsin, built an additional structure on the property in 1980—a "prayer tepee." The small building is open twenty-four hours a day for prayer, is occasionally used for meetings and classes, and has become something of a symbol for the Apache church. The structure was dedicated March 27, 1981.

The following year, on May 9, 1982, the Apache church joined the Comanche church for a combined seventy-fifth anniversary celebration—the two congregations having been organized on the same Sunday, May 7, 1907. The two congregations held combined anniversary worship services in the morning in Lawton and in the evening in Apache, with a potluck meal in between. On hand were the Reverend Richard Vander Voet, mission secretary for the Americas; the Reverend Harold Colenbrander of Denver, representing the Classis of West Central; mayor Wayne Gilley of Lawton; chaplain William Harbour of Fort Sill; and the Reverend Herman Van Galen, former pastor at Comanche.

The Kamphuises retired in 1985, after twenty-nine years of service in ministry among Native Americans, six at the children's home in Winnebago and twenty-three in Apache. The Kamphuises retired to Pella, Iowa, where Andy began working part-time as a representative for Portable Recording Ministries, and where rumor has it that he became nearly as well known on the streets of Pella as he was on the streets of Apache. Marjorie Kamphuis died December 2, 2004, in Pella.

Slow but Steady Growth

Over more than two decades of Kamphuis ministry, the Apache church experienced slow but consistently steady growth—from 14 families and 20 communicants in 1962 to 55 families and 98 active communicants in 1983. Meanwhile, Sunday school enrollment also gradually increased, from 48 in 1962 to a high of 120 in 1981, and then back to 105 in 1983 and 1984. The absent/inactive list remained fairly consistent, between 5 and 12. Seldom was anyone dropped from the

Third grade vacation Bible school class in 1973

rolls; they just disappeared from the statistical reports.

Church attendance statistics were not reported to the denomination at that time, but during the tenures of administrators Brown and Vander Voet, the mission churches were required to submit monthly attendance and financial reports. A sampling of these reports indicates a relatively strong ratio of attendance to reported communicant membership. For February of 1969, for example, Kamphuis reported an average morning attendance of 80, an average evening attendance of 48, an average Sunday school attendance of 56, an average junior youth fellowship attendance of 13, and an average senior youth fellowship attendance of 8.

Fourteen years later the church reported average January attendances of 173 at the morning worship, 64 at evening worship, 71 in Sunday school, 24 at junior youth fellowship, and 12 at senior youth fellowship. The men held a monthly prayer breakfast, the women held monthly guild meetings, and twenty to thirty children sang in the junior choir. No senior choir was reported.

During the Kamphuis years confessions of faith ranged all the way from one in 1962 to twenty-two in 1971, with an average of about six per year. New members received by letter of transfer averaged about two per year. This is a relatively high figure for an American Indian church, no doubt influenced by its non-reservation setting.

Vacation Bible school was held every May during much of this period, with volunteer leaders coming from several Reformed Church congregations. In 1982, for instance, 163 students were enrolled and 80 had perfect attendance. Other volunteers came during the summer to work on church property and to conduct Bible story and activity times in the town park.

Kamphuis, like most of the pastors of the Reformed Church's American Indian ministries, came to be the unofficial "burier and marrier" of the community. Over his twenty-three years at Apache he conducted 173 weddings and 310 funerals. Among the funerals were many of the Christians who had been the backbone of the church over the long years of struggle since 1914: David and Helen Chinney, Robert Gooday, Mary Simmons, Blossom Haouzous, and several members of the Kawaykla family—James, Sr., Mason and Lottie, and Pearl. The vast majority of those "old saints," as they often were called, were well into their eighties when they died.

When the Kamphuis's moving van pulled out in 1985, the Apache congregation experienced a major void. Andy Kamphuis was the only pastor the majority of its members had known. He had been worship leader, Sunday school teacher, janitor, bus driver, record keeper, and policy maker. Marjorie Kamphuis had been church secretary, organist, Sunday school teacher, Women's Guild leader, and hostess for visiting guests. The Apache church was without a pastor for about a year. For this congregation, which had depended so completely on its pastor and his wife, it was an agonizingly long time, and attendance dropped precipitously.

The Gearharts Arrive

The pastoral gap at Apache was filled by the Reverend Carl and Kathy Gearhart, who had previously served Reformed congregations in Aplington, Iowa, and Lennox, South Dakota. A native of Gary, Indiana, where for a time he was a member of a street gang, Carl had graduated from Hope College and Western Theological Seminary, and Kathy came with credentials as a medical technician and special education teacher. The immediate need at Apache was a larger home for the Gearhart family, which included three children. It was determined that it was impractical to remodel a two-bedroom home that had been moved from an army base more than twenty years earlier, so plans were drawn up to build a new parsonage. This also assured the congregation that

Carl and Kathy Gearhart

the Reformed Church was committed to a continuing ministry there.

Having determined that a $81,500 bid from a contractor was too high, it was decided to use volunteer help whenever possible. The Pella, Iowa, Classical Union of Reformed Church Women contributed $24,500; the General Program Council provided approximately $25,000; and several volunteer groups from the Pella Classis participated in construction work. The four-bedroom home, which cost about $58,000, was later appraised at $92,000. The following year volunteers installed showers at Hospers Hall, making it no longer necessary for visiting work groups to take showers at the town jail.

During the summer of 1987 Darrell Dalman, a student at Reformed Bible College in Grand Rapids, Michigan, began a three-year off-and-on stint as volunteer and intern at the Apache church. While in Apache he met and married Dawn Tsatoke, a Kiowa who was a member of the Methodist church there. Dalman later graduated from Western Theological Seminary and became pastor at the Winnebago Reformed Church in Winnebago, Nebraska.

During this time Steven and Cathleen Boint also worked as assistants at the Apache Church, but they moved on in less than a year to serve churches in Bismack, North Dakota, and Sioux Falls, South Dakota. While working at Apache, Boint and Gearhart conducted extensive research on the Oklahoma mission work, which they later contributed to the writing of this volume.

Gearhart's immediate emphasis was on Bible teaching and developing native leaders while continuing ministry to alcoholics and other marginalized people. While he was pastor, the second non-Apache Indian (the first being Leeds Soatikiee) was elected to the consistory—Rose Attocknie, a Comanche. Meanwhile, the tradition continued of giving Christmas boxes. In 1987, for instance, those who had been attending church on a regular basis received a hat, gloves, paper, pencils, pens, toothbrush, toothpaste, soap, shampoo, and articles of clothing. Younger children received crayons, coloring books, and toys; and older children received a devotional booklet and a wallet, necklace, or purse.

From October 17 to 20, 1988, nineteen inches of rain flooded the Apache area. No lives were lost, but sixty-five families were forced to leave their homes, several of whom stayed for a time at Hospers Hall. Twelve families associated with the Apache church lost most of their possessions. Reformed Church World Service distributed financial aid through the Apache church.

In the summer of 1990 Gearhart accepted a call to serve the Reformed church in Dumont, Iowa. During his four years at Apache, he had seen the church rebound from its post-Kamphuis slump to about sixty-five active communicants. Confessions of faith ranged from four in 1986 to a high of twenty-three in 1989. The number of members reported as inactive ranged rather erratically between twenty-two and fifty-one. Average worship attendance was reported as ninety-eight in 1988 and 1989.

The Ministry of George and Mary Anne Montanari

After the Gearharts left for Iowa, the Apache church only had to wait a few months for a new pastor. The Reverend George and Mary Anne Montanari, fresh out of seminary, moved into the parsonage in November 1990 with their son Michael (Sarah and Mark were born later). George Montanari had grown up in Riverdale, New Jersey, where his family was active in the Pompton Reformed Church in Pompton Lakes. He had graduated from Lynchburg College (1987) and Western Theological Seminary. Mary Anne had grown up in the Presbyterian Church (PCA) in Wilmington, Delaware, and also graduated from Lynchburg College.

Montanari began emphasizing leadership development for consistory members and others, adult discipleship, and a sense of ownership in the ministries of the church. He also encouraged family

George and Mary Anne Montanari

solidarity with couples retreats at a nearby conference grounds and at the church. In June of 1992 three women of the church traveled to Albany, New York, where they played a role in the "Rainbow Festival" in connection with the annual General Synod meeting.

For two years, from 1998 to 2000, Montanari assumed additional responsibilities as interim associate for the American Indian Council. There he helped "jump start" the newly configured Native American Indian Ministries Council and assisted the search for a new (Indian) staff person.

Several interns served in Apache during the 1990s. These included Bruce Hole, a doctoral student of missiology at Reformed Theological Seminary in Jackson, Mississippi; and Theda and Ellis Jefferson, Choctaw Indians who had recently graduated from Cook College and Theological School in Tempe, Arizona.

Continuing ministries included the Kids Club (after-school program), vacation Bible school, children's church on Sundays, youth groups, and participation in the annual youth camp of the American Indian Council. The vacation Bible school was particularly successful, with average daily attendance of forty-two in 1992, seventy-three in 1995, ninety-three in 1996, and eighty-six in 1997. Outreach efforts included assisting the White Eagle Nazarene Church in Ponca City, in northern Oklahoma; volunteering in a chaplaincy program at the Lawton Indian hospital; and participating in a new food pantry in

The church van still plays an important role in
the ministry of the Apache Reformed Church.

Apache. Among the volunteer work groups that came to Apache in
the summer of 2000 was a teen group from the Shin Kwang Church
(Korean) in Bayside, Queens, New York.

In a video interview in 1996, Mary Anne Montanari told of a
poignant time in a worship service:

> When we sing, "I Have Decided to Follow Jesus," there's one
> Comanche woman [Geraldine Koosochony] in our church who
> at the very end picks it up in her native language and the piano
> drops out and most of the other voices drop out, and generally
> she's with herself or her sister.[52]

Another Flood

Another flash flood devastated the low-lying areas of the
community in October of 2000. Fifty homes were destroyed or heavily
damaged, nine of them belonging to people associated with the
church. Members of the Apache church set up a clothing distribution
center, cooked meals at the local senior citizen center, and distributed
furniture, clothing, food, and clean-up supplies to the victims, many of
whom were not Indians.

52. Video interview with George and Mary Anne Montanari, April 1996.

Reformed Church World Service immediately sent $3,500 to help members of the Apache church. Church World Service (an interdenominational agency with which Reformed Church World Service works closely), sent $5,000 to help form an interfaith group to develop a long-term plan to rebuild the community. Subsequently, Reformed Church World Service and the Mennonite Church worked out a plan for equipping, housing, and sending work groups that may be needed in the future. For nearly two years the church hosted ecumenical work groups.

Janine Dekker Joins Staff

For several years the Montanaris had believed the church needed a second full-time staff member to work with children and youth, and in March 1999 the Reverend Janine Dekker joined the staff. Dekker, who was raised in the American Reformed Church in Worthington, Minnesota, graduated from Central College in 1986 and spent the next three years teaching music in Clinton, Iowa. After spending several summers at Inspiration Hills conference center near Inwood, Iowa, where she interacted with teens from Winnebago and Macy, Nebraska, she enrolled at Western Theological Seminary, from which she graduated in 1993. One of the highlights of Dekker's ministry at Apache was taking a group to her home church in Worthington, Minnesota, and then to the First Reformed Church in Hospers, Iowa. The teens performed songs in Native American sign language, sang Apache hymns, and told about the ministry of the Apache church.

Montanaris Leave Apache

Quoting Ecclesiastes 3:1, "For everything there is a season, and a time for every matter under heaven," George Montanari resigned as pastor of the Apache Reformed Church in June 2002 after having served there for eleven years. The Montanaris left on good terms with the congregation, having received sixteen new members that spring and seeing a surge in congregational financial support. Montanari later accepted a call to the Middlebush Reformed Church in Somerset, New Jersey. After the Monanaris left, tensions emerged between the consistory and Janine Dekker, and her tenure was terminated by the consistory in February 2004.

Since the departure of the Montanaris, interim pastoral care has been provided by retired pastors Herman Van Galen and

The Apache Reformed Church

Roger Bruggink, as well as by seminary student Brenda Snowball of Winnebago, Nebraska.

Reported statistics during the eleven Montanari years were remarkably consistent. Communicant membership made slow gains, beginning at fifty in 1991 and gradually increasing to fifty-nine in 2001. Average worship ranged from a fifty-two to a high of seventy-seven, with an average of sixty-one. The absent/inactive list was forty-eight or forty-nine the entire time. The number of adherents gradually increased from forty-one in 1991 to seventy in 2001, but average Sunday school attendance remained low during the entire period, usually ranging between fifteen and twenty. Meanwhile, significant strides were made in Montanari's goal of developing leadership within the congregation.

The Apache Reformed Church continues to be a small congregation in a dusty little nonreservation town. Yet the congregation is a continuing witness to the vision of the women's board that sent a missionary to Oklahoma, the early courageous converts such as Noche and Naiche, the handful of Native Christians who maintained the ministry during the fifty years without a full-time pastor, spiritual giants like Leeds Soatikee and Mildred Cleghorn, the congregations who contributed financial and work group support, and the pastors and spouses who labored over the years with patience and diligence.

CHAPTER 5

The Comanche Mission at Fort Sill and the Comanche Reformed Church in Lawton, Oklahoma

The Comanches, often referred to as "Lords of the Southern Plains," were at one time one of the most powerful tribes of the American West. Once nearly twenty thousand strong, they controlled parts of what is now Colorado, Kansas, Mexico, New Mexico, Oklahoma, and Texas.

The Comanches originally were hunters in the Rocky Mountains and were the only tribe to move into the Great Plains. It is likely that they received their name from a Ute Indian word meaning "one who fights me all the time," but they called themselves *Kumunab*, meaning simply, "the people." Whereas the Apaches were one of many branches of the Athapascan linguistic family, the Comanches had roots in the Shoshone language—and the one could not easily communicate with the other.

Tepees made of buffalo hides enabled the Comanches to move quickly to follow the buffalo herds, their primary source of livelihood. They gleaned fruits and berries from the land but never settled down to plant crops. The Comanche people were among the first tribes to own horses, which had been introduced to the Americas by the Spanish in the late 1600s. They soon became known as the most skillful horsemen of the American plains, perfecting the skill of riding on the side of a horse at full gallop, thus protecting themselves from enemy arrows or bullets while shooting arrows from under the animal's neck. One band of two thousand Comanches was reputed to own more than fifteen thousand horses. Their horsemanship added greatly to their prosperity, as the onrush of Mexican and white settlements simultaneously reduced the opportunity to hunt buffalo and enhanced the opportunity for plunder. Plundering often included taking captives, and by 1900 as many as a third of the Comanches, including chief Quanah Parker, were of mixed blood.

The Comanches, like several other tribal groups, placed a high priority on the "vision quest," a process by which young men at puberty made a solitary trip into the wilderness. Here they spent four days and four nights without food or water, praying and meditating until they received a personal vision from a supernatural power, often identifying a certain animal as the conduit of this power.

Like other tribes—including the "five civilized tribes" transplanted from the east—the Comanches were relegated to what was then known as Indian Territory. In 1867 they agreed by treaty to an assigned reservation in southwestern Oklahoma, but continued white settlement, disappearing buffalo, and harsh living conditions led to continuing rebellion. Wars and disease decimated their numbers, and by the turn of the century only about fifteen hundred survived.

The Comanches Come to Fort Sill

In June 1875 a band of four hundred starving Comanche Indians, led by chief Quanah Parker, rode into Fort Sill and surrendered to the military authorities, the last of the Comanches to do so. They never were held as prisoners of war, but agreed to live on allotted land adjacent to the military base. Although the Comanches and Apaches had in years past been enemies, Parker convinced his people to cede some of their holdings to the Apaches when they were brought from Alabama in 1894.

Quanah Parker, one of the most colorful of the Indian chiefs, was the son of a Comanche chief and a white captive, Cynthia Ann Parker. After his surrender Parker urged his people to make the most of reservation life and to adopt many of the white man's ways. He took his mother's last name, learned Spanish and English, became a prosperous farmer, and built a twelve-room white house with huge stars emblazoned on the roof, surrounded by a white picket fence. But he never gave up such traditional accoutrements as buckskin, long twin braids, and multiple wives (seven). Parker also introduced the tribe to the use of peyote as a religious activity designed to induce visions—a practice that later became more or less combined with Christian theology and eventually led in 1918 to the founding and legalization of the Native American Church.

Blankets and Smallpox

Mention should be made here of the smallpox epidemic that roared through the Comanche encampment during the winter of 1898-99, taking the lives of some two hundred Indians and nearly decimating the tribe. To this day the Comanches think it is more than a coincidence that the plague spread (a) shortly after the soldiers distributed blankets and (b) just before the planned allotment of lands to Indians and the opening of more territory to white settlers. That charge is denied by Fort Sill officials, and the truth will probably never be known.

Many of the bodies were buried in a Comanche cemetery maintained by the Reformed Church until Fort Sill annexed it in 1917. Missionary Richard Harper compiled a list of 109 people buried there, but Reformed Church publications never mentioned the epidemic. The site was subsequently forgotten by whites, then rediscovered, although the Comanches knew about it all along. The crude grave markers, which are below ground level, are now covered with tall grass near a Fort Sill airstrip. The markers include such inscriptions as "Woeddie," "Caper Tissoyo's Children," "Karty's Brother," and "Clark Twins." Long-time Reformed Church members Philip and Gladys Narcomey were active in the cemetery rediscovery project. When a memorial service was held at the site in 1995, participants included the Reverend Robert Chaat and Raymond Nauni of the Comanche church.

The Comanches Today

Today the majority of the eight thousand Comanche people live in Oklahoma, where their tribal headquarters are in Lawton. They are closely associated with their long-time allies, the Kiowas and the Apaches. Many Comanches live intermingled with white citizens and make their living by raising livestock, leasing mineral rights, and working in the marketplace and factories. A large casino also provides jobs and income.

Early Converts, 1895-1905

Remembering his initial calling to establish a mission work at Fort Sill, the Reverend Frank Hall Wright made frequent trips from Colony to Lawton and began holding evangelistic meetings among the

Dorothy, the first Commanche convert, died at the age of 16.

Apache and Comanche Indians living there. Among the Comanches who attended was a teenage girl with the anglicized name of Dorothy, the niece and adopted daughter of a leading Comanche medicine man, Nahwats (also spelled Nahwatz, especially by Elizabeth Page).

Dorothy and Nahwats

Nahwats, convinced of the value of learning English, had sent Dorothy to the government Indian school in Lawton but had forbidden her to have anything to do with the white man's religion. Dorothy, however, was entranced by the missionary's message and after coming several times to the meetings, requested baptism. (One oral version of the story says that Wright took her to the school in Colony, where she became a Christian, then brought her back to her uncle in Lawton.) When Dorothy told her uncle of her desire to declare herself a Christian, he became angry. Finally, Nahwats agreed to the baptism, although reluctantly, and a service was planned under the trees near the missionary's camp, with Wright and the Reverend Walter Roe officiating. A number of Indians, including Nahwats, gathered in curiosity.

According to the account by Elizabeth Page, before the baptism could take place Nahwats made his way forward and, through the interpreter, confronted the missionaries:

You must not go on until you have heard from me. Dorothy tells me that now, today, she is going one way and I am going another. While we live we can look into each other's faces, but when we die the ways go ever apart and we shall never meet again. I cannot have Dorothy walk in one road while I walk in another. I want to go with Dorothy, I don't know the road but Dorothy does. Your guidebook there—I can't read it, but she will teach me. I don't know what I am to do in this new road, but she will show me. Take me too if you must take her. I cannot walk in the old road while Dorothy walks the new.[1]

This posed a dilemma, because at this point Nahwats knew little or nothing of the Christian faith. After consulting with each other, Roe and Wright spoke to Dorothy, explaining that they could not go forward with the baptism at this time. They would go back to Colony for six weeks, they said, and then return. "Meanwhile you take your Bible and teach Nahwats all about this new road. Read the story to him and teach him, and then, when we return, if he understands and still wants to walk with you, we will take you both."[2]

When the missionaries returned six weeks later they were told by the Indians that they could hear the voice of Dorothy late into the night, reading the Bible and explaining it to Nahwats and other members of her family.

"At the first service that was held," reported Page, "Nahwatz showed an insight and aptness of understanding that delighted the missionaries."[3] Roe explained the way of salvation to Nahwats and other members of the family and asked if they were willing to leave behind their heathen worship and follow Jesus. The answer was positive. Not only did the missionaries baptize Nahwats and Dorthy, but also Dorothy's mother and father, two of their younger children, two of Dorothy's grandmothers, and another old woman. Thus, under a brush arbor in 1897 did evangelist Wright baptize the first Comanche believers.

Nahwats did not take his new commitment lightly. When the church was organized ten years later, Nahwats was elected as one of the two elders. He also became a generous giver, tithing the income from his

1. Elizabeth Page, *In Camp and Tepee: An Indian Mission Story* (New York, Chicago, and Toronto: Revell, 1915), 63.
2. Ibid, 64.
3. Ibid.

farm. On one occasion, when the Women's Board of Domestic Missions made an appeal to wipe out a deficit, Nahwats determined to make a contribution. He sold some cattle, called his family together (cattle being a family or tribal possession), and announced his intention. The family agreed, and he made a gift of $100—a significant contribution at that time. Many years later, in 1912, he gave this testimony, presumably at a camp meeting:

> I know sin, and I will follow the Christian road and try to get right, and when I see the people here come and bring their children to follow the Jesus Road it makes me glad, and if we go straight the children will follow....Whenever I become a Christian I put on Jesus rope (making a sign for a lariat). At first I could not get straight, but Jesus put the rope on and make it straight. Jesus leads me straight and I cannot get away or jump aside."[4]

Dorothy, fluent in English, became the interpreter for religious services and for classes at the government's Comanche school. With the permission of her parents and her uncle Nahwats, Dorothy was brought into the missionary cottage under the care of Maud Adkisson and F. A. Mosely. These women, as mentioned earlier, had been hired primarily to teach at the Apache school and to call on the Apache Indians, but they also included the Comanches in their ministry.

Tragically, Dorothy died at the age of sixteen, the cause of her death and the exact date never having been made clear. Dorothy's youngest brother, Robert Chaat, who was born about the time of Dorothy's death, became the Reformed Church's first Native American pastor. Dorothy's name lived on in Dorothy Chaat Tomah, a daughter of Robert and Elsie Chaat who died in 2003.

Tocsi

According to Page's account, Nahwats came to Adkisson after Dorothy's death and said, "Now, today, we have no one to read to us from God's book. There is no one to tell us the words of the missionary. We walk just the same as in the dark. Here," and he drew the little five-year-old forward, "is Tocsi, Dorothy's sister. We give her to you. Teach her the white man's talk. Teach her to read God's book that she may lead us, just the same as Dorothy."[5]

4. "Indian Testimony," *Mission Field*, August 1912, 151-53.
5. Page, *In Camp and Tepee*, 135.

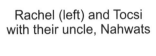

Rachel (left) and Tocsi with their uncle, Nahwats

Tocsi became a favorite subject of personal interest stories in the *Day Star*, a mission publication for children published by the Reformed Church. Adkisson, the presumed author of one of these articles, described her as a "bright, pretty, child" and tells a somewhat different story about why Tocsi was taken into the missionaries' home. Adkisson described at length Nahwats's primitive home, that included an arbor and cots made of rough poles. At meal time people sat around an oilcloth spread on the floor and ate out of a dish in the center, and their wardrobes did not include nightgowns. "This is the life we wish to keep away from Tocsi," said Adkisson, "and it is surprising to see how quickly she adapted herself to white people's ways."[6] The article is accompanied by two photos of Tocsi, one of her in full Indian dress, and the other in her school clothing consisting of a dress with long sleeves and a white smock.

Adkisson even took Tocsi on a vacation with her, traveling by train to South Carolina. Even though she was a child, Tocsi became the Comanche mission's primary interpreter. Eventually the little girl was renamed Maud, after her surrogate mother. As Maud Blevins she

6. "Tocsi," *Day Star*, January 1900, 3.

The Nahwats family on the way to church

remained an active and faithful member of the Comanche church until her death in 1984 at the age of one hundred.

Tocsi's younger sister Rachel, age six and with no knowledge of English, was also brought into the cottage. Rachel was supported by the First and Suydam Street Reformed churches in New Brunswick, New Jersey, and Tocsi was supported by the Hamilton Grange Reformed Church (later merged with Fort Washington Collegiate) in New York City.

Otipoby

Another early Comanche family to be brought into the church was that of Otipoby, who later assumed the first name of Bob. Otipoby was born in Indian Territory, the son of an early white settler and a Comanche woman. His mother died when he was only two years old, and he was given to the care of his grandmother. Although an ardent user of peyote, he was converted through the influence of the missionaries at Fort Sill.

Otipoby was a respected member of his tribe and an efficient farmer. He, with Nahwats, was one of the two elders of the Comanche church when it was organized in 1907, and he held that position for nearly twenty years. One son, James, became an ordained minister in the Reformed Church and was the first Indian chaplain in the U.S. Army. Another son, Hugh, served on the Comanche consistory for many years and contributed land for the Otipoby Comanche cemetery at Fort Sill.

Periconic

Among the Comanches, more than any other tribe the Reformed Church worked with, it was the leading men of the tribe who became Christians and subsequently provided much-needed leadership. Among these early leaders was Periconic (also spelled Perconnic), son of the Comanche chief Tabananaica. Periconic was described in the *Mission Field* as "at least six feet tall and very good looking for an Indian."[7]

By his own testimony, Periconic had been a heavy drinker and an enemy of Christianity, but after he began observing believers like Nahwats and Chahtinneyackque (one of several spellings of the name of Robert Chaat's father), he said of them, "I look at them and their hearts are not on the ground. I look at them and their faces are like the sun."[8] After coming to Wright for instruction, he made his decision:

> At first your words came to my ears, but I would not let them in. Then after a while they came in and came down and lay in my heart....Just one thing I can do. I can give myself to This Man who died and took my sins away....I want to walk in this new road with Nahwatz and Chataneyerque.[9]

At one point Periconic and Nahwats sought out Quanah Parker in his big home. After a lengthy conversation and a challenge to take his place with them on the "Jesus road," Parker (according to Elizabeth Page) gave this response, speaking slowly in English:

> You ask me what do I think of the road. It is a good road. For the children it is a good road, but for me—you are too late. Why didn't you come before? Were you too busy to come?...While you have been waiting many of us have died and the rest of us have turned to stone.

Then, said Page, in a chilling conclusion to the chapter, "He stood a moment dominating them, then he turned and went into the house."[10]

Periconic continued to be faithful, served as a deacon, and frequently gave his testimony at camp meetings and in the church. He industriously farmed the 160 acres allotted to him through the Dawes Act of 1887. He also wrote songs in Comanche, some of which are still used by the Comanche Reformed Church. His wife, Arlene (or Allena),

7. "Our Comanche Mission," *Mission Field*, January 1904, 333.
8. Page, *In Camp and Tepee*, 151.
9. Page, *In Camp and Tepee*, 151-52.
10. Ibid., 179.

was baptized several years after her husband, but the missionaries were deeply disappointed when she decided to hold a coming-of-age dance for her daughter, Annie. Periconic died in 1922, and a granddaughter, Gladys Narcomey, continues to be a faithful member of the Comanche congregation.

A Church Built and a Congregation Organized, 1906-1914

In 1903, after a camp meeting, several Comanche leaders came to Wright and requested that the Comanches be granted a church and missionary of their own. That fall three men—Nahwats, Periconic, and Howard Whitewolf (educated at Carlisle and the Comanche's interpreter), accompanied by field secretary Elizabeth Page, made a trip east to visit Reformed churches and raise money.

Their message was, "We want our children to have the privileges we have been deprived of. You have told us of the 'Jesus road,' and we long to walk in it; send us a minister who will be our teacher and friend, and give us a church where we may worship the great Heavenly Father."[11] They repeated this message in thirty-six churches, and by the time they were ready to return home they were assured that they would indeed have a church and a minister.

Vermilye Chapel Dedicated in 1906

This was one promise the white man kept. The government had granted some 120 acres of land for mission work just south of Fort Sill, and work began on this property in 1905 as soon as roads became passable. Periconic and Nahwatz, said Page in her history, "camped by the enlarging hole and watched operations with proprietary interest."[12] Saying it was not good for white men to do all the work, they organized teams of Indians to haul the lumber.

The church was dedicated May 6, 1906, and was named the Vermilye Memorial Chapel, for Elizabeth B. Vermilye of Albany, New York, in memory of her father and mother. Her gifts were contributed through the First and Madison Avenue Reformed churches in Albany. (The Madison Avenue church, also called Second Reformed Church, merged with the First Church in Albany in 1938). The church was painted yellow and was referred to locally as the "Yellow Mission."

11. *Annual Report of the Women's Executive Committee of the Board of Domestic Missions*, 1905, 21.
12. Page, *In Camp and Tepee*, 163.

The "yellow mission," the original Comanche church

L. L. Legters Becomes Pastor

Although Frank Hall Wright played a key role in founding the church, he believed that his calling was to be an evangelist rather than a pastor. The duties of pastor fell on the Reverend L. L. Legters (whose first name, Leonard, was seldom used). A native of Clymer, New York, he had graduated from Hope College in 1900 and from New Brunswick Theological Seminary in 1903. He had served briefly at Colony after the sudden death of the Reverend Arthur Brokaw.

Although the exact sequence of events is not clear, a romance with Maud Adkisson at the Apache mission developed during this time, possibly while Legters lived on the Apache mission compound while waiting for the parsonage to be built. Legters and Adkisson were married June 28, 1906, at the Colony church, with much celebration by the mission staff, and the newlyweds moved into the newly constructed parsonage. One of their first responsibilities was to visit churches in the east. This trip resulted in funds for the construction of an interpreter's house and the purchase of a "sweet-toned" bell.[13]

13. *Annual Report of the Women's Executive Committee of the Board of Domestic Missions*, 1907, 32.

A 'Significant Incident' Concerning Child Care

A short item in the *Mission Field*, revealingly titled, "A Significant Incident," illustrates the importance of Anglo customs to the missionary endeavor. The author pointed out that from time immemorial, Indian women have carried their babies. But one of the missionaries said to a young mother, "See here, look at your small shoulders, and then look at the big ones of your husband; he ought to be carrying that heavy load." After the service of the next Sunday evening, "Up rose the lusty brave, and carried the black-eyed baby with seeming pride, if not with so much grace as the little brown mother."[14] Another article, apparently referring to the same or similar incident, mentions the derision the husband had endured from other Indian men.

The Comanche and Apache Churches Organized

On May 1, 1907, two sister churches were organized on the same day—the Comanche Reformed Church in Lawton and the Apache Reformed Church in Apache.

The Comanche church was organized in the morning, and the Apache church was organized in the afternoon.

Leading the services at both sites were Walter Roe and Frank Hall Wright, Richard Harper of Colony, L. L. Legters, and Edgar Tilton of New York City. Tilton was pastor of the Harlem Reformed Church, which long had supported the Indian work. He also represented the Classis of New York, which had held the informal membership of the Indian churches.

The Classis of Oklahoma had been founded the previous October, and the two new Indian churches became members of that classis. Five years later, in 1911, the ill-fated Classis of Oklahoma was dissolved. At that time the two Indian churches reverted to the Classis of New York, and the twenty white Reformed churches in Oklahoma were either dissolved or transferred to the Presbyterian Church.

The Comanche church was organized with sixty-three members, eight more than the Apache church. These included Nahwats and his wife, Otipoby and his wife, Periconic, Chiwooney, Howard Whitewolf, Karty, Chatasy, Tahmahka, Fred and Leslie Tice-ah-kie, and Chahtinneyackque. The elders were Nahwats and Otipoby, and the deacons were Periconic and Chahtinneyackque. All of these elders and

14. L. A. McClurken, "A Significant Incident," *Mission Field*, September 1905, 184.

deacons lived in the same general area seven miles north of Lawton, where they farmed. Two sons of these charter members later became Reformed pastors—Robert Chaat, son of Chahtinneyackque, and James Ottipoby (he spelled it with two t's), son of Otipoby.

The interpreter of the Comanche congregation, Walter Komah, also served as Sunday school superintendent, pastoral visitor, and stable hand. On Sunday evenings, while Legters was at Apache, Komah often took charge of the Comanche meetings, which included prayer, Bible reading, and testimonials. Komah's wife was a daughter of Quanah Parker, and his story illustrates the dilemma of many Indian youth who went away to distant Indian schools.

Against the will of his parents, Komah enrolled at the Carlisle Indian School in Carlisle, Pennsylvania, where he stayed five years. He then went to Boston, where he worked by day and attended high school at night. After a year and a half in Boston, he returned to Carlisle with the intention of completing his education. But this was not to be. Three months before commencement he returned home for a short vacation, and, yielding to family pressure, he never returned.[15]

The work at the Comanche church continued with considerable success. Twenty-three new members were added in 1908, sixteen in 1909, and nineteen in 1910, for a total of 115 communicant members in 1910. It seems that Maud Legters, even more than her husband, was the moving force of the ministry. She taught a Sunday school class of more than fifty women, "the largest class of Indians in the state," and when in the summer of 1909 she became quite ill her husband reported that "we accomplished but little."[16]

Meanwhile, laypeople continued to show self-sufficiency, undertaking the repapering and repainting of the church. Otipoby, a relatively wealthy man, asked permission to provide lighting for all of the Indian churches under the women's board. By 1910 he had sent $95 to pay for the lighting at Winnebago and later did the same for Comanche and Mescalero.

Legters Succeeded by Sluyter

In 1910 the Legterses moved to California, where Leonard assumed an administrative position with the California Indian

15. Walter Komah, "A Letter from an Interpreter," *Day Star*, May 1908, 2.
16. *Annual Report of the Women's Executive Committee of the Board of Domestic Missions*, 1909, 23.

Association and was dismissed to the Presbyterian Church two years later. He later moved east to become field secretary for the Pioneer Missionary Agency in Philadelphia, but he returned from time to time to conduct camp meetings at various Reformed Church missions. One of the couple's sons, David Brainerd Legters, became well known as a missionary in Yucatan and wrote the book *Maya Mission*.

After Legters left, the Reverend Henry Sluyter served the Comanche church for three years. Sluyter arrived in 1910 after having served several churches in upstate New York. During his tenure a parish house was built as a social center for the Indians. Sewing machines were brought in, and Jennie Lewis was hired as matron and field worker. Howard Whitewolf continued as interpreter.

Sluyter, who also served the Apache church part-time, accompanied 163 Apaches to Mescalero, New Mexico, when they were released as prisoners of war. He preached there the following Sunday, Easter of 1913, as 89 Apaches joined the Mescalero church. Sluyter left the Indian ministry shortly afterward to serve briefly at a Presbyterian church in Anchorage, Alaska, and then at Reformed churches in College Point and Paterson, New Jersey.

Sluyter was followed at Lawton by the Reverend James Dykema, who arrived shortly after his graduation from New Brunswick Theological Seminary. He left a year later to undertake a pastorate in East Orange, New Jersey. After the three short pastorates of Legters, Sluyter, and Dykema, the Comanche church enjoyed fifty-five years under the next three: the Reverends Richard Harper (1915-23), John Read (1923-31), and Robert Chaat (1931-69).

Photo of the Joint Consistory

The *Mission Field*, in its February 1913 issue, published a remarkable photo of the joint consistories of the Comanche and Apache congregations, together with pastor Sluyter. All nine men are dressed in suits and ties except for Cooney, an Apache who is dressed in his scout uniform. All of the Apaches have short hair, while three of the four Comanches have long braids. The exception is Howard Whitewolf, who was educated at Carlisle. The accompanying article included a thumbnail sketch of each of the elders and deacons:

Nahwats, a Comanche elder, is described as "the pastor's assistant" who has done much for the upbuilding of the church. He is also called a tither who reportedly gave $100 to help wipe out a deficit for Kentucky and Indian mission work.

The Apache and Comanche consistories in 1913. Front row, left to right, are Carlos, Apache deacon; Benedict, Apache elder; Nahwats, Comanche elder; and Chatasy, Comanche deacon. Second row, Cooney, Apache deacon; James, Apache elder; the Reverend Henry Sluyter; Howard Whitewolf, Comanche deacon; and Otipoby, Comanche elder

Otipoby, also a Comanche elder, is described as the "Indian Mission Light Giver," both because he is "a light among his people" and because he equipped the Mescalero, Winnebago, and Comanche church buildings with complete lighting systems.

Howard Whitewolf, a Comanche deacon, is described as having a record for long and faithful service as an interpeter for both the church and the tribe.

Chatasy, the other Comanche deacon, is most colorfully described. He is usually greeted, says the caption, with *"Euch poy,"* a Comanche expression of sleep, when he enters the consistory meeting late, as he usually does. He has no viciousness or bad habits, says the caption, "unless inertia in his case can be termed one."[17]

Benedict, an Apache elder, is described as a humorist and a man "respected by his tribe with considerable influence among them." (In

17. "The Apache and Comanche Consistory," *Mission Field*, February 1913, 406.

later accounts Benedict is also identified by his last name, Jozhe. His son, also named Benedict, became a long-time member of the Apache church and was one of the last surviving Chiricahuas who were born as prisoners of war.)

James, the other Apache elder, was a government scout. He was a son-in-law of the war chief Naiche (described as "a beloved member of the church") and had been the interpreter at the mission. The interpreter at the time the photo was taken is identified as Uncas, who was almost totally blind.

Coony, an Apache deacon, was held as a prisoner despite his service as a government scout. He is described as "one of the most beloved members of the tribe" who "eagerly seizes every opportunity to speak a word of praise" for the mission and its workers."

Carlos, the other Apache deacon, was the youngest member of the consistory and also a scout. He is described as faithful in church attendance and as one who does many favors for workers at the mission.[18]

The Pastorate of Richard Harper, 1915-23

Richard Harper assumed the Comanche pastorate in 1915. Like Frank Hall Wright, Walter Roe, and L. L. Legters, Harper came from outside the Reformed Church in America. (Up to this point only Henry Sluyter and James Dykema had come through the traditional ranks of the Reformed Church, and those two pastorates were short and probably unhappy.)

Harper, who had been born in Plymouth, England, had come to America at the age of sixteen and had graduated from Chicago Theological Seminary. In 1891 he was ordained in the Congregational Church, under which he undertook Indian missions in Oklahoma. He entered the Reformed Church ministry in Colony (1907-09) and then served in Mescalero, New Mexico, before coming to Lawton. While in Mescalero, one of the Harpers' daughters, May, married J. Denton Simms, who subsequently founded the Jicarilla Apache Reformed Church in Dulce, New Mexico.

Harper continued the tradition of annual July camp meetings, often led by Frank Hall Wright. For two years, in fact, Harper added a December evangelistic event led by the Reverend Elmer Lindquist and an Indian gospel group from the Roe Indian Institute in Wichita,

18. *Mission Field*, February 1913, 406.

Richard and Ella Mae Harper with unidentified woman (center),
perhaps one of the mission workers

Kansas—the Christian training institution founded by Henry Roe
Cloud, the "adopted son" of Walter and Mary Roe.

Trouble with Peyote

At this time a new problem began to cause serious problems for
the mission—the use of peyote, more or less combined with Christian
beliefs, as a religious exercise. As Harper expressed it:

> A false worship has grown up, whose followers believe that the
> Holy Spirit dwells in the mescal bean. They even go so far, we are
> told, as to administer the rite of baptism with water in which the
> mescal bean has been soaked. This form of worship has a strong
> hold on many of the young Indians, especially the men, and on
> some of the older ones.[19]

Losses to the peyote cult were mentioned in nearly every annual
report, and concerns increased even more in 1918 when the Native
American Church, which used peyote as a sacrament, was officially
incorporated in the state of Oklahoma. Quanah Parker, incidentally,

19. *Annual Report of the Women's Board of Domestic Missions*, 1915, 41.

was one of the chief advocates of the use of peyote, becoming a virtual missionary of the cult among other Indian tribal groups.

In 1916 Harper reported that the members of the consistory were "faithful and earnest," that twenty-five had been converted, and that attendance at Sunday morning services had increased from fifty-six to eighty-two. But then the tone began to change. He described 1917 as a year of "steady, earnest, persistent effort" in which nine persons were received.[20] In 1918 he reported that the "total number of Indians is 162" (although it is not clear what he meant by that), but that "a much smaller number than that usually partake of the Communion service."[21] The following year Harper reported, "Though the past year has been one of the hardest of our ministry, there is little in figures to show for the work, the planning, the hoping, the determining."[22] He attributed the difficulties to several causes: the influenza epidemic, peyote, and the war.

Wider Ministries

With American involvement in World War I, Fort Sill suddenly became a very active military base, and airplanes buzzed above the mission every day from dawn to dusk. Indian soldiers attended the Comanche church nearly every Sunday, and Harper began to hold worship services for native servicemen at Fort Worth and other locations in Texas.

Because some of the Indians, both Comanches and Apaches, lived in the town of Fletcher, twenty miles to the northeast, Harper sent Jennie Lewis to open a mission there. The work was discontinued in 1923 when the Methodists began a ministry in Fletcher. The church's ministry also extended to the government Indian school, a mile to the east, where staff members were involved in YMCA and YWCA groups. They also directed a Sunday school, with Harper himself teaching a class of boys.

In 1921 the consistory met with the Reverend G. A. Watermulder, who at the time was superintending all of the denomination's Indian work in addition to serving as pastor to the church in Winnebago, Nebraska. Watermulder convinced the consistory to agree to undertake more self-support—namely to pay for the interpreter, the janitorial

20. *Annual Report of the Women's Board of Domestic Missions,* 1917, 29.
21. *Annual Report of the Women's Board of Domestic Missions,* 1918, 33.
22. *Annual Report of the Women's Board of Domestic Missions,* 1919, 32.

work, a larger share of the lodge expenses, and a full quota of the denomination's Progress Campaign.

Lawton's 1921 report contained a litany of difficulties. Jennie Lewis, under the strain of her work at Fletcher, returned to Grand Rapids, Michigan, for rest and did not return. Ella Mae Harper struggled with a serious illness, so her husband labored alone. The 1921 report also gives a rather negative report about the weekend activities of the Comanches, which included some of the unintended results of adopting the "civilized" white culture:

> Every Friday they leave their little farms and come into the mission grounds, where they camp until the following Monday or Tuesday, leaving their belongings, such as chickens, pigs, and sometimes a cow, uncared for until their return. This is not the way to inculcate habits of thrift and industry, and ought not to be encouraged. On Saturday they spend a portion of the day in Lawton, where they amuse themselves in various ways, being constantly exposed to the vices and temptations incident to a town. Then they return to the Mission, attend the services on Sunday [and on] Monday or Tuesday go back to their homes and the weekend history repeats itself....Something must be done to counteract the evil influence of the weekly trip to Lawton.[23]

But there were bright spots as well. After two years of only one new member, fifteen made confession of faith on Easter Sunday of 1922. James Ottipoby, son of elder Bob Otipoby (previously referred to only as Otipoby), enrolled at Hope College in Holland, Michigan, to prepare for the Christian ministry. Ella Cox, granddaughter of Quanah Parker, was also mentioned as studying in high school in preparation for Christian service.

In September of 1922 an event occurred that would have long-term significance for the Comanche church. The Reverends H. B. Dinwiddie, of Philadelphia, and L. L. Legters, formerly pastor in Lawton, upon their return from a preaching tour in Central America, conducted a camp meeting under the tent in Lawton. Dinwiddie spoke of the ancient training of young Indians for warfare and drew an analogy to modern preparation for spiritual warfare. In the words of Mary Roe's report:

---

23. *Annual Report of the Women's Board of Domestic Missions*, 1921, 27.

He...asked the Indians why there were none to carry the banner of Christ from tepee to tepee here, and down to those waiting Indians afar....He pleaded with them for the needs of their own race, not to be evangelized by others, but to be led into the Light by the hands of their own people. At the end, eight Indian young men and two Indian young women rose to offer their lives for permanent Christian service. Among them was Robert Chaat, nephew of our dear elder Nahwats, one of the boys educated at the Indian Institute at Witchita, and from his birth a child of our Reformed Church.[24]

The summer student at the Comanche church in 1928 was the Reverend John R. Kempers, who two years later, with his wife Mabel, founded the Reformed Church mission in Chiapas, Mexico, where the Kemperses stayed for forty years. Kempers was just one of dozens of Reformed missionaries and ministers who received their first taste of cross-cultural work at these Indian mission sites.

Harper's statistical reports to the General Synod, like so many reports from the Indian churches, were a crazy quilt of confusion. During his first year (1914) he increased the number of families reported from 85 to 110, a figure that remained constant for nine years until being raised to 113 in 1923. (Pastor John Read reduced the figure to 83 the following year.) Despite several years of gloomy overviews, the reports of communicant members ranged from 118 to 185. Reported Sunday school enrollment bounced up and down between 100 and 225, again displaying no patterns. The "absent" category ranged from 3 to 35. (This figure jumped to 78 in the first year of Read's pastorate, 1924.)

In July of 1923, after three years of painful illness, probably cancer, Ella Mae Harper, mother of six, died and was laid to rest in the Indian section of Highland Cemetery in Lawton, near the church property. She was fifty-three years old. Soon after this, Harper left Lawton to serve the Women's Board of Domestic Missions. His duties there are unclear, but no doubt he went on speaking tours on behalf of Indian mission work. He was honored by Central College in 1939 with a Doctor of Divinity Degree. Harper died April 8, 1941, at the age of seventy-five, and was buried next to his wife in Lawton.

24. Mary Roe, "Campmeeting at Lawton," *Christian Intelligencer and Mission Field,* October 25, 1922, 678-79.

A Period of Growth, 1923-30

With the eight-year pastorate of the Reverend John Leighton Read and his wife, Betty Lou, another era in the life of the Comanche Reformed Church began. Read, born in 1879, had originally come out of the Southern Presbyterian Church, graduated from Austin Theological Seminary, and served several Presbyterian churches in Arizona before coming to the Colony mission in 1917, where he stayed for six years.

Read began his work in Lawton in September of 1923, and a few months later he announced what he considered a minor victory in the form of the annual Thanksgiving dinner in which turkey was served:

> An Indian feast without "wohaw" is an almost unheard of thing, but there was no beef to be seen....All this is mute evidence that the Indian is taking up with the white man's ways more and more.[25]

The Thanksgiving dining schedule was an interesting one: non-Christians were admitted first, then visiting Christians, and, last of all, church members. The meal was served after the worship service, but attendance at worship was not a prerequisite for the meal.

Robert Chaat Hired as a Student Missionary

The next summer Robert Chaat, then a student at Cook Christian Training School in Phoenix, was employed as a student missionary at the mission. Beginning a pattern he would follow throughout his ministry, Chaat immediately began reporting through the pages of the *Christian Intelligencer and Mission Field*:

> Twice a week I would accompany one or more of the missionaries on one of these trips. We would cover from five to fifty or more miles a day....We brought Sunday school papers and tracts to those who could read. Sometimes the older Indians would open up and tell us their reasons for not being Christians. One of the most frequent excuses is that they are praying to God and believe that things will turn out all right in the end, and that they are afraid of failure in the Christian life. After we hear their excuses we show them the necessity of accepting Christ as their Saviour

---

25. John J. Leighton Read, "Thanksgiving at the Comanche Mission," *Christian Intelligencer and Mission Field*, Dec. 10, 1924, 793.

and there is only one way of salvation and that all that they can do will not save them.[26]

Chaat also said that his duties included calling on the sick, teaching children, and preaching. He had harsh words for Indian dances, which he said keep people from worship services and "are used by the devil to lead my people down the broad road that leads to destruction."[27] Among the converts in 1924 was White Parker, son of chief Quanah Parker.

Under Read, the ministry continued at the government Indian school at Fort Still. This included teaching Sunday school, preaching or teaching on alternate Sunday evenings, conducting YMCA and YWCA meetings during the week, and leading Bible classes for catechumens. Boys and girls were required to take three months of instruction before making confession of faith. Read reported that, on Easter Sunday of 1924, "all of the 165 students of the Government School attended the morning service in a body and, with other visitors, filled the house."[28]

Scheduled events included Sunday morning and evening worship services, a Friday evening social at the lodge, a weekly meeting of the Women's Missionary Society, and weekly Bible training classes for teachers and officers. In addition, the missionary traveled twice a month to conduct Sunday afternoon services at the Apache chapel. Home and hospital visits were ongoing, conducted largely by the female field workers. In 1925 the consistory was expanded by two, for a total of three elders and three deacons, described as "all active, consistent Christians."[29]

The first daily vacation Bible school was also held in Lawton in 1925, about the same time these summer ministries were popping up throughout the country. The Bible schools became a regular part of the ministry, with an average of about twenty students enrolled in those early years. The mission staff conducted the school; it was not until four years later that Indians became involved in teaching.

The year 1925 also marked the passing of one of the most faithful of the Comanche elders, Nahwats, described by Harper as "standing on

26. Robert P. Chaat, "A Summer at Lawton," *Christian Intelligencer and Mission Field*, Oct. 8, 1924, 649.
27. Ibid.
28. Mrs. Leighton Read, "Resurrection and Reclamation at Comanche Mission," *Christian Intelligencer and Mission Field*, May 7, 1924, 291.
29. *Annual Report of the Women's Board of Domestic Missions*, 1925, 27.

Comanches at a camp meeting in Lawton. Mission workers seated on the grass include (left to right), G. A. Watermulder (with hat), John and Betty Lou Read, Robert Chaat, and Jennie Dubbink.

the right no matter what other Indians thought; fearless in word and deed; glad to be known as a Christian."[30] Nahwats died of an apparent heart attack and was found by a nephew when he did not return from working in his field.

Camp Meetings Continue to be Important

Camp meetings also continued, but with more musical sophistication, including solos, duets, quartets, and the use of a violin and saxophone—provided largely by Indians. Preachers included men like Henry Roe Cloud, Peter Van Es, G. A. Watermulder, and former pastor Harper, with Indian testimonies following the traditional pattern of "once I was..." and "the Jesus Road is the only road." Read also initiated "little camp meetings" some distance from the mission, on the property of church members. One such meeting in June of 1925 attracted over a hundred people, and twenty people came forward, mostly for recommitment. These one- and two-day camp meetings were held enthusiastically for several years, with families issuing an invitation and the consistory giving approval.

30. Richard Harper, "Some Indians Leaders, Past and Present," *Christian Intelligencer and Mission Field,* September 30, 1925, 616.

In 1927 the church discontinued the custom of issuing beef at camp meetings, and instead provided noon and evening meals at the lodge for all who came. The next year the Indians decided to entertain visitors in their own homes and camps. This experiment apparently received mixed reviews, and in 1930 the camp meeting again featured a beef issue. But two years later the beef was discontinued again in favor of family hospitality, and this time the new policy stuck.

Weckeah Bradley Remembers Church Life

Many years later, elder Weckeah Bradley, in one of the few printed Indian recollections at the time, related these childhood remembrances of the camp meetings:

> Many Indians camped; some would come on horse-drawn wagons. There were other tribes. Cheyennes and Arapahoes; Fort Still Apaches; Kiowas and more Comanches. Each tribe had their own interpreter and after the speaker would say about a paragraph each interpreter would relate it to his tribe. Each tribal member sat with their tribe for this convenience and we would sing hymns sung from these other tribes. We children learned at least one song from each of the other tribes. We were all under the big camp meeting tent. The Comanches always butchered beef the Indian way. When the gall was removed without being punctured it was held high for all to see. Women would KAHTAHTAHKIINH (give the victory cry). It was compared to sin being removed to give unsoiled food for the people.

Bradley also recalls, "On Tuesday was the sewing meeting and the ladies would have a devotional and then make beautiful quilts. Sometimes they would be taught how to cook." Another important aspect of these women's meetings, according to Bradley, were prayers for "the fourteen men":

> No one ever mentioned who they were as I remember. When I grew up my mother and I were reminiscing one day and it was brought out that the fourteen men took the "Jesus Road" one by one and became what they used to call strong Christians.

Bradley remembered this about midweek meetings and Sunday services:

> On Wednesday evenings either the bell would ring or the camp crier would call out where the mid-week prayer meeting would

be. Many times in the summer the people at the mission would meet for this service under someone's brush arbor. Sometimes coal oil lanterns were used for light. There would be campfire smoke on the south side to keep the mosquitoes away. Since there was no electricity the Bible messages were from memory and the Comanche hymns resounded down the hillside to the creek…

On Sunday morning the camp crier could be heard calling the people to come to church.…Somehow he found his way to the church. He had shoulder length flowing hair and used a cane. He was blind.

Bradley also remembered Friday night socials at the lodge:

Carrom boards would be set up on saw horses and the adults would have a jolly time playing carroms. They called it *tsipotse*, which means bounce.…We children played Biblelotto, button button, hot potato, and other games the missionaries taught us. The social would be closed with a devotional and Comanche hymns and prayer. On Saturday it was cleanup day at the mission. Trash was hauled to a certain place and burned.

In Sunday school, recalled Bradley, "our names were written on a large chart and according to what we learned, gold, red, and blue stars were placed by our name. Naughty children got black stars by their names."

Regarding Christmas, which Bradley remembered fondly, there was always a program telling of the birth of Jesus.

One Christmas more shepherds were needed. I was about seven years old and my aunt who didn't speak English was about fifty years old were fixed up like shepherds. She showed me how to fall back when the angel appeared.[31]

A Far-Flung Ministry

Robert Chaat, who had attended Cook school, now began working full time as "assistant missionary," the first Indian so employed. The church first paid $10 a month toward his salary, then increased it to $20. (The records don't indicate his total salary.) Among other things, he directed, with Jennie Dubbink, the vacation Bible school, superintended the Sunday school and the intermediate

---

31. Weckeah Bradley, typewritten ms., Nov. 11, 1991.

Christian Endeavor Society, took charge of the weekly YMCA meetings at the Indian school, led and interpreted the Sunday evening service on occasion, played the organ and piano, and made field trips.

An article by Chaat in the *Christian Intelligencer and Mission Field* gave an idea as to how far-flung were these trips. The Comanches, he said, were to be found in five districts: (1) Mount Scott (named after the highest peak in the Wichita Mountains), twelve miles to the northwest; (2) Richard's Spur, ten miles north; (3) Fletcher, twenty-five miles northeast; (4) Geronimo, ten miles south; and (5) Beaver, twenty-seven miles northeast.

As native culture changed, the mission changed with it. A second service, this one in English, was added to the camp meetings for the younger Indians. Instead of camping in tepees, the Indians set up rectangular tents. Moccasins gave way to shoes, and shawls and blankets were gradually replaced by "white" clothing.

A spirit of ecumenism also became apparent. Fourth of July picnics included Indians from other missions, followed by ball games between the groups. These, in turn, led to the organization of the Inter-Mission Athletic League in 1930. Street meetings were held for a time on Saturday afternoons as Indians came to do their trading in Lawton. These meetings, which included Comanche and English songs and a message by Read, did not continue long.

Christmas continued to be a major event, with more than three hundred gifts being received from churches throughout the denomination. These were sorted, wrapped, and tagged for individuals. Programs included songs, Scripture readings, a pageant of sorts, and "stereoptican" pictures from the life of Christ. The Sunday before Christmas was always "Giving Sunday," with the special offerings being designated for such denominational mission causes as Southern Normal School in Brewton, Alabama, and mission schools in the Middle East.

Read was one of the first pastors in any of the Indian mission sites to exhibit consistency in statistical reporting. His first report after taking over from Harper indicated a drop in communicant membership from 160 to 116 and an increase in absent/inactive members from 30 to 78. It is possible that some of these losses can be attributed to more accurate reporting, but it is also likely that the Lawton church, like most Indian congregations, suffered a radical drop-off in church activity between pastorates. During Read's pastorate the church took in an average of 14 members per year by confession of faith, about half of whom were students from the government school. Communicant membership grew gradually from 116 to 138, but about 40 percent of these were listed as absent or inactive. Hardly anyone was ever listed as having been dropped or transferred.

The use of peyote continued to be a concern. In 1929 a prospective new member, Morgan, was questioned about whether he was willing to give up peyote. He said he was willing to give up peyote meetings but wished to continue to use peyote for medicinal purposes. After considerable discussion, the elders voted to receive him into church membership.[32]

Beginning in 1927 the church listed one Sunday school instead of two, and enrollment dropped from 249 to 124. Actually, the Sunday school at the government school continued, but it was no longer listed as an Reformed Church school because by then its teachers came from various churches in Lawton. Enrollment at the remaining Sunday school continued to drop precipitously, from 124 in 1927 to 104, 90, and 60 in subsequent years. These figures were duly recorded in annual reports but never explained in the mission board's annual reports or in the denomination's periodicals.

In 1931, after having served in Colony for six years and Lawton for eight years, Read left the employ of the Reformed Church in America. He moved to Norman, Oklahoma, to found an interdenominational training center for Indian and white students. About this time Jennie Dubbink also left, returning to Grand Rapids, Michigan. She had served as field worker and lodge matron for thirteen years, from 1917 to 1930.

Robert Chaat, the First Native American Pastor

The departure of John Read opened the door for the long pastorate of the Reverend Robert Chaat, the first Native American to be ordained as a pastor in the Reformed Church in America.

Robert Paul Chaat was a son of the Comanche mission. He was born September 6, 1900 (or 1899; the records are not consistent), the youngest of five children of Christian parents. We have already met his three sisters in these pages, three girls who were initially in the care of their uncle, Nahwats—Dorothy, the first convert among the Comanches, who died at age sixteen; Tocsi, later known as Maud

32. Consistory Minutes of Comanche Reformed Church, Aug. 31, 1929, 11.

Blevins; and Rachael (Akers), also raised at the mission. Robert had one brother, Ralph, who also became a member of the Comanche church.

The family name was Chahtinneyackque (spelled differently in various records), but it was shortened by one of Robert's sisters to Chaat. Robert was later to tell this story of his early dedication to Christian service:

> From the beginning of their work, the missionaries had observed the custom of having the Sunday before Christmas as "Gift Sunday." On this day the Indians brought their gifts of money to be used to help others. On one such Sunday, when I was a tiny baby, my father and mother were very sad because they were quite without money to give. One by one the others took forward their gifts until only my parents were left. Then my father took me in his arms and went forward.
>
> Standing before the missionaries, Dr. and Mrs. Roe, of the Reformed Church, he said, "We have no money to give, but here is our baby which we give to the Lord."
>
> Dr. Roe took me in his arms and prayed that God would accept this gift and raise me up to be a Christian leader among my people.[33]

Chaat's parents died when he was seven or eight years old, and like his sisters he went to live with his uncle Nahwats and his aunt Tsiwanny. Robert and the other children in his family were the only Comanches to attend the mission school established for Apaches. He was the second person to enroll in the American Indian Institute in Wichita, Kansas, the Christian school founded by Henry Roe Cloud.

Meanwhile, Elsie Tahkofper, who had attended the government school in Fort Sill, was enrolled at the Haskell Institute in Lawrence, Kansas, and the two began seeing each other on holidays and during the summer. They decided to marry (Robert at age twenty and Elsie at age seventeen), dropped out of school, and began farming on the land allotted to Robert's family.

Chaat's call to full-time Christian ministry was awakened in the 1922 incident already described, when two missionaries addressed the annual Lawton camp meeting and told of their work among the Indians of Central America under the auspices of the Pioneer Mission Agency in

33. *From Medicine Man to Minister*, brochure (Home Missions Council of North America, 1944), 2.

Robert and Elsie Chaat
in their early years

Philadelphia. The Chaats sold their farm implements and moved with their infant son, Robert, Jr., to Philadelphia, where Robert enrolled in the National Bible Institute. Unable to cope with the cold northern climate, the family soon moved back to the southwest, and Chaat enrolled in Cook Christian Training School in Phoenix, Arizona.

Chaat graduated in 1924, and the couple returned to Lawton, where Robert was hired as assistant to pastor John Read. Chaat worked alongside Read for six years, also serving as an elder and clerk of consistory. In 1930, after Read left, Chaat was called to become the pastor of the Comanche church. By this time the Chaats had five children: Robert, Jr., Samuel, Theodore, Dorothy, and Pauline (also called Paula).

Chaat was pastor of the church, and had moved into the parsonage with his family, but he had not been ordained as a pastor in the Reformed Church. He had not graduated from an accredited college nor attended a theological seminary. But on the basis of his studies at Cook School, his six years of experience under a pastor at Lawton, and the personal tutoring of Professor Milton Hoffman of New Brunswick Theological Seminary, the General Synod granted Chaat a dispensation in 1934 that cleared the way for his ordination.

Chaat Is Ordained in New York

Robert Chaat, aged thirty-four, was ordained to the gospel ministry of the Reformed Church in America by the Classis of New York at the Marble Collegiate Church in New York City, November 20, 1934, in conjunction with the fifty-first anniversary of the Women's Board of Domestic Missions. The event, the first ordination to the ministry of a Native American, took place a little more than three hundred years after the Reformed Church was founded on Manhattan Island.

At the service, Chaat recounted several acts of providence that had brought him to the point of ordination and expressed appreciation to the Women's Board of Domestic Missions and the missionaries who had brought the message of Jesus Christ to the Indian people. He concluded with a paraphrase of his text, Ephesians 3:8, "Therefore unto me who am less than the least of all saints, is this grace given, that I should preach among the Comanches—and others, the unsearchable riches of Christ."[34]

Elsie Chaat, with her five children at home, was unable to attend—nor, apparently, did the Reformed Church offer to pay for the family's travel to New York. Two weeks later, on December 2, Chaat was installed at the Comanche mission lodge (used at the time for worship services) as pastor of the Comanche Reformed Church. Pastors Richard Harper and G. A. Watermulder conducted the service, which included inspirational comments by Mary Roe.

James Ottipoby Also Ordained

A second Comanche pastor was ordained by the Reformed Church four years after Chaat. James Ottipoby, the son of long-time elder Bob Otipoby (originally simply called Otipoby, without the first name and with one *t*), was born October 26, 1900. At the age of twelve, with his parents' approval, James went to live as a white boy with Mr. and Mrs. P. Van Donselaar in Sioux Center, Iowa, where he attended the local junior high and high school. He first went to Central College and then to Hope College, from which he graduated in 1925.

After one year at Western Theological Seminary he left school and served for several years at various Indian schools and churches. In 1938 he accepted the invitation to serve as assistant minister with pastor Watermulder in Winnebago, Nebraska.

Ottipoby was ordained by the Classis of New York November 15, 1938, in connection with the fifty-fifth anniversary celebration of the Women's Board of North American Missions. The service, like Chaat's, was held at the Marble Collegiate Church in New York City. Robert Chaat read the scripture and the Reverend Norman Vincent

34. Robert Paul Chaat, "Fulfillment," *Intelligencer-Leader*, Feb. 20, 1935, 12-13.

James Ottipoby

Peale delivered the sermon. Following the service, Ottipoby noted that both Chaat and he had been dedicated by their parents to the service of God.

Ottipoby and his wife, Lucille, served in Winnebago for two years, and then in Mescalero until 1943, when James resigned to become a military chaplain in the closing years of World War II, reportedly the first Indian chaplain in the U.S. Army. Although this is not confirmed by a written record, the Reverend Reuben Ten Haken, who served as pastor in Mescalero and Macy, stated in a letter that Ottipby carried the documents of unconditional surrender (unaware of their contents) to the battleship *Missouri*, to be signed by Emperor Hirohito.[35]

As a chaplain Ottipoby attained the rank of major, and after the war he served for twelve years at three churches on the Laguna Reservation in New Mexico. He died October 5, 1960, at the age of fifty-nine and was buried at the Santa Fe National Cemetery in Santa Fe, New Mexico.

Robert Chaat's Views on Indian Religion and the Christian Religion

One might expect that Chaat, as a Native American, would attempt to incorporate some traditional elements of Indian culture into Christian worship and practice, but this apparently was not the case. Although he received no formal training at a Reformed Church seminary, he followed the example of the white missionaries before him in shaping a church not unlike that of his white counterparts, calling for a clean break with the past.

35. Letter from Reuben Ten Haken to Eugene Heideman, Dec. 18, 1980.

Chaat was careful not to identify Christianity with white culture, although he did believe that Christianity was better able than the old Indian faith to prepare the Indian for living in the dominant culture. "Will his own religion and worship help him to be a better citizen?" he asked. "Does it make him more industrious, honest, and upright? Does it give him a forward look or does it keep him looking back to the past?"[36]

Chaat was a frequent speaker at various conferences on Indian missions, both Reformed and interdenominational. At one of these, the National Fellowship of Indian Workers, he espoused what might be called a creed by describing three roads open to the Indian people of his day. "The Indian Road," he said, "was a good road in its time. Many fine traits are found in Indian life, honesty, truthfulness, loyalty, and a religious spirit. The best should be kept from the past. But the old Indian way of life cannot meet the needs of today and a different generation, no more than a dirt road can meet the demands of modern traffic."

"The White Man's Road," he said, "has contributed much to the spiritual welfare of the world" and "has done wonders in the development of the God-given resources of the earth." Yet, he said, this material greatness "has not helped the white man's road to be the Jesus Road." Indians and whites, said Chaat, must join together in walking the third road, the Jesus Road:

> Jesus, the Son of God, came that He might make a better road for the tired, weary, and heavy-laden of every race. Love and service are the guiding principles of those who walk this way. Jesus lived and worked and died and rose that He might make complete the best way of Life for all who will walk in the way....Today we look forward, not back—not with fear and dismay but with steadfast faith and courage.[37]

The Comanche Ministry under Chaat

Chaat continued, as had Read before him, to direct the Christian education work at the Fort Sill Indian school. Chaat reported in 1932 that the school was attended by about 180 students, mostly Comanche,

36. Robert Chaat, "The Indian Needs Christ," *Intelligencer-Leader*, Sept. 30, 1938, 5.
37. Robert P. Chaat, "The Road Ahead," *Church Herald*, Nov. 2, 1945, 13.

in grades one through nine, and that eight teachers from various churches in Lawton conducted the religion classes.

On Monday evenings the Chaats conducted special religious instruction classes for children of the Reformed Church, about fifty in number, in preparation for church membership. Some students from the school, he said, also came to the church services every Sunday (attendance was no longer required), and the Chaats often invited two or three for Sunday dinner. At that time the superintendent and all the teachers in the Sunday school conducted by the church were Indians, as were all the members of the consistory. Chaat also provided limited pastoral services to the small group of Apache Christians twenty miles to the north, as had the missionaries before him.

Early in 1932 the consistory discussed what to do about a local church (unnamed) that had "encroached upon our field" and taken about twenty members. It was agreed informally that "we should show a Christian spirit of tolerance and Christian love." There is no record, however, of members being transferred to that church.[38]

In the fall of that year, Chaat reported an average July attendance of thirty to thirty-five at the morning worship service, with about twenty-five in Sunday school. He said that Christian Endeavor attendance had fallen off somewhat, but gave no statistics. It is difficult to say whether these attendance figures were higher or lower than before, since attendance was not reported in annual statistical reports and seldom reported in *Christian Intelligencer* news stories.

Ecumenical summer social events expanded. The annual picnic on the grounds of the government Indian school grew to include seven Comanche churches representing five denominations. Contests were held in foot races, tugs of war, and horseshoes, with women as well as men participating in these events.

The annual camp meetings continued as usual, resulting in new commitments and recommitments. A notable example of the latter came in 1932, when Howard Whitewolf, an early interpreter and church leader who had fallen away because of a dispute with the missionary then in charge (probably Read), came forward with a testimony:

> I want to thank God for being so patient with me in my willful neglect. He has loved me so much....Now I want to forget the past

38. Minutes of the Comanche Reformed Church, February 21, 1932.

and want the Holy Spirit to make my religion a religion of the heart and not merely outward.[39]

Whitewolf and his wife came before the consistory the following March and were reinstated. Later that year they invited members to hold a camp meeting at their home, fifteen miles away. In 1934 he was again elected as an elder. In the consistory minutes of July 16, 1933, Chaat noted that "a very fine spirit has characterized the consistory meeting for the last two years. There have been no divisions or anything to mar the harmony and good will."[40]

Bob Otipoby died in late 1937 after a six-year illness, and Howard Whitewolf died in the spring of 1939, having remained true to the recommitment he made seven years earlier. His death marked the end of an era of outstanding leadership by capable and devout Comanche laymen who in the earliest days of the mission chose the "Jesus Road."

In 1939, for the first time, the members of the Comanche church voted on a double slate of nominees for elder and deacon. That was also the first year that Ralph Chaat, Robert's brother, was elected as a deacon.

Denominational reports on the mission over the next several years included such observations as "the new attitude of the Indians toward the mission";[41] numerous activities and meetings "in all of which the leadership is entirely Indian";[42] and "young people play a greater role in the life of the church."[43]

In 1939 the Comanche church accompanied its camp meeting with its first youth conference. The leaders were the Reverend and Mrs. Raymond Drukker. At the time, Mr. Drukker served as the denominational secretary for young people's work. Also present and leading the camp meeting was the Reverend James Dykema, who had served the Lawton church in 1913-14. Of the thirteen living charter members of the church, eleven were present for this tent meeting.

39. Robert Chaat, "Comanche Camp Meeting," *Christian Intelligencer*, Oct. 5, 1932, 688.
40. Minutes of the Comanche Reformed Church, July 16, 1933.
41. *Annual Report of the Board of Domestic Missions and of the Women's Board of Domestic Missions,* 1936, 41.
42. *Annual Report of the Board of Domestic Missions and of the Women's Board of Domestic Missions,* 1937, 37.
43. *Annual Report of the Board of Domestic Missions and of the Women's Board of Domestic Missions,* 1938, 40. (In 1938, incidentally, the report that had been previously called "Report on Indian Work," was called "Rum-tum-tum-tum!" The next year it was called, "Indians in the United States.")

The Comanche Reformed Church, dedicated in 1941

A New Church Building Is Erected

The original wooden church building, the "yellow mission," had fallen into disrepair to the point of being unsafe and was torn down in 1932. Worship services were then held at the lodge. Eight years later the church had not yet been replaced, so the consistory appointed a committee and established a church building fund. Men pledged their labor, and plans were drawn up. Several Indian families were generous in their contributions. Mrs. Pahdapony, a faithful member for many years, said she wanted to pay her pledge before she died. Three sons of the Nauni family petitioned the government to release bonds being held for them totaling $1,000, then turned the money over to the church.

Four more years elapsed, but construction began at last in 1941. The building was a unique one, incorporating various shades of brown and tan stone taken from a quarry west of the church. Some of the lumber was salvaged from the old church, and both whites and Indians donated much of the labor. The new church building, named on its cornerstone the Comanche Memorial Reformed Church, was dedicated December 7, 1941, on the tenth anniversary of the installation of pastor Chaat and—as it turned out—the Sunday of Japan's attack on Pearl

Harbor. Of the total cost of $10,000, only $2,000 remained to be raised at the time of dedication.

World War II

During the years that followed, some fifty young men and two young women with some connection to the church volunteered or were inducted into military service. Of these, one man, Thomas Chockooyah, Jr., was killed in action in France. His aged father, reported Chaat, "made an eloquent plea to the large congregation for a closer walk with God."[44]

In addition to its fighting men, the Comanches also contributed code talkers, seventeen in all, to form the Army's 4th Signal Company in Europe. Although not as well known as the Navajo code talkers in the Pacific, the Comanches, by speaking their own language (with modifications like "sewing machine" for "machine gun"), communicated war strategy in a code the Germans were never able to break. There is an irony here that few people grasped at the time: the language that the U.S. Government and sometimes the church had tried so hard to squelch eventually made a significant contribution to America's victory. It was not until 1999, when only one member of the original seventeen was still alive, that the U.S. Defense Department offered special recognition to this group of code talkers.

Over the long term, the war was a mixed blessing for the Comanche people and for the church. Some Indian soldiers worshiped at the Comanche church while stationed at Fort Sill. Indians found work in war-related industries. But the presence of thousands of soldiers nearby resulted in a large number of mixed race, single-parent children, and many young Indian women were arrested for prostitution. Some Indian servicemen took up drinking on a large scale. Many became adept at assimilating with the white culture and sought further education under the G.I. Bill of Rights. Some came home from the service better prepared to provide leadership in the church, while others who were active in the church before the war showed little interest when they returned.

In January of 1949 Chaat gave a rather somber report in the pages of the *Church Herald:* "The need today is just as great....The present generation seems, to a large extent, spiritually indifferent. The post-war

---

44. Robert Chaat, "A Comanche Prayer Meeting," *Church Herald*, Nov. 24, 1944, 8.

period has been one of tragedy for some, confusion and frustration for others, and a falling away from the church for some."[45]

The Camp Tent Is Destroyed and Replaced by an Arbor

A sudden and violent windstorm in the summer of 1948 brought down the old camp tent and brought an end to an era. The large tent had been put up and taken down each summer for forty years. In the camp's early days, those who attended included Comanches, Apaches, Cheyennes, and Arapahos, all with their shawls, blankets, and moccasins. All the pioneer missionaries had preached there. It had provided a place of renewal and commitment for Indian Christians who had drifted away, and a place of ingathering for those who throughout the year had been instructed in the faith.

Chaat, who had made confession of faith in that tent when he was eleven years old, said that the tent "could not be restored, even if we wanted to keep it. It has served its purpose well....The old Indian life can never be brought back: the manner of dress, the language, social and economic ways of life are giving place to the modern. Even the first generation of old Christian Indians has gone."[46]

To replace the tent, Chaat hoped to build a permanent pavilion that would be used not only for camp meetings but also for social and recreational events. There, he said, "The Indians who will gather under it will wear modern clothes and speak English; there will be no interpreters."[47] That vision was fulfilled in the summer of 1949 with the construction of an arbor, open on all sides. Two years later the congregation raised $258 to put in a concrete floor, and the Board of Domestic Missions contributed fifty folding chairs. The first camp meeting held there used the services of the Reverend Herbert Gee of Dulce, as well as the usual Indian testimonies. Although the term "camp meeting" was still used, it was no longer accurate. Whereas in years gone by Indian families camped nearby—first in tepees and then in white men's tents—now nearly everyone either drove in for the day or stayed with relatives or friends who lived in the area.

Gradually the influence and importance of the camp meeting waned. As the camping experience diminished, so did its significance

---

45. Robert P. Chaat, "The Big Tent is Gone," *Church Herald*, Jan. 14, 1949, 11.
46. Ibid.
47. Ibid.

as a family reunion and community social event. No longer was the distribution of beef a motivator. Whereas in earlier days Indian people, moved by evangelistic sermons and personal testimonies, made confession of faith during this week of special meetings, now people united with the church one or two at a time throughout the year.

Emphasis on Indian Leadership

The emphasis on Indian leadership continued in Lawton, with an all-Indian consistory and all Indian teachers in the church's Sunday school, the government's Indian boarding school, and the church's vacation Bible school program. Indian leadership was stronger at Lawton that at any of the other Indian congregation for several reasons: (1) the presence of an Indian pastor; (2) the influence of an integrated community that, unlike a typical reservation at the time, encouraged self-determination; and (3) the historical example of early devout leaders such as Nahwats, Periconic, Otipoby, and Whitewolf.

Whereas previously the missionaries had identified "pagan" Indian customs and rituals as the primary hindrance to Christianity, now attention was turned to the "evil" of modern civilization as the primary detractor to Christian commitment in general and to church attendance in particular. This was Chaat's observation in 1953:

> The problems and difficulties of our missionaries today are largely related to the impact of modern life with its sins and distractions: radio, cheap magazines, beer taverns and rodeos compete for the interest and time of our people. Many are confused with no sense of real values. Sunday used to be a sacred day with our early Christians, many of them driving long distances to attend the little Mission church. Today, with cars and buses, and even without them, Sunday is a holiday for many of our Indians—a day to go visiting, take a drive to the mountains, go to the ball game or rodeo, to an Indian dance or anywhere else except to church. There are, however, a goodly number who follow their elders in church attendance; many are children or grandchildren of those who were so faithful in the early days.[48]

One might observe that one of the major goals of the early missionaries—the adoption by Indians of the white culture, which was

48. Robert P. Chaat, "Comanche Contrasts," *Church Herald*, Dec. 11, 1953, 5.

Robert and Elsie Chaat in 1954

especially successful in a multicultural nonreservation setting such as Lawton—proved in the end to be counter-productive.

Chaat also mentioned peyote as a negative influence. "Eventually they become addicted to the drug and are completely demoralized by it," he said.[49] But he acknowledged that peyote was not as serious a problem at Lawton as it was elsewhere.

From 1930, when Chaat took over the pastorate, to 1938, the number of communicant members remained virtually unchanged at 132 to 135. From 1939 until 1957 (when both churches were transferred to the Classis of West Central), Comanche's membership reports included the Apache membership, so it is impossible to determine the membership of either congregation.

A 1954 report, first published in the *Lawton Constitution and Morning Press*, and later in the *Church Herald*, indicated that approximately eighty people regularly attended morning services, at which times Chaat preached the sermon in English and followed with a short summary in Comanche. Music was provided by a fifteen-voice choir. Additional organizations included the Women's Missionary Society, youth fellowship, a younger adult group, a men's brotherhood, and a group

49. Ibid.

Men's group at the Comanche church, 1955

for older Comanches. The church had purchased a new Hammond organ, and plans were being made for a new brick parsonage.[50]

That article and a 1955 *Historical Highlights* booklet, published by the Board of Domestic Missions, include photos that indicate that the Chaat family was represented in nearly every aspect of the congregation's life. Robert, Jr., taught a Sunday school class of young men; Elsie Chaat was the organist, choir accompanist, and a Sunday school teacher; and Lawrence Tomah, Jr., married to Dorothy Chaat, was the Sunday school superintendent.

Difficult Times in Lawton

Then, in November of 1956, an article by Chaat, called, "Testing Times in the Comanche Church," appeared in the *Church Herald*. In it Chaat wrote:

---

50. "Indian Pastor Sees His Mission Expand," *Church Herald*, Jan. 7, 1955, 5; rep. *Lawton Constitution and Morning Press*, Nov. 28, 1954.

The past months have been times of real testing for the Comanche Church. Through the fall and winter the work had been going forward, then Satan began to do his work. Sin thrust its ugly head into our midst, involving some of the most faithful. It was felt in the whole church and some few began to stay away. Others lost the zeal they once had.[51]

Although some members expressed repentance at the camp meeting, said Chaat, the conflict continued throughout the remainder of the summer. Chaat gave no hint regarding the nature of the problem, but some members who remember those days say that peyote was becoming increasingly popular, and that some members of the church had begun advocating its use. Chaat took a strong stand against the use of peyote, saying that the peyote cult and the Christian faith were mutually exclusive.

In a *Church Herald* article one year later, Chaat did not specifically mention the church's problems, but he did point out that "tribal politics and other tribal business have created conflicts and caused a division among the Comanches. Some have even left the churches." Chaat also said that the Indian people "are in a desperate period of struggle to survive," and that "poverty, disease, frustration, prejudice, and sin prevail."[52] In November of 1957 the church transferred several members, including elder Wilson Tahmakuah, to the Hunting House Methodist Church in Lawton. This was an unusual action, since transfers were uncommon among Indian congregations.

Sale of Church Property Becomes an Issue

Another cause of tension may have been the sale of church property by the Board of Domestic Missions. At one time the Reformed Church owned 120 acres, granted by the government for the mission, about a mile and a half from the town of Lawton. But as Lawton expanded to a city of more than fifty thousand, the mission found itself surrounded on three sides by housing developments. Some of the land had to be sold to make room for the highway that runs in front of the church. In 1929 the denomination had sold thirty-seven acres to the city of Lawton for $2,775. Of this, $1,375 had been used immediately for a piano and various repairs to the church, lodge, and parsonage.

51. Nov. 16, 1956, 9.
52. "Our Ministry to the Comanches," *Church Herald*, Nov. 15, 1957, 12.

Over the years several Indian families associated with the church had moved to the church property without any formal agreement or sale. They simply became more-or-less permanent squatters by mutual consent, and the church charged them twenty cents a month to pay for city water. But eventually the church needed additional Sunday school space and a new parsonage. The solution, it seemed to the mission board and administrators, was to sell some of the property not needed by the church. By that time, the property had become much more valuable because of the adjacent housing. This meant, of course, removing the people who had lived there for many years and had come to regard the place as their home. The sale was made in 1955, although no announcement was ever made in the annual reports of the Board of Domestic Missions or in the pages of the *Church Herald*. The church addition and parsonage were then built. A motel and apartment complex, as well as private homes, were built on the vacated church property.

The sale of the property and the subsequent removal of Indians from their homes caused strains in the life of the church. Several church members left, and the issue is still a sore spot in the minds of some who believe that the Reformed Church sold land that was rightfully theirs.

The Comanche Congregation Becomes Self-Supporting

In 1957 the American Indian churches were at last transferred from the Classis of New York to a classis in the general geographical area. The two Oklahoma churches—Comanche and Apache—as well as the Jicarilla Apache Reformed Church of Dulce, New Mexico, were transferred to the Classis of West Central in the Particular Synod of Iowa.

In 1962 the Comanche Reformed Church took a step that no other Reformed Native American congregation has taken—it moved beyond mission status and became self-supporting. For some years the congregation had been carrying its own operating expenses, but now it also assumed responsibility for the support of its pastor. The new status meant that the Comanche church was no longer under the jurisdiction of the Board of North American Missions and was amenable only to its classis in matters of church polity.

How, with a congregation of only 121 communicant members, could the church take a step like this? For one thing, it applied for and received a salary supplement, as did many new or smaller congregations of the Reformed Church. A second source of financial confidence lay in the bequest of a faithful member of the church known throughout most of her life as Lucy Sixteen. Herein lies a fascinating tale.

Charlie Hot Coffee, John Sixteen, and Lucy Sixteen

Among the early Comanche converts was a woman named Tahwatistahkernaker, but who was given the name of Lucy by an early mission worker, Jennie Lewis. Lucy married a Comanche man, Chattahsy, who, when he visited the cow camps, always asked for hot coffee and became known by Indians and whites alike as Charlie Hot Coffee. Chattahsy and Lucy attended the camp meetings each year, and eventually Chattahsy was converted. He joined the Comanche church in 1907, the year it was organized, and became a deacon two years later.

Chattahsy died in 1922, and Lucy married another Christian Comanche man, Wuthtakwah, better known as John Sixteen because he so often quoted John 3:16. Now Lucy became known as Lucy Sixteen, and she became something of a legend in her own time. The story is told that she and her husband owned an automobile, but that every few miles she ordered John to stop the car, saying, "Him get tired just like horse. Rest him a little."

John Sixteen died in 1951, and Lucy continued to live in the small house they had built on church land just west of the mission. She died in 1960 at the age of ninety-three, having refused to the end to have her dirt-floor dwelling wired for electricity, preferring kerosene and wood, which she gathered herself. She left behind a fortune of more than $100,000, a staggering amount in that day, amassed primarily from oil royalties from the land allotments of her mother and two husbands. Her only child had died in infancy, and her will stipulated that half of her fortune should go to the Comanche church. Over the years some of these funds were used for building projects, and the rest were used to support the program of the church.

Chaat, the Communicator

From the very beginning of his ministry, even as a student assistant, Robert Chaat was a frequent and skilled communicator, his articles appearing at least once a year and often twice a year in the pages of the *Church Herald*. These regular communications stopped in 1958, a year after he had announced a "time of real testing" in the church.

One more article, "Growing in Maturity," appeared in the November 9, 1962, issue of the *Church Herald*. In this piece, Chaat announced that the Comanche church had left mission status to become self-sufficient. After that, no articles by Chaat appeared in the *Church Herald*. The magazine's Mission of the Month articles were assigned to promote the mission projects of the Reformed Church, and since the Comanche church was no longer a mission, Chaat was not requested to contribute.

Property Transferred to the Comanche Church

Shortly after rescinding its mission status, the church began suggesting to mission administrators and the Board of North American Missions that the board ought to transfer to the church the remaining thirty acres adjacent to the church and parsonage. Apparently there were verbal agreements followed by delays and changes, a source of annoyance and confusion to the consistory.

Early in 1967 the Reverend Albert Van Dyke, newly appointed as the director of Indian work for the Board of North American Missions, met with the consistory of the Comanche church to hear its request for the transfer of property. The church was mature enough to handle the property responsibly, the consistory argued, and they were afraid that if the board kept possession it would continue to sell the land until there was nothing left.

Van Dyke sympathized with their concern but pointed out that all the proceeds of the property sale in 1955 had been used for the Comanche church. He also expressed concern that "some sharp man would take it away for a song."[53] Nevertheless, he was personally inclined to honor the request, an opinion he relayed to the board.

The Board of North American Missions responded by voicing several concerns and considerations, namely that the land was originally given to the Reformed Church by the government and that it had never been tribal or Indian land; all proceeds from the previous sale of the land had been used for buildings and programs at Comanche; most new congregations have to pay for their land through loans; the area of the church is adequate for present and future needs; numerical growth has been small; and there is a danger that the church will sell off land to support programs, as it did with some of Lucy Sixteen's legacy. In addition, the board suggested the possibility of joint control and administration of the property. It also pointed out that even if the church were given the property, it would need classis permission to sell it.

53. Letter from Albert Van Dyke to Beth Marcus, Feb. 3, 1967.

After several more years of discussion, correspondence, and debate, the consistory of the Comanche Reformed Church took formal action. In a letter dated June 13, 1971, the consistory addressed the General Program Council of the Reformed Church in America. Drawing on a recent action of the council, the consistory employed a new tactic in its request:

> In accordance with policy of the General Program Council to transfer all properties to local institutions, thereby divesting the National Church of any holdings in local areas, and because we feel that it would be of great benefit to the work of the church, the consistory and congregation of the Comanche Reformed Church, Lawton, Oklahoma, requests that the parcel of land now held by the General Program Council, R.C.A., be transferred to the Comanche Reformed Church.

The letter was signed by moderator Robert Chaat, elders Lawrence Tomah Jr. and Philip Narcomey, and deacons Weckeah Bradley and Ted Chaat. Three of the five, incidentally, were members of the Chaat family—Robert, his son Ted, and son-in-law Lawrence Tomah.

In response, the General Program Council in November of 1971 voted:

> To recommend to the General Synod Executive Committee that real estate property now owned by the Board of North American Mission, used by the Comanche Reformed Church for church purposes and cemetery purposes in Lawton, Oklahoma, be deeded to the Comanche Reformed Church.[54]

This was done, the document goes on to say, in keeping with World Mission objectives that local congregations have full charge of the resources involved with their programs. The land in question was about thirteen acres. The Board of North American Missions then deeded the property to the Comanche church.

Chaat Retires

As noted above, Chaat signed the property request as moderator rather than as pastor. In 1969, when he was sixty-nine years old, rather reluctantly and with some urging by the classis, Chaat retired from the

54. Minutes of the General Program Council, Nov. 9-11, 1971, 71-34.

Albert Van Dyke, director of Indian work, presents the deed for
the Comanche church property to Robert Chaat and Comanche
consistory members Philip Narcomey, Lawrence Tomah, Ted Chaat,
and Wells Blevins.

gospel ministry of the Reformed Church in America. He stayed on for
two more years as moderator. When he finally stepped down entirely in
1971, he had spent all forty-seven of his ministry years at the Comanche
Reformed Church—six as assistant minister, thirty-nine as ordained
pastor, and two as moderator. Robert and Elsie Chaat retired to a home
they had built in Medicine Park, a few miles north of Fort Sill.

Statistics reported to the General Synod indicate a gradually
declining membership from 1957, when reliable statistics were first
available, to 1971, the last year of Chaat's tenure as pastor and then as
moderator. Communicant membership was reported as 135 in 1957,
and by 1971 had dropped to 73. The number of church-related families
dropped less dramatically, from 58 to 50. Members in the inactive
category remained fairly constant in the mid thirties, with few people
ever being dropped. Sunday school enrollment dropped gradually, with
some fluctuations, from 84 in 1957 to 46 in 1971.

In the same year, it was discovered that the church bell was in
danger of falling. The bell had been cast in Troy, New York, presented
by Louise Runk of New York, chairman of the Committee on Indian
Missions, and brought to the first building site in 1905. Weckeah
Bradley, in his reminiscences of the church, tells of the women of the
church, who when they heard of the bell being carted away with the
lumber, quickly hitched up the horses to a wagon and brought the bell

back to the mission, where it was put on a sturdy scaffolding on the south side of the lodge. Then, when the new church was built in 1941, the bell was placed in the steeple.

Now the bell was moved once more, this time to a wishing-well pedestal matching the stone on the church. The bell was dedicated in its new location May 30, 1971. Participants included Chaat and representatives from the Institute of the Great Plains (which contributed to the project) and the Fort Sill Museum.

On October 26, 1974, Northwestern College in Orange City, Iowa, conferred on Chaat the honorary Doctor of Divinity degree, recognizing him for his long service at Lawton and as the first American Indian to be ordained by the Reformed Church in America. The degree was conferred by Northwestern's president, Lars Granberg, at a meeting of the American Indian Council in Winnebago, Nebraska.

The Reverend Robert Chaat died October 7, 1992, at the age of ninety-two. At the funeral the Reverend Eugene Heideman, secretary for program, represented the Reformed Church General Program Council, and Arvilla Craig of the nearby Apache Reformed Church expressed condolences on behalf of the American Indian Council. The Chaat family established on his behalf the Reverend Robert Paul Chaat Memorial Scholarship Fund at Cook College and Theological School in Tempe, Arizona.

Elsie Tahkofper Chaat died January 25, 1998, at the age of ninety-three, leaving five children, eleven grandchildren, twenty great-grandchildren, and two great-great grandchildren. A daughter, Dorothy Tomah, who died in 2003, was active not only in the Comanche church but also served on the Reformed Church's American Indian Council. She also served on the General Program Council for two three-year terms, 1982-88, representing the American Indian Council. A Chaat grandson, Paul Chaat Smith, is the founding editor of the American Indian Movement's *Treaty Council News*. He is also the author, with Robert Allen Warrior, of *Like a Hurricane: The Indian Movement from Alcatraz to Wounded Knee* (New Press, 1996).

Comanche Reformed Church after Robert Chaat

With the retirement of Robert Chaat, there began a period of uncertainty, confusion, controversy, and sometimes chaos—an era that lasted nearly fifteen years. It was signaled by the hiring of a Methodist layperson, John Pahdocony, with a one-year contract. As a youth attending the Fort Sill Indian School, Pahdocony had joined

Children with Herman Van Galen
at an Easter egg hunt in 1975

the Comanche church and later joined a Methodist church. When his contract was up, the congregation wished to keep him, but the consistory voted to let him go. This action ignited animosities that had been smoldering for some time, and the situation became so hostile that members of the vying factions refused to sit down with each other at church suppers.

Van Galens Arrive, 1973

The calling of the Reverend Herman Van Galen in 1973 marked the first white pastorate at Lawton in forty years. Herman and Joyce Van Galen had served for twelve years (1957-68) as lay missionaries in Mescalero, New Mexico; then Herman decided to pursue the ordained ministry. He obtained a bachelor's degree from Northwestern College in 1970 and a Master of Divinity degree from Western Theological Seminary in 1973, after which he accepted the call to Lawton.

In an effort to create a climate of reconciliation in the church, Van Galen made numerous visits on Saturdays, held church dinners on Sundays, and tried to make sure that no one was ostracized. He received support from retired pastor Chaat, who declined invitations by parishioners to conduct funerals and weddings but was willing to participate with Van Galen when invited to do so. Finding the church financial records in disarray, Van Galen took over financial responsibilities for the church but required that checks be cosigned.

Although reported communicant membership remained constant at about seventy during this time, Van Galen reported that church attendance increased from about thirty to about sixty.

The inactive category held at about thirty-two, and Sunday school enrollment hovered at about twenty-eight. An average of four new members joined the church each year, about half by confession of faith and half by letter of transfer. At a time when accessions by transfer were rare among Indian churches, the ten new members received by transfer between 1973 and 1978 reflected a significant increase.

Gerald Dykstra Arrives

The Van Galens left Lawton in 1978 to undertake the pastorate of American Reformed Church in Hull, Iowa. Earl Smith, a student at New Brunswick Theological Seminary, came as a student pastor in the fall of 1978 and served until the spring of 1980. The congregation urged Smith to stay, but he moved on to complete his theological education at Western Theological Seminary. He later served the Reformed Church in McKee, Kentucky, and then Umonhon Reformed Church in Macy, Nebraska.

In 1981 the church called the Reverend Gerald Dykstra, who was aged sixty at the time. He and his wife, Dorothy, had last served a thirteen-year pastorate at Primghar, Iowa. At the time of his arrival tribal rivalries, which had erupted twenty years before and had simmered under the surface, began to heat up. These political struggles for power soon spilled over into the church.

Dykstra initiated a regularly published "Letter to Church Members and Friends," sent to 125 homes of members, adherents, and others who in the past had shown an interest in the church. The letters shared current news, urged contributions, included a prayer list, and announced upcoming events. Among the specific items mentioned in the letters were outdoor worship services in the Wichita Mountains and the construction of a handicap ramp, made possible by a gift by long-time church member William Karty. During this time, Ruth Irwin, a white woman whose entire family was active in the church, served as church treasurer, and Charlotte Mullen, a white woman married to an Indian, was the Sunday school superintendent.

The Indian school at Fort Sill closed in 1980, bringing to an end the church's ministry at that institution—although in later years the church's ministry had been limited. The Mission of the Month prayer requests, sent to the denominational offices, can be revealing. Some of Dykstra's requests included thanksgiving for the families who were attending vacation Bible school but also included prayer requests for more faithful attendance at worship, concern over the church's financial needs, and continuing concern about tribal rivalries spilling over into the church.

Seventy-fifth Anniversary, 1982

Since the Comanche and Apache churches had been organized on the same Sunday, May 7, 1907, they celebrated their seventy-fifth anniversary on the same Sunday—May 9, 1982. They held combined worship services in the morning at Comanche, followed by a potluck dinner, and held an evening service at Apache.

Guest speakers were the Reverend Richard Vander Voet, mission secretary for the Americas; and the Reverend Harold Colenbrander, pastor of the Christ Community Church in Denver, Colorado, representing the Classis of West Central. Greetings were brought by Wayne Gilley, mayor of Lawton; William Harbour, chaplain at Fort Still; and the Reverend Herman Van Galen, former pastor. Special recognition was given to the Chaats for their lifetime of service and to Maud Blevins (Tocsi), the only living charter member. Blevins died two years later, in February of 1984, at the age of one hundred.

A photo of the current Comanche consistory, printed in the anniversary book, pictured Charlotte Mullen; Elsie Chaat, the first woman elected to the Comanche consistory; Schley Tahkofper, brother of Elsie Chaat; Lawrence Tomah, husband of Dorothy Chaat; Philip Narcomey; Norman Nauni, and Gerald Dykstra, pastor.

Decision to Eliminate Full-Time Pastorate

In 1985 the consistory of the Comanche church made some decisions that would have long-time consequences. After years of dipping into the bequest left by Lucy Sixteen, the church had completely depleted the fund and found itself unable to meet its expenses. The consistory asked the General Program Council for financial help, and its request was approved. But before that aid could begin, the consistory, unwilling to return to mission status and lose its independence, voted to withdraw its request. Then, in order to meet its budget, it voted to reduce expenses by terminating the services of its pastor and to rely on hiring a Sunday preacher week-by-week. Dykstra, by that time aged sixty-four, decided to retire, and he and Dorothy moved to the site of their previous pastorate, Primghar, Iowa.

Open Hostility

With Dykstra's retirement, the congregation, which had been showing growth in communicant membership (seventy-five to eighty-five over four years) and especially in attendance, again entered a period of uncertainty in leadership. Dr. Seesaran, a retired pastor and dentist, took the pulpit for a year. Seesaran, who was born in India, had converted to Christianity in the United States and had been ordained as a Presbyterian minister, later becoming a dentist.

When Robert Chaat, Jr., a lay pastor in the Methodist denomination in Lawton, was asked to take over, a longstanding tension broke into open hostility. The tension was between the Chaat family and its followers and the Nauni family and its followers. The chief critic of the Chaat family was Raymond "Dink" Nauni, Jr. The Nauni family had a long association with the church, Raymond's father and uncles having been active members and having contributed generously to the church building. Raymond Nauni's Christian testimony includes the story of how a vision brought him to the point of recommitment. He had been strongly influenced by the Christian charismatic movement and was an advocate of including Indian customs and practices in the church. These include "cedaring," in which the ascending cedar smoke is interpreted as symbolic of prayers rising to God.

The critics of Robert Chaat, Jr., said that he didn't visit parishioners often enough, and Chaat said that they were jealous that he had been selected. The Nauni group said that the Chaat family believed they owned the church and that under them the church had become stiff and formal, following the pattern set by the white missionaries and refusing to incorporate Indian culture and distinctiveness. The Chaat group said that the Nauni group wanted power, didn't conform to Reformed policies and theology, and advocated non-Christian Indian practices.

A struggle took place for the control of the church's books, including financial records and the church's checkbook, and there were accusations from both sides about financial impropriety. Many members dropped out, not because they were involved in the dispute, but because they were disgusted and confused by it. Chaat had considerable support in the congregation, which for so many years had been nurtured by his father, but after less than two years he was informed by the consistory that his services were no longer needed. This decision, of course, sparked further unrest.

Next came the Reverend Robert Graham, a pastor originally from Canada but not from the Reformed Church, who claimed to be a chaplain's assistant at Fort Sill, a claim that the chaplain's office later refuted. Graham had filled the pulpit at Comanche on several occasions, and after several months the consistory offered a part-time contract. Graham tried to mitigate the church's divided loyalties by conducting two worship services: one for the Nauni contingent and the other for the Chaat group. Unfortunately, this exacerbated the problem. The split widened, and Graham left in 1993 to do mission work among the Kiowas in nearby Medicine Park, then later returned to Canada. He left behind a seemingly hopeless situation.

Even though the church was no longer a "mission church," the Reverend Robert Terwilliger, the Native American mission administrator for the Reformed Church, together with the Reverend Barbara Nauta, president of the Classis of Red River, met with members of the two factions. The meeting, as a whole, they reported, was positive.

The Ministry of Charles and Judy Spencer

In May of 1994 Charles and Judy Spencer of Oklahoma City visited Lawton, and Charles, as a layman, preached at the Pentecost service. The response of the congregation was positive, and in the fall of that year Spencer entered into a part-time contract to provide services as a student intern.

Spencer, a certified public accountant, had in past years become an alcoholic and had entered the twelve-step program of Our Lord's Community Church in Oklahoma City. Though the ministry of that church he had become a Christian believer. Wishing to be better prepared for Christian service, he enrolled with the Reformed Church's Theological Education Agency and began studies through Phillips Theological Seminary (Disciples of Christ) in Tulsa while helping at Comanche.

Spencer was ordained as a Reformed Church minister in 1996 and shortly thereafter was installed as pastor of the Comanche Reformed Church on a part-time contract. Spencer, who is still the pastor at Comanche as of this writing, works two or three days a week for the church while maintaining an accounting business in Oklahoma City, where his wife Judy is a high school teacher.

When Spencer arrived, members of the Chaat family had long since left the congregation and few of the original Chaat supporters remained. Spencer was, however, able to maintain a good relationship

Pastor Charles Spencer with worship leader
Raymond Nauni, Jr., in 1997

with Robert Chaat, Jr., and at Spencer's invitation the two conducted several funerals together.

As of this writing Raymond Nauni, Jr., frequently assists in worship services, leading the singing of Comanche hymns, sharing congregational concerns, and leading in prayer. Spencer, with a background in the charismatic Our Lord's Community Church, is open to all spiritual gifts and supports Nauni's emphasis on free-spirited worship, but at the same time he places a strong emphasis on Reformed theology. He has led the adult Sunday school class in a study of the Heidelberg Catechism, frequently preaches from the catechism, and recites with the congregation the Apostles and Nicene Creeds.

Although the annual statistical reports did not indicate it, attendance dropped to less than twenty during the darkest days of the church's struggles. Attendance has gradually increased to about sixty on an average Sunday morning, with several confessions of faith each year. Sunday school continues to struggle, often with less than twenty in attendance, as does the youth ministry. Reaching children and youth is made difficult in this nonreservation setting by the fact that the youth of the church are scattered among eight to ten area schools.

Several other denominations maintain Indian congregations in the Lawton area, including the Methodist, Baptist, Nazarene, and Roman Catholic churches. The Native American Church maintains a presence but is not a major religious factor in this area of Okalahoma. Several members of the Comanche congregation participate in an

Long-time members Philip and Gladys Narcomey. Mrs. Narcomey is a granddaughter of early leader, Periconic.

interdenominational Comanche hymn-singing class in an effort to keep alive that part of the Indian/Christian heritage.

In recent years the ministry of the Comanche Reformed Church has inspired at least one member to follow full-time Christian service. Ralph "Butch" Seahmer, who grew up as a Baptist, was employed by the church to do roof work. He began to attend services and joined the church shortly thereafter. He was encouraged by the congregation to attend Cook College and Theological School, from which he received an associate in arts degree in 1999. He began work that year as a ministry assistant at Umonhon Reformed Church in Macy, Nebraska, a position he held for two years before moving on to do youth work in Nevada.

The Comanche Reformed Church, like the nearby Apache Reformed Church, continues its ministry as evidence of the labors of such legendary missionaries as Frank Hall Wright, Walter and Mary Roe, Maud Adkisson, and Richard and Ella Mae Harper. The church maintains the distinction of not only raising up, but also thriving for nearly forty years under the ministry of the Reformed Church's first Native American pastoral couple, the Reverend Robert and Elsie Chaat.

To this day it is the only one of the Indian congregations that does not depend on financial support from the Reformed Church in America. At the advice of the Advisory Committee on Church Vocations, the 2003 General Synod passed this recommendation: "To urge the General Synod Council to explore possibilities for working with the Comanche Reformed Church in Lawton, Oklahoma, in developing a model for a ministry with the RCA's Native American Indian congregations," one reason being that "This ministry in Oklahoma is a model of a self-supporting indigenous congregation."[55]

55. *Minutes of the General Synod*, 2003, 112.

CHAPTER 6

The Mission in Mescalero, New Mexico, and the Mescalero Reformed Church

The Mescaleros are one of six bands of Apaches who descended from the Athapascan-speaking peoples who migrated to the Southwest from Canada some time between 1300 and 1500 A.D. , the others being the Western Apache, Chiricahua, Jicarilla, Lipan, and Kiowa. The name, "Mescalero," comes from the clan's use of the mescal cactus for food, drink, thread, and fabric.

The Mescaleros traded peacefully with the Spaniards when the latter advanced into the area. The Spaniards traded horses, weapons, and liquor, and the Indians provided buffalo hides, robes, and food. But as the buffalo disappeared and other sources of food diminished, the Mescaleros turned to raiding in order to survive. Unable to stop the raids, the Spaniards introduced a program of free food and alcohol, which solved the problem for a while.

Then Mexico gained independence from Spain in 1821, and Mexico adopted a new approach to the Apache problem: extermination. The Mexican government offered rewards for Apache scalps, and the Apaches retaliated by murdering settlers and stealing livestock.

When the United States acquired the Southwest under the Treaty of Guadalupe Hidalgo in 1848 following the Mexican-American War, it appeared that peace might return. But when it came to justice for the indigenous peoples, Americans proved to be no better than the Spaniards and Mexicans before them. A new wave of land-grabbing and treaty-breaking led to increased violence.

The government gradually rounded up the Mescalero people and located them in a semi-arid area of New Mexico known as Bosque Redondo. Here the Mescaleros planted crops and seemed to be willing to stay, until the government relocated thousands of Navahos—traditional enemies of the Apaches—in the same area of forty square miles. On the night of November 8, 1864, all of the Mescaleros vanished, and for several years the military forces found it difficult to find them, much less to round them up.

The Mescalero Reservation

In 1871 the U.S. Government brought an end to the Apache wars and began the peace process by establishing reservations for the Indian people. One of the first of these (1873) was a reservation for the Mescaleros in south-central New Mexico, between present-day Ruidoso and Alamogordo, about thirty miles northeast of the White Sands National Monument and about one hundred miles from the borders of Texas and Mexico.

Ironically, the Mescalero reservation is one of the most attractive pieces of real estate in southern New Mexico. Located in a rugged, high-altitude area adjacent to the Sacramento Mountains on the south, its relatively cool summer days and cooler nights are in stark contrast to the heat of the surrounding desert. The highest point is Sierra Blanca, "White Mountain," 12,003 feet above sea level, traditional sacred mountain of the Mescaleros, and its lowest elevation is Three Rivers, with an elevation of 5,450 feet. Its rugged terrain is covered with forests of Ponderosa pine, Douglas fir, white oak, and juniper.

For reasons that are not clear, the tribe was exempted from the evils of the Dawes Act of 1887, and the Mescaleros did not receive separate allotments. The population numbered about four hundred when the reservation was first established, and it was augmented modestly in 1903 with the arrival of Lipan Apaches from Texas and Mexico. Then, as we have previously described, 163 Chiricahua Apaches chose to move to the Mescalero reservation in 1913 when they were released from their twenty-seven-year captivity in Florida, Alabama, and Oklahoma.

Dance of the Mountain Gods

The Mescaleros share many traditions, such as coming-of-age ceremonies, with other tribes. One dance—the dance of the mountain gods, also known as the crown dance because of its distinctive headgear—is a favorite of the Apaches.

The Mescalero tribe's welcome sign features a crown dancer.

The dance is based on the legend of two young men, one blind and the other lame, who, when the tribe was attacked, were hidden by their families in a mountain cave until the tribe could safely return. As their provisions were running out, according to the legend, the two men were visited by four figures with black masks and great headdresses that represented north, south, east, and west. The two men were then joined by a fifth mountain god—for that is what they were—this one dressed in white. The gods led the fugitives out of the cave, healed them of their blindness and lameness, and reunited them with their tribe. The dance that reenacts that story has become a regular feature of the coming-of-age ceremonies.

The Town of Mescalero Today

The present town of Mescalero is the only town on the reservation. U.S. Highway 70, the primary route between Alamogordo, to the southwest, and Roswell, seventy-five miles to the east, runs through Mescalero. The Reformed church, built in a distinctive southwestern style, together with the parsonage, workers' home, and arbor, sit on a hill overlooking the highway.

Other churches on the reservation include the Church of the Latter Day Saints, the Apache Assembly of God, the nondenominational Carrizo Fellowship, the First Baptist Church, and the historic St. Joseph's Catholic Church. There is no Native American church here because of restrictions against the use of peyote.

Mescalero's facilities are typical for a reservation town: a tribal center, the Bureau of Indian Affairs headquarters, a general store, a museum, tribal police headquarters, and a small hospital. Historic settlements remain in outlying areas such as White Tail and Carizzo, and the tribe has developed several additional clusters of new homes. Mescalero has its own school and school board, the K-12 facility having been completed in 2002.

Sources of income for the tribe include a ski resort and timber and cattle businesses. The plush Inn of the Mountain Gods, with its 230 guest rooms, golf course, and complete recreational facilities, together with the Apache Casino, are the most lucrative of the tribe's businesses. With the exception of a few privately owned acres, the tribe owns all of the land on the reservation. Specific tracts, called "assignments," are granted for use by individuals, but even these are owned and regulated by the tribe. About four thousand people are enrolled as members of the Mescalero tribe, but not all of them live on the reservation.

Mission in Mescalero Begins, 1907

The ministry of the Reformed Church in Mescalero began upon the recommendation of the Reverend Walter Roe, a missionary in Colony, Oklahoma. During one of his winter trips, Roe visited the agency and school at Mescalero, which he described as "a valley surrounded by mountains of grandeur and beauty unspeakable."[1]

Agent James Carroll encouraged Roe to begin a mission near the school, and Roe brought the proposal to the Women's Executive Committee of the Board of Domestic Missions. Approval was immediate and enthusiastic. In a letter dated May 21, 1907, Carroll responded to the board's decision by writing, "I can safely assure you of the hearty cooperation of the Hon. Commissioner of Indian Affairs; and as regards the attitude of this office, so long as I shall remain in charge, you may rely on me absolutely to lend you every possible assistance, personally and officially." Carroll went on to urge that the mission be established very near the agency, offering lumber at the cost of manufacture and water and light at nominal cost and perhaps free. Carroll ended the letter with a postscript that contained a threat that was only slightly veiled (underlines are his):

1. Elizabeth Page, *In Camp and Tepee: An Indian Mission Story* (New York, Chicago, and Toronto: Fleming H. Revell, 1915), 216.

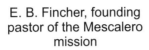

E. B. Fincher, founding
pastor of the Mescalero
mission

I will go to any length to help a fellow who shows a disposition to attend to <u>his own business;</u> I should have little patience with the one who assumed that 'twas his prime duty to become the censor of my official conduct, and much less for one who showed a disposition to <u>openly</u> criticize me because forsooth, my private life failed to measure up to his standard.[2]

In August of that year Roe addressed a letter to "Dear Fellow-Workers of the Reformed Church." Of the Mescalero Apaches he said that civilization "has laid but a light hand upon their aboriginal life and character," and that when he had preached there it was only the second Protestant sermon the children had heard in four years. These people, he said, are "absolute heathens in a Christian land, but deserted by the Church of Christ in that land and without hope of missionary succor from other lands."[3]

E. B. Fincher Arrives

The response of Reformed congregations was generous and immediate, and by November of that year (1907) the Reverend E. B.

2. Letter from James A. Carroll, Supt. of the United States Indian Service of the Department of the Interior, to Walter C. Roe, Colony, Oklahoma, May 21, 1907.
3. Page, *In Camp and Tepee*, 217.

Fincher and his wife (neither of whose first name, to this author's knowledge, was ever revealed), arrived by wagon to begin work there. Fincher came from the Southern Presbyterian Church and had served for the prior two years as pastor of the First Presbyterian Church in Amarillo, Texas. The initial contact, no doubt, had been made by Roe, himself a Presbyterian from Texas.

Fincher was supported in this new work by the Classis of Iowa. He hired as his interpreter a young educated Apache, Solon Sombrero, who was to become one of the church's most stalwart members. Sombrero not only interpreted Fincher's Sunday sermons but also traveled with him as he went on horseback from camp to camp. The Mescaleros called Fincher *etenadiglish*, "the man who prays for us," and gave all subsequent missionaries that same name.

In 1908 Fincher gave this report of his work:

> I spent about three days in each week among the camps trying to win their confidence, or reading the Bible to them and praying with them. I have ridden about seventy-five miles each week in reaching these people.
>
> Each Sabbath morning I hold service for the camp Indians through an interpreter. To this a few old people and some thirty or forty of the school children come. We make singing quite a feature of the night service and after some ten hymns I preach in English to a mixed audience of forty or fifty people. The work is extremely difficult and sometimes discouraging.[4]

Fincher's acceptance among the Mescaleros may have been enhanced by one of their legends that forecasts (to summarize), "there will be coming a white man carrying a black book that contains the words of life. Listen to him."

The Mescalero Church Is Organized

The parsonage was built in the summer of 1908. A tent was secured as a place of worship until lumber could be secured for the new church.

The Mescalero Reformed Church was organized January 3, 1909, just two years after the work began. Fincher reported nineteen members but did not indicate how many were adults, youth, or children. Juan

---

4. *Annual Report of the Executive Committee of the Women's Board of Domestic Missions*, 1908, 29.

The original Mescalero church, dediated in 1910

Sanspeur, a man of mature years and one of the three chiefs of the Mescaleros, was elected elder; and Solon Sombrero, the interpreter, was elected deacon. There is no evidence that classis representatives were present for the service of organization. A young people's service was soon added on Sunday afternoons, as was an additional meeting on Tuesday evenings.

The Church Building Is Dedicated

It was not until the following Thanksgiving Day that the congregation was able to move out of the tent and into a new wooden church building. Gone were the "two years in the tent, with dust and dogs and dead odors."[5] The building was dedicated March 13, 1910, with Roe preaching. The morning sermon used the services of Sombrero as interpreter; and the evening sermon was given without an interpreter for the benefit of government employees and other English-speaking people of the area. Meanwhile, the Iowa Classis was continuing to meet its pledged support.

Fincher Is Succeeded by Harper

Shortly after the new building was dedicated, Fincher left Mescalero to serve the First Presbyterian Church in McKinney, Texas. Here, according to that church's website, "he endeared himself to the children by visiting the public schools regularly to tell them stories of the Apache Indians with whom he had worked."[6]

5. L. L. Legters, "The New Mescalero Church," *Christian Intelligencer*, Dec. 5, 1909, 814.
6. Website of the First Presbyterian Church in McKinney, Texas, July 2002.

Original mission site in Mescalero

The reasons for Fincher's leaving after less than three years were reported only as "owing to family reasons and the pressure brought to bear by old friends."[7] Fincher later became superintendent of Home Missions for the Dallas Presbytery, retiring in 1946.

The Women's Board now turned to the Reverend Richard Harper, another Presbyterian clergyman, who had served briefly as assistant to Roe in Colony and for a year at the short-lived white Reformed Church congregation in Shawnee, Oklahoma. Harper assumed the pastorate in Mescalero in November of 1910 and immediately set in motion a drive for a lodge, patterned after the prototype established in Colony ten years earlier. That dream was achieved two years later, with help from $1,536, raised by the Women's Board. The building was named the Mrs. S. A. Sandham Memorial, after an early benefactor of Indian missions. The eight-room building with a huge front porch served as a social center for the Indians and included a room for the sick as well as centers for teaching homemaking skills to women and woodworking to men.

Twenty-five members were received by Harper that first year. Electric light fixtures were installed at the church, a gift of Otipoby, an elder of the Comanche church. The following few years were much more difficult, with brave reports about making a "faithful effort" to teach the catechism, and Indians who were "thinking seriously" about the gospel.[8] The Roman Catholic Church began work on the reservation, building an impressive church not far from the Reformed mission, with the immediate effect of attracting some of the Reformed church's Sunday school children.

7. Page, *In Camp and Tepee*, 221.
8. *Annual Report of the Women's Board of Domestic Missions of the Reformed Church in America*, 1913, 28.

One modification made during Harper's time was the hanging of a curtain in the church, shutting off part of the sanctuary. Older women could then sit behind the curtain, in deference to the old taboo that forbade mothers-in-law from looking into the eyes of sons-in-law. Early in 1913 an effort was made to employ the camp-meeting approach, following the pattern set by the church in Colony. Former pastor Fincher came as the speaker, and seventeen people made confession of faith.

A mission study lesson in the children's mission publication, the *Day Star*, gives insight into the life of the Mescalero Apaches, at least from the white missionary's point of view:

> The Mescalero tepees, tents, and houses are not as clean as they should be, nor do they take proper care of themselves. But they are learning the ways of civilization. The women attend a sewing class which Mrs. Harper has for them on Thursday afternoons. They wear a dress more like that of their white sisters than the "camp dress" of Indian tribes, while the men wear citizen's clothes and cut their hair.
>
> They are not lazy, but generally industrious. Unlike many Indian tribes they own no land, but cultivate tracts which they are permitted to use. In a good season thousands of bushels of oats are grown and some potatoes. Hundreds of cords of wood for fuel are cut and sold, and a few men of the tribe own sheep and goats whose wool and hair they sell. The women are basket-makers and do some bead work. Then there is "grass money" paid by white men for the privilege of grazing cattle and sheep on the reservation. But the Mescaleros have a small income all told, and were it not that deer and wild turkeys are plentiful, would have a hard time. Yet out of their poverty they gave forty dollars toward the support of their own services and thirty dollars to missions last year....The government maintains a free boarding school. The children attend school a half day and are taught to work with their hands the other half.[9]

The Chiricahua Apaches Arrive, 1913

In April of 1913 the long-rumored and long-negotiated event finally happened: the Chiricahua Apaches, who had been detained as

9. "The Mescalero Apaches," Red Men IX segment of "Our Mission Study Lessons," *Day Star*, June 1912.

prisoners of war at Fort Sill, Oklahoma, were released after twenty-seven years of captivity. They had been given a choice: receive an allotment of 160 acres in Oklahoma or join their Apache cousins in Mescalero, on their reservation in southern New Mexico. About two-thirds of the Apaches, despite their mistrust of the government, their separation from family and friends, and fear of the unknown, chose the Mescalero option.

The Reverend Henry Sluyter, pastor of the Comanches and Apaches at Lawton, accompanied the Apaches on a special train to their new home. He and T. E. Brents, a special enforcement officer from the U.S. Department of the Interior, were prepared to face threats of violence from white people along the way. They had been warned by U.S. senators in Washington and cattle barons in the Mescalero area that they would fall victim to a wild band of cutthroats whose sole object was to destroy and plunder. As it turned out, the only incident was the discovery of a small dog that had been smuggled on board in a blanket, against railroad orders. Here are excerpts from Sluyter's personal account:

> At four o'clock on Wednesday afternoon [April 2, 1913] the special train of five tourist cars, eight freight and stock cars and two baggage cars pulled out of the Fort Sill station. Beside the 170 Apaches on board, there were Major Goode, who has had charge of the prisoners of war the last two years, Sergeant Branch, one of the major's aides, a doctor, a nurse, three private soldiers, Mr. Brents, the writer of this article, Miss [Hendrina] Hospers and Miss [Martha] Prince [the two women transferred by the Women's Board of Domestic Missions from the Fort Sill Mission to the Mescalero Mission]. At Tucomari, N.M., the first stop of importance was made. Here the train was greeted by crowds of people who thronged around the station to get a glimpse of the famous Geronimo band. Young and old, rich and poor, white and black—all were there. The schools had been dismissed for the occasion. [Some] pointed out Miss Hospers and Miss Prince as daughters or captives of Geronimo. The wife of Geronimo was with us but she kept herself quite in the background. Such beadwork as the Indians had was bought up eagerly by the sightseers....

> It was a great relief to the Mescalero agent, C. S. Jeffries, his deputies, and our missionary, Rev. R. H. Harper, to see the

Dismission certificate from the
original letters of transfer of the
Fort Sill Apaches to the Mescalero
Reformed Church

A **Certificate of Dismission**

Was Granted

Mrs. *Hannah B. elatchu*

Mar. 21st 1913

to the *Reformed*

Church of *Mescalero N'Mex*

Given at *Fort Sill Okla*

Henry Slinyler
                        Pastor.

Register Number of
Dismissed Member.

Baptized children of the above were also dismissed:

NAME.	Register Number.	AGE.

headlight of the special train in sight about 2:30 o'clock Friday morning. In a remarkably short time the horses were unloaded and fed. The closest vigilance was kept up the remainder of the night.

A large camp of Mescalero Indians awaited our coming to truck household goods, baggage, etc., up the winding road for eighteen miles to the Mescalero agency, situated 6,600 feet above sea-level....It gave a thrill of satisfaction to know that we were accompanying a band of Indians not cutthroats but men, women, and children, clothed and in their right mind, a model lot, and in the words of the government special enforcement agent, "the best bunch of Indians in the country."[10]

Eighty-seven of the Apaches and the two white mission workers carried with them transfers of membership from the Apache mission church to the Mescalero mission church.[11] Among them were George Martine, an interpreter; his wife, Lillian; and their daughter, Evelyn Gaines. Also present were Christian Naiche, the hereditary chief of

10. Page, *In Camp and Tepee*, 237-39.
11. Their original membership documents are housed in the Archives of the Reformed Church in America, in New Brunswick, New Jersey.

Uncas Noche, long-time
interpreter, and his wife, Mary

the Chiricahuas; Uncas Noche, the blind interpreter; and Eugene
Chihuahua, leader of Apache singing.

The government had provided tents for the new arrivals, and these
were set up in the vicinity of the agency, with the promise of relocation
to a more permanent location on the reservation. Hospers and Prince,
who had brought a tent with them from Oklahoma, camped alongside
the Apaches.

Despite dire predictions of Apache carnage from New Mexico's
Senator Albert Fall, the most serious conflict occurred a few months
later, when the Chiricahua Apache baseball team defeated the city team
of nearby Cloudcroft, 22-2.

Assimilation Not Easy

The blending of the two tribes was neither easy nor immediate.
Although united by blood and language, they brought contrasting
life experiences. The Mescaleros, about 450 in number, were largely
untouched by the dominant culture or the Christian religion, having
lived as nomads except for the last six years, when they dwelled in an
isolated reservation. The Chiricahuas, on the other hand, had spent
twenty years in close proximity with the white culture at Fort Sill, had
lived in wooden houses, were better educated, and counted at least half
of their number as Christian believers. One religious difference emerged
immediately: the Mescaleros participated in traditional celebrations
while the Chiricahuas—influenced for decades by the strict missionaries
and the mission school at Fort Sill—did not.

The situation in the church was no easier. Suddenly the majority
of members were newcomers from Oklahoma, and Harper reported:

> ...one effect of their coming, which could not be foreseen,
> developed; the Mescalero adults almost abandoned our services.
> Various reasons were given, but none of them were of any value.
> For many months this condition continued, but now we are

happy to say the Mescaleros are slowly returning to the Church; some of them have become professing Christians during the past winter and the two bands are getting along harmoniously.[12]

The Mescalero Church Is Organized (Again)

Harper said in the same report that in June 1913 he and Henry Sluyter, having been appointed by the Classis of New York to do so, met at Mescalero and officially organized the Reformed Church in Mescalero. This report gives credence to the suspicion that Fincher's organization of the church in 1909 was his personal action without classis approval or participation. The consistory members included Juan Sanspeur, Naiche, and Solon Sombrero, elders; and John Shanta and Quinah, deacons, with a third deacon to be elected later.

Within a year after accompanying the former prisoners to their new home, the two female staff members left Mescalero. Martha Prince left to get married, and Hendrina Hospers was invited by J. Denton Simms, Harper's son-in-law, to accompany him to Dulce, New Mexico, to help found a mission there among the Jicarilla Apaches. Hospers would continue to serve in Dulce for thirty-two years.

Economic Difficulties

The Chirichua Apaches lived for nearly a year in tents surrounding the agency then gradually began moving their tents to White Tail Canyon, a narrow, eight-mile valley in the northeastern part of the reservation, about twenty miles from the agency and the mission. Harper purchased a large tent for church services at White Tail and also began a Sunday school there. For a time he also conducted a Sunday school for white people who worked at the government sawmill. In 1914 he reported a total enrollment of 225 at the three schools and a total church membership of 180. The Fort Sill Apaches had brought several Apache hymns with them, and these were added to the worship service format.

While the social and religious integration of the two Indian groups caused some difficulties, the economic situation proved to be more problematic. The government had sold nearly seven thousand head of Apache cattle in Oklahoma, with the promise that these funds would be used to purchase livestock at Mescalero. With very little

12. *Annual Report of the Women's Board of Domestic Missions*, 1914, 32.

tillable land available in their new homeland, raising sheep and cattle was about the only viable option for making a living. But some of the grazing land had been leased again to white men, and the cattle funds were not forthcoming. These funds, which were to have been deposited in a special account with the U.S. Treasury, somehow disappeared. Elizabeth Page tells of Naiche's travail as he waited for the arrival of their rightful funds from the government:

> Every morning Naiche, who was holding his people to their work with an iron grip, rode up to the agency to see if it had come, and every morning he returned, a pathetic figure in his stoical disappointment, to face the jeers of his waiting camp. Late in August came a belated payment and twelve hundred cattle were purchased against the seven thousand left behind....The Indians, inured to injustice, accepted the inevitable.[13]

These were trying times for the Indians, with several epidemics sweeping through the reservation. A long siege of whooping cough in 1915-16 took the lives of more than half the babies. Crop failures were common on the small common family acreages allotted for agricultural purposes. In addition, the Indians did not receive a $16,000 fund promised for general resettlement purposes, allocated in 1913, until 1918. Many of the Chiricahuas wished they had remained in Oklahoma.

Arthur Conducts Ministry in White Tail

To help with the Chirichuas in White Tail Canyon, the mission board turned to James Arthur and his wife, Katherine, Presbyterian workers who had served for two years at the West Side Chapel in Winnebago, Nebraska. They began work in mid-1914 and lived in a tent for several months until a house could be erected.

Harper, acknowledging that the past year had been "one of testing,"[14] ended his service in January of 1915 to accept the pastorate of the Comanche Reformed Church in Lawton, Oklahoma. The next two pastors came and went with alarming speed, hardly receiving mention in either the board reports or the denomination's periodicals. The Reverend James Dykema, a 1913 graduate of New Brunswick Theological Seminary, served from 1914-15 before moving on to

13. Page, In Camp and Tepee, 240-41.
14. Annual Report of the Women's Board of Domestic Missions, 1915, 43.

East Orange, New Jersey. The next pastor was the Reverend Norman Curtis, of whom little is known except that he was received from the Association of Congregational Universalists in 1916 and left in 1918 for a Presbyterian church in Phoenix, Arizona.

Of concern to the missionaries was the use of a native brew called *tiswin*. Seemingly specific to the Mescaleros, tiswin was made by the older women of the tribe, who buried corn in the earth, then dug it up when it was partly decayed and put it through a secret process. Tiswin was outlawed by the government, but it was very intoxicating and provided a good source of income, and therefore it was hard to control.

It appears that James Arthur, who, according to the *Historical Directory of the Reformed Church in America*, was ordained by the Classis of New York in 1916, was the key leader in the work of the mission. He reinstated annual special meetings and began work on a building to replace the tent church at White Tail, where the Chiricahuas were concentrated. He and several Indian men cleared the ground and hauled building materials from the nearest railway station, thirty-eight miles away. In June 1916 Arthur, one Indian worker, and one white carpenter began to build, and before winter the White Tail chapel was finished. The Indians themselves purchased a bell several years later. Arthur stayed at White Tail until 1919, five years. He transferred to the Presbytery of South Oregon in 1928.

Reported communicant membership spiked from 61 in 1912 to 180 in 1913 because of the arrival of the newcomers, then increased to 192 two years later. The number of reported confessions of faith see-sawed wildly, from a low of three in 1914 to a high of thirty in 1915. The next four reports were identical in all categories, including 189 communicants, indicating that no reports were sent in and that the compilers simply repeated the figures of the previous years.

The local government school for elementary students was a boarding school, which required that children be taken from their parents at age six to live in the dormitories. Attendance at the mission worship services and Sunday school was obligatory, which accounts for attendance of nearly two hundred during most of this time.

A Time of Stability, 1918-30

Stability in ministry was finally achieved in the person of the Reverend Nathan E. Overman and his wife, Melissa, who arrived in 1918 and stayed until 1930. Although the mission had been in existence since 1907, Overman was the first missionary pastor to stay more than five years—the first five pastors having stayed an average of 3.2 years.

Overman came from outside the Reformed Church, as did most of the early missionaries who served the Indian people. He had graduated from Atlanta Theological Seminary in 1909, pastored several Congregational churches, and served as principal of Toccoa Falls Institute, a Presbyterian College in Toccoa Falls, Georgia. He was fifty-eight years old when he arrived in Mescalero.

One of Overman's first policy changes was to require more extensive instruction of candidates for membership. He made no report of new members in 1918, he said, for a reason: "We have been reluctant to take anyone into church membership until there is satisfactory evidence of real conversion, so while several were willing to come as a result of our special meetings in February, we agreed it would be better to put them to the test."[15]

In 1919, influenza took the life of Naiche, hereditary chief of the Chiricahuas when they were first made prisoners of war. He was one of the first converts at Fort Sill and was for many years a quiet yet faithful elder of the church. He had adopted, appropriately, the English name "Christian." Other key leaders during this time were Uncas Noche, the blind man who was mentioned in several accounts as a faithful interpreter and occasional preacher; and Solon Sombrero, interpreter and consistory member.

Mission life settled into something of a routine during these years, with ministry continuing at two sites—in Mescalero itself, near the agency, and in White Tail, where most of the Chiricahua Apaches were settled in their wooden homes.

Special services continued to be held, although attendance gradually declined over the years. In Mescalero these meetings were called special services rather than camp meetings, as they were called elsewhere, and they were held in January or February instead of the more common July and August. Speakers included people like Dirk Lay, a Presbyterian missionary to Indians in Arizona, John Read from Colony, and evangelist Frank Hall Wright. Mary Roe, now a widow, often came to assist.

Christmas was also a highlight each year. The celebration included gifts of toys, books, and clothing given by Reformed Church congregations, a huge dinner, Santa Claus, decorations, a Christmas

---

15. *Annual Report of the Women's Board of Domestic Missions,* 1919, 34.

Camp meeting tent in Mescalero

tree, programs, and candy. Up to three hundred children and adults attended. The lodge continued to be a busy place, and sometimes there were not enough sewing machines to go around. The women also took up beadwork for additional income.

Ministry at Four Settlements

Now the government began to take more interest in the economic development of the tribe, calling for a conference of government and church representatives. The conference included pastors J. Denton Simms of Dulce, G. A. Watermulder of Winnebago, Richard Harper of Lawton, and Overman. There is no hint, however, that any Indians were invited to talk about their financial future. A five-year plan was adopted, a significant segment of which included the allotment of sheep to each family. This changed the dynamics of the reservation, as the sheepherders began to scatter around the reservation.

Three primary centers were established, in addition to the one at Mescalero: White Tail, Carizzo, and Elk Silver (the junction of Elk and Silver canyons). Twenty to thirty small houses were built at each location, each with a chicken house and twenty to forty acres of land for gardening and farming. A small day school was also built at each location, making it unnecessary for children to be shipped away to a boarding school.

In response to this new alignment, the mission established a circuit schedule which, although grueling, made it possible to bring

The White Tail chapel

the services of the church to where the people lived. A typical Sunday schedule, as reported several years later by summer student J. Robert Swart, involved traveling over a hundred miles over winding roads: Sunday school at 10 a.m. and preaching at 11 a.m. at Mescalero; preaching at 1 p.m. at Carizzo; Sunday school at 2:30 and preaching at 3:30 at White Tail; and preaching at 5:30 at Elk Silver.[16]

The facilities included a small chapel at Carizzo and the home of the Sombrero family at Elk Silver. (A rustic log chapel was built there in 1953.) The original White Tail Chapel, together with its church records, was destroyed by a mysterious fire in 1935, and services were held subsequently in the renovated parsonage first used by the Arthur family. In 1940 the White Tail building was renovated further and dedicated as the Scholten Memorial Chapel. The project was underwritten by the women of the Particular Synod of Iowa and named after Mrs. Dirk Scholten, who with her husband had founded several new churches in Iowa. A 1943 photo of the White Tail group, published in the fiftieth anniversary booklet of the Mescalero Reformed Church, shows fourteen women, one man, and four children.

16. J. Robert Swart, "Student Service at Mescalero," *Intelligencer-Leader*, Nov. 5, 1943, 7.

The Ministry Diversifies

In addition to the Sunday schedule, the Reformed and Roman Catholic churches were permitted to conduct released-time classes at the four day schools—Tuesdays at Elk Silver, Wednesdays at Carizzo, Thursdays at White Tail, and Fridays at Mescalero. About eighty-five students were reached in this way. The Reformed mission also conducted Ladies Aid meetings (quilting, embroidering, and Bible study) on the same days.

At this time there were three churches in Mescalero—Reformed, Roman Catholic, and what was described as an "Indian church," a combination of Protestant, Catholic, and native religion—but apparently without the use of peyote. This church, said summer student David Laman in 1937, is "perhaps a greater menace to the cause of Christ than outright heathenism."[17]

It would seem that there was little emphasis at this time on cultivating Indian leadership. It was not until 1925 that mention was made of Indians teaching Sunday school, although it is possible that this was taking place all along. Nor was there much mention of the Indian elders and deacons. Robinson Fatty enrolled in 1926 at Cook Christian Training School in Phoenix, Arizona, taking with him his wife and two children, the first Apaches from Mescalero to prepare for Christian service. The outcome of this effort is not known.

Daily vacation Bible school was also part of the work. Typically, the minister's wife was in charge, but most of the teachers were Indian. Attendance, as reported at various times, was about fifty, with white and Indian students participating. Scouting made its debut at Mescalero during this time, with Boy Scout, Girl Scout, and Cub Scout troops. At least some of these activities took place at the lodge, now called the Community House. Much of the ministry continued to be done on a personal level, with the Overmans welcoming to the parsonage as many as twenty callers a day seeking help, advice, or sociability.

In 1925 the first Indian-owned automobile appeared on the reservation, a sure sign of gradually increasing prosperity. Prosperity, however, did not solve all problems. Many in the older generation became regular gamblers, and many in the younger generation lost old traditions without learning how to use money wisely. Throughout this time the Indian agency seems to have been in a constant state of flux,

17. David Laman, "Work at Dulce and Mescalero," *Intelligencer-Leader*, Oct. 15, 1937, 13.

if not confusion. Every year or so Overman announced the advent of a new superintendent, each with a promise of reform and new-found concern for the welfare of the Indians.

Less Criticism of Indian Customs

Conspicuously absent from the reports of Overman and even of his numerous predecessors were criticisms of Indian dances and other customs. Words like "pagan" and "godless" simply did not appear. If attempts were made to prevent Christian Indians from attending powwows and coming-of-age ceremonies, they were not published. This is in sharp contrast to several of the other fields, where nearly all Indian traditions were associated by the missionaries with drunkenness, lechery, and wanton godlessness. Competition for the Indians' loyalty continued, however. On at least one occasion (in 1924) Overman took a small organ and Uncas, the interpreter, into the tribal grounds and conducted a Christian service during an Apache feast. The experiment was apparently dropped, as no subsequent mention was made of this approach.

Overman Leaves Because of Ill Health

During the winter of 1929-30, Overman, now seventy years old, became quite ill, although the nature of his illness was not announced. He spent the winter in the warmer climate of California, leaving his wife in charge of the mission. Melissa Overman made pastoral calls and preached at worship services, but because she was not ordained she called on pastors for baptismal, wedding, and Communion services. But Nathan Overman's health did not improve, and he retired from the ministry. He died seven years later, at the age of seventy-seven, in San Luis Obispo, California.

It is difficult to evaluate Overman's twelve-year ministry statistically, simply because he rarely reported numbers to the Reformed Church in America. Camp meeting conversions ranged from fifteen to twenty-five each year, but they apparently had little impact on the bottom line, for it seems that communicant membership declined from about 180 to about 135.

The Short but Innovative Ministry of John Mixon

Overman was succeeded by yet another missionary pastor who came from outside the Reformed Church, the Reverend John

Mixon. Little about his personal or professional life is revealed in denominational reports. He stayed only a short time but introduced many new community-oriented services to the ministry.

Shortly after arriving in Mescalero, Mixon launched a three-point program with a view toward (a) Christian community, (b) Christian homes, and (c) Christian people. Noting that the infant mortality rate was 60 percent, he preached on health issues from the pulpit. He built a basketball court adjacent to the community house and organized sports teams for both boys and girls. Discovering that the library of the local boarding school contained only thirty books and that the community house had none, he appealed to Reformed Church congregations. They responded by adding over 450 books, as well as magazines, newspapers, and phonograph records to the library of the community house. Recognizing the need for profitable employment, he initiated a taxidermy class for men and a silver jewelry class for women, the latter taught by Solon Sombrero. The women also made beadwork, rugs, and blankets for sale.

Mixon encouraged self-determination by putting Solon Sombrero in charge of the community house and convincing the congregation to pay the interpreter, buy the fuel, and purchase their own songbooks. But Mixon's tenure was short-lived; he resigned after two years to return to his studies in Chicago. He apparently sent no statistical reports to the denomination while in Mescalero.

Lay Leader Solon Sombrero

Sombrero, who had attended the government boarding school in Mescalero, had been an interpreter nearly from the beginning of the mission. As we have seen, he extended his leadership to other areas as well. In 1932 his testimony was published in the *Christian Intelligencer*:

> In the midst of tradition and superstition have come many devoted Christian families. Although different religions have come to us and been tried, they have all ended in failure. The Christian religion stands firm today! The Christian religion is the only religion for my people![18]

Edith, a daughter of Solon and Katrina Sombrero, later married

18. Solon Sombrero, "A Quarter Century at Mescalero," *Christian Intelligencer*, May 18, 1932, 307.

Solon Sombrero, interpreter
and lay leader at Mescalero

Jonah Washington, a Pima Papago who was later ordained as a
Reformed Church pastor.

The Van Eses Arrive

The mission responsibilities in Mescalero were next undertaken
by the Reverend Peter, Jr., and Henrietta Van Es—only the second
missionaries to stay more than five years (they stayed twelve, from
1932 to 1944) and only the second pastorate (of eight) to come from
Reformed Church roots. Van Es, a native of Orange City, Iowa, had
graduated from Hope College and Western Theological Seminary and
had spent the two years after ordination with the Reformed Church's
Indian ministry in Colony, Oklahoma.

One of the first priorities of the Van Eses was to strengthen the
Sunday school, which apparently had been neglected. They organized a
school of eight classes with two Indian teachers and six white teachers.
Henrietta Van Es organized a Ladies Aid, at which Indian women
conducted the devotions. Like the missionaries before him, Van Es
relied heavily on Uncas Noche as interpreter and Solon Sombrero as
assistant at the community house.

Peter and
Henrietta Van Es
and family

Shy Choir Members

Henrietta Van Es, a frequent contributor to the *Christian Intelligencer*, was also active in organizing choirs. Leading choirs was difficult in Indian congregations, she reported, because singing vocal parts is not a part of the Indian heritage. "But the biggest drawback in our choir work," she said, "is a large practicing group, but a small rendering group on Sundays."[19] A few months later she said that both the junior and senior choirs were preparing Easter music, but that when the older groups face a congregation they display "such pathetic shyness."[20]

Three Outstanding Members

Also in 1933 the Van Eses mentioned the marriage of Belle Baheda, "our outstanding Apache girl, one who has fine training," to David Kazhe, "a worthy young man."[21] They expressed great hope for

19. Henrietta Beyers Van Es, "Here and There at Mescalero," *Christian Intelligencer*, March 1, 1933, 140.
20. Henrietta Byers (sic) Van Es, "News from Mescalero Mission," *Christian Intelligencer*, May 3, 1933, 284.
21. Rev. and Mrs. Peter Van Es., Jr., "Christmas Letter from Mescalero," *Christian Intelligencer*, February 1, 1934, 38.

Belle and David Kazhe

this young couple, whose names would appear frequently in years to come, Belle as a leader in Sunday school and women's work and David as a deacon and "doer of kind deeds."

The year 1936 marked the coming of Dorcie Kazhe, a Pima who moved from Arizona to marry Isaac Kazhe, an Apache from Mescalero whom she had met at the Indian school in Phoenix. Dorcie taught Sunday school for fifty-nine years at the Mescalero Reformed Church, played the piano and organ, and spoke throughout the denomination on behalf of Indian missions. She died in 2000 at the age of eighty-six, having taught Sunday school until five years before her death. Lynette Kanseah, one of her three children, has served for many years as principal of the Mescalero High School as well as giving leadership in the church.

Another long-time faithful member who came to the forefront during this time was Walter Scott. Born of Christian parents in 1911, he was very short and had physical limitations that made it difficult for him to walk. Scott served on the consistory, sang in the choir, and was a translator for Peter Van Es and Reuben Ten Haken. When his services as translator were no longer needed, he became the mission's maintenance man, a position he held for many years. Scott died in June of 2002 at the age of ninety.

Isaac and Dorcie Kazhe and family

Mary Broomhall joined the staff in 1936 as the first community worker to be employed at the Mescalero church. Her responsibilities included teaching Sunday school and midweek classes, sponsoring the Girls' Club, and visiting people at the hospital and in their homes. She was pleased that at her first Christmas in Mescalero the Indians decided to change the holiday dinner menu from the traditional Indian food to one that included roast beef, mashed potatoes, cabbage salad, escalloped corn, ice cream, and cake.

Broomhall left in 1939, in all likelihood to make room for the Reverend James Ottipoby, a member of the Comanche Reformed Church who had been ordained by the Reformed Church and had served two years as an assistant in Winnebago, Nebraska. Ottipoby served in Mescalero from 1940 to 1943, at which time he entered the military chaplaincy.

New Indian home on the Mescalero reservation, 1938

The Mescaleros Organize as a Tribe

The epic Indian Reorganization Act, passed by the U.S. Congress in 1934, made it possible for native peoples to organize tribal councils and therefore take a major step toward self-government. The Mescalero Apaches were one of the first tribes to take advantage of this new freedom, and they did so almost immediately, in 1936, incorporating the Lipan and Chiricahua bands as part of the Mescalero tribe. Oddly enough, denominational periodical accounts and annual mission reports, voluminous as they were at the time, never mention this significant action. The Jicarilla Apaches, in northern New Mexico, followed suit in 1938. "For peoples who had never been organized on a tribal basis," wrote Gordon C. Baldwin, author of *The Apache Indians, Raiders of the Southwest*, "this was a dramatic step to take. Most of the Apaches had never thought of themselves as tribes."[22]

John Collier, U.S. commissioner of Indian affairs and architect of the Indian Reorganization Act, wrote exuberantly, "The Mescaleros are now a chartered corporation. What a future is theirs in this land in the sky!...Not an acre of the reservation is now under lease. Nearly the whole tribe is in the live stock business."[23] Yet denominational reports

22. Gordon C. Baldwin, *The Apache Indians: Raiders of the Southwest* (New York: Four Winds Press, 1978), 190.
23. "The Mescalero Apaches Make Progress," *Intelligencer-Leader*, Dec. 30, 1936, 12, quoting an editorial by John Collier in the Sept. 36, 1936, issue of *Indians at Work*.

over the following years referred to continuing hardship and near-starvation among the Indians on the Mescalero reservation.

Summer Students Become Missionaries

We have mentioned J. Robert Swart as having served as a summer student in Mescalero in 1943 while studying at Western Theological Seminary. Later he and his wife, Morrie, served for forty years as pioneer missionaries in Africa. Two years later, in 1945, Harvey and Hilda Staal spent the summer in Mescalero. Harvey graduated from Western Theological Seminary the following year, and, after a short pastorate in Webster, New York, the Staals spent thirty-eight years as missionaries in the Middle East.

Van Eses Leave Mescalero for Macy

The Van Eses left Mescalero in 1944 to accept a call to the Indian congregation in Macy, Nebraska. They stayed in Macy for eight years, bringing their total years of service in Native American ministries to twenty-two. Their son Rowland, a career Reformed Church missionary in Taiwan and the Philippines, was born in Mescalero in 1939.

During the Van Es tenure at Mescalero, statistical reports exhibited the mysterious confusion that had become common among American Indian churches. The Van Es pastorate ended in 1944 with a reported 165 communicant members. In that year, the reported absent members were only 11, down from 90 just seven years before. Reported Sunday school enrollment was about 50.

A New Church Building, 1949

Ten Hakens Arrive

The Van Eses were followed by the Reverend Reuben and Bernice Ten Haken, who were to stay in Mescalero nine years (1944-53) and who gave an additional nine years to Indian ministry in California and Macy, Nebraska.

The Ten Hakens were both natives of Wisconsin (Gibbsville and Cedar Grove), and both attended what was then the Wisconsin Academy in Cedar Grove. Reuben graduated from Hope College in 1937, the couple married, and Reuben enrolled in Western Theological Seminary.

After graduating from seminary in 1940, Reuben accepted a call

Reuben and Bernice Ten Haken and their family

to Newton Zion Reformed Church in the rural community of Erie in northwestern Illinois. In 1944, while attending the General Synod, the Ten Hakens were invited to enter Indian work in Mescalero. They readily accepted, even though they had never met an Indian in their lives.

On their journey to New Mexico they took with them an eighteen-year-old young lady, Bernice Tegeler, as household help. Tegeler, the thirteenth of sixteen children, had recently lost both parents and possessed only an eighth-grade education. She saw an opportunity both for employment and Christian service and went on to dedicate the remainder of her life to mission work among American Indians, primarily in Winnebago, Nebraska.

The Ten Hakens' preparation for Indian ministry consisted of four days of visiting on location with former missionary Hendrina Hospers, at the close of which Hospers said, "You'll get along all right."[24] The Ten Hakens related their early impressions of the people of Mescalero in a 1945 *Church Herald* article:

> We were all eyes and ears when our Indian mothers, fat and pudgy, puffed their way into our home, with their babies tied securely to their backs. Rickety wagons rumbled down our streets drawn by a pair of skeleton nags. Indian cowboys with rustling leather chaps, bright silk shirts, and jangling spurs came to sit in our

24. Interview with Bernice Ten Haken, June 1997.

A typical cottage meeting in the 1940s,
this one in the Coarizzo district

upholstered chairs while in their hands they held their embossed bridles and nicely circled lariats. Old Indian grandmas shuffled along, puffing away at hand-rolled Bull Durham cigarettes....The coyotes sing us to sleep at night, and we are awakened at early dawn by the chant of the devil dancers and the beat of the tom-tom just outside the town where some of our people are having an all-night feast for one of their boys in the service who has become a hero by capturing a Nazi flag. At school, church, or on the street, it's Apache you hear. Many of the children know no other language until they begin school. You wave an enthusiastic greeting to a passing friend and yell a hearty hello and get in return a dubious look and a stubborn nod and a grunt. Little black-eyed children smile shyly and run at your approach.[25]

The Ten Hakens continued the multisite ministry established by the Van Eses, traveling over a hundred miles on a typical Sunday, preaching four sermons, and teaching in two Sunday schools. On weekdays they taught Bible at the four day schools on the reservation in addition to making family calls and conducting other typical activities of a country pastor. Ten Haken proved to be a quiet and sympathetic counselor, and over the years built a considerable legacy of affection and trust.

25. Reuben H. Ten Haken, "Mission in the Mountains," *Church Herald*, Nov. 23, 1945, 11.

The Atomic Bomb

On July 15, 1945, two years after the Ten Hakens arrived, Mescalero and the surrounding area were rocked by a distant explosion that was first reported to have been caused by a munitions dump in Tularosa. In reality, the people of the area had experienced the first detonation of an atomic bomb, just fifty miles to the northwest at the Trinity Site of the White Sands Missile Range. Three weeks later, on August 6, the "Little Boy" atomic bomb was dropped on Hiroshima, Japan.

New Church and Parsonage

The church building and parsonage in Mescalero were by this time nearly forty years old and dilapidated beyond repair. The church had been built adjacent to the government agency, and for some years the missionaries had believed that the implied association was not always desirable. Besides, the Reformed Church was launching the United Advance, an effort to raise $2.5 million over and above regular benevolent giving, designated for (in that order) Reformed Church colleges, post-war world relief, foreign missions, and domestic missions. The Women's Board of Domestic Missions was scheduled to receive $57, 706, over half of which ($30,000) was designated for Mescalero. The United Advance goal was a staggering amount for its time, and the fund drive took in nearly $2 million, or 83 percent of its goal.

The U.S. Department of the Interior had provided the initial mission site, and now the government negotiated the relocation of the mission property. The result was better than anyone in the church could have imagined. The new site was on a hillside overlooking the highway (now U.S. Highway 70), which at the time went to Los Angeles. To the rear of the church property were the tribal store and post office, which the Indians visited frequently. In addition, the new property covered four acres, compared to the one and one-half acres of the original site.

The Ten Hakens went back to the scene of their first pastorate, Erie, Illinois, and presented the need for additional funds, speaking not only to the Reformed church there but to other congregations as well. In the winter of 1948-49 Fred Slocum, a building contractor and member of the Methodist church in Erie, brought a contingent of builders and their families to Mescalero. Most of them lived in government housing, and Slocum paid his workers their normal wages. The Kohler Company donated the fixtures, and the Mescalero tribal council voted to give $1,000 in tribal funds, despite the fact that the majority of the council's

The Mescalero Reformed Church, dedicated in 1949

members were Roman Catholic. Church members contributed $2,000, and an unnamed visiting woman gave $1,000. The old bell was removed and placed in the bell tower of the new building.

The attractive stucco building, seating about seventy-five, was designed in the style of the southwest and cost about $50,000. The church was dedicated in June 1949, forty years after the completion of the first church. E. B. Fincher, the founding pastor, now eighty years old, gave the dedicatory address, and Dorcie Kazhe, accompanied on the organ by Belle Kazhe, sang "Open the Gates."

Two years later, on April 8, 1951, the congregation dedicated three stained-glass windows that grace the front of the sanctuary, a gift of the children of missionaries Richard and Ella Mae Harper, who served the church from 1910 to 1915. At this service, former pastor Peter Van Es preached the dedication sermon. The tall center window depicts the Good Shepherd. The window to the left, with the caption, "Put on the whole armor of God," pictures an Apache warrior with his Bible, the sword of the Spirit, in his hand, and a shield and broken spear at his feet. The window on the right pictures a missionary with Bible in hand and an Indian interpreter in front of him, with the caption, "And he interpreted to them all the Scriptures."

"We Know Very Little"

Ten Haken did not hesitate to report the negatives as well as the positives:

There's shouting, drinking, gambling, adultery, fornication, and fighting....A very high percentage of the Indian babies that come to our reservation are born out of wedlock. As many grow up they develop a philosophy of life which has as its basic principle, "do as little as you can, with as little as you have, and get as much as you can." "It's no use trying to help an Apache" is a common expression on the lips of my white neighbors, and I think I'd say the same if I weren't a missionary."[26]

We've been with them seven years. It would seem that in that perfect unit of time we ought to know perfectly. The perfect truth of the matter is that we really know very little of the people we love. But we do try to "sit where they sit."[27]

One of the emphases of the Ten Haken era was the encouragement and cultivation of Indian leadership, including giving the consistory responsibility for all aspects of their work, such as keeping the books, making deposits, receiving and transferring memberships, and praying with members who needed spiritual help.

A photo of the consistory in 1949—the year the new church building was dedicated—indicates that all except Ten Haken were Indian. Pictured, in addition to the pastor, were Southerland Comanche, David Kazhe Jr., Eugene Chihuahua, Solon Sombrero, Jonah Washington, George Martine, Jasper Kanseah Jr., and Walter Scott.

The Ten Hakens left Mescalero in 1953 and took two short pastorates in Mesquite, Nevada, and Chino Valley, California, before returning to Indian ministry, this time in southern California. The government had developed a program to encourage Indians to leave the reservations and move to the cities. The Southern California Council of Churches undertook, with the government, to help Indians with housing, jobs, and social services, and Ten Haken directed the program from 1957 to 1960, when he went to Macy, Nebraska, to serve the Reformed church there.

Unlike the Mixon and Overman pastorates, statistical reports were submitted annually during most of the nine Ten Haken years. Communicant membership increased by about forty during this time, and Sunday school enrollment increased by about fifty. The number of

26. Reuben Ten Haken, "Mission in the Mountains," *Church Herald,* Nov. 23, 1945, 11.
27. Reuben Ten Haken, "I Sat Where They Sat," *Church Herald*, Nov. 9, 1951, 5.

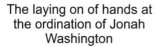

The laying on of hands at the ordination of Jonah Washington

inactives hovered at about twenty-five. Attendance statistics were not required for the statistical tables at the time, but Ten Haken reported in a *Church Herald* article in mid-1951 that during that year attendance had ranged from forty to ninety.

A Recurring Membership Pattern

The Mescalero statistics revealed a pattern—common among many American Indian congregations—of a substantial drop in reported membership after a pastor left, followed by a gradual increase during the next pastorate. A couple of possible explanations of this pattern come to mind. Perhaps the new minister revised the records to reflect reality more closely, or perhaps active church participation dropped off precipitously after a minister left and took time to be restored, or perhaps both were true.

Jonah Washington and Wendell Chino

Two future Indian pastors were gaining experience at Mescalero during this time: Jonah Washington and Wendell Chino.

Jonah and Edith Washington

Jonah Washington was born in 1916 into a Pima Christian family in Mesa, Arizona. He attended Indian schools in Phoenix, Arizona, and

Albuquerque, New Mexico, then enrolled at Highlands University in Las Vegas, New Mexico. He left Highlands in his junior year to join the U.S. Air Force, where he stayed five years. While stationed near Mescalero, he met and married Edith Sombrero, daughter of Solon and Katrina Sombrero. Edith had attended the Indian high school at Albuquerque and studied at Cook school in Phoenix, but came back to Mescalero when her father became ill.

After Jonah's discharge from the Air Force, the Washingtons served for five years, from 1946 to 1951, as lay assistants to Ten Haken in Mescalero. Jonah completed his college degree at Highlands and went on to attend Austin (Presbyterian) Seminary, spending his summers working in Mescalero. In a 1954 article in the *Church Herald*, he is pictured with the nearly completed log church at Elk Silver, and he writes about "false shepherds" coming into the flock, without being specific.[28] Washington graduated from Austin in 1958 and was ordained as a Reformed Church pastor that same year.

After ordination Washington was called to become the first full-time pastor at the Apache Reformed Church in Apache, Oklahoma, but left less than a year later. He then directed the religion program at the Indian school in Chilicco, Oklahoma, from 1958 to 1968. Edith Washington died in 1960, in Chilicco, after seventeen years of marriage. A year later Jonah married Harriette Johnson, of Caucasian and Mohawk ancestry, a guidance counselor and teacher from Sidney, New York. Washington served the Jicarilla Apache Reformed Church in Dulce, New Mexico, from 1968 to 1972, then left to serve a Presbyterian church in Okemah, Oklahoma. He died in 1987 in Laveen, Arizona.

Wendell Chino

The Reverend Wendell Chino served for four years as associate and pastor of the Mescalero Reformed Church, but he is best known for his four decades as a tribal leader and for his outspoken defense of Indian rights at the national level. As one Indian-based website succinctly states it, "Chino was a nationally recognized Indian leader who fought for tribal sovereignty and ruled Mescalero with an iron fist while successfully building and diversifying the tribe's economy."[29]

28. Jonah Washington, "A Chapel at Elk River" (sic), *Church Herald*, Nov. 19, 1954, 10.
29. "Wendell Chino, Mescalero Apache Leader," in "Passing of Elders," internet site dickshovel.com., April 2001.

Wendell Chino

Chino was just sixteen years old when he was first mentioned in a Reformed Church publication. The 1939 annual report of the Board of Domestic Missions, highlighting Indian leadership, identified him as "a school boy who is being trained to be a general helper at the mission and whom it is hoped will develop into a leader as he grows older."[30]

After graduating from the Indian school in Santa Fe, New Mexico, Chino received generous help from the Reformed Church to continue his education. He attended Central College, boarding in Pella with an elderly woman. Upon returning to Mescalero after his first college year, he was hired by Ten Haken to visit families, assist with vacation Bible school and the annual camp meeting, and evangelize. Disillusioned by the personal lives of some of the men who had initially encouraged him, he wished to resign, but Ten Haken pointed out that Christ depended on Christian workers to solve problems, not run away from them. So he went back to school, but this time to Cook Christian Training School in Phoenix.

After graduating from Cook he attended Western Theological Seminary, from which he graduated in 1951. He was ordained in June of that year and accepted a call to become associate minister with Ten Haken. He stayed on when Ten Haken left and worked with the next pastor, the Reverend Harvey Calsbeek, for about a year, but by then he was becoming more and more involved in tribal leadership. Chino was elected to the tribe's Business Committee, which at that time conducted the business affairs of the tribe.

---

30 *Annual Report of the Women's Board of Domestic Missions,* 1939, 36.

Chino Becomes Tribal Leader

In 1955 Chino was elected chair of the Business Committee, at which time he resigned as pastor in order to give full time to tribal leadership. He chaired the committee from 1955 to 1965, when the tribe adopted a council form of government. He easily won the first election as tribal chairman under the new system and went on to be elected to sixteen more two-year terms. He demitted (voluntarily resigned) the Reformed Church ministry in 1972.

During his tenure as tribal chairman, Chino led the tribe to new levels of economic prosperity, with the development of a school, community center, ski run, lumber industry, fishing industry, and the well-known Inn of the Mountain Gods resort, with its adjoining Casino Apache. When he succeeded in winning reparations from the U.S. Government, he resisted pressure to distribute the funds to individual tribal members and insisted that the money be used to develop tribal industries. He was often quoted as saying, "The Navajos make rugs, the Pueblos make pottery, and the Mescaleros make money."

National Influence

Chino's influence reached far beyond the boundaries of the reservation, however. A fierce advocate for Indian self-determination, sovereignty, and rights, he demanded that the federal government honor its few remaining treaties with Indian nations regarding lands and resources. He was elected to two terms as president of the National Congress of American Indians, the largest and oldest national Indian organization in America, representing 130 tribes. In a 1969 article in the *New York Times Magazine,* Chino is pictured flanked by vice president Spiro Agnew and secretary of the interior Walter Hickel.[31] Chino's most controversial action was negotiating an agreement with the U.S. Government to store nuclear waste on a remote corner of the Mescalero reservation. This never came about, but it created a major conflict on the reservation.

Throughout his political career Chino maintained a cordial, albeit loose, relationship with the Reformed Church. He continued to subscribe to the *Church Herald* and maintained friendly relationships with Reformed pastors. His first wife, Patricia, was originally a Catholic but became a member of the Reformed Church. His second

31. Vine Deloria, Jr,., "The War Between the Redskins and the Feds," *New York Times Magazine,* Dec. 7, 1969, 82.

The Inn of the Mountain Gods on the Mescalero reservation

wife, Rita, was also a member of the Roman Catholic Church, which became Chino's primary affiliation. Yet when he died, the pastor of the Reformed church was asked to preside at his funeral.

Chino Dies at Age Seventy-Four

Wendell Chino died November 4, 1998, at the age of seventy-four, in Santa Monica, California. He suffered a heart attack after working out on a treadmill. His popularity with the tribe seemed at last to be slipping. Two of his supporters had been voted off the council, and he had hinted that in another year he would retire. Chino's funeral at the Mescalero Community Center was attended by more than two thousand people. Among those who spoke during the two-and-a-half-hour service were Peter Domenici, U.S. senator; Gary Johnson, governor of New Mexico; and Manuel Lugan, former secretary of the U.S. Department of the Interior.

Despite the fact that Chino was no longer a member of the Reformed Church, members of the Mescalero Reformed Church sang two Apache hymns and its pastor, the Reverend Robert Schut, was asked to preach the sermon. Using Joshua 1:1-9 as his text, Schut said, "Moses took the people of Israel to the edge of the Promised Land. Mr. Chino has taken his people to the edge of the *Promising Land*. Who will lead the people into that Promising Land? I do not know, but that

Harvey and Angeline
Calsbeek and their
family

person must be 'strong and courageous' and also depend on God for
spiritual direction."[32]

Waves of Peace and Stress, 1954-84

After the Ten Hakens left Mescalero, the church turned to a
young couple that would give twenty-two years of service in American
Indian churches—the Reverend Harvey and Angeline Calsbeek.

Calsbeeks Enter Indian Ministry

Harvey Calsbeek, a native of Sibley, Iowa, had attended
Northwestern College, then a two-year institution, and had graduated
from Hope College and Western Theological Seminary. Angeline
Calsbeek was a native of Davis, South Dakota, and also attended
Northwestern College. The Calsbeeks went to Mescalero in 1952 as
summer students while the Ten Hakens were away on deputation
and vacation. During this time they took complete responsibility for
the mission. They resolved to go into Indian work, but when Harvey
graduated in 1953 and was ordained by the Classis of Germania
(consisting of German-heritage Reformed churches in Iowa and South
Dakota), no Indian congregations were open. They took a call to the
Logan Reformed Church, a small country congregation near Dell
Rapids, South Dakota. A year later, when the Ten Hakens left Mescalero,
the church called the Calsbeeks. The Dell Rapids congregation, knowing
the Calsbeeks' desires, sent them to Mescalero with their blessing.

The Calsbeek years (1954-62), reflecting the Calsbeeks themselves,
were quiet and diligent. Harvey was always a low key man and seemed
to have endless patience. The work at Mescalero settled into something
of a routine, including worship services, Sunday school, vacation

32. Letter from Robert Schut to LeRoy Koopman, Nov. 11, 1998.

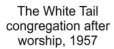

The White Tail
congregation after
worship, 1957

Bible school at three locations, women's meetings, weekly children's clubs, prayer meetings, summer youth camps, community recreational programs, special Lenten services, summer camp meetings, and rounds of calling at hospitals, homes, and jails. Integral to the ministry was the ever-present "open parsonage" for people who had various needs or just wanted to visit. The guest room at the parsonage also provided lodging for visiting board personnel and other mission visitors. In these years, the ministry faced problems brought on by alcoholism, as well as the challenge of Mormon elders who were working hard to make inroads on the reservation.

Angeline Calsbeek recalls that her husband and Wendell Chino (and later, Wilbur De Cora) held prayer meetings at homes in the outlying areas:

> The men, elders of the tribe, would interpret the Scriptures into the Apache tongue and explain it to those in attendance. Many times after the mission personnel left, these older men would spend time composing songs to the beat of the tom-tom, expressing the message they had heard and/or telling about some of their pilgrimage when they were imprisoned by the U.S. government. Some of these ballads are still used in the church services. One I remember was entitled, "Jesus Is My Light." Jasper Kanseah, one of the elders, would begin singing an Apache hymn

and others would join in. Younger people were encouraged to sing along in order to learn the words and melodies.[33]

Angeline Calsbeek and the wives of the pastoral assistants also traveled to the outlying areas at least once a month to meet with the women for Bible study, quilting, crocheting, and refreshments.

Speakers at the annual evangelistic meetings, held after the July feast times, included the Reverends Roe Lewis, an Indian pastor and teacher who later led the Reformed Church's American Indian Council; Robert Chaat of Lawton; and Henry Bast, the *Temple Time* (now called *Words of Hope*) radio minister. The church celebrated its fiftieth anniversary in 1959 and produced an attractive brochure, complete with many historic photos.

Calsbeek stressed self-support and self-determination. For some years the church had used folding chairs in the sanctuary. When members asked Calsbeek to request that "New York" send money for pews, he recommended that they get a loan and buy the pews themselves. They secured a thirty-six-month loan from the mission board and paid it off within twenty months. Two women's groups—the Ladies Aid and the Ruth and Naomi Society—purchased new equipment for the kitchen and also made contributions to the Board of North American Missions.

Chino left the pastorate about a year after the Calsbeeks' arrival, so Calsbeek immediately invited another potential Indian leader, Wilbur De Cora, and his wife, Lupita, to join the staff. De Cora, from Winnebago, Nebraska, had for many years been a professional boxer and had attended Cook Christian Training School. The De Coras worked two years at Mescalero (1955-57), then left for New Brunswick, New Jersey, so Wilbur could attend seminary there. He attended one year, was ordained in 1958, and went on to serve twice at Winnebago.

Van Galens Join the Staff

After the departure of the De Coras, Calsbeek invited Herman and Joyce Van Galen to assist at Mescalero, thus launching another long-time career in Indian service. The Van Galens, who came as newlyweds, were originally from Waupun, Wisconsin. Herman had attended Central College for three years, had served in the U.S. Army, and was working in a factory when they received the invitation to come to Mescalero. The Van Galens were one of many lay couples—mostly white—who served in the dual capacity of maintenance work and

33. Letter from Angeline Calsbeek to LeRoy Koopman, Jan. 1, 2002.

The Van Galens
in Mescalero

Christian education, especially youth work. Herman also took the responsibility of preaching at the White Tail chapel.

Statistics During the Calsbeek Years

For the most part, the church's annual statistical reports made sense during the Calsbeek years. After a low of seventy-six in 1955, communicant membership climbed to about 135, while the reported number of inactives remained at about fifty. Sunday school enrollment remained fairly steady, mostly in the 120 to 150 range. These figures reflect the total of the four worship locations, although only a few families were ordinarily involved in each of these outlying sites. The statistics do not include actual attendance.

The Passing of 'Grandma Mary'

Mrs. Uncus Noche, known to everyone as "Grandma Mary," died in 1961 at the age of ninety-six after being severely burned when her small home burned to the ground. A tribute to her, as it appeared in the 1962 *Annual Report of the Board of North American Missions*, is included here as an illustration of the several Indian people who kept the faith over the years at Mescalero and elsewhere:

Although she spoke no English and understood very little, she was faithful in attendance at all [Ladies Aid] meetings as well as at the church services. Her sincere faith and active interest was an inspiration to all. Her fine humor and bits of wisdom gained from her years of experience encouraged others. Even though her body was becoming weak, she felt that she had to be in the Lord's House on Sunday. Many times she literally crawled on her hands and knees to get into the church bus, refusing offers to help.[34]

During all of this time the Reformed Church's six Native American congregations had been members of the Classis of New York, reflecting the time when all mission work was directed from the headquarters in New York City. Finally, in 1957, the Indian churches were transferred to classes in their general geographical area, and the Mescalero church was transferred to the Classis of California.

The Arrival of Robert and Joyce Zap

In 1962 the Calsbeeks left Mescalero to continue their Indian ministry at the Jicarilla Apache Reformed Church in Dulce, New Mexico. Later that year the Mescalero church and the Van Galens welcomed the Reverend Robert and Joyce Zap. Zap had come out of the Faith Community Church, a largely Czech Reformed Church congregation in Stickney, Illinois. He had graduated from Wheaton College in Wheaton, Illinois in 1953 and from Western Theological Seminary in 1957, then had served for five years at the Reformed church in Williamson, New York.

During Zap's time at Mescalero, one of the summer seminary interns was Harold "Shorty" Brown, who some years later (1972-79) served as the Reformed Church's area secretary for Indian Ministries and Chiapas. Brown, during this short time, took Apache language lessons from Amelia Naiche and Sarah Kanoi, and by the end of the summer was able to give his farewell speech in the Indians' native tongue. None of the full-time pastors had ever seriously studied the language, and older people from Mescalero still mention Brown's accomplishment with appreciation.

Ministerial Tensions

Three years after the Zaps' arrival, in keeping with the denomination's policy of encouraging Indian leadership, another staff couple joined the Zaps and the Van Galens—the Reverend Frank and

34. *Annual Report of the Board of North American Missions*, 1962, 30.

Mary Patricia (Pat) Love. Frank Love, of Omaha and white lineage, with roots in Macy, Nebraska, had graduated from Cook Christian Training School, Hope College, and Western Theological Seminary. He was ordained January 28, 1965, by the Classis of California and subsequently installed as minister of education at Mescalero.

In this new staff, the members clashed almost immediately, fueled by differences in personality and mission philosophy. Within two years Zap submitted his resignation to the Reverend Albert Van Dyke, director of Indian work for the denomination, citing his wife's ill health but also a perceived lack of support by the Reformed Church's mission administration. He subsequently accepted a call to a Southern Presbyterian church in Andrews, Texas, and transferred his membership to that denomination. Love was appointed moderator and temporary pastor, and in the fall of 1967 the Mescalero congregation voted to call him to become their pastor, albeit by a slim margin.

In August of 1968, the Van Galens left Mescalero after eleven years of service there, and Herman enrolled in Northwestern College to complete his college education. He graduated from Northwestern and then from Western Theological Seminary, so he could continue Indian ministry as a pastor. After his ordination in 1973, he became pastor of the Comanche Reformed Church in Lawton, Oklahoma, following the retirement of Robert Chaat. The Van Galens later returned to Mescalero for three years, 1996-99, and also served on an interim basis at the Apache Reformed Church after the Montanaris left in 2002.

Love left Mescalero shortly after the Van Galens' departure and went immediately to Macy, Nebraska. His pastorate there lasted two years, and from that point Love launched a career that took him to several Indian religious, social, and political agencies throughout the western states.

Communicant membership at the Mescalero church dropped from 129 to 108 during this time of tension (1962-68), and Sunday school enrollment went from 150 to 45. Actual attendance during these years is unknown.

Those unhappy times in Mescalero were followed by another brief and strained pastorate, that of the Reverend Thomas Beech. A graduate of Westminster Theological Seminary, Beech had served short pastorates in several denominations, including the Bethany Christian Reformed Church in Gallup, New Mexico. He served in Mescalero from December of 1971 until 1974, when under pressure he left to take a call from the Community Reformed Church in Hawarden, Iowa. He

Roger and Adilee
Bruggink

stayed at Hawarden two years, then was dismissed to the Presbyterian
Church. Reported communicant membership in Mescalero dropped
catastrophically in 1973, from 107 to forty-eight. Since that time,
membership has increased very slowly over the years and has never
again reached the one hundred mark.

In 1968 the Wycliffe Bible Translators produced the Apache
language in written form for the first time. Despite criticism that
Christian organizations destroy native cultures, these organizations
often play a key role in preserving native languages that otherwise
might forever be lost.

Roger and Adilee Bruggink

After twelve years of upheaval, the Mescalero church was ready
for a measure of tranquility. They found it in the Reverend Roger and
Adilee Bruggink, who arrived in 1974 and stayed six years.

Roger, from Oostburg, Wisconsin, and Adilee, from Oskaloosa,
Iowa, met at Central College, from which they both graduated. After
Roger graduated from Western Theological Seminary in 1961, the
couple spent six years in Jackson County, Kentucky, and seven years
in Midland Park and Oakland, New Jersey. Adilee, trained to teach
secondary school, soon found herself teaching kindergarten at the local
school. The Brugginks were well received and carried on a ministry to
the entire community, including involvement in the alcohol and drug
abuse recovery program. At this time more than a dozen people who
had been born in Fort Sill as prisoners of war were still living in the
community.

One youth project, the Brugginks recall, involved scavenging the reservation for old and broken bicycles, "cannibalizing" them, and getting them back in working order. Another youth project converted an unused attic room above the sanctuary into an "upper room" for youth.

Outlying Mission Posts Close

The late 1960s marked the closing of the three outlying mission centers. Many people moved from the outlying areas to Mescalero, and, as roads improved, church members who lived at a distance could drive to church on Sundays. The chapel at White Tail had earlier been moved to Carizzo because the building was in such bad shape. The Inn of the Mountain Gods was built in the Carizzo area, and the church building, which had not been used for several years, was in the way. Soon after the Brugginks arrived, the congregation held a final service in Carizzo, with the people who had once worshiped there giving testimonies and reliving their experiences. The building was sold for $300 and moved halfway between Mescalero and Cloudcroft, where it is still used as a house. The log cabin at Elk Silver, which had never been used extensively except for summer youth camps, was purchased by a family in Ruidoso and houses a tourist shop.

After the other sites closed, the Mescalero people continued to remember them by closing the Mescalero church for a few Sundays and gathering instead at the sites of the former churches. As the Brugginks remember it:

> This proved to be popular as people willingly loaded their pick-ups with tables, chairs, food, etc. and we had truly remarkable services at the sites named. In White Tail we gathered literally on the ruins of the former community there, and people shared wonderful stories, pilgrimage tales, etc. At one or more of these services we asked people to bring back rocks from the sites, which we then fashioned into a fireplace located in the arbor next to the church. This nearly was a mistake as we had tons of rocks! It was intended to be a reminder, as it was for the children of Israel, who made a pile of rocks so that when their children asked, they could be told the story.[35]

35. Email from Roger and Adilee Bruggink, Dec. 14, 2002.

The Arbor Is Built

The Memorial Arbor was built in 1976 by work crews from Hudsonville, Michigan, and Albuquerque, New Mexico. The arbor is an open structure, thirty-six feet square, with a wooden roof. The building also incorporated the aforementioned stone fireplace and the bell from the Carizzo church. A concrete floor replaced the "sawdust trail" in 1997. It continues to be used for the annual camp meeting, youth activities, noon lunches, and other outdoor meetings.

Indian Ceremonies

When it came to Indian ceremonies, the Brugginks did not raise an issue with tribal dances, the coming-of-age ceremonies, or the activities of medicine men, but at the same time emphasized the "all-powerful Christ." To Indian people the spirit world is very real, and people who moved into new homes often wanted to have their homes blessed. "We developed," say the Brugginks, "a simple ceremony not taught at Western Seminary, including the lighting of candles in four directions. We then read Scripture and offered prayers for the Spirit of Christ to protect against any other spirit that might try to enter. What seemed to be quite simple to us became very significant to them."[36]

The Brugginks Leave

In 1980 the Brugginks moved on to the First Reformed Church in Yakima, Washington, after which they became missionaries in Oman and Yemen. They retired in 2001 and since then have been doing interim pastoral work, including the Apache Reformed Church. During the Bruggink years, the Mescalero church showed slow but steady growth from fifty-three communicant members in 1974 to sixty-six communicants in 1980. The number of reported inactives declined from the high of 118 in 1973 but remained substantial at seventy-five in 1980. Sunday school enrollment was steady, from fifty-six in 1974 to sixty-five in 1980. An unusually high number of church members died during that six-year span—an average of more than seven per year.

Clarence and Helen Van Heukelom

After the Brugginks left, the church reverted to another short pastorate—that of the Reverend Clarence and Helen Van Heukelom,

36. Ibid.

Clarence Van Heukelom picked up children for
vacation Bible school in a horse-drawn surrey.

who served from 1981 to 1984. Van Heukelom, a graduate of Central
College (1949) and New Brunswick Theological Seminary (1952), had
served as a hospital chaplain in Denver and as pastor of Reformed
congregations in Minnesota, California, and Iowa.

Van Heukelom became known in Mescalero as the pastor who
transported vacation Bible school children in a surrey with a fringe
on top—specifically a black surrey with two red seats and a red fringe
on top, pulled by a horse named Tonka. Vacation Bible school was
big during those years. In 1982, for instance, more than two hundred
children were enrolled in three schools—one held at the church and two
held in the yards of members.

Van Heukelom also became known as a critic of native customs. He
became increasingly concerned about what he saw as a new eclecticism,
a willingness to accept traditional Indian beliefs alongside Christian
beliefs. He was especially concerned about what he called "spiritism,"
involving witch doctors and medicine men and women. Several
consistory members, including Berle Kanseah, were strong advocates
of Indian traditionalism, and the situation became increasingly tense
until Van Heukelom accepted a call to the First Reformed Church in
Sibley, Iowa, in 1984. Reported statistics were virtually unchanged from
1981 to 1984, with about seventy-five active communicants, sixty-five
inactives, and eighty-five enrolled in Sunday school.

At this time five of the Chiricahua Apaches who were born as prisoners of war were still alive. One of those who died in 1983 was Amelia Naiche, the daughter of chief Naiche and always an active member of the church. Her son, Silas Cochise (who took the name of his great-grandfather), served for several years as a consistory member and occasional preacher.

The Schut Era, 1984-

After twenty-two years of rapid change, uncertainty, and sometimes animosity, the Mescalero church was ready for peace and continuity. They found it in the persons of the Reverend Robert (Bob) and Linda Schut. The Schuts came in 1984 and as of this writing are still serving there.

The Schuts both grew up in Clinton, Wisconsin, where Bob was a member of the Emmanuel Reformed Church and Linda was a member of the First Presbyterian Church. They were married in 1969 and graduated from Northwestern College. The Schuts then moved to New Brunswick, New Jersey, where Robert attended New Brunswick Seminary. They accepted a summer assignment to the Indian congregation in Macy, Nebraska, and the internship stretched to two years.

After their service in Macy the Schuts moved to Holland, Michigan, where Robert finished his theological training at Western Seminary in 1976. He worked as associate pastor of the Sixth Reformed Church in Holland from 1976 to 1978, then served for six years at the First Reformed Church in Colton, South Dakota. At Colton the Schuts began what would become a long-standing tradition. Ever since 1979, members of the Colton Reformed Church, sometimes accompanied by members of other Colton churches, have helped with the summer Bible school program in Macy, Nebraska. In 1984 the Schuts accepted an invitation to serve the Mescalero Reformed Church.

Difficulties Shared

In their letters to supporting congregations, the Schuts have made no effort to hide the fact that they sometimes become discouraged in their work. In a letter of October 1985, a little more than a year after they arrived, Schut wrote, "I am coming to the realization that all my efforts, good intentions, gifts and abilities, and personality will not necessarily carry out the ministry that is needed here. I have been humbled through mistakes and poor choices that I have made in ministry." This

Robert and Linda Schut

humbling, he said, offers him the greatest hope. "David needed to be humbled so he would look to God *alone* for his strength....God is trying to show me the same thing." He concluded by saying, "We have not 'turned Mescalero upside down' with the message of salvation. But God is beginning to turn *me* upside down. I am grateful for that."[37]

In the spring of 1989, the Schuts wrote, "In Indian culture, living for Christ is often referred to as 'walking the Jesus road.' That road has been difficult for us in recent weeks. As we share this letter with you, we thank you for your prayers that uphold and strengthen us. In this way, you are walking on the road with us."[38]

Several letters in subsequent years reflected Schut's wry humor as well as his concern for the many tragedies in the community, many of which were related to alcohol. Schut wrote in May 1986, for instance, that since February five people of the community had died—ages thirty, twenty-six, thirty, eighty-four, and twenty-six. But he also reported that worship attendance was better than ever and that more than half of the worshipers were under twenty-five years of age. It was not unusual, he wrote, to have sixty students in Sunday school and twenty to twenty-five young people attending youth groups.

Over the years, the Schuts have adopted five children, all of whom have some percentage of Indian lineage. Three of the five suffer from

37. Bob and Linda Schut, letter to supporting churches, October 1985.
38. Bob and Linda Schut, letter to supporting churches, April 1989.

a fetal alcohol effect, with its accompanying learning and behavioral problems. The Schuts have freely shared these incidents with their supporting churches. "One of the things I've really appreciated about Mescalero," Bob Schut has said, "is that as we have gone through some of our struggles as a family, we have had tremendous support and understanding."[39] The Schuts also have one child by birth, Robbie, who after graduating from Northwestern College became a military intelligence officer with the U.S. Air Force.

Hundredth Anniversary Observance

In 1986 the Apaches of Mescalero, New Mexico, and Apache, Oklahoma, together with representatives from several other Indian tribes and white friends, gathered at the ceremonial grounds in Mescalero to observe the one hundredth anniversary of the beginning of the twenty-seven-year imprisonment of the Chiricahua Apaches. Events included traditional Indian dances, Apache hymns sung by members of the Mescalero Reformed Church, a speech by tribal chairman Wendell Chino, and a prayer led by Schut. Narcissus Gayton, one of the Chiricahuas, presented a plaque that included a U.S. flag and the Mescalero flag. A similar observance took place at Geronimo's grave in Lawton, attended by three hundred Apaches. Chino and Gayton also participated in that event.

The Associates of Mescalero

A veritable parade of associates passed through Mescalero during the Schut era, each serving a year or two and then moving on. Almost all of them followed the familiar pattern of working in maintenance and in Christian education and youth programming.

The associates from 1982 to 2003 included Terry and Rachel Meekma (1982-83), Harry and Judy Willemstyn (1983-84), Stan and Cheryl Deelstra (1985), Luke and Chris Schouten (1985-86), Wayne Peterson (1986-87), John and Elizabeth Maynard (1988-90), Keith and Linda Burton (1991-94), the Reverend Herman and Joyce Van Galen (1996-99), Bethany Graves (1999-2002), Bethany Buege (2002-03), and Janice Merino, a young woman of the tribe (2004-).

The long tradition of Anglo work groups traveling to Mescalero was reversed in November 1999 when eight high school students and two adults traveled to Holland, Michigan, for a work project at the

39. Video interview by John Grooters of Robert and Linda Schut, July 1997.

Calvary Reformed Church, which two years earlier had sent a work group to Mescalero. "We want to begin making a change in the attitude of 'being helped,'" said Schut, "and begin to reach out to others."[40]

Building Addition in 1998

The Mescalero church, built in 1948, was a practical and attractive building, but it had several shortcomings, including the lack of an entryway off the parking lot, restrooms on the sanctuary level, and overflow seating for special occasions. For several years the church had been saving money for a special building project. In April 1997 the congregation voted to proceed with a major sanctuary renovation that would double the seating capacity, remodel the basement, and correct the aforesaid deficiencies.

Beginning in January of 1998, each of eight congregations from Washington, Iowa, Minnesota, Missouri, Oklahoma, and Michigan contributed a week of work and $2,000. The Mescalero church contributed about half of the $53,000 total cost. Volunteers Klaas and Betty Groen from Spencer, Iowa, supervised the project. The addition and renovation was dedicated April 26, 1998.

Christianity and Traditional Indian Faith

In the Mescalero church, as in many other places, tension sometimes exists between those Christians who believe it is important for Indian believers to cut off all association with traditional Indian practices, and those who wish to blend the two. One of the outspoken proponents of the latter point of view is Berle Kanseah, a long-time member of the Mescalero church, one of the Apaches featured in the PBS film, *Geronimo and the Apache Resistance* (1988), and a member of the Mescalero tribal council.

Kanseah and others still tend to see Christianity as the white man's religion, or, more specifically, the way of the "dominant society." Even though they have declared a degree of allegiance to it, they are not ready to say it is the only way. "Christianity is the church," he says. "Our way is in the open. In our way, God is in the air, the trees, the mountains. These things are sacred to us." Kanseah has high regard for the Apache legends and for such rituals as the coming-of-age rite for girls. "The Apache way is the deepest way that faith works," he says. "We need to choose the best of the two—Christianity and the Apache way.

40. Bob and Linda Schut, letter to supporting churches, December 1999.

My wife and I feel we can go to church, pray, and sing in the dominant society's way."[41]

Clarence and Dolores Buurma

No history of the Mescalero Reformed Church would be complete without mention of Clarence and Dolores Buurma. The Buurmas, originally from Holland, Michigan, came to Mescalero in 1966. Clarence taught school for three years, then worked for the tribe as education director and education counselor until his retirement in 1988. They moved to Alamogordo, thirty miles away, but continued to attend and serve the church. The Buurmas were involved in the Mescalero church the entire time, Clarence serving as elder and church treasurer, and Dolores as a teacher and women's group leader. The Buurmas have eight children, two of whom are adopted Mescaleros.

Clarence Buurma was highly trusted by the tribe, so much so that he was honored by being declared an "Indian" and thereby eligible to receive a pension from the tribe. "I honestly believe," wrote Robert Schut in a 1984 letter to supporting churches, "that [Clarence] has been the best 'missionary' this church has ever had."[42]

Statistics During the Past Twenty Years

Statistics have been reported faithfully during the Schut years and have been remarkably consistent. Communicant membership was seventy-five in 1984, went to eighty-two in 1986, and has varied little since then. From one to six new members have made confession of faith each year. Sunday school enrollment has averaged about seventy-five. Average worship attendance was first reported in 1988 and has averaged about eighty-five. The average number of reported inactive members has been fairly consistent at about fifty.

Present Ministry at Mescalero

Life on the reservation continues to be difficult. The use of alcohol continues to be rampant, and its attendant calamities— including accidental death, violence, fetal alcohol syndrome, and infidelity—touch nearly every family. Despite the casino and other tribal businesses, unemployment remains at about 30 to 35 percent. Nearly 75 percent of the children drop out of school before graduation,

41. Interview with Berle Kanseah, July 1997.
42. Bob and Linda Schut, letter to supporting churches, November 1984.

although a few students have gone on to attend such schools as MIT and Stanford. Diseases such as diabetes are pervasive.

At the Mescalero church, as in most Native American congregations, attendance is often erratic. Families attend regularly for a time, drop out for a while, and then resume worship with no predictable pattern or discernable reason—at least not to the white pastor.

The number of tribal and family feasts has increased substantially in recent years, and this has hurt church attendance. During a typical summer, only three or four weekends are free of feasts. These include the increasingly popular coming-of-age feasts during which the families spend twelve days on the feast grounds—four days in preparation, four days for the feast itself, and four days for dismantling, all with elaborate ritual.

As of this writing, Indian tradition is reflected to a moderate degree in worship services. An Apache song and prayer, led by someone from the congregation, are part of nearly every service. Indian baskets are used for the offering. The use of drums and flutes in the worship service was requested by some members in the 1960s, during the "red power" days, but at that time the older men turned it down, saying that these were part of the feast, not of the church. The use of these instruments in the church has not been suggested in recent years. These are more commonly used in the Roman Catholic congregation, which not only uses drums, flutes, arts, and crafts, but also has incorporated the crown dancer headdress into the décor of the church.

The Apache hymnal of the Mescalero Reformed Church contains twenty-four hymns (text only), of which seventeen are translated from the English. Among the seven hymns of Apache origin are several that speak of following Jesus, coming to Jesus, and taking the Jesus road. The Apache hymn, "I Came Back to Jesus," is typical:

> Chorus: I came back to Jesus. It was good when I came back to Jesus.
> Verse 1: My friends, it is good to walk the Jesus road with him.
> Verse 2: My friends, it is good to walk according to Jesus' word.
> Verse 3: My friends, it is good to live according to Jesus' book.
> Verse 4: My friends, it is good to stand with the strength of Jesus.

The children's message has become an integral part of the service, and creative services on such occasions as Thanksgiving, Christmas,

The children's sermon is a highlight at the Mescalero church.

and Maundy Thursday are greatly appreciated. A few contemporary praise songs are used alongside traditional hymns.

The church van travels about 350 miles each week to pick up children and youth for Sunday school, youth meetings, and Kids Klub. More than 70 percent of the children and youth do not have a background in the church. At one time the church was the social center of the community, with "fun night," board games, and other activities, but now that role has been preempted by the tribe's community center, pool, and gymnasium, to say nothing about every family's own television sets.

Camp Meetings Emphasize Christian Growth

After sixty years the camp meeting is still alive, although it has changed drastically from the times when Indians came by wagon and pitched their tents for a week or more. The camp meeting is no longer the one great climactic event of the Christian year when many confessed how they had gone astray during the past year and where they made a new or renewed commitment to Christ. "I have known people who have gone to three or four camp meetings a summer and have 'given their lives to Jesus' at each meeting," said Schut. "Now the emphasis has changed somewhat. We look at the camp meeting as a time of growing in our faith—of learning how to live as disciples."[43] The meetings are

43. Robert Schut email, Dec. 13, 2002.

Mescalero youth group social event

held in the church's permanent arbor during the second full week of July, and they feature an outside speaker or group. In recent years the Mescalero church has called on several speakers from the C.H.I.E.F. organization of Phoenix, Arizona. These have included Craig Smith, author of *Whiteman's Gospel*.[44]

Emphasis on Discipleship Rather than Leadership

Robert Schut has come to a strong conviction regarding leadership development. One of the goals of the pastors and of the Native American Indian Ministries Council, he says, has been to train Indian leadership—but it hasn't worked very well. The solution, Schut believes, is not to train leaders but to develop disciples. This, he said, is what Jesus did; he emphasized discipleship rather than leadership. When Christians strive to become true disciples, when they experience spiritual victory in their lives, leaders will emerge.

In a June 2002 *Church Herald* article Schut called on the Reformed Church in America to "stop barking up the wrong tree" (leadership development) and emphasize discipleship above all:

Leadership development is a program to implement. Disciple making is a process of growth. Leadership development is

44. Craig Stephen Smith, *Whiteman's Gospel* (Winnipeg: Indian Life Books, 1997).

taught. Disciple making is done through mentoring. Leadership is learned. Discipleship is a way of life. Leadership is relatively simple. Discipleship is the hardest thing that we can ever be called to do.[45]

Schut took a three-month sabbatical in the summer of 1998, primarily for the purpose of learning how best to develop discipleship. The sabbatical included mission studies with the Reverend Dr. Charles Van Engen at Fuller Theological Seminary in Pasadena, California.

But training in discipleship, says Schut, is not a one-way street. "Our people," he says, "have a tremendous sense of spirituality. And that's one thing they can—and need—to share with the rest of the denomination, and the denomination needs to hear what they have to say."[46]

Early in its history the Mescalero mission succeeded in blending the incoming Chiricahua Apaches with the resident Mescalero Apaches into a viable Christian community. In the political realm, it provided in the person of Wendell Chino, an Indian leader who not only led his tribe into relative prosperity but made substantial progress in gaining Indian rights nationwide. The congregation is the only Indian church that during the past decade has felt it necessary to build an addition to its worship facility. After nearly one hundred years of ministry, the Mescalero Reformed Church is still held in high regard even by those who do not attend, and it continues to be a stabilizing force in the community.

45. Bob Schut, "The Importance of Discipleship," *Church Herald*, June 2002, 7.
46. Robert and Linda Schut, video interview with John Grooters, July 1997.

CHAPTER 7

The Jicarilla Apache Mission in Dulce, New Mexico, and the Jicarilla Apache Reformed Church

The Reformed Church's mission among the Jicarilla (pronounced Hick-a-REE-ya) Apache people in northern New Mexico was unique in several ways. Its pioneer missionary didn't have a high school diploma, much less a college degree or theological training. The mission certainly was the most isolated of all the denomination's Indian sites. Unlike the other mission plantings in the Southwest, it had no direct connection to the Apache imprisonment at Fort Sill. Yet it is safe to say that the mission in Dulce would not have begun if it had not been for the other ministries in the Southwest. It was the Reverend Walter Roe who discovered the critical needs of the Jicarillas and urged the Women's Board of Domestic Missions to take up the work, and it was the son-in-law of the Reverend Richard Harper, J. Denton Simms, who pioneered mission work there.

Like the other Indian missions of the Reformed Church in America, this one had its share of crises and tensions; and also like the other missions, the work in Dulce has been a significant stabilizing force in the community.

Modern Dulce

Today's out-of-state visitor to Dulce, New Mexico, ordinarily arrives by air in Albuquerque, heads north on Interstate 25, then takes U.S. 550 to the northwest. Just north of the town of Cuba, about one and one-half hours from Albuquerque, one sees a sign, "Entering the Homeland of the Jicarilla Apaches." Highway 550, then State Road 537, and finally U.S. 64 take the travelers eighty miles through

267

spectacular mountains, narrow valleys, mountain streams, rugged mesas, purple sage, and rock formations called dikes. As the travelers round a mountain less than ten miles from the Colorado border, they see the town of Dulce, nestled in a valley. Rising up behind Dulce on the northwest—behind the Reformed church—is Dulce Rock, a landmark sandstone butte that is the town's most prominent geological feature.

About 3,500 people make their homes in Dulce, accounting for 95 percent of the Jicarilla Apaches who live on the reservation. At one time the Jicarillas were spread throughout the reservation, raising sheep. Over the years most of the sheep have died because of the bitter winters, and most of the people have moved to the town nestled on the extreme north side of the reservation. Its name, Spanish for "sweet," is presumably an illusion to the "sweet spring waters" that flow down from the mountains of the area.

An Isolated Tribe

Dulce is the most isolated of the mission sites, being an hour-and-a-half drive from the nearest mall, movie theater, and McDonald's, all of which can be found in Farmington, ninety miles to the west, population 38,500. The reservation is a relatively large one, extending about eighty miles south of the Colorado border and averaging about twenty miles wide in an irregular configuration. Elevations range from 6,000 to 10,000 feet, which means that even here in the Southwest the summers are cool and relatively dry. Temperatures can drop to 50 degrees below zero in the north, and snows can be very deep. Two prehistoric sites—the La Jara and Cordova Canyon cliff dwellings—are located on the reservation.

One who logs on to "Dulce, New Mexico" on an Internet search engine will find dozens of articles claiming that the Jicarilla reservation is an extraterrestrial site. No other-worldly creatures have actually been sighted yet, according to these claims, because the aliens live two miles under the mountains.

The northern two-thirds of the reservation, consisting of timbered ridges and broad valleys, has a wealth of ponderosa pine, interspersed with fir, oak, aspen, and cedar. The southern third is characterized by sandstone mesas, pine, juniper, and sagebrush. Hunting and fishing are major industries, and visiting big game hunters are required to hire a Jicarilla tribal member as a guide. Limited game permits are also available for black bears and mountain lions.

The primary agricultural activity is cattle ranching. Few crops can be raised here, as frost can be present every month except July and August. Temperatures on any given day can fluctuate widely. On July 2, 1997, the low temperature was 29 and the high was 92. The Jicarillas have expanded their land holdings in recent years by purchasing several large ranches adjacent to the reservations. These holdings include the Chama Land and Cattle Company, a 32,000-acre range and hunting lodge. The Jicarilla Apache tribe, in fact, was the first tribe in the U.S. to offer a tax-exempt tribal bond issue secured solely by the tribe and not guaranteed by the government or any other agency.

The General Allotment Act of 1887, commonly known as the Dawes Act, decreed that land be allotted to families and individuals for agricultural purposes. The Jicarilla reservation is a prime example of how misguided and unfeasible this policy was. Most of the Jicarilla land consisted of mountains and forests. Some of it on the southern end was suitable for grazing, but very little could be used for growing crops. Some allotments were made, and a few succeeded, but allotments never became widespread on the Jicarilla reservation. While other tribes lost their acreages through sale and fraud, the Jicarillas maintained their holdings.

The Indian Reorganization Act of 1934 opened the door to Indian self-government. The Jicarilla tribe approved its Constitution and By-Laws July 3, 1937, one day before the country's Independence Day. On August 4 of that year the U.S. secretary of the interior approved the Jicarilla Apache tribe as a federal corporation.

In the early 1950s natural gas and oil was discovered on the reservation. In early negotiations the government grossly undervalued the leases, which is still the case with many tribes. But the Jicarillas have won several lawsuits and have now taken charge of all leasing contracts. More than two thousand active wells continue to be an important source of tribal income. The Jicarillas received a boost in 1970 when the federal government awarded nearly $10 million in restitution for lands taken in 1883. The Jicarillas have been leaders in securing skilled legal counsel in pressing their claims.

About seventy percent of the able-bodied adults are employed, which is remarkably high for a reservation community. A great many of these are employed by the tribe for road maintenance, social services, public works, law enforcement, fire protection, and the casino.

Many Jicarilla Apaches have Spanish names such as Martinez and Vicenti, but this does not necessarily mean that they have Hispanic

The Go-Jii-Ya races at Sand Lake in the 1930s

blood—although some do. When Indians had to come up with names for a census, they often took the names of Mexican Americans they liked or even lived near.

Two major tribal events punctuate the year—the Little Beaver Round-up in July and the Go-Jii-Ya harvest festival in September. The Little Beaver Round-up is held in honor of the young Indian boy, reputedly a Jicarilla, who accompanied Red Ryder in his comic book and movie adventures. The Go-Jii-Ya (pronounced Go-GEE-Ya), always held at Stone Lake, eighteen miles south of Dulce, continues the custom of an ancient ceremonial relay race between two bands of Jicarillas—the Llaneros, or plains people, and Olleros, or mountain-valley people.

The Jicarilla Apache tribe was the first—and perhaps the only—American Indian tribe to produce its own newspaper. The *Jicarilla Chieftain* published its first issue January 8, 1962, and has been in business ever since, supported by tribal funds. Mary Polanco, for many years its editor, has been a long-time member of the Reformed Church and also served for six years on the editorial council of the *Church Herald* magazine.

As the common symbol for the Mescaleros is the unique headdress of the Dance of the Mountain Gods, so the symbol of the Jicarillas is a hand-woven basket. The traditional hand-made baskets, woven from sumac, are of a unique design and can cost as much as several thousand dollars. The tribe's promotional brochure says that the name *Jicarilla* comes from a Spanish word meaning "little basket maker."

The Town of Dulce

The town of Dulce is a sprawling community unofficially divided into several neighborhoods: Rivertown (nearest the river); Ghost Town (near the cemetery); Mosquito Flats (swampy area), and Chinatown (houses which have an Asian look when seen from a distance at night).

Along "main street," Highway 64, is the Jicarilla Inn, which serves the many hunters who come to the area and includes a small casino. The walls of the motel lounge and restaurant (the only one in town) display several historic black-and-white photos of professional quality. These were taken by Marguerite Rymes, who with her husband, Albert, served at the mission from 1928 to 1940 in food preparation and maintenance. Mrs. Rymes also left a rare legacy of motion pictures, a remarkable record of tribal customs and mission activities during the time she served.

Across from the business area are the rodeo and powwow grounds. The powwow area is surrounded by a large, round, branch-covered arbor, under which people sit on lawn chairs to watch the dances. Here and there are subtle legacies of the early Dutch Reformed presence. Several of the homes have lace curtains, a style adopted from the missionaries who introduced their culture as well as their faith.

At one time the Reformed church was the only church in Dulce, and most residents still consider it to be the "tribal church," whether they attend or not. But the Reformed church has since been joined by Mormon, Assembly of God, Roman Catholic, Southern Baptist, and independent Baptist churches. A few people who belong to Bahai meet in homes. Conspicuously absent is the Native American Church, which is not active in the area.

Beginning of the Jicarilla Mission, 1914

The seeds of mission work among the Jicarilla Apaches were planted, not in Dulce, but in Mescalero, New Mexico, nearly three hundred miles to the south. In 1910, twenty-year-old J. Denton Simms began managing the store at Mescalero. Simms's father, a medical doctor in Texas, had moved with his family to the drier climate of New Mexico after contracting tuberculosis. When the doctor died, his funeral was conducted by the Reverend E. B. Fincher, who in 1907 had begun mission work in Mescalero.

Fincher left in 1910, and the Reverend Richard H. Harper came to take his place. Harper arrived by wagon from Colony, Oklahoma, with his wife, Ella Mae; daughters, May, Alberta, and Mabel; and sons, Richard and Wilbur. "In a day or so," wrote Simms in his memoirs, *Cowboys, Indians, and Pulpits*, "Mary came to the store with a note from her mother, inviting me to dinner. That was a memorable experience and a turning point in my life."[1]

A Conversion and a Wedding

The arrival of the Harpers also proved to be a turning point in Simms's spiritual life. "Before long," he wrote, "I knelt beside an old Indian man at the altar in that church and was baptized, uniting with the Reformed Church in America."[2] May Harper and Simms were married in the parlor of the parsonage in 1911, and Simms began to feel called to the Christian ministry. As he told it:

I saw Reverend Harper at work, performing these kinds of Christian services at Mescalero and was convinced that there was no higher calling. I learned from Mrs. Walter C. Roe, a leader in the church, that a mission was being established to serve another tribe of Apaches, the Jicarillas, cousins of the Mescaleros, in northern New Mexico. I asked for and received an appointment to the mission."[3]

The calling agency, of course, was the Women's Board of Domestic Missions, then under the direction of Elizabeth M. Page. The board had acted upon the recommendation of Walter Roe and Reese Kincaid, pastor and director of the Mohonk Lodge in Colony, who had come to that part of the Southwest looking for a sanatorium site for Indians with tuberculosis. Roe had found, said Page, "a tribe located on a mountain reservation, with poor land, no work, and in dire need, surrounded by ignorant Mexicans whom they regarded with fixed and indomitable hostility bred of outrage and oppression. They were absolute pagans all."[4]

1   J. Denton Simms, *Cowboys, Indians, and Pulpits* (Roy, New Mexico: privately pub., Floersheim Printing, 1982), 55.
2. Ibid.
3. Ibid., 62.
4. Elizabeth Page, *In Camp and Tepee: An Indian Mission Story* (New York, Chicago, and Toronto: Fleming H. Revell, 1915), 242.

J. Denton and May
Simms, founders of
the Dulce mision, with
daughters

The records are not clear, but apparently Roe and Kincaid found some initial private funding (perhaps from Roe himself, who appears to have had substantial financial resources) to send food, clothing, and a worker (never named) to help the eight hundred Indians who were lacking both food and clothing.

Roe and Kincaid then went to New York to present the plight of the Jicarillas to the Women's Board. The board responded positively and set about to find financing. The board had earlier decided to build a "Walter C. Roe Memorial School" in Winnebago, Nebraska, and more than $4,500 had already been collected. But the board had problems securing title to the land it wanted, so it decided to transfer the funds to the Jicarilla mission. (Although the organized congregation is the Jicarilla Apache Reformed Church, the community building at Dulce still bears the name "Walter C. Roe Memorial Mission.")

The government granted a tract of land near the agency, and in 1914 work was begun on the church and parsonage—both of which are still in use and in good condition. In the fall of 1914 the Women's Board agreed to appoint Harper's son-in-law and daughter to temporarily conduct the mission under the supervision of the Reverend G. A. Watermulder, then serving in Winnebago. Simms, however, had no theological training, and, in fact, because of his father's illness, had never finished high school. He agreed to attend Torrey Bible Institute in Los Angeles, but after three or four months at the school the board asked him to go directly to Dulce and to pursue his training later. There is no evidence that he ever pursued any further theological studies, even though he was later ordained by the Southern Presbyterian Church.

Hendrina Hospers Arrives

In the fall of 1914 the Simms family, now consisting of Denton, May, and twenty-two-month-old Harper, arrived in Dulce via narrow-gage railroad, with all of their family possessions packed in two suitcases and a trunk. The family lived in a guest room of the Indian boarding school while Simms worked with carpenters to finish the parsonage.

One of the upstairs bedrooms of the parsonage was soon occupied by Hendrina Hospers, a coworker from Mescalero who Simms had asked to come and help him. Hospers, originally from Orange City, Iowa, had served the Chiricahua prisoners at Fort Sill as a field worker (community caller), then in 1913 had accompanied them on the train to Mescalero after their release. She was to serve the Dulce mission for thirty-two years and was the first of a legendary group of unmarried women to serve at Dulce.

A Dying Tribe

The Jicarilla Apaches were one of six related tribes of the Southwest, the others being the Western Apache, Chiricahua, Lipan, Mescalero, and Kiowa. These Athapascan peoples had migrated out of Canada sometime between 1300 and 1500 A.D. and had settled in New Mexico and southern Colorado. About 1700 the Jicarillas were "discovered" by the Spanish, and it was the Spanish who had given them the name Jicarilla. The name they gave themselves was *Didee,* meaning "the people."

The Jicarillas farmed as well as hunted, raising the three Indian staples—corn, beans, and squash. Their homes were of several types, including dome-shaped *wickiups* made of bark and thatch, flat-roofed adobe houses of the *Ollero* (mountain) band, and the tepees that the *Llaneros* (plains) band used on hunting excursions.

In 1841 the Mexican government gave 1.7 million acres—including Jicarilla land—to two of its citizens. The U.S. annexed the region in 1848 after victory in the Mexican War, then sold the land. The Jicarilla Apaches defeated the U.S. Army at the battle of Embudo Mountain, but then were defeated in 1854 and placed on a reservation in northeastern New Mexico. This land was also sold from under them, and during the next thirty years they were moved from one place to another a half dozen times. One idea was to remove the Jicarillas to the Mescalero Apache reservation, but the Jicarillas, who were scattered over a wide area, resisted. One agent wrote that it was more possible to round up a flock of wild turkeys than to move the Jicarillas. Reservations were

Early Jicarilla home

promised and then withdrawn; provisions were promised and not delivered. Periods of peace were followed by violent skirmishes as the Jicarillas responded in kind to treachery and as they resorted to their only means of survival—raiding the settlers' lands.

Finally in 1887 the Jicarillas were assigned to the reservation that is still theirs—415,000 acres in northern New Mexico. In 1907 another 300,000 acres at a lower—and warmer—altitude were added to the southern part of the reservation to provide grazing area for sheep, and since then the tribe has purchased additional land.

It soon became evident that Simms and Hospers were serving a dying and disillusioned tribe. When the missionaries arrived, the Jicarillas had been living on their own reservation for about thirty years, but their condition had deteriorated rapidly. Once free to migrate with the wild game, they were now confined to one place, and they soon depleted their source of food. They could no longer rely on cattle raids for a livelihood. Forced to stay in the high country, they suffered severe winters with little protection from the elements. Nearly 90 percent of them had tuberculosis, and their death rate was so high that they faced extinction as a tribe in twenty years. "Leave us alone," they said. "God is angry with us and we are a dying people."[5]

5. Edna Vande Vrede, "New Life for the Apaches," *Church Herald*, December 14, 1956, 4.

First Act of Witness: Burial 'the Christian Way'

In his memoir, J.Denton Simms told in some detail how he instigated an "opening wedge into the confidence and friendship of the Jicarillas"—an incident that today sounds simply bizarre. Hearing of the death of a little girl, Simms sought out the father, Reuben Quintana, and offered his services. "At Mescalero," he said, "the missionaries helped the Apaches begin a new custom of burial—the Christian way. I wonder if you would like to have me help you in that way." [6] The Apache way of burial was to wrap the body in blankets, carry it up the mountains, place it beside a fallen tree or large rock, and cover it with brush, rocks, and leaves.

Surprisingly, Quintana agreed to have Simms bury the child in the "Christian way." Simms arranged for the construction of a pine coffin and the digging of a grave, his wife made a white dress for the dead child out of the skirt of her wedding dress, and Simms read scripture and conducted the service. "It heartened me," he wrote afterward, "to see that, contrary to the pessimistic predictions of the Indian agent, I had not been rebuffed by the family I sought to help, nor were there visible signs of objection or opposition by others to what had to be a radical departure from one of the Apaches' sacred customs." Within a few years, he said, "most Apache burials were in the cemetery, with Christian ritual (sometimes in addition to certain of their own) instead of the old way."[7]

First Worship Service, 1914

The church building in Dulce was nearly completed by the time the Simms family arrived, and, by Christmas of 1914, it was ready for its first worship service. One of the first people to arrive, says Simms in his memoir, was a slightly drunk Apache man who tried to ride his horse up the steps and into the church. After convincing the man that he was welcome in church, but without his horse, Simms went ahead with the worship service, "encountering only minor interruptions as the Apaches, totally unaccustomed to the conventions of a white man's church service, wandered in and out, talked aloud to each other, cuffed crying children, nursed babies, and otherwise acted naturally.[8]

6. Simms, *Cowboys*, 68-69.
7. Ibid., 71.
8. Ibid., 85.

In the 1916 report of the Women's Board of Domestic Missions, Simms reported:

> We are gratified to say that these Indians, though backward and slow to take hold of the "New Road," are almost to a man in favor of our work among them and willing to be led...and it is now only by the simple but bold and fearless preaching of the Gospel, followed by kindness and much friendliness, that we are driving a wedge here and there into the breaking up of their evil ways."[9]

Questionable Statistics

The same report indicated that in the first full year of ministry (1915) Simms conducted forty-two worship services at the church with an average attendance of 111, as well as twenty-four services at the government school for the students and government employees. This seems to imply that the school children and employees attended their own Sunday services apart from the services at the church, but this was probably not the case. In a June 1915 article in the *Day Star*, Hendrina Hospers said that the missionaries felt much encouraged by the fact that "last Sunday, beside the school children, there were eighteen camp Indians at our morning service."[10] It is likely that the "average attendance of 111" included as many as a hundred children and workers from the government school, and that the twenty-four services at the school were additional Sunday or weekday events.

Statistical reports in subsequent years were vague, saying such things as, "Church services have been held regularly," and, "Among the converts a goodly number are living faithful to their vows and there are others who would be more frequent in their attendance if they did not live so far away."[11]

First Camp Meeting

In September 1916 the Dulce mission initiated a camp meeting, following the pattern originated by Walter Roe in Colony. E. B. Fincher, the first pastor to the Mescalero church, was the principle speaker, with additional help from the recently widowed Mary Roe and from the

---

9. *Annual Report of the Women's Board of Domestic Missions*, 1916, 43.
10. Hendrina Hospers, "With the Jicarilla Apaches," *Day Star,* June 1915, 1.
11. *Annual Report of the Women's Board of Domestic Missions*, 1917, 36.

entire Harper family of Mescalero. Simms reported that "thirty-one Indians gave themselves to Christ, among them one who is naturally a leader, the most intelligent and advanced member of the tribe."[12]

Simms reported enthusiastically in 1919 that there were by then sixty-five professing Christians. An old man had told him, he said, that "you missionaries are surely not children of white men but of God; for no children of white men have done for us what you have done." In addition, said Simms, white people employed by the government who had greeted them with such words as, "Why do you waste your time in coming to these Indians? They can never be Christianized nor civilized," had begun to take part in the Sunday school and church.[13]

The published reports continued to be upbeat, bright, and positive, but as Simms looked back in 1926 he cast quite a different perspective on those early years:

> There were days so dark that it seemed we sought in vain for signs of life and increase of its power. Days, months, and years went by and we worked and watched and wondered. Then came definite signs of growth. The "infant" is growing.[14]

The Ministry of Hendrina Hospers

Meanwhile, Hendrina Hospers, wiry and seemingly indefatigable, carried on a horseback ministry to the Indian camps, which were widely scattered around the reservation. Simms described her work in the 1917 report:

> Miss Hendrina Hospers, faithful, consecrated, wholly devoted to the Indians, has been busy from morning to nightfall, going on horseback when the roads are passable, to visit the Indians who live far from the Mission; she always carries with her the Sunday school picture cards which are sent to her, and the children love to receive them; even the older people put them up on the walls."[15]

Most communication, both from the pulpit and face to face, was done through interpreters. Dulce was unique in the number of

12. Ibid., 35.
13. *Annual Report of the Women's Board of Domestic Missions*, 1919, 38.
14. J. Denton Simms, "A Matter of Growth," *Christian Intelligencer and Mission Field*, Oct. 20, 1926, 677.
15. *Annual Report of the Women's Board of Domestic Missions*, 1917, 36.

Hendrina Hospers visiting an Indian family

Mexicans it had living in the area, and since some of the Indians as well as Simms spoke some Spanish, this third language became another vehicle of communication. Simms was never completely certain that his sermons were being accurately conveyed. "Many's the time," he wrote, "I have heard my interpreter compress a long English sentence of mine into a couple of guttural Apache words. And then when I might deliver a dramatic three-word phrase, he would ramble on for a full minute in the other language."[16]

The Mission School Opens, 1920

In 1918, at Simms's urging, the government school in Dulce was transformed into a sanitarium because so many children were dying of tuberculosis and other diseases. The influenza epidemic that encircled the globe reached Dulce as well, and church services were suspended for a time. H. M. Cornell, a medical doctor who had been coming to the tribe a few days a week, later served the tribe full time.

With the closing of the government school, however, the reservation was without a school for healthy children, so Simms contacted the Women's Board of Domestic Missions with a request to open a boarding school. The board approved, as did the U.S. Government, and Simms went on a speaking tour in Hospers's home country in northwest Iowa, raising $10,000 for a school building and dormitory. The government supplied food, clothing, school equipment,

16. Simms, *Cowboys*, 86.

The Dulce mission in winter

fuel, and the salary of one teacher (appointed by the Reformed Church), with the remainder of the personnel and plant being supplied by the Women's Board.

The mission school opened in 1920 with just twenty-four children able to attend classes, while sickly students attended classes in the sanitarium. The school operated for twenty years, until 1940, when a new government school was opened. For most of the 1920s and 1930s the school had five teachers, and the dormitories held about seventy students.

A Typical School Day

In 1922 Edna Vande Vrede, one of the long-time teachers, described a typical day at the boarding school:

> The children's day begins at 6.15 in the morning to be ready at 7.15 for breakfast, at which time we worship. After breakfast some of the girls are detailed to the kitchen to wash dishes and pare potatoes. Each boy and girl makes his or her own bed. Part of the girls and part of the boys are detailed to sweep the dormitories. At nine o'clock school begins and continues until 2.30 for the smaller and until 4.00 for the larger children. Seven o'clock finds the little girls and boys saying their prayers preparatory to being tucked in bed. Oh, that they may learn to say and understand with their hearts as they now say with their lips and understand not at all.[17]

17. Edna Vande Vrede, "Glimpses of Our Dulce School," *Christian Intelligencer and Mission Field*, January 4, 1922, 10.

Schoolboys and schoolgirls dressed in their Sunday best

Vande Vrede, as well as others, made quite a point of the fact that the Apache children "are fully as bright as white children," but said that "the smaller ones speak no English and have to be taught the names of every object." Both boys and girls, she wrote, are good at clay modeling; the boys are clever at making simple toys, and the girls make cloth dolls and dress them in Indian dress. But, she said, many of the children are physically weak and need constant monitoring.[18]

Parents brought their children to the mission school at the beginning of August and did not take them home again until May 1. The boys and girls were given English names at school but retained their Apache names at home. The mission provided all of their clothing, the exception being the boys' large hats, which fathers took pride in giving when the boys left home. Vande Vrede acknowledged the trauma of children and parents as they were separated for long periods of time, and that "their standards of what is best and our standards differ widely,"[19] but said that the Indians have learned to trust the mission.

18. Ibid., 10.
19. Ibid., 9.

As has been mentioned, Marguerite Rymes, who with her husband, Albert, did maintenance and kitchen work at the mission from 1928 to 1940, not only took remarkable black-and-white photos of Indian life but also took moving pictures, which was rare at the time. These included Indian children being transported from their dormitories in open-bed trucks on Sunday, then marching into the church, the girls wearing white dresses and the boys wearing dark suits, white shirts, and ties. The children are followed into the church by several white people and a few Indians, the women dressed in blankets and the men sporting large hats and braids. Movie footage shows school children crying as their hair is cut short, and forlorn-looking run-away girls being returned to the dormitory in a wagon.

Other footage includes Christmas trees being brought in by sled and boxes of Christmas gifts arriving by train. Mission teachers are pictured sledding, throwing snowballs, making faces at the camera, and sorting and wrapping huge piles of Christmas gifts. Simms is pictured occasionally, a little man wearing glasses, always dignified, and always dressed in a suit. Indians are featured in the Rymes movies rounding up cattle, branding and dehorning them, and herding sheep from pens into railroad cars. Included is remarkable footage of the Go-Jii-Yah races, including people arriving by horse and wagon, setting up arbors and tepees, drying meat on lines outside, marching with boughs, running in the relay races between lines of cheering onlookers, and good-naturedly taunting each other after the race.

In order to overcome the unwillingness of Indian children to stand up before others and give expression to their thoughts, teachers placed emphasis on dramatization and other forms of expression before an audience. Teachers encouraged interest in geography by instructing students to write letters to Sunday school classes in Dutch Reformed congregations and to send Indian dolls to the Netherlands and Japan. Cecilia Harina, a long-time Jicarilla church member who was raised at the school, recalls that at bedtime the "misses" gave each child a hug, and that the children would hang on to their housemothers.

The school's schedule and discipline were strict, which the Indian children often resented and to which they responded with mutiny. Harina recalls that two boys ran away from school after being punished by being made to wear girls' clothing. She also remembers that girls who ran away were punished by being locked in the school basement. This, she says, given the Jicarillas' fear of ghosts, was a terrifying experience.

The boys had their own dormitory, as did the girls, and all the beds were in one large room in each building. The children made their beds and scrubbed their rooms under the supervision of the matron. Bells rang ten minutes before each meal, which meant "wash your face and comb your hair." The matrons lined up the children, and at the second bell marched them to the dining hall, which was in the basement of the boys' building. Seats were assigned, with five boys seated on one side of the table and five girls seated on the other side.

An Emphasis on English and Faith

The children were allowed to speak Apache to each other in all places except the dining hall (a liberal policy in its day), with the result that the dining hall was a very quiet place. Lessons were taught in English, of course. In the eyes of the mission matrons and teachers, the Indian children were exceptionally timid, had little desire to learn, resisted singing, and sometimes had to be coaxed to say anything at all.

The school placed a strong emphasis on the (English) memorization of scripture, and a 1925 report says that "one recognizes a decided note of prophecy expressed as they sing in a meaningful manner, 'The old time religion will save the Jicarillas.'"[20] A notable exception to the English-only policy came in 1928, when at the annual Christmas program the Indian boys and girls sang "Jesus Loves Me" in their native tongue, translated and taught by Cevero Caramillo, an "outstanding Christian Indian and worker at the sanitarium"[21] Christmas programs always included the appearance of Santa Claus, played by one of the mission workers.

The mission's work at the school was so effective, said Simms, that "we closed the year with every child in our school a professing Christian, save five."[22] Eight youth, he said, have gone to other schools for training: two to Tucson, two to Albuquerque, and four to Santa Fe.

Even if the children became convinced that the new way was best, and even if they learned the skills of the new way, they encountered a major problem. The girls, for instance, learned how to sew dresses, cook carrots on the stove, make beds, and dress dolls like "American" babies. But when they returned to their tepees they found neither stove, sewing

20. "Our Future American Indian Leaders," *Christian Intelligencer and Mission Field*, August 5, 1925, 492.
21. "Christmas at Dulce," *Christian Intelligencer and Mission Field*, January 9, 1919, 20.
22. *Annual Report of Women's Board of Domestic Missions* 1929, 24.

The legendary "misses" of Dulce (left to right): Marie Van Vuren, Edna Vande Vrede, Gertrude Van Roekel, and Hendrina Hospers

machine, beds, carrots, nor white booties, and they again came under the authority of a very traditional grandmother.

The Legendary 'Misses' of Dulce

By 1924 the number of workers at the mission had grown to eleven. Alumni of the mission school are hard pressed to remember the names of any of the pastors who served there, but all of them have vivid memories of the "misses" who at the school were their teachers and housemothers and who called on their families at home. A host of mission workers came and went during these years, most of them unmarried women. We have mentioned Hendrina Hospers, who after eight years at Fort Sill and one year in Mescalero spent thirty-two years in Dulce. In addition to "Miss Hendrina," three other "misses" were especially well known: "Miss Edna" (Vande Vrede, 1920-54), "Miss Marie" (Van Vuren, 1929-59), and "Miss Gertrude" (Van Roekel, 1937-57). Together, these four women contributed 116 years of service in Dulce. In addition, Van Vuren and Van Roekel stayed and worked for the agency for several years after leaving the mission.

Miss Edna. Edna Vande Vrede came to Dulce in 1920 with the opening of the mission school. She was raised in Cedar Grove, Wisconsin, by her maternal grandmother, who instilled in her a love of missions. Vande Vrede taught school for a year in Corsica, South

Dakota, then worked for six years in an office. Her pastor urged her to go into mission work, and she at last found her life's calling in Dulce, where she stayed thirty-four years. Vande Vrede served as girls' housemother for three years, then put her business experience to work as business manager and assistant to Simms. When the mission school closed in 1940 and the children were transferred to a government boarding school, she became director of the newly opened community house.

Miss Marie. Marie Van Vuren arrived in Dulce in 1929, where she served as housemother in the girls' dormitory until the children were transferred to the government dormitories in 1940. But she stayed on in Dulce, serving in a wide variety of ways, including working with the village women, teaching Bible classes and Sunday school, and directing the vacation Bible school and the Home Aid Club.

Van Vuren was born and raised in Holland, Michigan, took classes at Holland Business College and Hope College, and worked in Holland as a secretary in a business office. She was active at the First Reformed Church, where through the Girls League for Service she became interested in Dulce, made clothing, and supported one of the Indian schoolgirls. In addition, an uncle (unnamed) had spent time as a missionary in Lawton, Oklahoma.

Miss Gertrude. Gertrude Van Roekel, who later was to write a memoir, *Jicarilla Apaches,* served in Dulce for twenty years, from 1937 to 1957. She was born on a farm near Monroe, Iowa (near Pella), attended the academy associated with Central College in Pella, then attended Central College. After graduating she accepted a position as boys' housemother in Dulce, which she held for three years, when she assumed duties as a field worker. After retirement she spent time in Ecuador with Wycliffe Bible Translators. Van Roekel died in 2002 at the age of ninety-two.

The Struggle to Subdue Indian Customs

Meanwhile, mission workers continued to be concerned about Indian customs and lifestyles. These included the marriage of girls as young as fifteen to middle-aged men, mistreatment of crippled children (regarded as "bewitched"), Indian dances, and debutant "coming out" ceremonies. Especially harmful, said the missionaries, was the Indian custom of destroying the house and belongings of people who had died, so the spirit of the departed one would not be able to return and haunt the relatives.

Concern for Babies

The missionaries were particularly upset by the medicine man's ceremonial ministrations and by the Indian custom of tightly binding newborns for several days. May Simms established a mothers' club to demonstrate the care of children in general and of newborns in particular. She boiled water, untied the "dirty new-born baby" from its "ever-so-tight wrappings," bathed it, washed out its eyes, and clothed the child in the "lovely soft white clothing" that had been supplied by women throughout the Reformed Church.[23]

In 1924 one of the missionaries, probably Simms, rejoiced that "some young men and women [are] now making homes where filth, ignorance, and heathen worship no longer hold sway, but where the cleanliness of civilization and the loveliness of Christian living abide."[24] Yet he acknowledged that "a very large majority live to the beat of the tom-tom in a world of feathers and paint; blindly, ignorantly, but after all really searching after the Heavenly Father if haply they may find Him."[25] Concerning the annual Go-Jii-Ya festival, Simms was more restrained in his evaluation, but he said that "as quickly as we can, we are trying to substitute wholesome fun and recreation, more appealing than crude feasts, so that these will die out for lack of patronage."[26]

Bernadine Vinkemulder, a boys' matron, tells of finding a group of boys squatting behind a clump of bushes, "busily talking in their native tongue of all the old Indian ideas, superstitions, and customs" and another group behind one of the barns, "staging an Indian dance with the tom-toms they have made." Subsequently, she said, basketball goals and a baseball field were set up; and "now that they are engaged in these clean sports, one does not have to be alert every minute to see that they are not busy with the old superstitions."[27] The clear implication is that the mission staff was often on patrol to uncover any regression to traditional Indian activities, which were carried out secretly behind bushes and barns. Baseball and basketball, on the other hand, were Christianized by missionaries as "clean sports."

23. Julia Williamson, "Help Us Save Our Indian Babies!" *Christian Intelligencer and Mission Field*, November 28, 1928, 765.
24. "Card of Thanks from the Jicarilla Mission," *Christian Intelligencer and Mission Field*, January 30, 1924, 75.
25. J. Denton Simms, "Out of the Mists of the Past," *Christian Intelligencer and Mission Field*, March 19, 1924, 186.
26. J. Denton Simms, "A Land of Fiestas," *Christian Intelligencer*, November 16, 1932, 733.
27. Bernadine Vinkemuler, "Which?" *Leader*, April 25, 1934, 13.

Schoolgirls in Dulce

Vinkemulder, in another article, told of an Indian boy who "has a sense of the finer things of life and has stepped out of many of the old crude ideas of his people." This year, instead of attending the fiesta, he "persuaded another boy to go with him and spend the day roaming in the hills instead."[28] A frequent publicity technique in those years was to publish a "first-person" testimony by an Indian child, describing and criticizing (in amazingly good English) the old ways and praising the new ways being taught by the missionaries.

The early missionaries in Dulce were especially harsh in their criticism of Indian dances. Simms repeated the accusation by government agents that dances and fiestas kept Indians from their work. "Perhaps," said Simms, "in years past these ceremonies had a religious significance for the Indians, but surely today they are but the excuse for doubtful and often sinful practices. How true that sinful man loves 'darkness rather than light.' The aftermath of these dances too often is unhappiness, sickness, and suffering."[29]

Edna Vande Vrede, in a letter to her friends and supporters, said of the beat of the tom-toms, "It would be well for our Indians if they, like a character in ancient mythology, would stuff their ears with cotton at the sound. But instead they bend to listen—and are lost!"[30]

28. Bernadine Vinkemuler, "Daniel of the Apaches," *Christian Intelligencer*, November 23, 1932, 748.
29. J. Denton Simms, "Summer Work with the Jicarillas," *Christian Intelligencer and Mission Field*, August 24, 1927, 53.
30. Letter from Edna Vande Vrede to "Dear Friends," n.d.

Christian Indians Identified by Anglo Clothing

In Dulce, more than anywhere else, Christian Indians were identified by Anglo clothing and short hair:

> At the church on Sunday we see side by side, young Christian Indians, clean and neat, and long-haired Indians with paint on their faces."[31]
>
> "Cevero, who cut his hair during Christmas week—which means the cutting loose from the old Indian road—reminded me of the old men of old, for his face shone like an angel's as he spoke."[32]

One of the most blatant identifications of Christianity with white culture is found in a short, unsigned news item in a 1923 issue of the *Christian Intelligencer and Mission Field,* which tells about a christening Sunday, noting that the couples involved would be ridiculed by others in the tribe:

> There were six little Indian babies, the children of six young couples who are trying to live like the white man and to "walk the Jesus Road." Any white mother would have been proud of the fine, clean little tots, dressed in white lace-trimmed garments for the event that is to mean so much in their lives."[33]

Sheep and Faith: A Church Is Organized, 1924

With the mission boarding school separating the well children from the sick children at the sanitarium, and with medical care available, fewer people were dying from tuberculosis. But the tribe was still dangerously undernourished. Their numbers had dwindled from 800, when the missionaries had first arrived, to 558 in 1920, with no end in sight.

Timber from the reservation was regularly being sold, with the money being placed in a government "trust fund" for the Indians, but the Indians were receiving no benefit. (Later investigations revealed

---

31. Edna Van De Vrede and J. Denton Simms, Letter to "Dear Friends," n.d.
32. Hendrina Hospers, "Christmas Celebration in Dulce, New Mexico, Jicarilla Apache Indian Mission," *Christian Intelligencer and Mission Field,* January 12, 1927, 30.
33. "One Step Forward," *Christian Intelligencer and Mission Field,* October 3, 1923, 646.

Alfred and Lincoln Velarde with their sheep

that millions of dollars placed in trust funds for Indian peoples remain unaccounted for.) Simms, trader Emmet Wirt, and local Indian agent Chester Faris requested that these funds be used to purchase sheep for the Jicarillas. There was no response.

Simms finally went to Washington to meet with Cato Sells, commissioner of Indian Affairs. Sells told him, in effect, to mind his own business. Simms persisted, threatening a publicity blitz. Finally, in 1920, Congress approved a measure to assign twelve sheep to every Jicarilla family member, with Simms to conduct the census. Simms reported two years later that the sheep industry was not only providing more income but also "more outdoor exercise and fresh air."[34] The Women's Board of Domestic Missions reported in 1924 that the Indians have been "reasonably successful" with their sheep, and that the Indians' health had been good, and that for the third consecutive year their population had increased.[35]

An Incredible Snowstorm

But tragedy struck the sheep business during the winter of 1931-32, when up to five feet of snow fell in late November and temperatures dropped to more than 35 degrees below zero. Many Indian lives were lost, and about 15,000 sheep, 75 percent of the total, were killed. After

34. *Annual Report of the Women's Board of Domestic Missions,* 1922, 31.
35. *Annual Report of the Women's Board of Domestic Missions,* 1924, 33-34.

the government replaced many of the sheep, the Jicarillas began making a long trek each fall to the southern end of the reservation, where they camped until spring. The missionaries followed them as best they could, often shoveling through deep snow banks, visiting the Indians in their camp homes, and conducting worship services. During May, June, and July the Jicarillas pitched their tepees in the north, where pasturage was best, as described by Simms:

> In far-off canyons extending to the reservations' limits, and sometimes beyond and hidden often by mountain walls, we find these tepees; sometimes singly, but more often in groups of two or three. The children and men are out herding the sheep while the women cook their meals over tiny fires outside or in the center of the tepee.[36]

The presence of the sanitarium, the introduction of sheep, and gradually improving living conditions and nutrition brought the Jicarillas back from the brink of annihilation. But various epidemics—including diphtheria, influenza, measles, and Rocky Mountain spotted fever—swept through the reservation on a regular basis. It made news, in fact, when the annual reports could say, "the mission experienced no epidemics this year."

Church Progress in the Early 1920s

Meanwhile, visitation work, carried on by Simms and Vande Vrede, together with the work of the mission school, was bringing results—although the precise nature and extent of these results are not always easy to ascertain. The 1924 report of the Women's Board of Domestic Missions, written by Simms, says that the average attendance for the entire year (1923) was seventy-eight, the highest ever. The report, however, does not indicate how many of these worshipers were government and mission staff. Nor does it mention the approximately forty students of the mission school, whose attendance was mandatory. In any case, almost all of the positive results among Indians were with the younger people. This same report speaks of the "ignorance and darkness in which these older Indians live; and the little progress, the few victories and the infrequent stepping out of the old life to the new." But the younger people "are showing unmistakable signs of Christian

36. J. Denton Simms, "Summer Work With the Jicarillas," *Christian Intelligencer and Mission Field*, August 24, 1927, 538.

advance and...desire for the good and precious things of Christian living."[37]

At one point the boys' dormitory was replaced by a larger building, and the old structure was remodeled as a lodge, supervised by Hendrina Hospers. Here mission visitors could be housed and Indians could camp out for a night or two. The lodge was especially busy on the first Saturday of the month, ration day. Indians from the camps came with their horses and wagons on Friday and rolled out their blankets to sleep on the floor of the large room of the lodge.

Jicarilla Reformed Church Organized in 1924

On October 25, 1924, ten years after J. Denton Simms began the work by burying an Indian baby in a white dress, the Jicarilla Apache Reformed Church was officially organized. Participating in the service, in addition to Simms, were G. A. Watermulder of Winnebago and Mrs. Tabor Knox, chair of the Indian Committee of the Women's Board of Domestic Missions.

The worship service was described in the December 17, 1924, issue of the *Christian Intelligencer and Mission Field*:

> The front seats of the church were occupied by the Indian girls and boys at our Mission School with their teachers and matrons; then the group of those who had come to present themselves for baptism and reception in the new church, several of them being Government employees; then the Government School children and back of them the friends and visitors, and in the rear the pagan Indians, who came to witness a very new sight, the acceptance in baptism of Indians of the Jicarilla Apache tribe....
>
> The white people were first received, some by letter and others by baptism...Several young Indian husbands and wives knelt together for the rite, their children in many instances having been previously baptized; then other young Indians, including five of our school girls and seven of our school boys, all of whom had taken the new road last Easter. Altogether fifty-seven members were received.[38]

---

37. *Report of the Women's Board of Domestic Missions*, 1934, 34.
38. "A Blessed Climax at Dulce, N.M.," *Christian Intelligencer and Mission Field*, December 17, 1924, 810.

But there was at least one major disappointment that day, an incident that illustrates the intensity of Indian opposition to the "Jesus Road." The crisis came when the time came for the baptism of Sixto, who "had long been walking the 'Jesus Road' and in very many ways had shown an unwavering devotion to Christ":

> Sixto arose and standing erect, made a sign with his hand over his head and said that he could not be baptized. It was an unspeakable disappointment to all who were interested in him and knew his faith. If he had been baptized that day he would have been the very first of the old Indians of the tribe to break with their tribal ceremonies and he felt that he could not take the step alone. He appealed to the Indians in the rear of the church to join him in the sacred sacrament, but they hurled back words in their own Apache tongue which we could not understand but the spirit of which was very evident. Men and women alike by sneers and suppressed laughter registered their disapproval of this new and unaccepted road.[39]

A report by Watermulder gave more specifics about the people who were received into membership. Twenty-four (including mission workers, government employees, and Mexican-Americans) were received by letter of transfer; three white people (a government employee and two Mexican-Americans living in the area) were received on confession of faith; and twenty-eight Indians were received on confession and baptized. One can deduce from other reports that many of those twenty-eight were children attending the mission school, so it is fair to say that relatively few of the fifty-seven charter members were adult Indian people. Had Sixto made the step, he would have been the only "old Indian" of the tribe to be baptized.

Although it was never explicitly stated, it is apparent that the vast majority of church attendees during these years were students at the mission boarding school, who were required to attend. Because of the health issues involved, it is not clear whether attendance was required of the students at the sanitarium/school. In 1927 about seventy students attended the mission school and eighty students attended the government school.

Sunday school lessons were taught to the children in English, but the adult class, like the church services, required an interpreter. Alfred

39. Ibid.

Velarde, one of the faithful interpreters, served for several years before his death in 1927. "We cannot see how they understand," wrote one of the mission teachers, "for the Apaches talk between their teeth and almost in an undertone." But they do come out to services, she said, and are eager, as one Indian expressed it, to "come out of darkness into the sunshine of God's love."[40]

The emphases of the church were revealed in the Dulce section of the 1927 Women's Board of Domestic Missions annual report. This report highlighted the leadership of a young man, Cevero Caramillo, who with four other young men—and with Simms's assistance—drew up "articles of organization for the furtherance of the activities of the church." These articles embodied such purposes as "earnest effort in the imitation of Christ, strict Sabbath observance, loyalty to the pastor, absolute abstinence from all Indian ceremonies and dances, kindly exerted influence in the prohibition of drinking and gambling." These young men also brought the Christmas message that year—"the first time the Gospel ever fell from the lips of a Jicarilla Apache."[41]

Church activities late in the decade included church and Sunday school, a mother's club, nursery (for children of parents attending the Indian Bible class), Christian Workers' Club, children's night at the church, socials for camp Indians, the Sheep Club (for boys), and sewing and cooking classes. The board's 1928 report illustrates Simms's meticulous record-keeping: 664 overnight stays at the lodge and 139 baths taken there. The staff made 2,693 camp calls. The fifty-two morning services were attended by 5,122, and the fifty-one evening services were attended by 2,693.

Evangelistic camp meetings with guest speakers continued each spring, but they were reported with less detail and enthusiasm than the camp meetings held at other mission sites. An exception was a ten-day series of meetings before Easter in 1934, which resulted in an ingathering of twenty-four new members at the Good Friday service—apparently without a waiting period of special instructions.

Daily vacation Bible school was added in 1935, with May Simms as director. Thirty-eight children were enrolled, of whom thirty were Indian children. The emphasis was on mission work in Japan, Mexico, Africa, and Arabia; and dimes and pennies were dropped into a Bible bank for missions.

40. Alice E. Scholten, "Our Indian Work at Dulce, N.M.," *Christian Intelligencer and Mission Field*, December 14, 1927, 795.
41. *Annual Report of the Women's Board of Domestic Missions*, 1927, 26.

The trading post in Dulce was run by Emmet Wirt,
a close associate of J. Denton Simms.

The End of the Simms Era, 1936

J. Denton Simms resigned in 1936, for reasons that had as much to do with politics and business as with faith.

In his twenty-chapter memoir, *Cowboys, Indians, and Pulpits*, Simms wrote relatively few pages about the twenty-four years he spent in Dulce. Of the eight chapters that covered his years there, he devoted one chapter to the white burial dress and three chapters to his best friend, Emmet Wirt, and Wirt's trading post on the Jicarilla reservation. Simms had been a trader in Mescalero, and in Dulce he soon began working at the store two Saturdays each month, when Indians came in from the camps to receive their meager allotments of beef, flour, bacon, beans, sugar, and coffee. Eventually there was also a family connection, for Simms's son married Wirt's daughter. When Wirt became too ill to work, Simms brought in his wife's brother, Dick Harper, from Mescalero, to carry on. After the store was sold to the tribe in 1937, Harper stayed on as store manager for another five years.

Simms Resigns

In his memoir, Simms states that President Roosevelt's administration had made changes that were making it more difficult for him as a missionary. "John Collier was appointed Commissioner of Indian Affairs and moved quickly to break up the alliance between the trader, the agent, and the missionary which had, we thought, brought about significant improvements for the Jicarillas." The tribe took over the trading post run by Emmet Wirt, and the new agent's approach was, in Simms's words, "to encourage the Indians to reinstate customs and religious ceremonies which he thought we had discouraged." Simms went on to say that "The new agent was shutting me out of discussion on Indian matters. I decided my usefulness as a missionary there was about over and resigned."[42]

Thus, Simms was forthright in making it clear that he could not accept (1) the new openness to Indian customs and (2) the loss of control that he and Wirt had enjoyed. In an age when most Christian missionaries to American Indians yoked Christian convictions with white civilization, Simms was among the most radical. It was not surprising, then, that the Indian Reorganization Act of 1934, with its legitimatizing of Indian culture and its legalization of tribal government, was a major factor in Simms's resignation.

The resignation of J. Denton Simms brought an end to an era. The daughter and son-in-law of pioneer missionaries Richard and Ella Mae Harper had come as virtual newlyweds in 1914, theologically untrained, without ordination, and in a temporary arrangement that smacked of nepotism. But they had stayed for twenty-two years and planted a church, opened a mission school, played a role in bringing a degree of health and hope to a dying tribe, and generated widespread support in the Reformed Church for Indian mission work in general and Dulce in particular.

A Review of the Simms Era

Veronica Velarde Tiller, a Jicarilla Apache who holds a Ph.D. degree in history from the University of New Mexico, in her book, *The Jicarilla Apache Tribe: A History*, gave a positive evaluation of the mission's influence on the Jicarilla people and on some aspects of the Simms-Wirt alliance:

> The mission exercised a strong influence over the Jicarillas not only because it had a monopoly over education for over two decades, but also because the Indian Office did not provide the people with community service facilities. The church filled this void and offered services such as performance of marriages and funerals, vacation Bible studies, recreational programs, and clothing drives for all newborn babies. The church became a

---

42. Simms, *Cowboys,* 126.

The Model A Ford replaced horses for calling on the scattered Indian camps.

fixture in the lives of most Jicarillas; it served as a place to turn when the government was unresponsive. It also had a way of ingratiating itself with the people. Parents were allowed to stay overnight at the mission at no charge when they had traveled long distances to get to town. Christmas gifts were given to all the people and they were appreciated since most were so poor....

The minister, Denton Simms, became a leading figure in the community. His son married one of Emmet Wirt's daughters and the two became a powerful duo. They were called upon to testify during investigations, served as advocates for the tribe, accompanied agency officials to important meetings, and in these ways they were able to influence affairs on the reservation.[43]

The Simms family, by this time including six children, moved to Albuquerque, where in 1939 Simms accepted a call to be pastor of the First Presbyterian Church. In all likelihood he was ordained by the Presbyterian Church at this time, although records are vague. A painful facial nerve malady forced his resignation in 1943. He turned to ranching near Chromo, Colorado, then returned to Albuquerque as associate pastor of the Immanuel Presbyterian Church. He served there for eighteen years until retiring in 1977 at the age of eighty-eight. Mary Simms died in 1973, and Denton died in 1979 at the age of ninety.

The Mission School Closes

With the close of the Simms era also came the close of the mission school. With tuberculosis largely contained, it was no longer

43. Rev. ed. (Albuquerque: BowArrow, 1983, 1992, 2000), 156-57.

John and Nina Keuning, with Kenneth and Audrey

necessary to maintain a sanitarium to keep sick children separated from the well ones, so in 1935 the government took back the schooling of all the children. The mission, however, continued to house the children in its dormitories for five more years, at which time the government built its own dormitories.

This meant, of course, major changes in staff responsibilities. Hendrina Hospers, in her twenty-sixth year at Dulce, continued her ministry of calling on Indian homes (now by automobile instead of horseback). Edna Vande Vrede continued much of her office and administrative work and later became director of the new Community House. She also called on Indian homes, taught Sunday school and midweek classes, and even assisted at funerals and worship services.

The Keuning and Gee Years, 1936-52

The Women's Board lost no time in calling a new missionary pastor to replace Simms. By September 1936 the Reverend John and Nina (Gosselink) Keuning arrived at the parsonage with their children, Audrey and Kenneth, later to be joined by Treva.

Keuning was the first pastor in Dulce to be raised and educated in the Reformed Church in America. Born in Pella, Iowa, in 1903, he graduated from Central College and Western Theological Seminary. He spent two years as pastor of the Hope Reformed Church in Westfield, North Dakota, and three years at the Central Reformed Church in Sioux Center, Iowa, before launching an eight-year stay in Dulce. The Keunings were not strangers to Dulce, Nina having taught the Simms children before her marriage, and John having visited the reservation in order to visit his fiancé.

A Change in Attitude toward Indian Customs

Articles in the denominational publication (now called the *Intelligencer-Leader* through a merger of the *Christian Intelligencer* and the *Leader*) and the minutes of the Women's Board of Domestic Missions revealed a gradual change in attitude toward Indian customs and ceremonies—at least on the part of the pastors. The "misses" who served the school and mission staff, however, continued to have serious misgivings about Indian dances and other observances. The primary thrust of reports to the denomination was on the progress of the ministry rather than on the shortcomings of the Indian culture. This change in viewpoint can in part be attributed to the nationwide change in attitude that precipitated the Indian Reorganization Act of 1934, which had been passed by Congress two years before the Keunings arrived.

This change also reflected, no doubt, the personal attitude of the new pastor and his wife. Both Keunings, for instance, undertook the study of Apache and Spanish. Many of the Indians could understand Spanish, still used widely in the surrounding Mexican-American population. How well the Keunings succeeded in their quest is unclear, however, since Keuning continued to use the services of an interpreter until he left in 1944.

When the Keunings arrived, the church that greeted them listed about 140 communicant members and sixty families. The staff consisted of a dozen people, including boys' and girls' matrons, housekeepers, and maintenance people. The Keunings' first letters to their constituency reflect pleasure at being received with a friendly spirit by the Indians, but also two major concerns: (1) the desecration of the Sabbath by the white people of the community, thereby setting a bad example for the Indians; and (2) the increased incidence of drunkenness among Indian people, despite laws against the sale or giving of alcohol. Heretofore little had been said about alcoholism on the reservation, but gradually it became a more common theme.

Dulce mission workers, 1936-37.

Ironically, the first funeral conducted in Dulce by Keuning was that of a sister of the little girl who had been buried by Simms when he arrived on the scene twenty-two years earlier—the child who to the astonishment of her fellow tribespeople had been clothed in the remnants of a white wedding dress and placed in a pine casket.

An entryway was added to the church, as well as a steeple—the previous steeple having been knocked down during an earthquake. The students were now attending the government school, but the dormitories, maintained by the mission, were overflowing with ninety boys and girls, ages five to seventeen. The entire mission complex, nestled at the foot of Dulce Rock, was featured on the front cover of the *Intelligencer-Leader* of June 25, 1937.

A Missionary Trailer

Soon after he arrived, Keuning determined that a mission house trailer would enhance the ministry, and in 1938 the Women's Board of Domestic Missions made a successful appeal to raise $1,000 for the vehicle. The fifteen-foot trailer, equipped with beds and cooking facilities, enabled mission personnel to travel to the south side of the reservation without returning home each evening. They carried with

The missionary trailer ready for a trip to the
south end of the reservation

them a small projector operated by the car battery, which attracted a lot
of curiosity. Increased attention to the southern side of the reservation,
where the Indians kept their sheep during the winter months, was also
evidenced by a Christmas service held in a store building in 1937, with
seventy-five Indians attending. Meanwhile, tepees were gradually giving
way to log cabins and Anglo-style tents, but still with dirt floors. Still
rare were cook stoves, double beds, and sewing machines.

Christmas continued to be a major event in the life of the
church, with as many as three hundred children and adults showing
up for Sunday school pageants, preaching services, staff dramas, and,
of course, the distribution of gifts provided by Reformed Church
congregations.

A New Community House

As the mission moved away from education (1935) and then
from student housing (1940), it looked for other avenues of ministry
to supplement the church work. In August 1940 the Women's Board
announced that the mission was to begin a "fine, Christian recreational
program" and that one of the buildings was to be remodeled into a
community house.[44] Work was begun immediately to provide a facility
that included a gymnasium, library, kitchen, dining room, women's
sewing/meeting room, and several rooms to be used by Indian families
when they came to the agency for their rations or to visit their school

44. Helen M. Brickman, "The Church That is Taking to Wheels," *Intelligencer-
    Leader*, August 30, 1940, 5-6.

A typical Indian camp

children. Edna Vande Vrede was appointed director, and it soon became known as "Miss Edna's Big House." Within a few years the gymnasium was used for basketball practice by the Lumberton Public School, the Dulce Public School, and by the Dulce Indian School.

It would seem that during the Simms years little effort had been made to train Jicarilla people for Christian leadership. Now the name of Bobby Ladd Vicenti, who had come up through the Sunday school and became Keuning's interpreter, came to the forefront. In the fall of 1939 he enrolled at Central College, the first college student from the Dulce church, but he dropped out after one year.

Visits to Indian Camps Continue

Visits to the far-flung Indian camps continued during all kinds of weather. Here are some excerpts from an account by Hedrina Hospers, who often made the trips with Gertrude Van Roekel:

> That night we slept at the Largo store. The next day was windy, but the roads were dry. Cevero had moved his camp but we looked carefully for tracks and finally found a dim road which we followed to the timber as far as we could. Then we got out and walked. We were about to give up when we saw fresh sheep tracks and heard dogs bark and found the camp. After we had visited our seventeenth camp that second day, the storm increased so that we could hardly see, and we had to quit for the day. We had very comfortable quarters at Albert Velarde's, a room to ourselves, as they have a two-room cabin....

Before daylight we were again on our way. Going down Wild Horse Mesa we met Ignacio on horseback. His stepson was very sick and he had had to ride twenty miles to get to a telephone to call the doctor....

At our next stop a grandmother, always pleasant, asked for a blanket. Hers was almost in shreds, so we gave her an outing blanket we had in the car. Her thanks were profuse.

We walked to a camp way up on the cliff by a winding trail....At Pine Springs...we stayed with a young couple who both were in our mission school. Lelia has two lovely children; she tries to train them aright and tells them the Bible stories we give them. She has an extra tent with an old tub for a stove, but it heats the tent well. This was our bedroom.

We were again on our way before sun-up, but we had car trouble once more....In all we visited forty-one homes during those four days, and we pray that at least some of the seed sown may bear fruit.[45]

Camp Meetings Are Revived

Annual evangelistic meetings, never as prominent in Dulce as they were in the other missions, apparently had been quietly discontinued. Then, in the summer of 1941, Keuning was invited to lead the camp meeting at the Comanche Reformed Church in Lawton, Oklahoma, and he took with him several Jicarilla consistory members. The Comanches took them into their homes and "talked with them earnestly about the duties and responsibilities and privileges of a consistoryman."[46] The Jicarillas were greatly impressed by the camp meeting, and upon returning to Dulce they requested a similar event.

The first such meeting was held the following summer, but it was called a Bible conference and held in the church rather than in a tent. The speaker was the Reverend Elmer Borr, pastor of the Trinity Reformed Church in El Monte, California. The conference began with an attendance of only fifteen on Thursday morning but grew to between 225 and 250 by Sunday. Attendance-keeping must have

45. Hendrina Hospers, "Forty-One Homes in Four Days," *Intelligencer-Leader*, May 14, 1943, 12.
46. Mrs. Bradley J. Folensbee, "To Serve the Present Age on Five Indian Mission Fields," *Intelligencer-Leader*, November 21, 1941, 7-8.

been meticulous; according to a very flowery report by the speaker, the meeting reached 291 persons at least once.

Annual Bible conferences followed, with speakers such as Robert Chaat of Lawton; James Ottipoby of New Laguna, New Mexico; Wendell Chino of Mescalero; and Reuben Ten Haken of Mescalero. Later the camp meetings again disappeared quietly, and they are no longer a regular part of the Reformed church's ministry in Dulce.

Military Service

Meanwhile, the Jicarillas were contributing substantially to the World War II effort, sending sixty-four men into the armed services. Of these, one was killed and others were seriously wounded. The social and cultural repercussions of the war became apparent as geographically and socially isolated young men were exposed for long periods of time to the culture and the lifestyle of the outside world, then returned to a tribe with little opportunity for earning a living.

Keuning Years Come to an End

The Keuning years—eight of them—came to an end in 1944 when, citing the health of their young son Kenneth, Keuning accepted a call to the Calvary Reformed Church in Ripon, California. The Women's Board of North American Missions heaped praise upon their work, saying they had "endeared themselves to the Indians scattered all over the reservation" and that their relationship to the board had likewise "ever been cordial and cooperative."[47]

Many years later, when the Keunings were in their late eighties, they reminisced on video about their years in Dulce. Their memories included finding runaways from the school, the mission trailer, worship services at the south end of the reservation, and the sheep industry. In the video John gave an illustration of Indian humor. He related how white people sometimes sniffed Jicarilla baskets before buying them, to see if they were genuine. An Indian woman, upon selling a basket, accepted the money and gave it a wry sniff before putting it in her pocket.

During Keuning's eight years the reported membership grew from 140 communicants to 230, with only six people listed as inactive. The number "Under Christian instruction" grew from 150 to 220. It is unclear, however, what "Under "Christian instruction" included. A 1944

47. M. O., "In New Fields of Service," *Church Herald*, November 3, 1944, 7.

Christmas service on the south side of the reservation

report by summer student Arnold Van Lummel stated that summer attendance in the Sunday school was fifty, with nineteen Indians attending the adult class. He made no mention of Sunday morning attendance. Van Lummel, incidentally, was disturbed by what he called the "moral instability of the people," saying that they can easily be led astray even after they have accepted Christ. He cited the example of a Christian leader who "will do anything to be the head man" and "will leave the church whenever he does not get his way."[48]

The Keunings later continued their ministry in Forreston, Illinois; Holland, Michigan; and Los Angeles, California. John Keuning died February 26, 1997, at the age of ninety-three, and Nina Keuning died three months later at the age of ninety.

The Gees Arrive

The next occupants of the parsonage in Dulce were the Reverend Herbert and Alberta Gee. Pastor Gee was an easterner, having been born in Paterson, New Jersey, in 1900, theologically educated at Colgate University, and ordained by the New Jersey Baptist Association in 1925. In 1940 he came to the Reformed Church, served Reformed churches in Saddle River and Waldwick, New Jersey, and graduated from New Brunswick Theological Seminary in 1942.

48. Arnold Van Lummel, "A Summer at Dulce, New Mexico," *Church Herald*, November 10, 1944, 11.

Worshipers leaving church in the 1940s

The Gees arrived in November 1945 and began their tenure by writing enthusiastically about their first Christmas in Dulce. By foot and wagon the Indian families began arriving two days before Christmas, filling "Miss Edna's Big House" with more than one hundred people on Christmas Eve and more than three hundred all-told. Four Christmas events were conducted. The first was a carol and candle-lighting service Sunday evening, December 23, attended by two hundred, with a chorus of Indian girls, teachers from the government school, and townspeople.

Then came a Christmas Eve service in the gymnasium, with a pageant and the distribution of gifts. Four hundred attended this event, of whom 230 were school children. The Christmas Day "camp tree" service was attended by 190, with gifts for adults and with Buster Vicenti leading the prayer in Apache and interpreting the message. Then on Thursday afternoon the camp tree service was held on the south end of the reservation, sixty miles from Dulce, with 70 attending as Lincoln Velarde interpreted the message and gifts were distributed. Offerings totaling $127 were received for the Reformed Church Emergency Fund, for the relief of war sufferers.

Activities of the church at this time included a Home Aid Club for mothers, a Girl Scout troop, a Boy Scout troop, a vacation Bible school, and roller-skating and movies at the Community Center. Calls continued at the far-flung camps of the 2,400-square-mile reservation.

Dormitory Children Attend Sunday School

In 1947 about 240 children were housed in the government dormitories, and nearly all of them walked down the hill every Sunday to attend Sunday school. In October of that year the Sunday school reported a record attendance of 234 on successive Sundays. The children were also required to attend Bible classes on Wednesday afternoon or evening. A high school education was not offered in Dulce at the time. In 1951 Gee reported that forty young people were attending the Indian High School in Santa Fe and that one girl was beginning a nursing course in Colorado Springs.

Dormitory arrangements remained largely unchanged. Children six years old and above left their homes in mid-August and did not return until early May except for occasional visits. Marie Van Vuren looked at it this way:

"Is all this sacrifice worth while?" the parents ask themselves. Those with an eye to the future answer "yes." The children must be enabled to make personal adjustments to the white man's world, to enjoy the wealth of materials through the use of the printed page, to earn a living and function as citizens of the nation.[49]

Hendrina Hospers retired in 1946 at the age of sixty-six, having given thirty-two years of service to the Jicarilla people following her eight years of service at Fort Sill and one year at Mescalero. In retirement, she made her home in Albuquerque, where she continued to work on a voluntary basis for a church and hospital. A community building, Hospers Hall, was named in her honor in Apache, Oklahoma, in 1966. She died in 1968 at the age of eighty-eight.

Statistics During the Gee Years

Herbert Gee was especially fond of citing statistics, and he sometimes arrived at totals in a curious way. For instance, when he reported on the four-day Bible conference held in October 1946, Gee said, "Our meetings were attended by 882 people."[50] Since the total membership of the tribe was about nine hundred, Gee's total must

49. Marie Van Vuren, "The Four R's," *Church Herald*, November 16, 1951, 8.
50. Herbert and Alberta Gee, "The Gift of Life to the Jicarilla Apache Indians," *Church Herald*, November 14, 1947, 5.

necessarily refer to the total combined attendance of all the sessions, which means that many people may have been counted several times. For Easter Sunday of 1951 Gee reported a record attendance of 346, which was several times the capacity of the church. Twenty-three were baptized, including three adults, ten young people, and ten children.

Despite the impressive statistics, Gee acknowledged that "the principal difficulty in our work is the seeming indifference of our people. In physical ways some have become independent and self-sufficient, which has caused them to feel that they do not need to depend on God and seek His Grace."[51]

Continued Discomfort with Indian Customs

Although pastors Keuning and Gee were much less strident than their predecessor in their criticism of Indian customs, the "misses" were only slightly less negative. Marie Van Vuren wrote in 1948 concerning the fiesta, which now included a rodeo:

> The beat of the tom-tom was heard all night for four nights, and each beat seemed to fall upon our hearts as we thought of the many who were giving themselves over to sin at that very moment. We could hear drunken shouts, and morals take a tremendous nosedive under the influence of liquor. Those were nights of prayer for us missionaries.[52]

Yet two years later, Edna Vande Vrede summarized the ministry by saying, "Paganism has given way to a nucleus of Christians. There has not been any mass acceptance of Christ but all have heard of the matchless love of the Redeemer." Vande Vrede was also encouraged by the fact that the Indian "hovels" had been changed to "one- or two-room crude houses" with stoves, beds, benches, and cupboards, even battery-operated radios.[53] That same year Gertrude Van Roekel wrote, "The Annual Fiesta which formerly gripped every soul, mind, and effort for weeks previous to the event, is less intense, for which we are thankful."[54]

51. *Annual Report of the Board of Domestic Missions*, 1951, 25.
52. Marie Van Vuren, "There Is Yet Much to be Possessed," *Church Herald*, November 19, 1948, 4.
53. Edna D. Vande Vrede, "Dulce—Then and Now," *Church Herald*, March 10, 1950, 4.
54. Gertrude Van Roekel, "Saul Versus Paul," *Church Herald*, November 10, 1950, 8.

Herbert Gee left Dulce in 1952 to accept a call to the Trinity Reformed Church in Amsterdam, New York, and his resignation was accepted by the Board of Domestic Missions with "deep regret."[55] He retired in 1964 and died in 1987 in Penney Farms, Florida, at the age of eighty-seven.

The statistical tables for 1952 show 271 communicants and 223 receiving doctrinal instruction. This compares to 203 communicants and 220 receiving doctrinal instruction at the end of Keuning's tenure eight years earlier. The major difference was in the category of "absent or inactive," which increased from six in 1944 to 150 in 1952.

Major Changes in the 1950s

In the 1950s, major changes took place in the community of Dulce. These in turn changed the role of the church profoundly. For years the Jicarilla Apache mission had offered a nearly total program of spiritual, social, and educational services, but during these years more and more of these functions were assumed by the government and the tribe.

The School Goes Public

A new high school opened in Dulce in 1956, making it unnecessary to send young people to Santa Fe. The entire school system became a public school not only for Indians but for all youth living in Dulce, elsewhere on the reservation, and in nearby Lumberton. It immediately became an interracial school, including Apaches, Navajos, blacks, whites, and Hispanics.

The mission had originally provided both the school and the dormitories, making religious instruction mandatory at both. Then, when the government took over the Indian school, the mission retained the dormitories and continued to give religious instruction at both the school and dormitories. Then the government also took over the dormitories, but it continued to require Indian students in all eight grades to attend religious classes at the school. However, when the school became a public school and included non-Indians, it could no longer include religious classes as part of its curriculum. Consequently, the church could only offer religious classes in its own community building during after-school hours. Bible school classes continued

55. *Annual Report of the Board of Domestic Missions*, 1953, 24.

every Wednesday, with 275 children being bused from the government dormitories, a mile and a half up the hill. Although students could choose what church to go to, they were still required to attend. Because of their own childhood associations, most parents chose the Reformed church, even though they were not themselves attending. As time went on, the Baptists, Assembly of God, Mormons, and Roman Catholics also drew students for after-school classes.

Fire Destroys Community Building

A serious blow was dealt to this after-school program five days before Christmas in 1954, when a fire completely destroyed the Community Building, along with the personal belongings of three Indian families staying there and hundreds of gifts stored for Christmas distribution. Faulty wiring was determined to be the cause of the fire. Plans were made immediately to replace the building, and in 1955 ground was broken for the new community center. The Church Service Center, as it was officially called, was built at a cost of $75,000.

Natural Gas and Oil Discovered

Another major development unfolded in the early 1950s: oil and natural gas were discovered on the reservation. Considerable income was generated by the newly found natural resources, each person receiving approximately $500 per year. Soon the tribe had a new office building and was assuming increased responsibility for the social and economic concerns of the people. Because many Jicarillas were immediately spending their entire checks, steps were taken by the tribe to make monthly instead of annual payments. As economic conditions slowly improved, horses and wagons gave way to pickups and automobiles.

The Dykstras Arrive, 1953

The fourth pastor in Dulce was the Reverend Harold E. Dykstra, who arrived in June of 1953 with his wife, Dorothy. Dykstra had been born in Holland, Michigan, and had received degrees from Hope College and Western Theological Seminary. After his ordination in 1952 he served for a year in Macy, Nebraska, before coming to Dulce.

Until this time the Reformed Church had been the only religious body in town, but that changed. The Mormons moved in, as they were doing on Indian reservations throughout the country, and their aggressive tactics included urging Indians to be rebaptized and to join the "only true religion." They most often targeted confessing Christians rather than the unchurched, thereby confusing church members. This prompted a new interest in teaching, not just to gain converts but also to strive for Christian maturity and spiritual stability. Said the Board of Domestic Missions in its 1953 report, "Many trust in the Savior without knowing why or how...the missionaries must be teachers as well as evangelists."[56]

With the passage of a law that loosened restrictions on alcohol sales to Indians, drunkenness went from bad to worse. Younger men began to scorn taking care of sheep, and, with few other industries available, idleness became an even greater problem than before.

Hassalls Join Staff

Significant changes in personnel took place in the 1950s. In 1948 James and Inez Hassall, members of the Reformed church in Hammond, Indiana, joined the staff—James as a maintenance worker, Inez as a teacher, and the two of them as directors of the religious education program. At a Women's Missionary Society meeting in DeMotte, Indiana, Inez had heard pastor Gee give an earnest appeal for a maintenance worker, and a month later they and their two sons arrived in Dulce via narrow gauge railroad. They later adopted a Jicarilla girl. James wrote positively about Indian people, relating proudly how his sons herded sheep and trailed wild animals with Indian friends. In 1955 he published in the *Church Herald* a virtual mission policy statement with thinly veiled criticism of past procedures and policies. Here are some excerpts:

> The mission's greatest need is an understanding heart....We are not trying to revive a dole system whereby we offer the Indians physical comfort if they will but enter our doors. Nor are we offering a "dole system of religion" in offering them the Gospel of Christ. The Indian must realize that it takes initiative to become a Christian; his reward—restoration of self-esteem...
>
> We must endeavor to erase the errors of the past which are prominent in his mind from past dealings with the "white" man....We, as missionaries, must erase the word "white" from his mind's eye so that he may see us only as Christian men.

56. *Annual Report of the Board of Domestic Missions*, 1953, 24.

We are not trying to force a "white" man's religion on a defeated nation, and the Indian must understand this point completely. The Indian, as a broken and defeated man, is hesitant to accept Christ. The Indian must realize that to accept Christ is to erase the prefix "de" in the word defeat, and create the word "feat,"—an act of esteem....

The Indian accepting Christ will again be able to take his rightful place in this great nation dedicated to the principle that all men are created equal—in the sight of God.[57]

More Optimism/Pessimism

As his tenure as pastor drew to a close, Dykstra penned another of those typical mixtures of hardship and hope. This one, in effect, negated the happy tales of mission success that had predominated the reports by the previous mission staff and the Board of Domestic Missions:

For forty years the foundations have been laid and groundwork has been done, and we can expect that fruits *should begin to be seen* [italics mine] in Dulce....There is a sense of expectancy for a genuine harvest in the years immediately ahead.[58]

The Dykstras left in 1956, having accepted a call to serve a circuit of small Presbyterian churches near Reserve, New Mexico. Record keeping and annual reports suffered a major breakdown during the Dykstra tenure, and no reliable figures are available.

Hesselinks Arrive

The Board of Domestic Missions added to the Dulce staff by hiring Derwin (Dick) and Edith Hesselink. Both Hesselinks had been born and raised in the area of Sheboygan, Wisconsin, and Dick had graduated from Reformed Bible College in Grand Rapids, Michigan. They served for about five years with the Christian Reformed Church in neighborhood ministry in Chicago, then came to Dulce with their two children in March 1956. The Hesselinks did maintenance work,

57. James R. Hassall, "Through Christ—The Understanding Heart," *Church Herald*, August 5, 1955, 5.
58. Harold Dykstra, "God Rules—and Overrules," *Church Herald*, November 18, 1955, 15.

The Dykstra Family

handled the Christian education program, and preached occasionally, maintaining a cordial relationship with the Indian people.

John and Helga Lucius

The fifth couple to occupy the pulpit in Dulce were the Reverend John and Helga Lucius, who four years earlier had begun a career of ministry to Native Americans that would span thirty years.

Helga Sawitzky Lucius spent most of her early years in the parsonage of the Reformed church in Canarsie, New York, where her father, Frederick, was pastor. She met her husband at Hope College and worked for several years as a social worker in New York City. A native of Long Island City, New York, John Lucius was educated at Hope College and New Brunswick Theological Seminary. After being ordained by the Classis of Schoharie in 1947, he served two churches in New York: Prattsville (1947-49) and Second, Astoria (1949-53). The Luciuses then went to Macy, Nebraska, where they served for four years before coming to Dulce in 1957.

Church Transferred to West Central Classis

In 1957 all six American Indian congregations were transferred out of the Classis of New York, where they had been since they were organized, and became members of a classis in their geographical area. The Jicarilla Apache Reformed Church and the Comanche and Apache churches of Oklahoma were transferred to the Classis of West Central.

Four Staff Members Phased Out

John Lucius, in his 1959 report to the Board of Domestic Missions, reflected on the changing role of the church in Dulce:

> Whereas we heretofore had been called on to extend our ministry into fields not usually the responsibility of the church, we could now see ourselves being able to confine ourselves to a truly vigorous ministry, and it is towards this goal that we now have set our sights....Tasks formerly performed by staff members can now be assumed by indigenous leadership.[59]

The staff members Lucius was referring to were James and Inez Hassall and the last of the "misses" of the Jicarilla mission—Marie Van Vuren and Gertrude Van Roekel, who had served the mission since 1929 and 1937, respectively. Lucius paid tribute to them as having "worked willingly and tirelessly during the past years, ministering in the name of Christ," but also made it clear that they would have no choice but to step down:

> Because they have labored so long and so well, those to whom they were sent can now assume some responsibility for their church, and these two devoted servants can enter some other area of service where they are needed and their talents can be used of the Lord.[60]

Van Vuren and Van Roekel found another "area of service" as employees of the Bureau of Indian Affairs—Van Vuren as secretary for education and welfare, and Van Roekel as an adult education teacher. They continued to attend the church and maintained cordial relationships with the Indian people, but they were deeply hurt by their termination, and their relationship to the mission became strained.

The Hassalls moved to Espanola, New Mexico, where James became an insurance agent. Said the Hassall's son, David (who married a Jicarilla woman in Dulce in 1958), "It really hurt him terribly, and I'm not sure he ever recovered from that."[61]

59. *Annual Report of the Board of Domestic Missions,* 1959, 25.
60. Ibid, 26.
61. Email from David Hassall, January 19, 2003.

Lucius Leaves

The Luciuses left the pastorate in 1961 to continue their ministry among American Indians in another context: high school education. John accepted an invitation to become chaplain and coordinator of religious activities at the Phoenix Indian School, a government high school. He stayed on for twenty-three years until his retirement in 1983.

Statistics for the four years of the Lucius pastorate indicate either a precipitous drop in active membership or (more likely) a policy of more accurate reporting. Reports for 1956, just before Lucius's arrival, boasted 295 communicants, and the 1957 report listed only eighty-two communicants. Simultaneously, the "inactive" column went from zero to 201.

Dick and Edith Hesselink resigned their position in 1961 to go to Chicago, there to serve with the Bethany Reformed Church and then with the World Home Bible League. After Lucius left for Phoenix, the pulpit was occupied for a year by a temporary pastor, the Reverend Robert Robinson, who had just graduated from Biblical Seminary in New York City.

The Calsbeek-Schouten-Hocking Team, 1960s

The Hassalls, Hesselinks, and Robinsons had all left; and Van Vuren and Van Roekel had retired, at least from official church work. Into the gap came newlyweds Stuart and Joan Schouten, who would contribute a measure of stability for the next nine years, even in the midst of storm.

Schoutens Arrive

The Schoutens had been born and raised in Wisconsin. Joan had a degree from Central College, and Stuart had only a high school diploma. They were not prepared, they said, for the void they stepped into when they arrived in Dulce in September 1961:

> We began with the prospect of 150-200 children in Sunday school and the Wednesday afternoon school release program. There were no teachers, no helpers (other than Steve Cata), no pastor, and no real direction.[62]

62. Stuart and Joan Schouten, "History of Mission Work, Dulce, New Mexico, September 1961-January 1971," private report, 1998, 1.

Stuart and Joan
Schouten

The Schoutens had been hired to do maintenance and educational work, but their roles quickly expanded. Stuart not only maintained the grounds, buildings, and vehicles, but also taught classes, drove the church bus, and led the Boy Scouts. Joan taught classes, directed the choir, did office work, managed the used clothing store, and led the women's work. Early in 1962 the Schoutens took training at Cook Training School in Tempe, Arizona, the first white people to attend a pilot program for missionaries who worked with American Indian people.

But they weren't alone for long. William and Marion Hocking, another lay couple who made major contributions to Indian ministries, arrived in Dulce a month after the Schoutens. William Hocking directed the Church Service Center (which was again being called the Community Center) and was custodian of the mission properties. Marion Hocking coordinated the weekday Bible classes and the Sunday religious education program.

Calsbeeks Arrive

Also in 1962 the church called the Reverend Harvey and Angline Calsbeek, one of the Reformed Church's most respected pastoral couples to serve American Indian congregations. The Calsbeeks came from Mescalero, New Mexico, where they had served for eight years. Calsbeek and other staff members launched an effort to train leaders and teachers, resulting in the commitment of three new teachers.

The gas, oil, lumber, sheep, cattle, and craft industries continued to alleviate poverty to a certain extent. Homes were being built or remodeled, complete with refrigerators and television sets, and pickups and cars replaced horses and buckboards. The *Jicarilla Chieftain*, supported by tribal funds, began publication in 1962. But alcohol continued to take its toll through auto accidents, cirrhosis of the liver, child abuse, divorce, and suicide. "During one six-month period," wrote Marion Hocking, "thirteen deaths, mostly of youth and mostly violent, wrapped our little community in a pall of gloom."[63]

In the midst of positive material progress and personal and community dysfunction, Marion Hocking saw a continuing role for the church:

> The Indian has inherited from the white man's dominance of the past a sense of inferiority, a broken family life, the use of alcohol to an alarming degree, a lack of pride in himself as a useful member of society, and a sense of futility about life in general that can continue to hinder his growth as a mature person, even in the midst of his economic advance. The church has it in its power to give the Jicarilla Apaches that inner sense of worth that can modify all his present adjustments to this space age and give them ultimate meaning.[64]

A 1965 photo brochure, *Dialogue in Dulce*, expressed similar sentiments. It did, however add an emphasis on dialogue (also drawing puzzling distinctions among "mission," "purpose," and "goal"):

> Our mission in Dulce is to effect dialogue—dialogue between church and community. Our purpose is to present Christ—to bear witness to His love, and to serve as an instrument of His grace....Our goal is to have His message so permeate every aspect of community life that together with physical, social, and economic improvement shall come spiritual strength and enlightenment.[65]

63. Marion Hocking, "Mourning and Dancing," *Church Herald*, June 1997, 31.
64. Marion Hocking, "The Changing Scene in Dulce," *Church Herald*, November 6, 1964, 30.
65. Published by North American Missions, Reformed Church in America, 1965, 1.

One of the photos in the brochure, incidentally, is an interesting study in denominational promotion. In an obviously posed photo of a worship service at the church in Dulce, all the worshipers are seated on one side of the church, making it look crowded. Of the thirty people present, eleven are children and nineteen are adults. Three of the children and six of the adults are white, indicating that only thirteen American Indian adults were present for the photo.

The Discouragements of Indian Ministry

Some of the difficulties of ministry—so seldom publicly aired—were voiced by the Hockings in a *Church Herald* article in 1965:

> Missionary life is sometimes so discouraging. Nobody seems to hear what you are trying to say....Oh, some do hear and respond—for a while. Then trouble comes, or failure in their Christian life, and they give up their new faith in Christ so easily. Sometimes it's not even trouble or failure that makes them give up. Sometimes it is too much money or the desire for too many material possessions.
>
> The children that you teach, so wide-eyed and eager, often go back to homes where the example and teaching of parents conflict with what you have taught, and the children forget, or become confused and bewildered by it all. And the seed planted seems to die before it ever gets a chance to take root.[66]

Marie Van Vuren, in a letter to a friend, wrote, "The church membership grows very slowly. Many consider themselves members of our church—who united with it as young people—but who enter the church about once a year—staunchly profess themselves members of the "Dutch Mission." [67]

Marie Van Vuren and Gertrude Van Roekel, incidentally, renewed their participation in the work of the mission after the arrival of the Calsbeeks, Hockings, and Schoutens. In the absence of Indian Sunday school teachers, they again volunteered their services. In the letter just quoted, Van Vuren also said, "The Indian people look to us for encouragement and help," and, since there was no field worker on the mission, "on weekends we try to visit a few homes."[68]

---

66. Bill and Marion Hocking, "...And So We Never Give Up," *Church Herald*, November 5, 1965, 4-5.
67. Marie Van Vuren, letter to "Dear Jennie," April 27, 1963, 2.
68. Ibid., 3.

An earthquake rattled the town in January of 1966, causing damage to many buildings in town, including the parsonage and Community Center.

Calsbeeks Leave

By all indications, the six members of the staff—the Calsbeeks, Hockings, and Schoutens—had outstanding professional and personal relationships, often referring to themselves as a "team." The team was reduced to four in 1966 when the Calsbeeks accepted a call to the Reformed Church in Silver Creek, Minnesota. They later accepted pastorates in Yankton and Willow Lake, South Dakota, before returning to Indian work in Macy, Nebraska, in 1978. After retirement they returned to Dulce for a one-year interim assignment in 1988.

During the Calsbeek's four-year tenure, active membership increased from seventy-two to eighty-four, and the number of inactive members decreased from 215 to sixty, primarily because many inactives were dropped from membership. The number of children in the weekday and Sunday school programs moved downward, primarily because children in the government dormitories began to move to their own homes as transportation became easier.

The Tribe Asks Missionaries to Leave, 1967

In 1967, apparently immediately after the Calsbeeks left for Minnesota, the remaining mission staff conducted a survey of community opinion. Thirteen responses were received from representatives of various agencies in the tribe. The survey consisted of four questions. To the first, "Has the Jicarilla Apache Reformed Church made any significant contributions to this community?" all except one said yes.

Question two, which dealt with the manner of contributions by the church, yielded such answers as religion, spiritual and moral guidance, education, living standards, organizations such as the scouting program, and the use of facilities for recreation and organizational activities.

Question three, which asked for perceived weaknesses, yielded a rather consistent pattern of "not enough personal contact," "pastors who feel superior," and "too busy taking care of a building and not busy enough taking care of people."

Question four, which asked how the church could better serve the community, emphasized getting to know the people, spending less time on buildings, developing Indian leadership, alcohol education, and greater emphasis on youth activities.[69]

Calvin and Janet Hays Arrive

After a vacancy of about a year, the Reverend Calvin Hays succeeded Harvey Calsbeek as the pastor in Dulce. Hays was a native of Gray Hawk, Kentucky, where his father, Ray, a lay preacher ordained in the Reformed Church, served as an evangelist for twenty-four years. Hays had served for two years at the Hope Reformed Church in Parkersburg, Iowa, after graduating from New Brunswick Theological Seminary.

The validity of the affirmations and criticisms of the community survey never had a chance to be evaluated, much less implemented. In the fall of 1967, the Dulce tribal council dropped a bombshell on the mission. In a letter dated October 23, 1967, tribal chairman Charlie Vigil addressed Beth Marcus, executive secretary of the Board of Domestic Missions:

> By unanimous action of the Representative Tribal Council of the Jicarilla Apache Tribe at its meeting of October 23, 1967, I was instructed to request of your Board that you take the necessary steps to cause the removal of the Reverend Calvin Hays as pastor of the Reformed Church here in Dulce. Similar action was taken in regard to request the removal of Mr. and Mrs. William Hocking.

The letter went on to say that the council's decision:

> will in no way affect the continued operation of your church here in Dulce. In years past there is no doubt but what your pastors and assistants have contributed in large measure to the welfare and betterment of our people. However, permit me to repeat that it is our collective hope that, in your wisdom, you will agree that the above named persons have outlived their usefulness on this reservation.

---

69. Typewritten report, "Jicarilla Apache Reformed Church—Mission Evaluation," 1967.

Contributing Factors to the Call for Removal

What could have triggered this unprecedented action? The Reverend Willis Clark, pastor of the Disciples Church in Farmington, had for some time been serving as director of the Community Action Program (CAP) in Dulce, which conducted four components of the poverty program. The CAP Committee and the Tribal Council had dismissed Clark, apparently without giving him a hearing or giving any reasons. The members of the Reformed mission staff—Hays, Schouten, and Hocking, as well as Mrs. Thaymeus B. Vigil (a Pueblo who had married a Jicarilla)—had sent a thirteen-page letter, with attached documents, to the CAP office in Washington, D.C., objecting to the action.

Word got back to Dulce through the local CAP office. The tribal council responded negatively, questioned the missionaries, and stated in the letter to Marcus quoted above that "the clergy and its assistants must not become so intimately involved in the governmental decisions of the tribe" and that "we do not believe it serves any usefulness for non-Indians to continue a controversy involving matters not within their jurisdiction, once a decision has been reached."

Several factors are likely to have played a role in this unprecedented action. The late 1960s were the zenith of the "red power" movement, a period of self-assertion, self-determination, and sometimes of militancy. The government, church, tribal councils, and individual leaders were sorting out their new roles as power was being transferred from the non-Indian minority to the Indian majority. The tribal council may have looked upon the missionaries' letter as a challenge to their authority and perhaps as an attempt to rein in their newfound independence. The fact that non-Indian missionaries had come to the defense of a non-Indian employee of the tribe may also have contributed to their unease.

Another factor in the case may have been the forthright personality of Hays, a fiery preacher who in no uncertain terms condemned the heavy drinking and other vices that were bringing so much devastation to the community. A sermon delivered April 2, 1967, for instance, was entitled, "The Scars of Irresponsibility." In it Hays stated that in the past two or three weeks eleven people had been hospitalized or buried "because of irresponsibility." His prayer of confession included that "nine of thy children are broken to pieces and two are dead because we have been irresponsible Christians." Hays took to task both the congregation and the community. To the congregation he said, "If there isn't some sadness in your heart—if there isn't any emptiness in your life this morning, a compassion going out, for those people whose lives have been badly damaged and may be destroyed, then the label 'Christian' doesn't fit you in the slightest." The community, he said, is "sick unto death with the vilest of sin in its life....We are responsible. Don't you forget it! And our children, yours and mine, will die, just like the others have died, unless we call a halt in the name of God!"[70] The Reverend Albert Van Dyke, the Reformed Church's newly appointed director of Indian work, said in a letter to Beth Marcus in December of that year that state officials believed that the preaching at the mission was the real issue.

It is important to note that although the Schoutens also signed the letter to the Washington CAP office, they were not included in the tribal request for dismissal. Perhaps the Schoutens were not perceived as a threat to tribal authority. Perhaps the tribe wished to retain the Schoutens in order to substantiate their expressed wish for the ministry to continue. Or perhaps the reason was simply that the Schoutens were expecting their third child and were at a doctor's appointment in Farmington when the Hayses and Hockings were asked to appear before the council.

The Church Responds

Ruth Peale, president of the Board of North American Missions, sent a letter to the tribe acknowledging its request. On November 29, 1967, a consultation was held with Indian leaders from other areas—Al Spence, Scott Redhouse, Wendell Chino, Robert Chaat, and Jonah Washington. Conversations apparently were not held with the Jicarilla consistory or congregation.

Mission administrators Marcus and Van Dyke made the decision not to appeal the decision or even to talk to the Jicarilla Apache Tribal Council. "If we go to talk to the Council before these folks leave," wrote Van Dyke to Marcus, "might it not appear that we are hoping they would reconsider and change their mind? This would only serve to irk them. I think we should remove the families and then talk."[71]

70. Calvin C. Hays, "The Scars of Irresponsibility," typewritten message delivered to the Jicarilla Apache Reformed Church, April 2, 1967.
71. Memo from Albert Van Dyke to Beth Marcus, Board of North American Missions, RCA, Dec. 2, 1967. Letters related to this incident are housed at the Archives of the Reformed Church in America in New Brunswick, New Jersey.

Acting quickly, Van Dyke wrote to Hays December 9, 1967. "In correspondence and conference with Dr. Marcus," he wrote, "it has been definitely decided that you and William Hocking will have to terminate your ministry at Dulce." He went on to say that efforts were being made to secure another area of service, and that "I'm sure that the messages you have brought to the community in this short span cannot easily be forgotten, whether they are heeded or not."

Hays subsequently moved to the denomination's Midwest office in Lansing, Illinois, where he spent six months doing promotional work. He subsequently founded the Calvin Hays Evangelistic Association and spent the next six years as an itinerant evangelist. He later returned to his roots in Jackson County, Kentucky, to do pastoral work there.

In August of the next year, after seven years in Dulce, the Hockings began a long ministry at Cook Christian Training School, which by that time had moved from Phoenix to Tempe, Arizona.

A Puzzling Follow-Up and Apology

Inexplicably, to the non-Indian mind at least, Jicarilla tribal chairman Charlie Vigil—who had written the letter asking for the missionaries' removal—wrote a letter to Ruth Peale (with copies to Stewart Udall, secretary of the interior, and other government officials), reprimanding the Reformed Church's Board of North American Missions for not supporting the Hayses and the Hockings and for not talking with the tribe about the matter.

"I am sorry," he wrote, "that you or a representative from the Board of Missions did not come to talk with us....We understood you would. I wish, too, that your church members here in Dulce would have come to talk with us, and that you would have consulted with them and gotten their reaction to all of this." He said that many who supported the missionaries had not come forward, "so I feel that these courageous people, the Hays and the Hockings, were left alone in their hour of need." The apology became more explicit as Vigil said that:

> most of us who sit on the Council, as well as others in the community, were embarrassed by all that has taken place....A lot of light has been thrown on this whole affair since the decision of our Council and by you. It is said that the decision was made at a time when all the facts were either not clear or not known....We have hurt the community spirit by our hasty action.

The Hayses and the Hockings, he said, "are the kind of people we need to help us move forward in this fast changing world." Vigil concluded by urging the Reformed Church to stay in Dulce and by pledging to work more closely together:

> I am most grateful to have the Reformed Church at work in our reservation. It has done much for our people, and I feel that my people do not want this fine relationship to be marred by this unfortunate incident that never should have happened. It is my desire that you will consult with us about any major changes in your program on this reservation. I feel that your program might be more effective if we worked together more closely.[72]

In response, Ruth Peale acknowledged that "in human frailty, no doubt, we all made some mistakes," expressed gratitude for the expression of concern, and pledged to work more closely together in planning the church's future role in the community.[73]

It was decided not to replace the Hockings, in hopes that the congregation would take more responsibility for teaching and leadership. The Schoutens were to train someone in the congregation for general janitorial duties, and the tribal maintenance department would be contracted to help with major repairs.

Meanwhile, Max and Wilma Phone were emerging as lay leaders in the congregation. Instead of boycotting the annual Go-Jii-Yah Festival at Stone Lake in September, the church conducted Sunday services at lakeside during the festival, with elder Phone leading the group. Wilma Phone later served a term on the General Program Council of the Reformed Church. Both served as elders and deacons, both taught Sunday school, and both were instrumental in keeping the Jicarilla language alive.

One of the promising young men of the congregation, Floyd Atole, attended Northwestern College and had intentions of studying for the ministry, but was killed in action in Vietnam.

72. Letter from Charlie Vigil to Mrs. Norman Vincent Peale, president of the Board of North American Mission, with copies to Stewart Udall, secretary of the interior; Dr. James Wilson, chief of Indian Desk, OEO; Mr. L. J. Kozlowski, superintendent, Jicarilla Agency, July 12, 1968.
73. Letter from Ruth S. Peale to Charlie Vigil, chairman of the Jicarilla Apache Tribe, August 5, 1968.

Irvin Max and Wilma
Phone, long-time church
leaders in Dulce, in 1962

Jonah Washington, First Indian Pastor in Dulce

After the departure of Calvin Hays, mission administrators
Marcus and Van Dyke believed the time had come to install the first
Indian pastor at Dulce. They turned to the Reverend Jonah Washington,
who for nine years had received denominational support as director of
religious education and campus pastor at Chilocco Indian School in
Chilocco, Oklahoma (see p. 45-46).

With Washington's arrival in Dulce in 1968, three of the six
Indian Reformed congregations were being served by Native American
pastors. Robert Chaat was pastor in Lawton, and Frank Love served the
Mescalero church.

"We are happy here...We have been kindly received," wrote
Harriette Washington in a February 1969 article in the *Church Herald*.[74]
But the Washington's tenure was a short (four years) and generally
unhappy one. The Jicarillas had difficulty accepting a Pima pastor. Even
more importantly, the relationship between Harriette Washington and
church and community members was less than cordial, and tensions
soon became evident. She also displayed irritation with non-Indians
from the Reformed Church who, she said, "visit the reservation for
two or three days and become 'experts' in Indian affairs overnight."
She welcomed non-Indian friends "who really care," she said, "but we
are too busy developing indigenous leadership to educate superficial
observers."[75]

74. Harriette J. Washington, "Dulce in Transition," *Church Herald*, Feb. 7, 1969,
   28.
75. Harriette Washington, "The New Indian," *Update*, a bulletin of the General
   Program Council, October 1970, 2.

Faced with increasing uneasiness at the Dulce church and the unpleasant prospect of removing an Indian pastor, the mission administrators came upon the idea of removing the Schoutens, the last-remaining non-Indian staff members, in hopes of clearing the way for a fully Indian leadership structure. So the Schoutens left in January 1971, having come as newlyweds nine years earlier and leaving now with three children. "We could find many excuses to stay longer," they wrote in a farewell letter to supporting churches, "but we know that if we did, the people would not grow as they should."[76] The Schoutens moved to Frankfort, Illinois, to take responsibility for Camp Manitoqua; later they assumed the directorship of Inspiration Hills, a Reformed Church camp and conference center near Inwood, Iowa, where they continued until their retirement.

Washington left Dulce the following year, 1972, at age fifty-six, and also left the employ of the Reformed Church. Two years later he became pastor of the First Presbyterian Church in Okemah, Oklahoma, where he served until 1981. He died May 7, 1987, in Laveen, Arizona.

Statistical reporting continued to be problematic during the Washington years, but in general the number of reported active communicants dropped from the eighties to the fifties. Sunday school enrollment dropped to the forties, no doubt reflecting the fact that fewer boarding students were housed in the government dormitories.

The Dykehouse and Bandt Pastorates, 1973-94

By this time the U.S. Government, by and large, had stopped making U-turns in policy, so Native Americans no longer had to make constant adjustments to Washington's whims. The "red power" movement cooled down, and tribal life settled into a routine. As mission schools and dormitories were no longer necessary, American Indian congregations lost what had been a major component of their ministry. They began to look more and more like other congregations, with a routine of worship, Sunday school, pastoral calling, and youth work. Church staffs were smaller—generally one pastoral couple and a youth worker. The churches no longer needed a phalanx of day school teachers, dormitory matrons, field workers, and maintenance people.

76. November 1970.

Genevieve and Russell Dykehouse

The Dykehouses Arrive

The Reverend Russell and Genevieve Dykehouse arrived in 1973, a year after the Washingtons left, to begin a fifteen-year pastorate, the longest since the twenty-two-year stint of founding missionary J. Denton Simms. A native of Kalamazoo, Michigan, Russell Dykehouse graduated from Central College in 1965 and then from Western Theological Seminary. He served for three years at the Reformed Church in Williamson, New York, and spent a year as chaplain at Baptist Hospital in San Antonio, Texas, before accepting the call to Dulce.

Genevieve Workman Dykehouse, originally from Blue Island, Illinois, gained her first missionary experience as a short-term medical volunteer in Mexico. She attended Moody Bible Institute in Chicago and earned a nursing degree from Chicago's Mt. Sinai School of Nursing in 1964. In Dulce she was employed as a nurse for the Indian Health Service and for the public school. The Dykehouses arrived with two small sons, Jonathan and Jason, and later adopted a non-Indian daughter, Cassie. Jonathan, the oldest, later married an Indian young woman and as of this writing works for the tribe and still lives in Dulce.

The number of inactive members was a concern to the Dykehouses, as it was to other pastors in Indian congregations. In a "Dear Friends" letter of November 1979 Genevieve Dykehouse wrote, "Recently I taught a Sunday school lesson three weeks in a row....I haven't even had one [student] who came twice at that time." Regarding worship attendance, she said, "I suppose it is hard for Russ to get excited about preaching when so few come. It seems, though, that when we are most discouraged a large group shows up....Even though many families have not been active for years, they expect baptism for their children, a free Christian wedding, and burial from the church." Although the people have high respect for the Reformed church and its workers, she said, "Unfortunately, there is very little commitment to Jesus Christ."[77]

The Dulce congregation also had to deal with "sheep-stealing" by the Good News Baptist Church, which moved in during the early 1980s. The group built a church just outside the reservation and thus out of tribal control. The two Caucasian couples in charge of the church began attacking other congregations publicly from the pulpit, and the new group soon filled its pews with members from other churches, including several families from the Reformed Church.

Hesselinks Return

Meanwhile, the experiment of dispensing with the second missionary couple at Dulce proved to be unproductive, and in 1978 Dick and Edith Hesselink were called back to Dulce for maintenance, youth, and educational work. In a letter of November 1979, they reported with enthusiasm on the church's activities, but also said, "We pray much for our Sunday service. We have few in attendance and pray constantly for revival."[78] The Hesselinks stayed four years, resigning as a matter of personal choice in May 1982 before having secured another field of service. Subsequently they moved to Mountain Home, Arkansas, where Dick was self-employed in a repair business and where they eventually retired. Dick Hesselink died October 18, 2003, at the age of seventy-five.

Robert and Bonnie Vander Schaaf

By October of that year the Hesselinks were succeeded by Robert J. and Bonnie Vander Schaaf, who came from Orange City, Iowa, with their three small children. The Vander Schaafs had both graduated

77. Genevieve Dykehouse, letter to supporting congregations, November 1979.
78. Edith and Dick Hesselink, letter to supporting congregations, November 1979, 2.

from Northwestern College in 1971 and were members of the First Reformed Church in Orange City. Robert's father, the Reverend Robert S. Vander Schaaf, was at that time pastor of the Trinity Reformed Church in Fulton, Illinois.

The Vander Schaafs' responsibilities were in the same areas as that of the Hesselinks—youth work, Christian education, and maintenance. Bob, a former high school basketball coach, used that sport to good advantage with the basketball-addicted Indian youth and for the first time fielded a church softball team in the town league. Bonnie drew upon her experience with the Christian Women's Club to take a vanload of women to a Christian Women's Club meeting each month in Farmington, ninety miles away. This came to be viewed as competition for the church's Women's Guild for Christian Service.

The Vander Schaafs' review of a coming-of-age feast, calling it a "delightful way to spend a beautiful summer evening,"[79] stands in stark contrast to the negative descriptions of the early missionaries, but they (and other missionaries) decried the custom of burning the home and belongings of the deceased, leaving the survivors (often a woman with several children) with little more than a tent.

The Vander Schaafs had been hired on a three-year renewable contract, which in 1985 they chose not to renew. A year later, Robert enrolled at Western Theological Seminary and was eventually ordained into the ministry. Bonnie Vander Schaaf died of a brain aneurysm February 19, 1997, at the age of forty-seven.

Emphasis on Local People for Church Work

The consistory recommended that instead of hiring a maintenance/youth/Christian education couple, the General Program Council designate funds for securing local people to do the work on a part-time basis. Native Americans were subsequently hired in the areas of maintenance/custodial, transportation/recreation, and secretarial work. Although this process did not always go smoothly, Dykehouse continued his emphasis on developing local leadership. He took pride in the fact that during his ministry the church never requested outsiders to conduct the summer Bible school and accepted a minimum number of work groups. Referring to the mission effort in general, he said in a *Church Herald* article, "We have failed in our efforts

79. Bob and Bonnie Vander Schaaf, letter to supporting congregations June 27, 1984.

Jicarilla worshipers in the 1970s

to change the 'mission mentality' we have promoted in the minds of Native Americans." Most Christian Native Americans, he said "still understand the 'church' to mean the denomination and whatever pastor or other staff the denomination places in their community."[80]

In 1984 the Jicarilla Apache Reformed Church celebrated its seventieth anniversary. Harper Simms, a son of founding pastor J. Denton Simms, preached a sermon that originally had been given by his father. Several long-time members were honored and subsequently pictured in the *Church Herald*: sixty-year members Charlie Cachucha and Kay Kly Harina, and fifty-year members Anna Baltazar, Columbia Vigil, Avis DeJesus, Edith Serafin, Manuelita Quintana, and Martha Gonzales.

About this time, Mary Polanco, member of the church and long-time editor of the *Jicarilla Chieftain*, traveled with Genevieve Dykehouse to Chiapas, Mexico, to see first-hand the Reformed Church's mission work among the Mayan Indians. In 1986 church member Sherryl Vigil was appointed superintendent of the Jicarilla Agency of the Bureau of Indian Affairs, the first Jicarilla to hold this federal office on the reservation. Three years later, Polanco, Vigil, and Ronald Julian, another member of the Dulce church, were all recognized by the New Mexico School Board Association for their service on the Dulce school board.

In 1985 the tribal lease for the mission site was about to expire, and Dykehouse filed a request for a twenty-five-year extension. The

80. Russell Dykehouse, "Moving Toward Self-Reliance," *Church Herald*, December 5, 1986, 16.

original lease had been executed with the U.S. Government as trustee for ninety-nine years at $1.25 per acre per year. The tribal council offered to lease the remaining 11.6 acres of the original land at $6.25 per acre, or approximately $70 per year, to expire June 9, 2010. The General Program Council happily agreed.

Dykehouses Leave in 1987

Meanwhile, it became apparent that there were tensions in the church and that the Dykehouses were frustrated. In a letter to supporting churches in November 1986, Russell Dykehouse told his supporting churches, "My own personal struggle now is whether or not to continue my ministry here in Dulce."[81]

A year later they reported again to supporting churches, "We need your prayers to keep us in a positive attitude, when all around us the forces of evil seem to be trying hardest to disrupt our Lord's Kingdom."[82] So it was no surprise when in August of the following year Dykehouse accepted a call to serve the Bethany Reformed Church in Clara City, Minnesota. He served there until 1993, when the couple moved to Kalamazoo, Michigan, and Russell became certified as an interim pastor. In 2001 the Dykehouses returned to New Mexico to serve as hospital chaplain and nurse.

Statistics during the Dykehouse years increased gradually from thirty-nine active communicants in 1973 to the eighties in 1988. Although the numbers were erratic, the average number of reported inactive members during those years was about fifty.

Congregational Survey

To provide a sense of stability while a new pastor was sought, the church called Harvey Calsbeek to serve as interim pastor. He was then sixty-three years old and had served in Macy, Nebraska, for nine years. Within a year, however, Calsbeek was diagnosed with colon cancer, and the Calsbeeks retired to their hometown of Sibley, Iowa. Treatment was successful, and Harvey served for several years as associate pastor at the First Reformed Church in Sibley. He died suddenly of a heart attack May 25, 1996, at the age of seventy. As of this writing, Angeline Calsbeek continues to live in Sibley.

81. Russell and Genevieve Dykehouse, letter to supporting churches, November 12, 1986.
82. Russell and Genevieve Dykehouse, letter to supporting churches, December 1, 1987.

At the urging of Calsbeek, the church's pastoral search committee conducted a survey of the congregation, revealing opinions about the health and future of the congregation. Responses to "Areas in Our Church Life Which We Do Not Feel Good About" included "unwillingness or inability to witness for our faith;" "not very close to each other as a church family and tend to stay close only to our families/clan;" "unwillingness of people to volunteer for church work;" and "parents desire the sacrament of baptism, but do not remain faithful."

The positives, stated in Indian style as "Areas in the Life of the Church Which We Do Feel Good About," included, "Attendance at the worship service has improved;" "We remained faithful to the church during its difficulties;" "The Sunday school and Bible school were led by the members of the congregation;" "Our church accepts the Indian culture and does not forbid it;" and "The Reformed Church in America has been faithful in maintaining a ministry at Dulce."

The qualifications expected of a future pastor were especially revealing. "Respect for Indian culture" headed the list, followed by "Understanding Indian characteristics." These characteristics included limited response to congregational singing, being reserved in verbally expressing themselves, knowing the importance of body language, knowing what Indian time is, being able to motivate quiet people, and having experience with Indian people.[83]

John and Phyllis Bandt Arrive

In 1989 the Reverend John and Phyllis Bandt of Shreveport, Louisiana, accepted a call to serve the Dulce church. John had served since 1981 as chaplain at the Schumpert Medical Center in Shreveport. Both were natives of Wisconsin. Phyllis, a registered nurse, was a graduate of Presbyterian St. Luke's School of Nursing in Chicago. John had graduated from Central College and Western Theological Seminary and later earned a Master of Theology degree from Colgate Rochester Divinity School with an emphasis on family ministry. The Bandts had served as missionaries from 1964 to 1971 in the Philippines and had served Reformed Church congregations in Roxbury, New York, and Mount Prospect, Illinois, before moving to Louisiana.

The Bandts were greeted with an average church attendance of barely twenty and a physical plant that badly needed repairs. The

83. "Dulce—Survey, Pastor Search Committee," typewritten document, February 1989.

Phyllis and John Bandt

Bandts again welcomed volunteer work groups—about one hundred people in approximately six groups each summer, all under Phyllis's supervision. In 1992 the church welcomed a recent Hope College graduate, Jerry Jansma, as a Putting People in Mission volunteer for a one-year assignment that included youth ministries and work groups.

Bandt seems to have been received well, and within a year he was asked to give a prayer at the installation of a new tribal president. He was also appointed by the tribe to be a leader in a new program called Decade of Hope, administered by the Indian Council in Washington, D.C., designed to instill pride in Indian history. Yet he wrote in 1990, "It is taking much time to build trust! By remembering the past history of white-Indian relations, and the past history of early missionary-Indian relations, I find it easier to be more patient. Indians still remind me of how those 'early saints' used to punish them for speaking Apache, for growing long hair and wearing braids, as well as wearing any form of Indian dress."[84] Almost all of Bandt's letters mention the continuing problems caused by the use of alcohol on the reservation.

Church life was stable, but in 1994, after less than five years in Dulce, the Bandts announced that it had become necessary for them to leave. About twenty years earlier, John had undergone brain surgery followed by radiation treatments for a pituitary tumor. The radiation had damaged his ability to remember, a problem that was now

84. John Bandt, letter to LeRoy Koopman, March 19, 1990.

becoming more severe, and his energy level was decreasing to the point where it was difficult to perform pastoral functions. "Phyllis and I are leaving at a high point in my ministry," he wrote, "since more people are joining the church and getting involved in church and community activities."[85] John's disability retirement became effective in May 1994, and the Bandts moved to Aurora, Colorado.

Throughout his tenure in Dulce, Bandt never mentioned attendance in any of his missionary letters, and apparently the church never submitted a statistical report to the General Synod from 1988 to 1993. For the first three years of the Bandt pastorate, in fact, the church's financial secretary refused to share any records. When a new person finally took over the books, the consistory decided that legal action would do more harm than good, so they simply closed the old account and opened a new one.

The De Boer Ministry, 1994-

Shortly before the Bandts left, a new "second couple" arrived in Dulce—Duane and Carol Peterson of Twin Falls, Idaho. Duane Peterson had taken an early retirement after working for twenty-five years as a corporate executive, and the Petersons had decided to devote the remainder of their lives to mission work. They spent their first three months living in the Sunday school rooms at Dulce.

Bill and Peggy De Boer Arrive

Faced again with a vacancy, the church and mission administrator Richard Vander Voet looked again to people with both missionary and pastoral experience. This time the path led to the Reverend William (Bill) and Peggy De Boer, who had served for ten years as Reformed Church missionaries among the Ch'ol Indians in Chiapas, Mexico. They had left Palenque, Chiapas, in 1993, convinced that the believers were now ready to carry on without foreign missionaries. Previous to that, the De Boers had spent eleven years working at Cook College and Theological School in Tempe, Arizona, where they served as dormitory supervisors and in the Theological Education by Extension program.

The De Boers were natives of Grand Rapids and Byron Center, Michigan, and had graduated from Hope College. Bill had two degrees from Western Theological Seminary—a Master of Religious Education degree in 1971 and a Master of Divinity degree in 1994. He was ordained

85. John and Phyllis Bandt, letter to supporting churches, April 21, 1994.

Peggy and Bill De Boer

to the ministry in September 1994 in Dulce, the first time a pastor had been ordained there.

The De Boers had the advantage of coming to Dulce with experience serving among indigenous peoples in Mexico, but like all white pastors of Native American congregations, they had to learn quickly about the culture of this particular people. And like most pastors of these churches, they are able to view these learning experiences with a wry sense of humor. The De Boers, for instance, learned that to the Jicarillas "good-bye" means that they will never see the departing person again, but that "bye" is acceptable. Another learning experience involved butterflies:

> As part of the crafts class for vacation Bible school (VBS), we had the kids make butterflies. On the last day of VBS when we told the kids to take home what they had made, one of the teen helpers said, "Jicarillas aren't supposed to touch butterflies. Tradition says it makes people go crazy." Nice to learn those things *after* the fact. As far as we know, the kids are as sane as ever.[86]

The De Boers, as most of the missionary couples before them, immediately looked for ways to serve the wider community. They

86. Bill and Peg De Boer, letter to supporting churches, May 2001, 1.

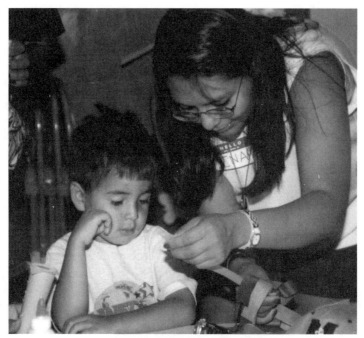

Ina Ramon Montoya helping a
vacation Bible school student

established ties with the community substance abuse agencies, served as an emergency first care family, and volunteered as tutors in the local public school. Peggy De Boer became a substitute teacher in the public school system, a piano teacher, and a helper in nearly every aspect of the church's ministry.

The Petersons left in 1996 after two years in Dulce to assume responsibilities in Appalachian ministries. Within a few years, Duane Peterson was appointed director of Jackson County Ministries in Annville, Kentucky, and Carol Peterson became one of the operation managers there.

Ina Ramon Montoya

After the Petersons left, the church again began a search for new staff, but this time they sought only a youth and Christian education worker, not combining these responsibilities with maintenance. These two skills, in the opinion of De Boer, are not necessarily complementary or even compatible. Most maintenance people are older men with experience in maintenance, and most youth workers don't have these skills. Besides, the denomination's $9.8 by '98 fund drive (which had a goal of raising $9.8 million by 1998) had designated $15,000 to hire a full-time youth pastor.

The search led them to their own congregation in the person of Ina Ramon, who was appointed in March of 1998 and the following year married Tilford Montoya. Ina had spent her early years in Dulce and had fond memories of the Calsbeeks. She traveled widely with her mother, as her mother's government job took her to various assignments around the country, and Ina thereby gained knowledge of the world beyond the reservation. This meant that she also attended a number of high schools before graduating with honors from Window Rock High School in Ft. Defiance, Arizona. She took courses at the University of Arizona and graduated with a degree in ethnic minority family studies from the University of New Mexico at Albuquerque.

Throughout her high school and college days, Ramon was active in youth groups and Bible studies, and when she returned to Dulce after college she became involved in the Children and Worship program, Sunday school, vacation Bible school, and youth groups. After being hired as a youth pastor, she continued these tasks and more on a full-time basis. In a letter of September 2001 she expressed her enthusiasm for the work: "Ministry is going great. Of course we have the challenges of teens in jail, teens pregnant, kids abused, and kids neglected. But that's why God put me where I am."[87]

In the fall of 2002 Ina enrolled in the Master of Divinity program at Denver Seminary, a course of study that she plans to pursue initially by correspondence. If she completes these studies she could be the first Native American woman to be ordained by the Reformed Church in America.

Present Church Life in Dulce

Although welcoming volunteer work crews each summer, the De Boers continue to emphasize self-determination and self-support. These efforts include local staffing for vacation Bible school, the training of several teachers in the Reformed Church's Children and Worship program, and one-day consistory retreats.

Worship services in Dulce are very much like non-Indian worship services of a decade ago, with the exception of music. The Jicarillas are

---

87. Ina Montoya, letter to supporting churches, September 2001.

The Jicarilla Apache Reformed church

not musical people. The local school has no vocal music program, the church has no choir, and the people don't particularly like to sing.

The church van is still widely used. A new fifteen-passenger van was purchased in 2001 to replace the 1990 vehicle, half the money being raised by the Dulce congregation and the other half raised by Reformed Church Mission Services. The van is essential to the children and youth ministry programs and is also used to take church members to workshops, retreats, and other events off the reservation.

As of this writing, attendance at worship services ranges from forty to eighty, following no logical or discernable pattern, and Sunday school attendance averages about twenty. At various times the entire consistory—three elders and three deacons—has been made up of women. The Jicarilla Reformed Church, in fact, is probably the first Reformed Church congregation to elect an all-female consistory.

Because of its isolation, social activities in Dulce remain limited, especially for young people. For this reason, the Jicarilla Apache Reformed Church continues to host roller skating in its gymnasium, with as many as seventy-five children raising noise to the "zillion decibel level" every week. "It's tradition," writes DeBoer. "For the past

Mary Polanco

forty years the thing to do in Dulce on Friday night is roller skate."[88] The facility is also used for private parties, youth group functions, and the ever-popular basketball.

Statistics during the DeBoer pastorate have shown slow but steady increases, avoiding the wild fluctuations that have characterized much of Dulce's history. From 1993 to 2003 active membership grew steadily from thirty to seventy-two; average worship attendance grew from thirty to sixty-three; and Sunday school enrollment dropped slightly from thirty to twenty-eight.

Ministry in Dulce continues to take place amid overwhelming social problems. In December 2000 the De Boers wrote:

> The reality of this spiritual warfare is obvious in Dulce. The death rate here from alcohol-related causes is twelve times higher than the Native American alcohol-related death rate in general—which is already much higher than the rate of the general population. This past Monday we went to the funeral of yet another teenage boy who took his own life....Ina Montoya is rejoicing with her husband over her pregnancy, but that joy is tempered by the fact that three thirteen- and fourteen-year-old girls are also pregnant.

"The point of all of this," said the De Boers in that letter, "is that we need to be on our knees more, pleading with the Lord, if these disturbing trends are going to be reversed and the good news of Jesus Christ is to be received. The pastors of our Native American Indian Reformed Church

88. Bill and Peg DeBoer, letter to supporting churches, March 8, 1995.

Vacation Bible School staff, 1997

congregations have made a commitment to do alternating, three-day periods of prayer and fasting for a couple of months, and we want to encourage you to spend even more time in the new year in prayer for us, for our churches, and for our communities."[89]

Said Mary Polanco, retired editor of the *Jicarilla Chieftain*, in a 1997 interview, "The vast majority of the people here hold the Reformed Church in high esteem, even if they don't come and even though they sometimes get angry when the church doesn't automatically marry everyone." She is proud, she says, to promote her own culture as well as her faith. "Because I'm a Christian doesn't mean I'm not an Indian."

89. Bill and Peg DeBoer, letter to supporting churches, December 2000.

CHAPTER 8

The Mission in Winnebago, Nebraska, and the Winnebago Reformed Church

While the drama of Reformed ministry among Geronimo's band of Chiricahua Apaches and the nearby Comanches was unfolding at Fort Sill in southern Oklahoma, another mission was quietly beginning five hundred miles to the north, in Winnebago, Nebraska.

Actually, the mission had been there for about twenty years, under the auspices of the Presbyterian Church. But things had not been going well, and the Presbyterians were more than happy to relinquish responsibility to the Reformed Church. The opportunity was ideal geographically, because the mission was just across the Missouri River from a major cluster of Reformed congregations in northwest Iowa, who could provide not only financial support but could also be involved personally. The Reformed Church took the opportunity, and for nearly a century it has maintained a viable and important Christian witness among the Winnebago tribe of northeast Nebraska.

A Short History of the Winnebago People

The Winnebago Indians learned about white people in 1634, just twenty-seven years after the first permanent English settlement was established in Jamestown, Virginia, and six years after the founding of the Dutch Reformed Church in New Amsterdam. At that time the French explorer and trader Jean Nicolet scraped ashore from the body of water now known as Green Bay, in eastern Wisconsin. Lake Winnebago, thirty miles off the tip of Green Bay, is a continuing witness to the people who once lived there. Another Frenchman, known only as

Decora, married a Winnebago woman, and that name has come down to the present day.

The Ho-Chunk

The name *Winnebago*, given by the neighboring Algonquins, means "people of the stinking water." Some believe the name is a reference to Green Bay's algae growth that smells bad in the summer, and some Englishmen dubbed the Winnebagos "stinkards." The proud name they gave themselves was *Ho-Chunk*, "people of the first voice" or "people of the big speech." Their speech was that of the Siouan language, and their dialect was close to those spoken by the Iowa, Oto, and Missouri tribes.

In their home in the woodlands of Wisconsin, the Winnebagos lived in lodges covered with bark and reed mats. The women raised corn, beans, pumpkins, and squash and gathered nuts and edible roots. The men hunted bear, beaver, and deer; speared fish; and on occasion ventured onto the prairies to hunt buffalo.

During the 1700s and 1800s the Winnebegos engaged in dozens of skirmishes, first with the French, then with the English, then with the United States, and intermittently with various Indian tribes. Three times the tribe contracted smallpox, brought to their land by the Europeans, and in 1836 they lost nearly a quarter of the tribe to that disease.

Four Broken Treaties in Thirty-One Years

Then the Winnebagos ran into real trouble; they began making treaties with the U.S. Government. Between 1825 and 1856 they signed no less than four treaties, an average of one every eight years. Each treaty moved them to a new "permanent home" in Wisconsin, Iowa, or Minnesota.

By the 1860s the Winnebagos were relatively content in extreme south central Minnesota, in the area that is now Blue Earth, where they had lived all of six years. Then in 1862 the Sioux staged a violent uprising, and white people demanded the removal of all Indians. Congress acceded to the people who could vote, and even though the Winnebagos had not raised one war club against whites, they were forcibly removed—at their own expense—to the desolate Crow Creek Reservation north of Pierre, South Dakota. This was done by the U. S. Army during the harsh winter of 1862, even as several Winnebagos were fighting as volunteers in the Civil War.

Escape to Nebraska

Without game to hunt, implements for farming, or adequate government rations, and having lost more than five hundred of their people in South Dakota to cold, starvation, and disease, the Winnebagos became desperate. Although they had been warned that if they tried to leave without the consent of the Great Father in Washington they could be fired on, the Winnebagos built canoes and escaped down the Missouri River.

By this time the Omahas were living along the Missouri on their reservation in southeast Nebraska, also having been removed from their previous reservation. The Omahas welcomed the bedraggled refugees as they came ashore, giving them food, clothing, and sympathy. A few years later, in 1865, the Omahas agreed to sell the northern part of their reservation, nearly half of their holdings, to the government for use by the Winnebagos. The new Winnebago reservation consisted of 128,000 acres, a tract roughly eight miles wide and twenty-five miles long. The deal was not entirely altruistic on the part of the Omahas. They had been raided for years by the Lakotas to the north. The Winnebagos, known for their ferocity in battle, created a buffer zone between the Omahas and the Lakotas, and the Lakota raids soon stopped.

The Omahas and the Winnebagos have been next-door neighbors ever since. The relationship of the two tribes could perhaps be described as strained but not hostile. There is some intermarriage. For a variety of reasons the Winnebagos have prospered more than the Omahas—a fact that has not gone unnoticed by either side. To over-simplify, the Winnebagos tend to look upon the Omahas as underachievers, and the Omahas tend to view the Winnebagos as uppity.

Of the two thousand Winnebagos originally deported from Minnesota to South Dakota, only about twelve hundred remained when they finally settled in Nebraska. Throughout the years of broken treaties and removals, and even after settling in Nebraska, several large groups of Winnebagos separated themselves from the tribe and found their way back to Wisconsin, where they remain to this day.

Later the U.S. Government enlisted the help of the Winnebagos in putting down a revolt by the more hostile tribes of the northwest plains. That campaign, led by Chief Little Priest, was successful, although Little Priest himself was wounded and died later. (Many years later, when the tribe purchased the children's home in Winnebago from the Reformed Church, it used the facility to house Little Priest Tribal College, named after its famous chief.)

The Long-Term Effects of the Allotment

The allotment policy of the U.S. Government was implemented in Winnebago even before being officially approved by the Allotment (Dawes) Act of 1887. By 1926 many of the original allotments were gone, the land having been sold to white settlers and the money quickly spent. With the exception of some Indians who leased their land to white farmers, and a few who still worked their own land, the younger generation was landless and without a means of livelihood. So the Winnebagos, like Indians of other tribes, began drifting away from the reservation to the cities, where they worked in stockyards, packinghouses, and factories. Some drove taxis and a few attended college. Ultimately, however, most of them drifted back to the reservation.

The Medicine Lodge

The religion of the Winnebagos most frequently referred to by the missionaries was the Medicine Lodge. Missionaries made little effort to explain its faith and practice, probably because the Winnebagos kept it to themselves and never really explained it to them. The non-Indian who searches for a Winnebago theology, in the sense of a creed or a system of belief, will find instead a collection of legends, practices, and ceremonies.

Chief among the legends of the Winnebagos were the stories of *Mauna*, ("Earthmaker"), who made the earth and everything on it. *Mauna* made a man and a woman, and then four men and four women, whom he sent to the four corners of the earth. They increased and were mighty, but they were evil. *Mauna* then sent four sons to the earth to save them from evil. The first was Turtle, who believed that courage was the answer to evil, so he led the people into war. But *Mauna* took him back, and his tracks are the Milky Way. Then Mauna sent his second son, Bladder, who believed that the answer was much thinking. The third son, Jester, who believed that the cure for all evils is mirth and good cheer, was also recalled by *Mauna*. The fourth son, Rabbit, believed that the answer could be found in religion, and the religion he brought is that of the Medicine Lodge. Rabbit called all the spirits of the universe into a wigwam and taught them, among other things, that the sun, moon, stars, animals, and plants are sacred; that the soul wanders four nights around the home after the body dies; that obedience to the spirits is the first virtue; and that vengeance is not necessarily a crime. At the center of the Winnebago religion was the Medicine Lodge chief, who meted out sacred and secret medicine, especially to those who honored him with gifts.[1]

The Peyote Religion

By the time the Reformed Church began its work at Winnebago in 1908, another Indian religious movement had become a major player there—the "mescal cult," recently imported from Oklahoma. Combining elements of Christian teaching with traditional rituals, it was subsequently called the peyote religion and later the Native American Church. Within the first few decades of the 1900s, the practice of using mescal as a spiritual experience had become popular on the reservation, capturing the loyalty of as many as a third of the Winnebagos. The mescal faith was considered by the missionaries to be somewhat more benign than the Medicine Lodge, but a formidable opponent nonetheless in the battle for the souls of the Indian people.

Winnebago Today

The Winnebago Indian Reservation covers approximately 120,000 acres of cropland, woodland, and pasture. About 2,600 people live on the reservation, one-third of them in the town of Winnebago. Highway 75, which connects Sioux City and Omaha, runs through Winnebago and thence through Macy to the south.

Several of Winnebago's tribal leaders have been educated at the mission school or cared for at its children's shelter, and this has likely contributed to the tribe's success in running a number of tribal business enterprises. In 1975 the tribe was awarded $4.6 million by the Indian Claims Commission for land it had lost in its 1837 treaty with the federal government, and the tribe used most of the funds for land acquisition and social development.

Present unemployment is about 20 percent, very low compared to most Indian reservations. The tribe owns ten auto service stations. Two of the stations are on tribal property and the others are in South Dakota,

---

1. Summarized from Henry Roe Cloud, "The Winnebago Medicine Lodge," *Christian Intelligencer*, Dec. 22, 1909, 833; other accounts of the legend are somewhat different in detail.

Iowa, and elsewhere in Nebraska. The station in town is a combination convenience store/service station/laundromat/lunch room/ATM station. The tribe also owns a buffalo herd and a gift shop that sells only traditional Indian items. The Winnebago Community Center houses a gymnasium, swimming pool, senior center, police station, and tribal offices. A new comprehensive medical complex, including a dental clinic and treatment centers for drug and alcohol abuse, was opened in 2004 to serve both the Winnebago and Omaha tribes. The Little Priest Tribal College now incorporates a cultural center. The tribe also maintains powwow grounds. As of this writing, a forty-acre plot is being developed north of town that includes retail stores, homes, and apartments. Much of the seed money for the commercial ventures came from the WinneVegas Casino, across the Missouri River to the east. The tribe now runs two daycare programs, enabling the Reformed Church to discontinue its daycare program.

Religious institutions, in addition to the Winnebago Reformed Church, include the Native American Church, the St. Augustine Roman Catholic Church, and a small Missouri Synod Lutheran church. The Episcopal, Mormon, and Presbyterian churches are now closed.

The Reformed Church Assumes the Presbyterian Mission, 1908

In 1889, twenty-three years after the Winnebagos settled in their sixth and final permanent home, the Board of Foreign Missions of the Presbyterian Church established a mission outpost in Winnebago (later transferred to the Presbyterian Board of Home Missions). If one can believe *Some Facts about the Nebraska Winnebago Indians*, a brochure published by the Reformed Church in America, this came about because the Winnebagos "were able to see the true value of Christianity and to desire it for their children" and subsequently appealed to the president of the United States "to have our children taught the Christian religion as before in Wisconsin."[2]

The Presbyterian Mission Has Limited Success

Shortly thereafter, a church and parsonage were built, and the Reverend William T. Findley was appointed missionary to the Winnebagos. If, indeed, the Winnebago's petition was their own, they must have changed their minds. The Reformed Church's Board

2. *Some Facts about the Nebraska Winnebago Indians* (Board of Domestic Missions, April 1954), 4.

of Domestic Missions reported that "Charles Mallory became the interpreter and convert of Mr. William T. Findley in a day when no one else turned to the Jesus Road. Years of bitter opposition followed."[3] The Reverend Henry Roe Cloud, who triggered the Reformed Church's involvement in Winnebago, reported that Findley "laid down his arms of battle...at the end of sixteen years of apparently fruitless toil."[4]

The Memorable Career of Henry Roe Cloud

Cloud should have known better, however, than to talk about the "fruitless toil of the mission," for he had been converted there through the personal witness of pastor Findley. Cloud was rapidly becoming a force to be reckoned with, not only in the Christian mission community but also in national education and politics. After completing his high school education at the Santee Indian boarding school in southeastern Nebraska, he went to Yale University in 1906. While there he attended a presentation by Mary Roe, who with her husband was serving as a Reformed Church missionary in Colony, Oklahoma. They talked at length after the speech, and Mrs. Roe invited Cloud to spend a summer at Fort Sill. He accepted the invitation and was greatly influenced by Comanche leaders Nahwats and Periconic. The Roes, who apparently were wealthy, virtually adopted Cloud as their son and paid his expenses at Yale, where he excelled and became its first American Indian graduate. Cloud earned a degree in theology and a master's degree in anthropology, and he was ordained as a Presbyterian minister. He assumed the Roes' last name as his own middle name and established the Roe Indian Institute in Wichita, Kansas, for training Christian leaders. He then moved into national leadership, being appointed to several government committees and agencies that were influential in establishing Indian policy, the most important being the panel that wrote the Meriam Report. This report laid the foundation for the historic Indian Reorganization Act of 1934, which established the rights of Indian peoples to practice their own traditions and to organize as self-governing tribes.

Cloud also was instrumental in introducing the Reformed Church to his tribe, the Winnebagos. In the summer of 1907 Mary

3. *Old Paths and New Trails*, bro. (Women's Board of Domestic Missions, circa 1932), 8.
4. Henry Roe Cloud, "The Winnebago Medicine Lodge," *Christian Intelligencer*, Dec. 22, 1909, 833.

Roe, who was on a speaking trip, spent a few days with Cloud at the Winnebago reservation. They prayed at the grave of pastor Findley, who had recently died, and Cloud pleaded with Mrs. Roe to influence the Reformed Church to fill the spiritual void at Winnebago. A few days later she went to the churches of Pella, Iowa, and the Pella Classis pledged to support the mission if it could be transferred to the Reformed Church.

The Board of Domestic Missions of the Reformed Church opened negotiations with the Presbyterian Board of Home Missions, and on July 1, 1908, the Reformed Church assumed responsibility for the Winnebago mission. On August 12 the church, parsonage, and eighty-five acres of the mission were transferred to the Reformed Church for "temporary use and occupancy for religious purposes."[5] In accordance with instructions by the Commission on Indian Affairs, the document bears the marks and thumb-prints of twenty-five "chiefs and head men" of the tribe, although it is not clear from the document whether the Indians had any choice in the matter. At this time the mission buildings were located one and one-half miles east of Winnebago.

A Formidable Task

The mission faced a formidable task. The Presbyterians had been frustrated because they had secured only a handful of converts over sixteen years of ministry. Cloud described the situation in language that exhibited the extent to which he had turned away from the traditions of his people:

> Dr. A. L. Riggs [missionary to the Dakota people with the Congregational Church] said, "if you convert those Winnebagos to Christianity it will mean that the religion of Jesus Christ can save any Indian tribe."...That patriarch very well knew the strength of the wall of heathenism among the Winnebago Indians. Miss Ida Scudder, missionary to India under the Reformed Church, after having spent a summer at Winnebago, said, "I never saw such heathenism in India." Miss Anna Beecher Scoville, once an interpreter of the United States Government to the Winnebagos, said to Dr. Roe, "The Winnebagos are a very hard people to reach. They are most degraded."...Dr. Wm. T. Findley's fruitless toil

5. Council Agreement signed at the Winnebago Agency in Nebraska, Oct. 3, 1908.

among the Winnebagos shows even more clearly the awful hold the Medicine Lodge has upon these people.[6]

But the Women's Board of Domestic Missions was not intimidated easily. In the summer of 1908 the board launched a mission *blitzkrieg*. Seven people—Cloud, the Reverend Walter and Mary Roe, the Reverend Frank Hall Wright, Elizabeth Page of the Women's Board, Johanna Meengs of the Colony mission, and the Reverend W. D. Barnes of Yale College—spent more than a month calling throughout the reservation in mission teams. They concluded the effort with a camp meeting on Flag Pole Hill, the site of Indian dances. Here they were challenged both by representatives of the Medicine Lodge and by the followers of the mescal cult, the latter having captured the loyalty of nearly a third of the Indians. But at the end, on a Sunday evening, twenty persons came forward to accept Christ.

The Winnebago Church Is Organized and Watermulder Becomes Pastor

Shortly thereafter, apparently without classis participation, the church was declared to be organized as a Reformed Church congregation. The church had twenty-three communicant members, two Indian elders, and two Indian deacons, but no pastor except the temporary services of Walter Roe. Mention was made later of eight members, all of whom were white or mixed race, who had come over from the Presbyterian church, but it is not clear whether these were included in the original twenty-three members. Although the facts are unclear, it would seem that the four Indian consistory members had been Christian believers for only a few weeks when they were given this responsibility. Almost immediately the church organized a Women's Missionary Society, and offerings were received at worship services for home and foreign missions.

The next task was to find a pastor. "For a time," said the 1909 report of the Women's Executive Committee of the Board of Domestic Missions, "it seemed impossible to find one willing to make the sacrifice and one competent for the work."[7] The search led them to Kalamazoo, Michigan, where a pastor with the imposing name of the Reverend Gustavus Adolf Watermulder (always referred to as G.A. Watermulder)

6. Cloud, "Winnebago Medicine Lodge," 833.
7. *Annual Report of the Women's Executive Committee of the Board of Domestic Missions*, 1909, 19.

Gustavus Adolf Watermulder

was presently unemployed, having taken a leave from the Second Reformed Church because of health concerns.

Tall and handsome, Watermulder had been born in Sheboygan, Wisconsin, in 1874 and had graduated from Hope College (1897) and New Brunswick Theological Seminary (1900). He had served several very short pastorates in Oyster Bay (now Brookville), New York (1900-02); Fairview, Illinois (1902-03); and at the First Reformed Church (later merged with Second Reformed to become Central Reformed) in Grand Rapids, Michigan (1903-05) before moving to Kalamazoo, where he stayed three years. He was married to Fanny Verbeck, originally from Holland, Michigan, and they had a six-year-old son, Louis, another son having died at ten months of age.

Watermulder Becomes Pastor

Despite the fact that Watermulder had served four churches in six years, Wright urged the board to call him, which it did, and Wright subsequently urged him to accept, which he did. This time Watermulder stayed thirty-four years and then served an additional four years at Cook Christian Training School in Phoenix, Arizona.

The first interpreter, George Smith, was converted in 1908 and sent to Moody Bible Institute in Chicago for a few years. In a personal report many years later, Smith said that when he went calling with the pastor in Indian homes, "often times they tell us to go on before we even get off the buggy. They tell us they don't want the white man's book, that they have their own religion."[8]

A "simple modest porch" was built at the front of the church at a cost of $75, given by the Indians themselves. Work also began immediately at the rear of the church, "where the Indians can gather between the services and eat their lunches, otherwise they can not remain for the second service, nor can the children be gathered in Sunday school."[9] The Indians, said the 1909 board report, were raising one-half of the money needed to buy the lumber and would help construct the building, since some learned the trade at the government school. The report went on to identify two additional needs: a "consecrated woman with the love of Christ in her heart, entering these homes with her Bible" and—most importantly—a boarding school for the children of the tribe. A memorial gift of $1,000 had already been designated for educational work among the Winnebagos.

Despite strong opposition from both the Medicine Lodge and the mescal group, more than a hundred Indians professed their faith at summer evangelistic campaigns over the next few years. As many as thirty-five converts were received into church membership at a time. Cloud said it with a poetic flair that probably included a tad of poetic license:

> God's countenance is not yet hid, and rays of light from heaven break through the cloud....The heathen is again turning from idols of wood and stone. Medicine Lodge is shaken to its foundation. Its members are breaking loose with a mighty struggle. Each one is taking Christ at the risk of losing this earthly life. Scores are being baptized and taken into the church....the once empty church is now taxed to the doors.[10]

Government authorities were most supportive of all of these evangelistic efforts, and phrases like "hearty cooperation" and "kindly and valuable assistance" were used to describe the attitude of the government agents. One of the early projects of the mission was placing in the hands of every Indian home a copy of *Foster's Picture Bible,* which was found to be "of inestimable value."[11]

8.   Handwritten report from George Smith to Auriel Aalberts, date uncertain.
9.   *Annual Report of the Women's Executive Committee of the Board of Domestic Missions,* 1909, 25.
10. Cloud, "Winnebago Medicine Lodge," 833.
11. *Annual Report of the Women's Board of Domestic Missions,* 1911, 29.

In February of 1910 another child was born to the Watermulders, and three days later, Fanny Watermulder died. The funeral was held at the Winnebego church, with Roe officiating. The casket was carried by relays of "sturdy Indian bearers, followed by a great procession of sorrowing friends" to the Indian cemetery on the hilltop overlooking the mission.[12]

Watermulder was not to remain single long. Just a little over a year later he was united in marriage with Hattie Hospers, a teacher at the Fort Sill Apache mission near Lawton, Oklahoma. The ceremony took place at the conference of Indian workers in Colony, Oklahoma, with pastors Wright and Roe officiating and which Roe described with a flair of whimsy:

> But ere our band scattered to the four winds of heaven, a most delightful experience fell to our lot. There was a sound of wedding bells. Loving hands were busy decorating with the wild vines of the woods and the myriad flowers of the prairie, the parlors of the parsonage, while others—and who shall question the dignity of their task?—were busy brewing and mixing for the coming repast....The bride was lovely, the groom handsome, the ceremony sweet and impressive, and "merry was the feast and long."[13]

By 1912 the staff at Winnebago had increased appreciably. Workers at the mission included the Watermulders; Mr. Harris, assistant; Mr. and Mrs. De Bruyn, field workers; Miss Muilenburg, housekeeper and general helper (first names were often unrecorded); and Henry De Cora and Frank Beaver, interpreters.

The mission buildings at this time consisted of a church valued at $3,000, a parsonage ($3,500), a hospital and rescue home ($2,500), an interpreter's house ($700), and miscellaneous barns and sheds ($1,200). The mission was still anticipating, however, the construction of a chapel on the west end of the reservation and a day school or boarding school. A chapel was, indeed, built a few years later, as was a YMCA building next to the church, complete with a reading room, game room, gymnasium, and other facilities. Among those who served at the chapel were Presbyterian laypeople James and Katherine Arthur,

12. Walter Roe, "Mrs. G. A. Watermulder," *Christian Intelligencer*, Feb. 23, 1910, 121.
13. Walter Roe, "Conference of Indian Workers at Colony," *Christian Intelligencer*, June 21, 1911, 402.

who worked there for two years. They then moved on to Mescalero, New Mexico, where they worked effectively for five years (1914-19) among the Chiricahua Apaches who had settled in the White Tail area. By 1918 most of the Winnebagos had moved to the east side of the reservation, and the chapel closed. The YMCA fell on hard times when young men volunteered or were drafted for World War I. Then, when the soldiers returned, they showed little interest in participating in the religious activities offered by the YMCA.

'Miss Anna' Berkenpas

The older Indians called her *He-nook-say-day-chga* ("tall woman"), the Indian children called her "Miss Anna," and she stayed at Winnebago thirty-one years. Anna Berkenpas came to the community as a nurse and community worker at the invitation of Watermulder in 1914. Like so many single women missionaries of the era, she came from the Midwest (Lafayette, Indiana), held a nursing degree (Chicago Social Service Training School), was fiercely self-sufficient, and was singularly devoted to God and the people she served.[14]

Berkenpas's job description changed over the years as the mission changed. In the early years she traveled widely by horse-drawn buggy to distant parts of the reservation, where she treated the sick, told Bible stories, chatted, and sometimes delivered babies. Once, when calling on a country family during the influenza epidemic of 1918-19, she was caught in a blizzard and suffered a broken arm when her wagon lurched and threw her out. When the boarding school opened, she was like a mother to the children—disciplining them, guiding them, and counseling with their mothers. She took a dim view of Indian traditions and ceremonies, regarding them as pagan, and she not only forbade the girls from going to the powwow but on occasion physically restrained them. When the Community House opened in 1926, she became the director, in charge of all its activities and programs. When Berkenpas left Winnebago in 1945 she joined the staff of Cook Christian Training School in Phoenix, Arizona. She died in Lafayette, Indiana, in 1974, at the age of ninety.

---

14. Berkenpas apparently insisted that her full name be used in Reformed Church publications. Whereas missionary wives in that era were given only a "Mrs." before their husband's last names, and unmarried missionary women were given only a "Miss" before their last names, this woman was always "Miss Anna Berkenpas."

A Property Dispute

About 1913 a controversy erupted between the Reformed Church and the tribe regarding the land occupied by the mission. The Presbyterian Board of Home Missions had originally been granted temporary occupancy of eighty-five acres of land, and that right was transferred in 1908 to the Reformed Church. It came to light that Indian people were buried on part of this land, and the Winnebagos let it be known that they wished to have it as a tribal burial ground. Three years later an agreement was finally reached in which the tribe traded fifteen acres of land to the mission for fifteen acres of burial ground, and the Women's Board of Domestic Missions paid $750 for improving and maintaining the ground as a tribal cemetery.

Early Converts

One of the early converts was Louisa Bear, whose first contact with Watermulder was in a drunken stupor while sitting in a wagon. A few years later Bear submitted five dolls in Winnebago costumes—a father, mother, boy, girl, and baby—to a contest sponsored by a Sioux City merchant. She was awarded the first prize of $100, sold the dolls for $50, and contributed the entire amount to the church—a sizeable contribution at the time. The purchaser, a woman from New York, gave the dolls to the mission board, which displayed them at the Reformed Church headquarters in New York City and took them on the road when making presentations to churches.

Another early convert was Charles De Cora (uncle of the Reverend Wilbur De Cora), whose testimony was recorded in the *Mission Field*:

> What I have to say to all these Christians is to pray for my people that they may be saved. Lots of my people live in darkness today of the gospel. The way I feel in my heart is, when I bought my ticket clear up to this place here I didn't have any trouble along the way; and the Bible is the same way. If you follow as the Bible says, then you will get to the Kingdom of Heaven without any trouble. That is what I have to say to my brothers and sisters.[15]

Watermulder Reports After Eight Years

In 1916 the Women's Board of Domestic Missions published a brochure by Watermulder, *At the Winnebago Indian Mission*, which was

15. Charles DeCora, "Indian Testimony," *Mission Field*, Aug. 1913, 151.

essentially a report to the denomination after eight years of ministry in Winnebago. Watermulder said that the Indians no longer camped together in groups of tepees, but lived in small frame houses on their own allotments. The Indians are learning to farm, he said, "although the nomadic instinct is still strong and it is difficult for many to keep up the steady hard plodding of the good farmer." Much Indian land had been bought by white settlers, and about forty thousand acres were leased by them, so that more white people were now living on the reservation than Indians. The allotment period of twenty-five years would expire in a few years, Watermulder said, and the Indians would be given full responsibility for their future. The question for him was, "Will they take care of their land or will they squander it?"

As for the church's ministry, Watermulder stated that the mission had begun with eight members (perhaps referring only to the carry-over members from the Presbyterian Church), all of whom had now been removed or left. But during the eight years of its existence, the church had received 309 people by confession of faith and had baptized 143 infants. Watermulder acknowledged that this was not the present membership, for during that time some had died, a few had moved away, and others had been suspended. He said that conflict with the Medicine Lodge still continued, and that the use of "mescal worship" still had a grip on at least a fourth of the tribe. Home life was still "sadly disorganized, and but few homes are training schools for children." He called alcohol "a terrible curse" and said, "Bootleggers are still with us."

"Then, too," Watermulder went on to say, "there is a sad lack of appreciation." Somehow failing to see the irony of criticizing native people for failing to appreciate the blessings of a white civilization that had taken their land, decimated their people, broken nearly every promise, and created a society of abject dependence, he quoted a government superintendent who had left Winnebago after a year, saying that he had found the Winnebagos to be "the most unappreciative people he has ever met."

"The Indian, too," Watermulder said in conclusion, "must seek first the Kingdom of God and His righteousness and all other things will be added to him. Christ alone can save! Christ alone can direct! Christ alone can prepare for greater responsibilities."[16]

16. G. Watermulder, *At the Winnebago Indian Mission*, bro. (Women's Board of Domestic Missions, 1916).

The Era of the Mission Boarding School, 1917-28

Soon after the Watermulders began their ministry in Winnebago, they began campaigning for a mission school. The government closed its school on the reservation, saying that the children could either attend the public schools of the area or be sent to such distant Indian schools as those in Carlisle, Pennsylvania; Genoa, Nebraska; and Flandrau, South Dakota. In 1914 the Women's Board announced that more than $4,500 had already been raised to build the "Walter C. Roe Memorial School" in Winnebago. The mission had difficulty, however, in securing title to the land where the school was to be built because of the cemetery controversy, and the funds were reallocated to the mission among the Jicarilla Apaches in Dulce, New Mexico.

But Watermulder did not give up. A few years later, in his important 1916 brochure, he pointed out the difficulty of carrying on the mission without a school: "The children we now influence must be reached by personal visitation and solicitation in their own homes, and remembering the scattered condition of the tribe it presents a difficult problem."[17] A year later the Women's Board of Domestic Missions quoted Wright's belief that "the best way to insure Christian manhood in the Indians is to give the little children early training in mission schools."[18]

So Watermulder the pastor became Watermulder the fundraiser. "His appeals," said the 1917 Women's Board report, "were most generously answered, mostly by friends in the Particular Synod of Chicago, and all the money raised, which amounted to over six thousand dollars, was given entirely as extra gifts, and did not detract from our general funds."[19]

The Mission Boarding School Opens

At last, in the fall of 1917, the mission boarding school opened for grades one through six, with Watermulder as the superintendent of the school as well as the pastor of the church. Thirty-nine students enrolled, including five day students. The federal government furnished much of the equipment and paid part of the operating expenses, while the Reformed Church supplied the teachers. Subsequent board reports indicated enrollments of sixty-one in 1918 and seventy in 1919, reaching

17. Ibid.
18. *Annual Report of the Women's Board of Domestic Missions*, 1917, 29.
19. Ibid.

one hundred in 1925. That report noted that "the children who come to us from heathen homes have surprised us by their alertness and ability to grasp, and the influence on their parents has been telling."[20]

Anna Berkenpas, now the school's superintendent, made it clear that one objective of the school was to wean Indian children from their tribal ways:

> With joy and pride parents tell us of prayers taught to baby brothers and sisters; of Bible stories told, of thanks offered for food so bountifully supplied, and fathers and mothers urged to keep away from Indian dances and ceremonies and "live like the Mission people," often little hearts troubled because "Uncle and Aunt" do not know about God, and a constant urging that fathers and mothers, grandfathers and grandmothers attend church.[21]

One account told of the closing school program in the spring of 1922, which included a musical program by twenty-eight girls; an exercise, "April Flowers," by twenty girls; and a pantomime by twelve girls. Then, as a grand finale on the following day, "a patriotic pageant was given, showing the discovery of America, the Colonial period, the Civil War period, and the progress to the present day."[22]

In a 1926 creedal-type essay, "The Spiritual Value of Christian Education among American Indians," Watermulder affirmed his agreement with the government's education policy of establishing Indian schools such as Carlisle, calling their accomplishments "commendable, inspiring, and hopeful." But he also said that the purpose of Christian education is not changing the Indians' cultural habits but introducing the power that changes hearts:

> If we develop the new Indian we need something more than new clothes and new paint. That is custom and convention. We need something more than new houses; the Indian's tent and tepee were not to be despised. We need something more than a new industry; the raising of Indian corn, the hunting of game, the weaving of rugs, the stringing of beads represented honest toil. We need something more than bathtubs and modern comforts;

20. *Annual Report of the Women's Board of Domestic Missions*, 1919, 36.
21. Anna Berkenpas, "What Hath God Wrought," *Mission Field*, March 1918, 502.
22. "Closing Exercises at the Winnebago School," *Christian Intelligencer and Mission Field*, Aug. 16, 1922, 523.

Mrs. Long Marsh,
Winnebago member

Mothers frequently came to
have their children receive
medical aid.

the morning plunge in the river made a hearty people. We need something more than a different form of pleasure. I prefer the Indian tom-tom to the modern vaudeville, and the powwow to a modern movie....The Indian needs the new heart, the implanting of the abiding elements of character by the Spirit of the living God.[23]

Emphasis on Indian Leadership

Early on, Watermulder emphasized the importance of self-support, introducing offering envelopes and reporting that all current expenses of the church were being met entirely by weekly offerings. His reports frequently included statistics on how many Sunday school teachers were Indian people and how he was trying to find an Indian superintendent. By the early 1920s, many of the early faithful members

23. G. A. Watermulder, "The Spiritual Value of Christian Education Among American Indians," Part I, *Christian Intelligencer and Mission Field*, June 2, 1926, 352.

like Louisa Bear and Grover Mallory had died, and he sought to replace them with promising young people. He said that if he had a great deal of money, he would "go through the various Indian reservations in the United States and pick up all the promising Indian boys and put them in our denominational schools to train them for Christian leadership."[24] The Women's Board of Domestic Missions, indeed, received a gift of $1,000 to set up a scholarship fund for this purpose.

Watermulder reported in 1922 that five Winnebago boys were attending Hope College: Owen White, Norval Tego, Edward Black Hawk, Charles Mallory, and Theodore Thomas. Two young women were attending nursing schools in St. Paul and Chicago. In addition, several young men and women were attending the academies (high schools) associated with Central College and Northwestern College, living with Reformed Church families. By the next fall, only one of the Hope students, Owen White, was still there, but another, George LaMere, a composer of Indian melodies, had enrolled. White left at the end of the 1924-25 school year, and LaMere left to accept a music teaching position at Haskell Institute in Lawrence, Kansas. One name that appeared frequently on lists of promising students was that of Alberta Rave, a talented singer and pianist who was also blind.

Christmas in Winnebago

Christmas in Winnebago, as in all of the Indian missions, was a very special time, one that never failed to be reported in the *Christian Intelligencer*. These accounts referred frequently to the importance of training the Indian children in voice projection, both for speaking and singing. The Christmas observance in 1921, said Watermulder, consisted of three parts: (1) Saturday morning festivities with a breakfast, a brightly decorated tree, recitation of the Christmas story, and the sharing of gifts; (2) a Christmas Eve cantata, "The Light of the World is Jesus," presented by the school children, followed by the distribution of gifts to adults; and (3) a Christmas dinner for mission workers. One of the gifts was particularly intriguing, and one wonders whether the teaching staff was duped by a classic example of Indian irony. As Watermulder described it:

> One gift from the older girls, rather large but carefully wrapped, for one of the workers was perhaps the most appreciated. After all

24. "Indian Boys Get a Wonderful Chance," *Christian Intelligencer and Mission Field*, Feb., 15, 1922, 106.

the tissue paper had been removed it was found to be the stave of a barrel, shaped into a sightly paddle, to be used for disciplinary purposes. We are glad to realize that the older children are beginning to respect authority.[25]

The phenomenal attendance at Christmas functions was no doubt enhanced by hundreds of gifts that poured in from congregations throughout the denomination. One year these included—much to the chagrin of the mission staff, one can be sure—a toy whistle for every boy and girl, donated by a business firm in Sioux City. In 1924, as a surprise to parents, the children sang Psalm 117 in the Winnebago language— one of the few times the native tongue was mentioned, and a radical departure from earlier times when children were forbidden to use their ancestral language.

The Community Center Opens

Following the example of the other Indian missions, the Winnebago Mission dedicated a community center December 7, 1926, with Anna Berkenpas in charge of all of its activities. The dedication was a community event, with addresses and comments by the pastor of the local Presbyterian (non-Indian) church, and representatives of the town board, public school, and government agency. The building was a geographic symbol, for it was built in town at a time when the rest of the mission buildings were located a mile and a half away. The other buildings were moved to town less than two years later, when Reformed Church involvement was reduced to running mission dormitories.

Businessmen from Winnebago contributed a radio, and businessmen from Sioux City gave a moving picture projector for the community center. Other equipment included a stereopticon (slide projector) and a piano, which a pianist from Sioux City used once a week to give lessons. The center housed a library—the only one in the community—to which the Nebraska State Library sent a new selection every three months. Adjacent to the library room was the girls' browsing room (the need for a separate room never having been made clear). Other facilities included a medical dispensary, shower baths, children's playroom, a reading room furnished with newspapers and magazines, and a game room equipped with carom, checkers, and jigsaw puzzles. The puzzles proved to be very popular, and soon there was a waiting

25. G. A. Watermulder, "Christmas at Winnebago," *Christian Intelligencer and Mission Field,* Jan. 25, 1922, 52.

list. "If jig-saw puzzles will keep our Indian people home in the evening," said a *Christian Intelligencer* report, "they have served a great purpose."[26] The center was also used by such community organizations as 4-H clubs, the Farm Extension Bureau, and county demonstration and home extension organizations.

During this time the Winnebago Reformed Church and the local Presbyterian (white) church displayed an increasing inclination to cooperate. This included, for instance, joint meetings in observance of the World Day of Prayer. The 1931 observance included seventeen girls, dressed in the costumes of many nations, coming forward and kneeling at the cross, then marching out carrying open Bibles while the leader read, "Go ye therefore and teach all nations."

Questionable Statistics

Meanwhile, Winnebago's statistical reports to the denomination included phenomenal numbers. The number of reported communicant members between 1910 and 1928 averaged 199, with a reported average of 18 people received each year by confession of faith. Reported membership reached as high as 231 in 1918, when 39 people made confession of faith. During these years the Winnebago church took in more than 300 members by confession of faith. Despite these phenomenal statistics, the 1928 annual report of the Women's Board of Domestic Missions contained this startling statement:

> We rejoice that in several cases this past year, after years of faithful sowing, the long overdue results have been experienced and some remarkable conversions on our Winnebago and Dulce fields have been witnessed among the older Indians who have turned from superstition and enslaving sins and accepted the cleansing of Christ and have been made new creatures in Him.[27]

One can only surmise that the great majority of these hundreds of new members were children, who responded positively to an invitation to accept Christ and were received immediately into membership, but who just as quickly fell away when they returned to their parents or left for Indian schools elsewhere.

---

26. "Community House Activities at Winnebago, Nebraska," *Christian Intelligencer*, Aug. 15, 1933, 458.
27. *Annual Report of the Women's Board of Domestic Missions*, 1928, 17.

The Era of Dormitories, 1928-40

In his essay, "The Spiritual Value of Christian Education among American Indians," Watermulder not only expressed his credo but also began to prepare the denomination for a major change in the nation's educational policy. Very soon, he said, Indian children will be receiving their training in public schools rather than in Indian schools. Watermulder embraced the new policy, saying, "Our Indian youth must as rapidly as possible find their place in our American school system. Isolation and segregation can only retard progress and perpetuate a vexing problem; but association and competition with the children of other races will bring about speedy amalgamation." The time will soon arrive, he said, "when the Church shall limit her education to schools of training for Indian leadership, and turn over secular education to the State and Federal schools, where it rightfully belongs. Christian leadership is our greatest need....Upon this type of work we must concentrate our efforts."[28]

The Public School Replaces the Mission School

The public school experiment began in 1928; Winnebago, in fact, was the site of one of the first public schools in the nation that welcomed Indian children. Although the mission school itself was phased out grade by grade, the dormitories—operated by the mission—continued to be used. Roads on the reservation were chronically bad and sometimes impassable, and the public school provided no transportation, so the dormitories still provided a valuable service. But there was a problem: the other mission buildings were one and one-half miles south of town. So the decision was made to move the buildings—four large dormitories, the parsonage, a staff cottage, and the church—a major operation.

Previously the dormitories housed children through the sixth grade, the highest grade in the mission school. Now the dormitories were opened to high school students as well, since these students could attend the local public school instead of going away to boarding school. (The high school curriculum, incidentally, included Latin, and some students were assigned to live in an area of the dormitory called the Gaul House.) The mission provided free room and board, requiring only

28. G. A. Watermulder, "The Spiritual Value of Christian Education Among the American Indians," Part II, *Christian Intelligencer and Mission Field,* June 23, 1926.

Dormitories in Winnebago

that the children provide their own clothing and help with the laundry, dishes, and housekeeping. On weekends they were allowed to go to their homes for only a few hours, and then only after they had finished their chores at school. Students were required, of course, to participate in all religious activities—worship and Sunday school on Sundays and dormitory devotions and Bible memory work every evening. How did the children respond? Anna Elenbaas, a worker supported by the Reformed Church in South Holland, Illinois, reported:

> We who have watched them make the change see the Indian natures developing; they no longer are a sullen, backward, frightened group of children; they are alert, wide-awake, energetic, ever-questioning, responsive. They are becoming more keen. Most of them are well able to take their place in the class room and many of them are leaders in the school work and show remarkable mental ability.[29]

One wonders: when the children were "sullen, backward, frightened"—was that when they were attending the mission school or does it refer only to their first days of public school? In any case, the mission staff approved of the new arrangement. "We believe," said Elenbaas, "our method is the only hope for the Indian race; segregation is wrong, amalgamation is the solution."[30] Another of the long-time mission workers was Marie De Keyser, who had served previously in Colony, Oklahoma. De Keyster left in 1937 after a total of fourteen years in Indian ministry.

29. Anna Elenbaas, "The Winnebago Indian School," *Christian Intelligencer*, Nov. 12, 1930, 740.
30. Ibid.

Timothy Cramer and James Ottipoby, Assistant Pastors

As Watermulder had since 1914 carried a measure of oversight responsibilities over the entire denomination's Indian work, at one point carrying the title, "Missionary at Large," assistant pastors were brought in from time to time. The Reverend Timothy Cramer came for two years (1930-32) after graduating from Western Theological Seminary; and the Reverend James Ottipoby, a Comanche from Lawton, Oklahoma, served for two years after his ordination in 1938. Ottipoby then moved on to Mescalero, New Mexico, to work with Peter Van Es.

Frank Beaver and John Smith

Frank Beaver, a graduate of Carlisle and the mission's interpreter, lived with his family in one of the mission buildings. Called a dependable worker and elder, he interpreted for Watermulder and also wrote a genealogy of every family of the tribe. In 1930 he was invited to the annual meeting of the Women's Board of Domestic Missions at the St. Nicholas Collegiate Church in New York City. He reviewed the changes at the school and mission, thanked the Reformed Church for its contributions, and concluded, "Forty years ago our people were looking down a dark trail, but today they are looking up a trail full of hope."[31]

Another of the outstanding Christian leaders of the church at this time was John Smith, a devoted church member and elder. Smith made several transitions in his religious path, first as a participant in the Medicine Lodge, then as a practitioner in the peyote religion. When he heard the Christian message, said Watermulder, "his mind and heart took in the life-giving message as a thirsty land drinks in the morning dew from heaven."[32] He came to every meeting, said Watermulder, and seldom failed to take part in prayer meetings. Watermulder told of calling on him early one morning and finding him alone in a quiet place in the yard, praying. Smith's testimony—at least as reported by Watermulder—was harsh in its condemnation of the old way:

> When I took Christ as my personal Savior, I had to struggle against one of the worst sins among the Indian people. That sin

31. "The Forty-Eighth Anniversary of the Women's Board of Domestic Missions," *Christian Intelligencer*, Nov. 26, 1930, 770.
32. Richard Harper, "Some Indian Leaders, Past and Present," *Christian Intelligencer and Mission Field*, Sept. 30, 1925, 616.

Elder John Smith

had been rooted down deep into my life. It was very hard for me to break away from it. It was the old heathen Indian religion....When I think of my past life I realize that I was a savage of the forest... Before I accepted Christ I tried to find a place of rest and leaned on the green oak tree. It looked strong and would not easily be uprooted, and yet at the end of its span of life it dried up and fell over. That was the way with my old heathen religion. But now I am resting upon Jesus and leaning upon Him and I know He will stand forever.[33]

Economic Hardship

Meanwhile, the tribe continued to experience dire economic conditions. The original Winnebago reservation had dwindled by Indian shortsightedness and white subterfuge from 130,000 acres in 1865 to 40,000 acres in 1930. Indian youth were bewildered, torn

---

33. G. A. Watermulder, "A Challenging Testimony," *Christian Intelligencer and Mission Field*, Dec. 31, 1924, 842.

between family loyalty and what they learned from their white teachers. A few went to college, but most returned within a year or two, confused by white culture and homesick for the tribe. Many more of the youth went to the cities to find work, but timid by nature and training, they felt intimidated by the dominant culture and longed for the security of family and tribe. Those who stayed on the reservation had little or no work and fell prey to the social pressure of alcohol.

Life was made even more miserable by the Great Depression; by a tornado that hit in the fall of 1929, killing seven, injuring forty, and destroying or damaging fifty homes; by a midwestern drought and grasshopper plague in 1935; by several major floods; by severe winter blizzards; and by a wave of influenza that swept through the Winnebago and Omaha reservations in the winter of 1936-37, killing twenty-five people. A fire destroyed the community building in 1937, including its library of fourteen hundred books. While the building was insured, the books were not, and the mission asked for contributions of books and magazines.

A New Emphasis on Tribal Development

Until this time the mission's stance was to oppose traditional Indian activities or at least to be aloof from them. Although the mission encouraged individuals and families to make a better life for themselves and rejoiced when individuals prepared themselves for professions through education, the church did not seek to work directly with the community as a whole in seeking economic development. (Actually, the church could not deal directly with the tribe, because official tribal governments did not exist until the Indian Reorganization Act of 1934.)

In 1927 the Reverend John Russell, a British evangelist, led meetings in Winnebago, following through with a flowery letter of appreciation to the Women's Board. He then made comments that might have been considered by some to be impertinent for an outsider:

> It seems to me that there is a great need for dealing in a dual way with the Indian field....I felt...that the only safe and effective way would be to work for the solution of the economic problem from the spiritual base....If I was a wealthy man I would say, "Launch out in the Canning Industry for Winnebago."[34]

34. John Russell, "An Appreciation," *Christian Intelligencer and Mission Field*, Jan. 18, 1928, 41.

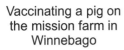

Vaccinating a pig on
the mission farm in
Winnebago

The minutes of the Women's Board of Domestic Missions for 1930 contain a new heading: "Economic." The report refers to the government's Meriam report (in which Henry Roe Cloud participated) that called for Indian economic development, and it goes on to mention such attempts on the part of the missions as bead and leather work in Oklahoma, sheep in New Mexico, and employment in neighboring towns and cities. "At Winnebago," the report says, "the mission is encouraging and in some instances helping to finance a chinchilla rabbit industry."[35] No further mention was made of the chinchillas, but the attempt was significant.

The Short-Lived Farm Program

Out of this new emphasis on economic development came the introduction of the mission's vocational and farm program in 1937. It seemed like a wise thing to do, since some of the Winnebagos still owned their acreages and had little or no training on how to conduct the business of agriculture. So the mission board built a barn and hired an agriculture teacher. The boys in the dormitory were assigned chores with the intention of teaching them how to care for hogs, cattle, and chickens. The girls were taught to milk, make butter, care for gardens, and practice homemaking. The government offered loans that would enable young men to purchase animals of their own. "Can you imagine the pride with which the boy will demonstrate to his family the proper care of his animal?" exuded Helen Brickman, general secretary of the Women's Board of Domestic Missions.[36]

35. *Annual Report of the Women's Board of Domestic Missions*, 1930, 21.
36. Helen Brickman, "The Great Conquest," *Intelligencer-Leader*, Nov. 10, 1939, 6.

But it was not to be. Within a few years the program quietly disappeared, and no mention was made of it again. One can only assume that the previously nomadic Winnebagos, having either sold or leased their allotments to white people and having never requested the program in the first place, simply showed little interest in feeding pigs or milking cows.

Membership and Camp Meetings

Reported communicant membership during the 1930s hovered at about two hundred members in eighty families, with about one hundred people listed as absent or inactive. Sunday school enrollment was listed at about 170, but with radical fluctuations. As was common among Indian churches at this time, there was little correlation between confessions of faith and membership, and no one was ever listed as having been dropped from the church rolls. Attendance statistics were not given, nor were they alluded to in news reports.

Meanwhile, annual camp meetings continued, but with changes. Beef distribution was phased out, and cafeteria-style meals, complete with paper plates, became common. With the exception of Anna Berkanpas—who seemed to be everywhere and to do everything—the Indians were in charge of preparing the food.

The Watermulder Era Comes to an End

Gustavus Adolf Watermulder retired from the Winnebago work in 1942 after thirty-four years of Indian ministry in one location. Watermulder's influence and responsibilities had reached far beyond Nebraska. Although he apparently carried no official title, he was the board's field representative for all the Reformed Church's Indian work for nearly thirty years. He was the first president of the National Fellowship of Indian Workers, had assisted in organizing the new mission in Dulce, New Mexico; had lobbied for the installation of the Reverend Robert Chaat of Lawton as the first Native American minister in the Reformed Church; and had been instrumental in the assumption of the mission in nearby Macy. He had been granted a leave of absence in 1923 to study mission possibilities in Central America and Mexico, and his report, together with that of Mary Roe, led to the founding of the Chiapas mission in 1925.

At the age of sixty-eight, Watermulder accepted the position of dean and Bible teacher at Cook Christian Training School in Phoenix,

Arizona, for a five-year term. He died there in 1946, one year before the expiration of his term and one day short of his seventy-second birthday. Hattie Hospers Watermulder stayed on for several years as a teacher at Cook, and she died in 1961.

The Era of the Children's Shelter, 1942-69

Gradus and Auriel Aalberts Arrive

The Reverend Gradus C. and Auriel Aalberts, who followed the Watermulders in Winnebago, were among the elite group of Reformed pastoral teams who served twenty years or longer in American Indian ministries. The Aalberts served in Winnebago from 1942 to 1958, left for six years to work with Native Americans in Minneapolis, Minnesota, and returned to serve in Winnebago from 1964 until Gradus's death in 1970.

Aalberts came from a Christian Reformed background in Orange City, Iowa, attended Calvin College, and graduated from Western Seminary in 1939. While living in Holland, Michigan, he visited his cousin Gradus A. Aalberts at the nearby Harlem Reformed Church. There he met Auriel Bakker, whom he married after graduation. Aalberts first served for three years at the American Reformed Church in Ireton, in northwest Iowa. After Watermulder's retirement, Aalberts was called to Winnebago in 1942. He had worked there one summer as a seminary student and frequently preached there while serving in Ireton.

Auriel Aalberts has stated that it took five years for them to be accepted, which is not surprising, considering the long tenure of the Watermulders and the reticence of Native Americans in their relationships with white people. The Aalberts did not make a major issue of peyote, which they regarded as a hallucinatory but nonaddictive drug. In fact, they maintained a somewhat amicable relationship with the local Native American Church. Auriel Aalberts has related that one of the leaders of that group sometimes came to the Reformed Church to listen to her husband's sermons, then went back to preach them in his own church—thus ensuring a significant amount of Christian theology in the Native American Church.

Most of the Winnebagos spoke English by this time, but Frank Beaver still interpreted for the older people who came to prayer meetings. Summer evangelistic meetings continued, with speakers like the Reverend Wendell Chino of Mescalero, Leon Grant of Macy, and the

Gradus Aalberts prays with
a Winnebago couple in their home.

Reverend Robert Chaat of Lawton. Vacation Bible schools continued to be popular, with several of the teachers being Indians. Picnics and special programs were held on the Fourth of July. From time to time Aalberts announced that one or more young men or women had enrolled in Cook Christian Training School, but he seldom gave follow-up reports. Worship attendance statistics were seldom announced, except that in 1947 Aalberts said that even during the summer powwow, seventy-five people attended the morning service and sixty-five came at night. Unlike his predecessor, Aalberts became very much involved in the life of the community. At various times he served as president of the local school board, member of the Community Development Committee, chairman of the local chapter of the Red Cross, and even the mayor of Winnebago.

A New Chapel

Up to this time the Winnebago mission never had a separate place of worship, Sunday services having been conducted in the community building. After the war, Aalberts and Reformed Church administrators negotiated with U.S. officials and arranged for the purchase (for $1) of a surplus military chapel. The building was moved from Lincoln, Nebraska, in six pieces. The community house was moved to the back of the lot and attached to the church. The new building was dedicated September 23, 1948. Robert Chaat came from Lawton, Oklahoma, to bring the message, "The Marks of a Christian Church," and several denominational executives, former Winnebago mission staff, and Peter Van Es, pastor at nearby Macy, brought greetings.

Dormitories Become 'Shelters'

Gradually the buildings that housed children at Winnebago began to be called "shelters" instead of dormitories. As roads became better and transportation improved, more and more children could live at home while attending the public school. But, simultaneously, wartime conditions and dysfunctional family life placed more children at risk. In the early 1940s the mission staff increasingly felt the need to provide care for children who had been abandoned, orphaned, or mistreated. The mission board endorsed the concept of providing a shelter for these children, and within a few years the facilities were operating at their full capacity of forty children.

Some children came for a short time, as when their mothers could not care for them because of illness, or when roads became impassable in the winter. Others stayed at the home while their parents left to find work in a city, or because of violence in the home, or because they had been orphaned. In addition to Sunday school and church attendance, the children attended Bible classes and practical classes such as sewing for the girls and "manual training" for the boys. "Naturally these children have an entirely new way of life to learn," said a board report in 1951. "They must be taught table manners, cleanliness, how to live with one another showing courtesy and thoughtfulness. They must be taught the value of truthfulness and honesty, and above all, we must instill in their hearts the feeling of God as their heavenly Father."[37]

The program was supported in part by the Baby Roll of the board, which encouraged parents and grandparents to enroll their own babies for a small fee, with the proceeds going to the children's shelter. A brochure, *Feed My Sheep*, promoted the cause by relating thumbnail sketches of children such as Edith, "a sweet little girl who craves affection."[38] In addition to financial support, churches in Iowa and Minnesota sent loads of potatoes, carrots, and onions, as well as

37. *Annual Report of the Board of Domestic Missions*, 1951, 28.
38. Typewritten promotional brochure of the Women's Board of Domestic Missions, circa 1944.

Bernice Tegeler with day care children in 1983

canned vegetables. Indian children often spent summers in the homes of Reformed Church people in Iowa. On two occasions, *Church Herald* articles about the shelter included photos of young Kenneth Mallory, who later became an elder in the church and a staff member of the American Indian Council.

Bernice Tegeler Comes to Winnebago

In 1951 the mission needed a competent housemother for the boys' dormitory, so the Aalberts asked for suggestions from Reuben and Bernice Ten Haken in Mescalero, New Mexico. They recommended Bernice Tegeler, the young woman they had brought with them from Erie, Illinois. Thus began a new chapter in a career of Indian ministry that is far longer than any other—officially forty-six years, but unofficially still counting.

Tegeler had gone to Mescalero to help care for the Ten Hakens' daughter, Beverly. However, within a short time Tegeler had acquired responsibilities with the Sunday school and Ladies Aid, eventually taking the title of community worker. When the call came from Winnebago seven years later, she was ready for a new challenge.

When Tegeler arrived in Winnebago, one of the boys said, "The other lady stayed three months. How long are you going to stay?" Tegeler's wards included Kenneth Mallory, who at that time was considered incorrigible. Mallory later looked on Tegeler as a mother.

Over the years Tegeler's responsibilities changed several times. She was appointed director of the shelter home in 1962, after Andy and Marjorie Kamphuis left to serve the Apache Reformed Church in Apache, Oklahoma. When the shelter was phased out, she became director of the tribe's group home (1972-75), then of the foster care program (1975-83), and of the day care program (1983-90). She continued her education by taking extensive college courses in Omaha, a hundred miles away. Tegeler retired June 30, 1990, at which time she was honored both by the tribe and by the General Synod of the Reformed Church. At the synod ceremony she was escorted to the platform by members of the Winnebago Reformed Church and presented with a plaque. Among the tributes to Tegeler upon her retirement was this one from the descendents of Mary Greywolf, from the Snake Clan at Winnebago:

> She came to us as a young woman filled with physical energy and spiritual love. Her visions and her dreams were not of power and prestige, but of humble service in her Holy Father's Name. She preached not, neither did she admonish or condemn. But through love and compassion she taught our children of Christ's love and God's promise....Truly she is one of us and has earned a place of honor for having her in our midst, and we pray to *Mauna* that He might bless her greatly for us because we love her as a mother, sister, and friend.[39]

As of this writing, Tegeler still lives in Winnebago, volunteering with the childcare program and residing in a home provided by the tribe. She has no plans to move away from the people she has lived and worked with for more than fifty years.

Bethel Reformed Church in Winnebago

The Bethel Presbyterian Church in Winnebago, the white congregation that sometimes worked with the Winnebago Reformed Church, actually became an Reformed congregation for a few years. The small congregation was transferred to the Reformed Church in 1951, with the Reverend Bernard Hietbrink as pastor. The Reverend David Wilson, a recent graduate of Western Seminary, followed Hietbrink in 1955. Wilson stayed just one year and was later dismissed to the

39. Typewritten document, "A Humble Tribute to an Honored Friend, from the descendents of Mary Greywolf, from the Snake Clan," no date, in the possession of Bernice Tegeler.

Presbyterian Church. The Bethel congregation was disbanded in 1957, and the tribe used the building for a time as a mortuary. It was torn down and replaced with a meditation garden in 2003.

The year 1957 also marked the transfer of all of the Indian congregations from the Classis of New York to a classis in their geographical area. The Winnebago Reformed Church became part of the Classis of West Sioux, while the Reformed Church in Macy, eight miles to the south, became part of the Classis of East Sioux.

Andy and Marjorie Kamphuis Enter Indian Ministry

In 1956 Andy and Marjorie Kamphuis came to Winnebago to do maintenance work and to serve as houseparents at the children's shelter—thus beginning a ministry among Native Americans that was to last more than thirty years. The Kamphuises had grown up in Waupun and Brandon, Wisconsin, and Andy had attended Moody Bible Institute in Chicago. After six years in Winnebago they were invited to Apache, Oklahoma, to deal with what was considered to be a lost cause—serving the tiny congregation made up of Fort Sill Apaches who had remained in Oklahoma after their release as prisoners of war. The Kamphuises revitalized the congregation there and stayed twenty-four years.

The Campaign to Expand the Shelter

In the early 1950s the mission began a publicity campaign to expand the shelter, citing examples of needy children who had to be turned away because of a lack of space. "Think of tiny Constance, six months old," wrote Gradus Aalberts in a 1953 *Church Herald* article. "Both parents are on the borderline of feeble-mindedness, and both are habitual drunkards. Practically every month the baby is taken to the government to be treated for malnutrition." And there was a threat of dire consequences if the shelter could not be expanded:

> I assure you that often our hearts nearly break when we learn that our children have been enrolled at the Catholic Mission...now snatched away, probably never again to return....We cannot afford to lose these young souls to Catholicism, where they are taught to reject and despise us, where they are told that everything we taught them is wrong.[40]

---

40. Gradus Aalberts, "The Sign of Promise," *Church Herald*, Nov. 13, 1953, 15.

Marion Klaaren, seated, and Gradus Aalberts at the laying of the cornerstone

The New Shelter Is Built

A denomination-wide Thanksgiving appeal in 1953 netted $35,000 toward the goal of $100,000 for the new shelter, and early in 1954 the Board of Domestic Missions approved the erection of a new structure. The building was constructed on the site of the old dormitories, so during construction Reformed Church families in northwest Iowa cared for the children. The building was dedicated January 10, 1955, and very shortly thereafter was filled to its capacity of sixty children. Soon an additional component was added—a preschool cottage for the care of four small children. Fund-raising brochures asked for $350 scholarships per year per student.

Edward and Eleanor Van Gent

When the Kamphuises moved to Oklahoma, Edward and Eleanor Van Gent moved in to take responsibilities for maintenance and Christian education. Both had grown up in the vicinity of Pella, Iowa, and graduated from Central College. They served in Macy for six years before moving a few miles down the road to Winnebago in 1962.

In Winnebago, the Van Gents were involved in remodeling the church, taught Bible classes, sponsored youth work, and engaged in a number of community activities such as the volunteer fire department.

The Van Gents left Winnebago in 1968, lived briefly in Kentucky, and then moved to Grand Rapids, Michigan, where Ed worked for Bethany Christian Services and Eleanor taught school. Ed Van Gent died November 23, 2000, and as of this writing Eleanor Van Gent lives in Waupun, Wisconsin.

The Aalberts Leave for Minneapolis

During and following World War II, many Native Americans moved away from the reservations to cities. The process was accelerated by federal legislation that ended much financial support and began a program to relocate Indians to urban areas and thereby assimilate them into the dominant culture. In the cities, the Indians often found work, but they also experienced an alien culture and intense loneliness for tribe and family, and several interdenominational agencies founded relocation ministries. In 1958, after sixteen years in Winnebago, the Aalberts moved to Minneapolis, Minnesota, where Gradus directed the urban Indian work under the auspices of the Minnesota Council of Churches. Nola Aalberts, who was one year old when her parents moved to Winnebago and seventeen when the family left, was later appointed to the Reformed Church's development and mission staff (1996-2001) with responsibilities for Native American Ministries. She and her sister Jan have been life-long members of the Winnebago church.

Wilbur De Cora Begins Ministry in Winnebago

After the Aalberts left Winnebago for city work, the church turned to one of its own, the Reverend Wilbur De Cora. Having been born in Winnebago in 1915, De Cora grew up as the town bully and then used his fighting skills for a career in boxing. He fought first as a Golden Gloves amateur and then as a professional, in a career that spanned eleven years and took him as far as Madison Square Garden. But near the end of his career he began drinking heavily, and after being severely injured in a bout he returned to Winnebago for hospitalization. There he met Lupeta (Lupe) Jojold, a Pueblo from New Mexico who had come to Winnebago as a nurse, and he soon astonished the populace by appearing in church with her. Through the influence of Lupe and pastor Aalberts, De Cora made a Christian commitment, gave up drinking, and in other ways turned his life around.

After getting married, the De Coras attended Cook Christian Training School, spent a year in Arizona working with the Maricopa

Wilbur De Cora

Indians, and then went to Mescalero, New Mexico, to work as assistants to the Calsbeeks. De Cora then attended New Brunswick Theological Seminary for a year and, although he did not graduate, was ordained by the Reformed Church in 1958. At that point he returned to serve his home church at Winnebago, first as stated supply and then as pastor.

Tensions soon arose, especially with the older members of the congregation. One point of view holds that De Cora insisted that parishioners become self-sufficient and self-determining; another point of view believes he failed to provide the kind of pastoral services the congregation was accustomed to receiving. He also got caught up in tribal politics, which alienated him from some members of the church. Attendance declined dramatically, and under pressure both from the congregation and the mission administration, he resigned in June of 1962. Although regular reports were not made, it would seem that during the four years of De Cora's ministry, communicant membership dropped from over two hundred to about sixty. The De Coras moved to Albuquerque, New Mexico, where Wilbur became a counselor at a government school. With the church vacant again after only four years, the Aalberts were invited to return from Minneapolis and to again take up the work at Winnebago.

The Children's Shelter Is Closed

The cornerstone of the children's home said "Shelter Home," and for several years the facility was referred to as the Children's Shelter. In 1963 the board decided to call it the Children's Home, with the explanation that "a shelter is not all that children without a home need." References were made to "the girls' family" and "the boys' family."[41] The home had originally been filled to its capacity of sixty children, but enrollment gradually declined to between twenty and thirty. By the mid-sixties major concerns were being raised about the long-term welfare of those who lived there:

> These were little children without the security of parents or a home of their own—unhappy, lacking in self-esteem, unable to trust adults, the world or even themselves....Many could not accept this love; some were suspicious and rejecting. Some grew strong; others remained weak.[42]

A committee consisting of social workers, church leaders, and local Indian residents conducted a comprehensive study for the Reformed Church, and in 1968 the committee reported its belief that long-term institutional care was not the best care for homeless children, recommending instead a foster home placement program. At its spring 1969 meeting, the General Program Council voted to close the home as a long-term care facility—just fourteen years after it had been dedicated. Foster homes were found for the children, a temporary short-term care center was opened at one of the homes on the property, and a community day care center was opened at the former shelter, with Bernice Tegeler as the director.

Church Renovated in 1966

The church had used a surplus army chapel for worship services for nearly twenty years. The need was now felt for a more adequate facility, so the church underwent major additions and renovations in the sanctuary and educational wing during 1965 and 1966. The remodeled facility was dedicated April 14, 1966, with the Reverend Garret Wilterdink, president of the Board of North American Missions, preaching the sermon.

41. Beatrice O. Gray, "More Than a Shelter—A Children's Home," *Church Herald,* Sep. 20, 1963, 9.
42. Beatrice O. Gray, "Our CCC (Church, Children's Home, Community) Ministry in Winnebago," *Church Herald,* Nov. 6, 1964, 20.

Another child-oriented service, the government-funded Headstart program, was initiated in 1967. Because the local school lacked space for the forty children involved, the church contributed space in its newly renovated facilities. Gradus Aalberts also acted as chair of the Headstart committee.

In 1968 the church celebrated its sixtieth anniversary. Former pastor Wilbur De Cora accepted the invitation to speak at the event, and retired long-time staff member Anna Berkenpas was also able to attend. In 1968 the Winnebago church also sent its first elder delegate, Gordon Beaver, to the General Synod, representing the Classis of West Sioux. Beaver was at the time not only the vice-president of the consistory, but also the chairman of the Winnebago Tribal Council.

'Red Power' Letter to the Reformed Church in America

In December 1969 Gordon Beaver cosigned an "Open Letter to the Reformed Church in America" with Edward Cline, who held similar positions in nearby Macy. The letter referred to a grant of $100,000 given by the denomination in response to a "Black Manifesto" delivered to the church's office in New York by a black activist. Cline and Beaver asked, "Is this the only way the church will listen to the requests of minority groups?...If you want 'Red Power,' we can furnish it."[43] The American Indian Council was organized three years later (see chapter 10).

The Era of Day Care, 1970-

Meanwhile, the work of the church continued. Church activities included vacation Bible school, two women's groups, and two choirs. Aalberts's community involvement included serving on the village board and helping set up voter registration after tribal members had been stonewalled. But person-to-person work remained high on his agenda. Aalberts, in a 1970 letter to his mission supervisor, the Reverend John Hiemstra, said, "Some of the greatest thrills of my ministry have come to me during conversations on a street corner...kneeling down in a prison cell...and entering a home at midnight to counsel with a disturbed couple."[44]

---

43. Gordon C. Beaver and Edward L. Cline, "Is a Show of 'Red Power' Next? An Open Letter to the Reformed Church in America," The *Church Herald*, December 26, 1969, 12.
44. Letter from Gradus Aalberts to John Hiemstra, March 23, 1970.

Aalberts Dies and De Cora Returns

Aalberts's second period of service lasted six years. He died suddenly of previously undiagnosed cancer at the age of fifty-seven April 23, 1970, having served all but two of his thirty-one years of ministry among American Indians. Aalberts was buried in the tribal cemetery, he and Watermulder's first wife being the only white people buried there who had not married into the tribe. Auriel Aalberts subsequently became a housemother at Annville Institute in Kentucky and later retired to Orange City, Iowa.

During the Aalberts's second pastorate, the church recovered some of the momentum it had lost during the previous four years. Reported communicant membership increased from about fifty to about seventy-five, with Sunday school enrollment increasing to about seventy-five. About twenty people were reported as inactive.

Now in this revolving door of Aalberts and De Cora, it was Wilbur De Cora's turn to return to Winnebago. Although there is no record that he had left the ministry of the Reformed Church, he was reordained September 21, 1970. Since Robert Chaat had retired the year before from his pastorate in Lawton, Oklahoma, De Cora was the only remaining Indian pastor serving a congregation in the Reformed Church.

A substantial number of De Cora's sermon outlines have been preserved, contributed by his wife to the Reformed Church archives in New Brunswick, New Jersey. The sermons follow unswervingly the homiletical pattern of the day—an introduction, three parallel points, and a conclusion. One sermon, "Christ in the World," for instance, is based on 1 Timothy 1:15 and contains three points: "The Person," "The Place," and "The Purpose." A review of dozens of these sermons revealed a great deal of biblical exposition but few applications to daily life and no specific references to Indian culture. It would almost seem that De Cora consciously avoided mention of Indian life of the past.

Children's Home Sold

In 1972 the children's home was closed entirely, and the day care center was transferred to the church's basement and community house. The General Program Council voted to sell the building to the tribe, and negotiations took place in Winnebago. Among those present were the Reverend Russell Redeker, secretary for church planning and development; the Reverend Harold (Shorty) Brown, Indian mission

The Children's Home was sold to the Winnebago tribe in 1972.

administrator; and Louis LaRose, tribal chair and elder of the church. After questioning Redeker about whether it was, indeed, on Manhatten Island that the Reformed Church offices were located, LaRose, without cracking a smile, made an offer for the children's home: a few beaded trinkets, $24, and a bottle of good whisky. Redeker was not amused. The next offer was $25,000, to which Brown agreed. Since that time the building has housed the tribe's Little Priest Tribal College, named after an early famous chief.

In 1974 the Winnebago congregation honored Cecilia Merrick for her forty years of service as church pianist, organist, and Sunday school teacher. Merrick, an Oneida, lived in South Sioux City but worked for the Bureau of Indian Affairs in Winnebago. She was eighty-one years old at the time of her retirement, but she continued to play the organ for the church on special occasions.

In terms of numbers, De Cora's second pastorate at Winnebago was also disappointing, with reported active communicant membership dropping from a high of seventy-six in 1970 to a low of forty in 1975. It ended in a manner reminiscent of Aalberts's second pastorate; De Cora died of a massive heart attack November 3, 1975, at the age of sixty-one. Lupe De Cora continued for many years to live in Winnebago as an active member of the church and as a member of the consistory, and as of this writing lives in Isleta, New Mexico.

Dirk and Linda Kramer

Next the congregation called the Reverend Dirk and Linda Kramer to the ministry in Winnebago. Dirk Kramer had been born in The Hague, the Netherlands, in 1950, but spent most of his early years

Dirk and Linda Kramer

in Zeeland, Michigan. He and Linda, also from Michigan, met at Hope College. Dirk had served as a summer intern at the Jicarilla Reformed Church in Dulce, New Mexico, while a student at Western Theological Seminary, and shortly after graduation accepted the call to Winnebago. "We tried," said Kramer, "to change the long-held perception of the work at Winnebago from that of a mission to a duly organized church fully capable of administering itself, albeit unable to support itself financially."[45] The Kramers served there three years, 1976-79, and since then have spent their ministry in Michigan and Ontario. During the short Kramer tenure, active communicant membership increased from about forty to about fifty.

Roger and Janet De Young

The Kramers were followed after a year of vacancy by the Reverend Roger and Janet De Young, who served from 1980 to 1986. Roger, from De Motte, Indiana, and Janet, from Manistee, Michigan, met at Hope College, from which they both graduated. Roger graduated from the joint program of Western and New Brunswick seminaries in 1976 and served at the Bushkill Reformed Church in Pennsylvania before accepting the call to Winnebago.

The De Youngs were well accepted and trusted as they tried to incorporate native influences into their lives while still maintaining their identity as white persons. One of the first things the church did after the De Youngs' arrival was to reinvigorate the faltering vacation

45. Letter from Dirk Kramer to LeRoy Koopman, Nov. 10, 2003.

Roger and Janet De Young in 1982

Bible school and the Sunday school, with predominantly Indian staffs. Roger De Young also worked closely with local church leaders such as Nikky Solomon and Kenneth Mallory. The De Youngs became involved in several aspects of community life, Janet serving on the school board and as a Girl Scout leader, and both teaching for a time at the Little Priest Tribal College.

In 1983 the church's senior high youth group visited Reformed Church young people in Indiana, Michigan, New York, and New Jersey, an experience that De Young called "an educational, faith-broadening two-week tour that our young people are still talking about."[46] The church also placed a high priority on sending youth to Inspiration Hills conference center in northwest Iowa during the summer. Stewardship included a continuing pledge to the Call to Commitment program of Northwestern College.

Meanwhile, Bernice Tegeler continued to work at the day care center in the church basement, taking care of business matters and helping with day-to-day operations. Twice, in 1979 and 1981, renovations had to be made in order to be licensed by the State Department of Public Welfare. In addition, Tegeler's home was always open to abused women and children who needed a temporary place to stay.

46. Roger and Janet De Young, letter to supporting churches, April 5, 1984.

Mention should be made of Arthur and Ann Sieplinga, who at different times filled three roles at Winnebago—houseparents of the children's home, group-home parents, and directors of the day care center. Art Sieplinga died unexpectedly in 1979, and his wife continued to work there until 1982.

The De Youngs left Winnebago in 1986 when Roger accepted a position on the financial development staff of the Reformed Church in America, later expanded to include North American mission supervision. During the De Young years in Winnebago, active communicant membership held strong at about fifty, with an average of six people making confession of faith each year. Sunday school enrollment increased from thirty-seven to seventy-three during that time.

Seventy-Fifth Anniversary

In November 1986 the De Youngs were called back to Winnebago for the church's seventy-fifth anniversary. Also present for the celebration were former missionaries Dirk and Linda Kramer and family; staff members Beth Marcus, Eugene Heideman, Richard Vander Voet, and Roe Lewis; and past mission workers and volunteers. The festivities were opened by Reuben Snake, tribal chairman and leader in the Native American Church, and closed by Kenneth Mallory, vice-president of the consistory and chairman of the American Indian Council.

David and Nancy Crump

In June 1987 the Reverend David and Nancy Crump began a ministry in Winnebago that continued for seven years. Nancy was part Cherokee-Creek, and David grew up in Brazil as part of a missionary family. He held degrees from Moody Bible Institute, the University of South Florida, and Memphis Theological Seminary. Both had children by previous marriages.

Both David and Nancy Crump were deeply involved with Indian history and culture. "There is a tremendous beauty, a richness that we experience here among the Winnebagos," they wrote shortly after they arrived.[47] More than any other missionary before him, Crump advocated "Indianizing" the church. In a sermon on Daniel 8:15-27, for instance, he compared Daniel's vision to Black Elk's vision and used

---

47. David and Nancy Crump, letter to supporting churches, Oct. 28, 1988.

David and Nancy Crump

Black Elk's emphasis on the sacred hoop: "In many ways the hoops of our Indian nations, and the hoops of many nations—including the United States—are broken today....But God's desire is for the hoops to be mended."[48] Long-time members of the church did not always celebrate these efforts. On one occasion Crump was advocating his cause with an elder of the church who said, in all seriousness, "You've got to realize that we are a Dutch Reformed Church."

Crump was also a political and social activist. In October 1992 he accompanied a group from the church and community to Washington, D.C., for an alternative Columbus Day celebration called "Celebrating Five Hundred Years of Native American Survival." In March of 1994 he and Christine Dyke, pastor at the neighboring Umonhon Reformed Church in Macy, traveled to El Salvador to help monitor the elections there.

Reuben Snake, Friend of Pastors

Some people of the church also believed that Crump's relationship with the Native American Church was entirely too close and sympathetic. In his farewell letter to supporting churches in June 1994, Crump made a special tribute to two of its leaders, John De

48. David Crump, "The Hoop Will Be Mended," typescript of sermon preached May 12, 1991.

Cora and Reuben Snake, calling Snake "a spiritual mentor and a good friend."[49] Crump's accolades were not unique, as Roger De Young before him had called Snake "a wise and good friend."[50] Snake, who often signed his letters, "Your Humble Serpent," served twenty-eight years on the Winnebago Tribal Council, most of them as tribal president, and he also served as president of the National Council of American Indians. As an early resident of the children's home, he had sat under the teaching of his houseparents and the preaching of Aalberts. De Young said, "When Reuben was asked to perform a marriage ceremony, he would borrow my RCA liturgy book. Finally I bought him one of his own."[51] Snake died in 1994 at the age of fifty-six.

David Crump left Winnebago in September 1994 to begin a doctor of ministry program in Chicago, and Nancy stayed behind to teach history and Native American studies at Wayne State College. The Crump's marriage dissolved, and David later became director of the National Farm Workers Ministry, an ecumenical ministry with headquarters in Chicago. As of this writing Nancy Crump Gillis continues to live and work in northeast Nebraska and is a teacher and elder in the Winnebago church.

Darrell and Dawn Dalman

The Crumps were followed by the Reverend Darrell and Dawn Dalman, who arrived in 1994. Darrell, from Hudsonville, Michigan, a student at Reformed Bible College in Grand Rapids, Michigan, spent the summer of 1987 at the Reformed Church in Apache, Oklahoma. There he met Dawn Tsatoke, a Kiowa member of the Methodist church, and Darrell's summer stretched, on-and-off, to four years. After marriage the couple moved to Holland, Michigan, where Darrell graduated from Western Theological Seminary in 1994, and from there they went to Winnebago.

Whereas Crump emphasized Native American culture and social justice, Dalman has stressed the charismatic gifts of the Spirit, including healing and the laying on of hands. His emphasis has been more on preaching than on the social dynamics of the tribe and church.

49. David Crump, letter to supporting churches, June 1994.
50. Email from Roger De Young to LeRoy Koopman, June 21, 2001.
51. Ibid.

Darrell and Dawn Dalman

At the 1998 Triennial Assembly of Reformed Church Women, held in Grand Rapids, Michigan, women from the Winnebago church met over breakfast with women from Reformed congregations in New York. Since that time, women of the two areas have interacted with each other on a regular basis, sometimes in New York and sometimes in Nebraska, culminating with a visit of ninety-nine New York women to Winnebago in conjunction with the 2001 Triennial Assembly in Sioux Falls, South Dakota.

Brenda Snowball, who spent her early years in Winnebago and later relocated to Chicago with her parents, returned to Winnebago in 1996. Feeling a call to the ministry, she entered Dubuque (Iowa) Theological Seminary, from which she graduated in August 2004. Snowball served two summers as a congregation-supported intern at the Winnebago church and has spent a summer at the Apache church in Oklahoma. She plans to continue her studies in the area of chaplaincy. Another intern supported by the church, Sumit Sen, from India, worked for the church for nine months in 2002 and 2003.

Darrell and Dawn Dalman were divorced in September 2002, and Dawn left the area. During the last several years, tensions concerning ministry style and priorities have affected the Dalman ministry, involving not only some church members but also the denomination's Mission Services staff. In September 2002 Mission Services terminated Dalman's employment as a General Synod Council employee.

The Winnebago Reformed church in 1997

The consistory and the Classis of Central Plains challenged this termination, charging that Mission Services had not followed proper procedural guidelines. Responding to a Mission Services ultimatum, the consistory met June 1, 2003, and voted to choose the pastoral relationship over denominational funding. The classis, on the advice of its Pastoral Relations Committee, supported the Winnebago church in its decision. The classis also encouraged the church to solicit direct financial support from the member churches of the classis and from other churches of the Regional Synod of the Heartland (upon classis approval) and to seek support from former Partnership-in-Mission churches throughout the denomination. In June 2003 the mission staff transferred administrative responsibility for the church to the Classis of Central Plains and set up a procedure for withdrawing financial support—one half to be withdrawn by October 2003 and the remaining half by October 2004.

The classis sent two overtures to the 2004 General Synod regarding the matter, and the synod responded by approving the advisory committee's recommendation to "instruct the General Synod Council, in consultation with the Commission on Church Order, to address the structural arrangement between a missionary pastor of a Native American Indian church, Mission Services, the classis, and the consistory of the local church in which the missionary pastor serves."[52] In addition, the synod appointed a committee to "listen to

52. *Minutes of the General Synod*, 2004, 189-90.

the pain of the Winnebago church and seek a transforming fellowship in which healing, restoration, and conflict resolution might occur."[53] In November 2004 a committee consisting of representatives from Mission Services, the classis, the regional synod, and the General Synod Council's Personnel and Evaluation Committee spent a weekend with Dalman and members of the church in Winnebago. The experience was positive, and progress was made toward understanding and reconciliation.

Reported statistics have remained fairly consistent during the Dalman years, with about fifty confessing members, an average worship attendance of about fifty, and Sunday school enrollment of about forty. The church has reported no inactive members in its annual reports.

Over the years, the Reformed Church ministry in Winnebago has adapted to the changing educational policies of the U.S. Government— first providing a mission boarding school, then dormitories only, then a children's shelter, then day care only, and finally limiting its work to traditional church ministries. Its first pastor, the legendary G. A. Watermulder, provided stability for the mission for thirty-four years and also acted as the field supervisor for all of the Reformed Indian ministries. As of this writing, the work continues in Winnebago with a refocusing process assisted by the regional synod, a new statement of goals and objectives, and regular worship services.

53. Ibid., 191.

CHAPTER 9

The Mission in Macy, Nebraska, and the Umo^{n}ho^n Reformed Church

While the stories of the Native American Reformed congregations in Oklahoma and New Mexico are rich in the lore of the old West, with echoes of the Apache wars and the exploits of Geronimo, in Macy, Nebraska, as in Winnebago, the history of Reformed mission work is more subdued. The Omaha tribe was one of the few that never raised a hand against the onslaught of white settlers and soldiers. The work in Macy on the Omaha reservation, like neighboring Winnebago, was inherited from a Presbyterian mission that faltered. The Macy work is the more recent of the two, with Reformed Church involvement dating back only to 1934.

The Reformed Church's work among the Omaha people in Macy has arguably been the most challenging of all of its Native American mission efforts. The Omaha reservation in northeast Nebraska is one of the most economically and socially depressed Indian communities in the United States. The Native American Church, with its "sacrament" of peyote, has competed vigorously for the loyalties of the Omaha people, and the membership of the Reformed church has always been small. Yet the Reformed congregation in Macy is the only viable Christian witness in town, and, after seventy years of faithful work, it is still providing a much-needed source of spiritual and social stability on the Omaha reservation.

A Trip to Macy

In former times, people who made the hundred-mile trip from Sioux City, Iowa, to Omaha, Nebraska, traveled U.S. 75 through the Winnebago and Omaha reservations. Now travelers take Interstate 29, which runs alongside the Iowa side of the Missouri River. Many of the people who drive U.S. 75 south of Sioux City today are Winnebagos, Omahas, the white families who farm reservation land, and the volunteer work groups who come every summer to upgrade the mission property and to become acquainted with the two Native American congregations in northeastern Nebraska.

About twenty miles south of Sioux City, they will drive through the town of Winnebago. About ten miles farther, as they pass through gently rolling hills and fields of corn, soybeans, and hay, they will see a sign that says "Home of the Original He-thu-shke Uh'mon'ha Pow-Wow." The reservation borders the Missouri River on the east, the Winnebago reservation on the north, and more farm country on the west and south. Except for some woodland, white farmers lease most of the reservation's 31,148 acres. About half of this land is owned by the tribe, about half is owned by individuals, and two thousand acres are owned by non-Indians. The tribe consists of about five thousand members, of whom about twenty-five hundred live on the reservation. Just beyond the reservation to the south, in Bancroft, is the home and museum dedicated to the memory of Nebraska poet John Neihardt, as-told-to author of *Black Elk Speaks*, the memoir of an Oglala Sioux holy man.

The Town of Macy

As visitors turn right off Route 75 into Macy, they will see the tribal police headquarters and court, and as they drive farther into town it will become apparent that this is not a prosperous community. Macy, population 836 at last count, is only about six blocks square. Several small buildings along the main street, formerly stores, are boarded up. The one place where groceries can be purchased, Jumps Food Barn, is a combination grocery store, general store, and restaurant. Also in the center of Macy are the tribal headquarters, a municipal swimming pool, and a set of brightly colored children's play equipment. To the west of the playground are the powwow grounds, a rather impressive area nestled under a circle of huge trees.

The newest structures in town are the U. S. Post Office, built in 2002, and the public school, which underwent a major renovation in

The town playground in Macy

2002. There also is the Wade Miller Memorial Field, a football field named after a respected Omaha teacher and tribal leader who was also an active member of the Reformed church. One of Macy's best-known citizens in recent times is Rodney Grant, a 1977 Macy High School graduate who played the role of the tribal warrior, Wind in His Hair, in the 1991 movie, *Dances with Wolves*, and in several other films.

The Umo^{n}ho^n Reformed Church

Across the street from the playground and the powwow grounds, just a few hundred feet west of the center of town, is the Umo^{n}ho^n Reformed Church,[1] a cement block and wooden structure painted grayish blue, with redwood stain under the arched roof that faces the road. Beside the entrance, towering above the church, stands a cross, together with a bell that was moved from the original church building. Above the door that leads from the foyer to the sanctuary is Indian art depicting rain, clouds, grass, and water, with the inscription, "May the Great Spirit watch over you as long as the grass grows and the water flows." Inside the church are found several pieces of art by the late Wade Miller.

---

1. The "^{n}" in Umo^{n}ho^n is a symbol for "to draw through the nose" and is not pronounced as an alphabet "n."

The Um^{n}ho^n Reformed church was dedicated in 1962.

Social and Economic Problems

The only major tribal industry is Casino Omaha, built on tribal land on the east side of the Missouri River, just off Interstate 29. Tribal members are also employed by tribal housing, maintenance, and health care services. The Carl T. Curtis Health Center is a full clinic that offers eye care, dentistry, pharmacy, medical care, nursing, and mental health services. Unemployment runs high on the reservation, between 65 and 75 percent. The reservation has high rates of heart disease and diabetes, and nearly every family is affected in some way by alcoholism or fetal alcohol syndrome. Spousal and child abuse are major problems, and death at an early age by accident, suicide, and disease is alarmingly frequent.

Some of the reservation's problems stem from a system of tribal government in which all seven members of the tribal council are elected at the same time—which means that there may be little carryover. Often the new council will negate everything the previous council did. One tribal council may begin a new business venture, and the next council will stop it and begin another. One building outside of town, for instance, became in succession a bingo hall, a fitness center, a bingo hall again, a cigarette factory, and a distribution center for government commodities such as food subsidies for the needy.

Relationship with the Winnebagos

The relationship between the Omahas and the Winnebagos on the adjoining reservation could be described as strained, although not openly hostile. The Winnebagos tend to look down on the Omahas, and the Omahas tend to view the Winnebagos as arrogant. Economic realities, as well as social, tribal, and historical factors, play a role in their attitudes. The Winnebago tribe is the more prosperous of the two, having a number of tribal businesses in addition to its casino. The Indian hospital is located in Winnebago, and Omahas who need certain kinds of treatment must travel there.

Some of the Omahas' resentment no doubt stems back to 1865, when the tribe gave up about half of its reservation to the homeless Winnebagos, who had escaped their near-starvation existence in South Dakota. The tension between the two tribes is present to a certain extent in the Reformed congregations, although the pastors of both churches have down through the years emphasized cooperation and acceptance.

An Overview of Omaha History and Religion

It is generally believed that before the colonization of North America by Europeans, the Dheghita-Sioux-speaking peoples (including the Ponca, Quapaw, Kansa, and Osage) flourished near the junctions of the Ohio, Wabash, and Mississippi Rivers in the general area of what is now southern Illinois. One segment, the Quapaw, moved down the Mississippi and settled in what is now Arkansas about 1500 A.D. The Omaha, whose name means "those going against the wind or current," moved in the opposite direction, north along the Mississippi to the mouth of the Missouri at what is now St. Louis. There they remained for a while, then began moving up the Missouri to the northwest.

The Omahas roamed and hunted in the areas of what are now Nebraska, Iowa, South Dakota, and Minnesota, engaging in frequent conflicts with their "cousins," the Sioux. The Lewis and Clark expedition found the tribe south of what is now Sioux City, Iowa, near its present location.

'Big Village'

About 1775, the Omahas built *Ton won Tonga*, or "Big Village," where the town of Homer was later established, about ten miles north of the present reservation. Omaha villages were comprised of fifty to one hundred dwellings. The standard living quarters were earthen lodges, with tepees used primarily for buffalo hunts. Buffalo were essential to the tribe's survival, but the Omahas also planted beans, corn, melons, and squash in garden plots. These were tended by woman and children, while a man's job was to hunt.

The Omahas moved again and again, sometimes because of smallpox and more often because of battles with the Sauk, Fox, and Lakota, but they always returned to Big Village. This was the village of Blackbird, the most famous of the early chiefs. Under him the Omahas became a military force. Blackbird, it is said, learned the use of arsenic and began poisoning those who opposed him. He died in 1800 of smallpox, along with about four hundred of his people, and the total Omaha population was reduced to about three hundred. Blackbird was buried upright on his favorite horse on a bluff overlooking the Missouri. The chief's skull was stolen in 1832 by artist George Catlin, who later displayed it as an artifact while touring Europe.

An even more famous chief, Ongpatonga, Big Elk, took over about 1810. The Omahas occupied Big Village until 1819, during which time they were met by several fur-trading and exploring expeditions. The tribe migrated to several new locations during the years following, including areas of what are now Iowa and Missouri. In 1831 they endured another devastating smallpox epidemic.

The next person to rise to the position of chief was Joseph La Fleshe, also known as Iron Eyes, the son of a French trader and an Omaha woman. La Fleshe believed that in order to survive, the Omahas had to adopt as much as possible the language and livelihood of white people. With him as their leader, many of the Omahas raised crops, attended the Presbyterian mission school, and learned trades—earning them the derisive name of "make-believe white men" by the more traditional Indians. Among Joseph's children were Francis La Flesche, author of *The Middle Five: Indian Schoolboys of the Omaha Tribe* and coauthor of *The Omaha Tribe*; Susan La Flesche Picotte, the first woman of her race to receive the degree of Doctor of Medicine; and Susette La Flesche Tibbles, activist for Indian rights and the subject of *Bright Eyes*, by Dorothy Clarke Wilson.[2]

Other Omaha names, like Fontenelle and Saunsouci, reflect contact with French traders who traveled up the Missouri, collecting furs, artifacts, and sometimes Omaha wives. The French were friendly with the Indian people, never trying to possess Indian lands or to disrupt Indian customs. The English, on the other hand, played the role of colonists, expecting the Indians to vacate the territory and find homes elsewhere. Tellingly, to the French the Omahas gave a name that

2. Wilson is also the author of *Dr. Ida*, the story of Dr. Ida Scudder, Reformed Church missionary in Vellore, India.

means "not strange," and to the English they gave a name that means "big knife."

Land Lost by Treaty

Although the Omahas often fought with other tribes, they were one of the few tribes who never engaged in violent conflict with white people, whether settlers or military forces. The Omahas lost their land not by war, but by treaty.

The first such treaty, in 1815, pledged peaceful relations with the U.S. Government and acknowledged that the United States was its "protecting power." The second, ten years later, authorized the government to send troops at its discretion to protect white trappers and traders, and also to prosecute crimes committed by tribal members.

In the third treaty, in 1830, the Omaha, Sac, and Fox tribes, along with bands of other tribes, ceded all of their territorial claims east of the Missouri River (Iowa) and established a large reservation in southeast Nebraska. In 1854 Omaha leaders were among nine tribes summoned to Washington D.C. to conclude treaty negotiations. At this time the Omahas ceded all of their land except 300,000 acres bordering the Missouri River and moved north to their new location in what are now Burt, Cuming, and Thurston Counties.

In 1865 the government purchased the northern portion of the Omaha's land and transferred it to the Winnebagos, after their escape from a desolate reservation in South Dakota. The Omahas received the Winnebagos with food, clothing, and sympathy, as well as with a new homeland. They sold additional acres to the Winnebagos two years later.

Land Lost by Allotments

In 1884, three years before the Dawes Act, but reflecting its philosophy, 76,000 acres of Omaha lands were allotted to families and individuals. The intent was that all Indians would farm the land in the same manner as their white neighbors, become self-supporting, and at last become citizens of the land that had originally been theirs. Unfortunately, most Indians knew little about this kind of farming and had no money to buy equipment or livestock.

Later, at the urging of the white citizenry, Congress passed a law that allowed individual Indians to sell their land. Many of them did so, quickly spent their money, and were as poor as before—but now without land. In addition, white people frequently loaned money to the Indians with land as collateral, which was later foreclosed. Other Omahas, not grasping the concept of taxation, failed to pay their taxes and therefore lost their property. A government bulletin of 1910 stated that 20,968 acres were owned by individual Indians and 6,694 acres belonged to the tribe. The remainder of the land, about 136,000 acres, had passed to non-Indians. The Omaha population at the time, says the bulletin, was about 1,200 people.

The Blackbird Bend Land Dispute

In 1854 the Omahas had made a treaty with the U.S. Government in which the tribe could retain three hundred thousand acres in eastern Nebraska (later reduced, by sale and subterfuge, to less than a tenth of that) if they would give up the rest of their homeland. The eastern boundary of their reservation was the center of the main channel of the Missouri River. Over the years the river flooded several times, and in 1923 a major flood shifted the channel of the river, leaving thousands of acres of Omaha land on the Iowa side. There was no bridge over the Missouri at the time, so the Omahas had no easy access to their eastern land. It was quickly claimed by a white man, Joseph Kirk, who in turn sold it to other farmers. Some of the land was eventually sold to the state of Iowa.

The loss of the land was not challenged until 1973, when several Omaha activists occupied the property. The Indians filed lawsuits, claiming that the land was rightfully theirs. The white farmers and the state of Iowa contended that the Indian land had simply eroded away by the action of the river. Initially a judge of the United States District Court ruled against the tribe, and from that point the case bounced back and forth through the legal system, including four times to the Court of Appeals and twice to the U.S. Supreme Court. Finally, in 1990, the District Court grudgingly awarded 2,200 acres to the Omaha tribe and 700 acres to the state of Iowa. Efforts to secure the remaining 700 acres were unsuccessful.

Among those who came to the defense of the tribe were the Reverend Harvey Calsbeek, pastor at the Macy church; the Reverend Richard Vander Voet, Reformed Church mission secretary for the Americas; the Reverend Gregg Mast, minister for social witness; and the denomination's American Indian Council. (See p. 48-49 for details of their involvement.)

As it turned out, the 2,200 acres reclaimed by the tribe became the most valuable piece of property on the reservation. The 1988 Indian Gaming Regulatory Act opened the door to casinos on reservations in states that permitted it. At that time Iowa allowed casino gambling but Nebraska did not, and in 1992 the Omahas opened a casino in Iowa.

The Historic Omaha Powwow and Other Traditions

American Indian peoples throughout North America have preserved their heritage through powwows, but the Omaha's annual dance is especially authentic. Long-forgotten Omaha songs recorded on wax cylinders at the turn of the century, discovered by a scholar from the University of Indiana, were taken in 1967 to the Library of Congress, where they were transferred to tapes. These tapes were played for the first time at the Macy powwow, and the Omahas heard songs as they had been sung by their ancestors. The Omaha powwow is a major event every summer, and "give-aways" are always a major component. Indians like to express gratitude, and they do so publicly with gifts and (to the non-Indian mind) very long speeches. Common gifts are blankets, shawls, pillows, and fruit baskets.

Unlike some other Native American cultures, the Omahas never burned down the houses of the dead in order to protect themselves from ghosts. Nor have they practiced coming-of-age ceremonies, common among many Indian groups.

The Sacred Pole

The most sacred object in the Omaha religion was the *Waxthe'xe*, the sacred pole. Legend has it that several hundred years ago the son of an Omaha chief, alone in the forest, discovered a tree that, reminiscent of Moses' burning bush, burned brightly without being consumed. The chiefs of the tribe cut it down and took it back to the tribe, where it became an object of veneration and was carried by the tribe wherever it went. The pole made its way to the Peabody Museum at Harvard University, where it was kept for more than a hundred years. "When the pole was taken away," said Dennis Hastings, the tribal historian, "the tribe lost the foundation....We had nothing to identify to ourselves why we were put on earth by God."[3] Through the efforts

3. "Tribe's Sacred Pole is on Journey Back to Nebraska," *Walthill Citizen*, July 6, 1989, 2.

of Hastings and other tribal representatives, the pole was returned with much celebration to the tribe in 1989 at the 185th powwow—an event documented by a video produced by Nebraska Educational Television.

Wako^{n}da, the Omaha Concept of God

One of the most difficult things for a non-Indian author to do is to describe Native American religion accurately. Non-Indian Christians whose body of faith has been colored, shaped, molded, and filtered by nearly two thousand years of conferences, catechisms, creeds, confessions, and controversies find it difficult to grasp the essence of a religion that has never been dogmatized, theologized, or formalized. Therefore, this discussion relies heavily on the book commonly accepted as one of the best tribal histories ever written—*The Omaha Tribe*, by Francis La Flesche, son of the tribal chief, and Alice Fletcher, noted anthropologist and advocate for the Indians. The book was first published by the Government Printing Office in 1911.

The Omaha word for God is *Wako^{n}da*, a word that Fletcher and La Flesche say "is not a modern term and does not lend itself to verbal analysis....The European mind demands a kind of intellectual crystallization of conception, which is not essential to the Omaha, and which when attempted is apt to modify the original meaning."[4]

"*Wako^{n}da*," say Fletcher and La Flesche, "stands for the mysterious life power permeating all natural forms and forces and all phases of man's conscious life."[5] It is neither synonymous with nature nor apart from nature. It is not accurate to define *Wako^{n}da* as "the Great Spirit," as if it were an objective god, but neither is it accurate to say that it is the same as nature. Native Omaha religion is not pantheism, at least as Greek-influenced theologians define pantheism.

"While the conception of *Wako^{n}da* may appear somewhat vague," say the authors, "certain anthropomorphic attributes are ascribed to it, approximating a kind of personality....All experiences in life are believed to be directed by *Wako^{n}da*, a belief that gave rise to a kind of fatalism. In the face of calamity, the thought, 'This is ordered by *Wako^{n}da*,' puts a stop to any form of rebellion against the trouble and often to any effort to overcome it."[6]

---

4. Alice C. Fletcher and Francis La Flesche, *The Omaha Tribe*, vol. 1 (Lincoln: University of Nebraska Press, 1992), 597.
5. Ibid.
6. Ibid., 598.

The relation of animals to humans and to *Wako^{n}da* is also difficult for the non-Indian mind to grasp. The Indian views the human not as the master, say Fletcher and La Flesche, "but as one of many manifestations of life, all of which are endowed with kindred powers, physical and psychical, and animated by a life force emanating from the mysterious *Wako^{n}da*."[7] Humans do not stand apart from nature; they are connected with nature physically and psychically. But neither is there a mixture or confusion of forms. "No Omaha believes that his ancestors were ever elk, or buffalo, or deer, or turtle, any more than that they were the wind, the thunder, or the sky."[8]

On the subject of morals, *Wako^{n}da* cannot be viewed as a god "up there" who sends down commandments. Nevertheless, "truthfulness in word and action was fundamental to the scheme of ethics taught among the Omaha....No untruthful report or evasion of responsibility was permitted to go unpunished, the penalty it was believed being inflicted supernaturally."[9] Old men have said, according to Fletcher and La Flesche, "*Wako^{n}da* causes day to follow night without variation and summer to follow winter; we can depend on these regular changes and can order our lives by them. In this way *Wako^{n}da* teaches us that our words and our acts must be truthful, so that we may live in peace and happiness with one another."[10]

The Native American Church

The most serious religious challenge to the church in Macy has been brought, not by the Omaha concept of *Wako^{n}da*, but by the Native American Church. The use of peyote to produce a "spiritual experience" arose in Oklahoma among the Comanches early in the nineteenth century, eventually resulting in the organization of the Native American Church. The key element in this worship is an all-night circular gathering that incorporates singing, praying, visions, and the use of peyote, a hallucinatory drug that is regarded as a sacrament and is sometimes equated with the Holy Spirit.

In some places the Native American Church embraces many biblical elements, and in other places it includes virtually none. In Winnebago, just eight miles from Macy, many of the leaders of the

7. Ibid., 599.
8. Ibid., 601.
9. Ibid., 598.
10. Ibid.

Native American Church were educated at the mission school, and they incorporate specifically Christian elements in their teaching and have maintained a largely cordial relationship with the Reformed pastors. In Macy the relationship has been more troubled, even confrontational, throughout its history. The Native American Church emphasizes "the Indian way" rather than "the white man's way," and it frequently pressures even church members to conduct funerals "the Indian way." Whereas at most Reformed reservation missions, most people will ask to be buried in the "Dutch Reformed Church," regardless of their affiliation or faithfulness, the Native American Church buries most Indian people in Macy.

The Reformed Church Takes Over the Presbyterian Mission, 1934

The mission work of the Reformed Church in America among the Omaha people in northeast Nebraska began in 1934, when the Reformed Church took over a work that was about to be abandoned by the Presbyterian Church—a mission that, oddly enough, was under the jurisdiction of the Presbyterian Board of Foreign Missions.

The Presbyterian Boarding School

The Presbyterians had begun the work eighty-nine years earlier, not in Macy, but about eighty miles south, in Bellevue, south of Omaha and at the heart of the original Omaha tribal territory. The church had opened a boarding school there in 1848, with a government contract to care for the Omaha's moral and educational improvement. Among the graduates of the Presbyterian mission school were several of the eight children of Joseph La Flesche. Life at the school has been recorded in poignant and sometimes humorous detail by his son Francis in, *The Middle Five: Indian Schoolboys of the Omaha Tribe.*

Just six years after the school's opening, the Omahas agreed to a treaty that relocated them to a 300,000-acre reservation to the north (a reservation that by 1960 had been reduced to 27,000 acres), and the mission moved with the tribe. The Presbyterians built a large three-story stone building on a bluff overlooking the Missouri River. The structure served as a day school and boarding school, with the assembly hall doubling as a worship center on Sundays. The missionaries also lived in the building, which means that the Omaha boarding students were under their full-time personal care. The children were given English

Lucy Sansouci at age 82

names, partly because the missionaries were unable to pronounce their names and partly because the missionaries regarded Omaha names as part of the pagan heritage the Indians were to leave behind.

An Emphasis on English

The academic emphasis was on the speaking, reading, and writing of English, in addition to geography and arithmetic. The boys were taught to farm, and the girls were taught to cook and sew. Vocal music was also taught, including the singing of parts, which is quite foreign to Indian music. Francis La Flesche, in his memoir, recounts lessons on the discovery of America and says that the students were always required to perform a song when visitors came to the mission, the chorus of which he still remembered:

Laura, Laura, still we love thee,
Though we see thy form no more,
And we know thou'lt come to meet us,
When we reach that mystic shore.[11]

The interpreter for the Presbyterian missionaries was Parish Saunsouci, the husband of Lucy Saunsouci, who became one of the most faithful members of the Reformed church. Parish Saunsouci translated about forty English hymns into the Omaha tongue, including "I Am Coming, Lord" and "My Country 'Tis of Thee." (There is no record

11. Francis La Fleshe, *The Middle Five: Indian Schoolboys of the Omaha Tribe.* Originally published in 1900. University of Nebraska Press, 1963, 101.

Blackbird Hill Presbyterian Church, the original church in Macy

of what the Omahas thought when they sang "sweet land of liberty.") About the only worship materials translated into Omaha since that time have been the Lord's Prayer and several hymns, translated by lay pastor Thurman Cook in the late 1990s.

The Reformed Church Takes Over

In 1885 the Presbyterian mission built a church on a hill northwest of Macy, and the congregation became known as Blackbird Hill Presbyterian Church. The congregation, made up of both Indians and non-Indians, flourished for several decades. But by the early 1930s the Presbyterian mission at Macy was faltering, the parsonage was vacant, and the Great Depression was jeopardizing denominational support. At that time G. A. Watermulder, from his post in the Reformed Church mission in Winnebago, contacted the Reformed Church offices in New York City, urging the Women's Board of Domestic Missions to consider taking over the work in Macy. The Women's Board entered into negotiations with the Presbyterian Church, and in 1934 the Reformed Church in America took over the work. In a report published in the *Intelligencer-Leader*, in 1935, Watermulder said:

> The need is very great. Outside of a Mormon and a Pentecostal group, and a small Catholic following, our mission is the only religious organization in the entire surrounding country,

comprising a population of an equal number of whites and Indian people, about 3,000 in number. It would be very difficult to find a more needy field anywhere in the United States.[12]

A Question of Credibility

One of the major problems of conducting a Christian witness in an Indian culture was credibility. This was articulated by Fletcher and La Flesche in *The Omaha Tribe*:

Regarding all white persons as Christian, he naturally looked to their lives for the exemplification of their beliefs...it is not surprising that the Omaha found it difficult to reconcile the precepts taught by the missionaries with the conduct of many of the white people whom he met. As a result he could not give hearty acceptance to a religion which seemed to have so little power over the lives of those who professed it.[13]

Laug Becomes First Reformed Church Pastor

The first Reformed Church pastor in Macy was the Reverend George Laug, who with his wife, Mildred, arrived in 1934. Laug, aged thirty-seven at the time, was a native of Coopersville, Michigan. After graduating from Hope College in 1921, he had served as a short-term missionary in Japan for three years, then came back to the U.S. to attend New Brunswick and Western Theological seminaries. Immediately after ordination in 1927 by the Classis of Muskegon, the Laugs had gone to Japan as missionaries, where they worked until beginning the mission in Macy.

The white clapboard church and the two-story parsonage were moved from the old site to the center of Macy, near the powwow grounds, the business district, and the new community building being built by the government. "Everyone who visits the village," wrote Laug, "is brought face to face with the attractive mission property, and everyone throughout the whole valley is within reach of the cheerful notes of the 'clear ringing bells.'"[14]

12. G. A. Watermulder, "A Report from Our New Omaha Indian Mission at Macy, Nebraska," *Intelligencer-Leader*, Aug. 7, 1935, 10.
13. Fletcher and La Flesche, *Omaha Tribe*, vol. II, 628-29.
14. G. A. Watermulder, "A Report from Our New Omaha Indian Mission at Macy, Nebraska," *Intelligencer-Leader*, Aug. 7, 1935, 10.

Frank and Daisy Tyndale,
early members

How much of a Presbyterian remnant greeted the Laugs is a matter of conjecture. Watermulder reported in the August 7, 1935, issue of the *Intelligencer-Leader*, "The work has opened with a faithful nucleus, and great results should come as the work is faithfully done in the future years," but he also reported that "there is practically no dependable nucleus of Christians to work with."[15]

Laug did report, however, a Sunday school average attendance of about fifty, and Sunday morning service attendance of nearly equal to that, with additional services on Sunday and Thursday evenings. Various social gatherings were held in the church basement, and several sewing classes were conducted each week in the church by a government employee. It was Laug's opinion that "true friendliness and consistent Christian living will do much in cooperation with the preaching and teaching of the Gospel to bring these people out into the 'glorious liberty of the children of God.'"[16]

A year later, at the height of the Great Depression, the Women's Board of Domestic Missions announced the motto of "No Retreat," citing great needs in many areas of mission work in its appeal for financial support. First among the needs was the work in Winnebago and Macy:

15. Ibid., 10-11.
16. Ibid., 11.

Our missionaries at Winnebago and Macy are carrying on their work in the face of distressing conditions. The depression has left the majority of the Winnebago and Omaha Indians in dire poverty. "Old Timers" at Macy say that conditions have never been so bad there as now.

In spite of the desperate economic situation, many Indians are able, somehow, to buy liquor, and this problem is growing by leaps and bounds. Both at Macy and Winnebago marriage rites are being discarded increasingly. This is nothing short of disaster, upsetting the entire home rehabilitation program.[17]

The use of peyote as a religious sacrament was also a concern to Laug, as it was to most of the pastors of American Indian churches, but Laug apparently avoided public confrontation and condemnation. The 1939 report of the Women's Board of Domestic Missions says that it was the policy of Laug "to treat these Indians with courtesy and kindness, to avoid speaking against them in public, and in private to patiently explain to them the true way. It is encouraging that even the most fanatic peyote followers call upon him in time of sickness and to conduct the funerals of their loved ones."[18]

Christmas in Macy

In Macy, as well as in the other Indian congregations, Christmas was a time of special excitement and overflow attendance. Each year Reformed congregations sent hundreds of gifts to its American Indian missions, and each year the pastors of those churches gave enthusiastic reports to the readers of the denominational magazine. Laug reported that the custom in Macy was to hold Christmas activities on the Sunday before Christmas Day, with the Sunday school program being held in the morning and a pageant or musical in the evening. In 1935 more than two hundred people packed the little church, and after the program an article of clothing and a toy top were given to each child who had come once or more during the year. Then, after the closing prayer, the children marched out in single file to receive a sack of candy and an apple. In the evening, reported Laug, a choir of thirty young people, with their pastor, the Reverend L. A. Brunsting, came from the First Reformed Church in Sioux Center, Iowa, eighty miles away, "to make Christmas more real and worthwhile for the Omaha people."[19]

17. "No Retreat in Domestic Missions," *Intelligencer-Leader*, Oct. 28, 1936, 12.
18. *Annual Report of the Women's Board of Domestic Missions*, 1939, 35.
19. "Christmas Among the Indians," *Intelligencer-Leader*, Dec. 16, 1936, 13.

At one point Laug became concerned about certain unnamed magazines on sale at the local store, considering them harmful to young people. Laug talked with the store's owner, who not only "graciously consented" to remove the offending periodicals but also agreed to place Christian literature in the window of the store. Some high school boys constructed a suitable rack, said Laug, "and although there have not been many sales as yet, the display has received considerable attention."[20] School authorities also cooperated with the mission program, and many teachers attended worship services and even taught Sunday school. The mission contributed a number of Christian books to the school library. It also secured the motion picture, *The King of Kings*, for use in the school, at the showing of which Laug opened and closed with prayer.

Laug reported in November 1939 that on almost every Sunday attendance was fifteen to twenty more than on the corresponding Sunday of the previous year, and that two Indian teachers had been secured to teach Sunday school classes. The Sunday school, he said one month later, had recently broken all records with 147 present. Laug also reported triumphantly that "Sunday is now being observed in the little community of Macy, and practically all places of business are closed on the Lord's Day."[21]

'The Cause of Much Evil'

In January 1941 there appeared in the *Intelligencer-Leader* a revealing article by an unidentified member of the Missionary Society of the Reformed Church in Rock Valley, Iowa:

As we approached our destination, we suddenly became aware of the absence of large and attractive farm buildings such as we had been seeing and instead saw scattered here and there, usually near a small clump of trees, a few old ramshackle sheds or even in some instances, old home-made tents which served as homes for the Omaha people. In many cases the only approach to these homes was a path or trail, and we wondered how they could tell which trail led to which homes.

20. "News Flashes from Domestic Mission Fields," *Intelligencer-Leader*, June 11, 1937, 11.
21. Helen M. Brickman, "The Great Conquest," *Intelligencer-Leader*, Nov. 10, 1939, 7.

After expressing appreciation for the hospitality of the Laugs, the author shared these observations about the tribe:

> This particular tribe of Indians seems to be carefree and irresponsible, many of them trying to do a little farming with the least possible effort and naturally with meager results. They still follow many of their old ways and customs, this being the cause of much evil among them as drinking, gambling, and very lax marriage relations.[22]

To what extent these opinions reflect those of other visitors to the mission, or even of the host pastor, we do not know. But one would like to have asked which of the evils of "drinking, gambling, and lax marriage relations" had their roots in Indian "old ways and customs" and which of these evils had been introduced by the white people who had come to introduce the Indians to civilization and straight driveways.

A Fire and a New Church Building

Continued growth in attendance at Sunday services and Sunday school prompted the building of an addition to the church structure that had been inherited from the Presbyterians. The project was completed in 1940.

Two years later, on a Sunday afternoon in February 1942, Mildred Laug looked out of a parsonage window and saw smoke pouring from the eaves of the church. Her husband ran to the church and rang the bell for help, and Indian and white neighbors came running with hand extinguishers. They were, however, unable to quench the flames that were licking the wall to the right of the pulpit. The Walthill Fire Department, ten miles away, responded but could no nothing because of a lack of water. Except for some of the furniture, the church building and its contents were a complete loss.

A little less than two years later, on January 10, 1943, a new church building was dedicated, made possible by insurance money, an advance from the Women's Board of Domestic Missions, and gifts from throughout the denomination. The *Intelligencer-Leader* reported that, in addition, "each Sunday a steady stream of pennies, nickels, and dimes have come from the Indian members," about $600 at the time of dedication.[23]

22. "A Visit to the Omaha Indian Mission at Macy, Nebraska," *Intelligencer-Leader*, Jan. 17, 1941, 12.
23. "Macy Church Is Dedicated," *Intelligencer-Leader*, Mar. 26, 1943, 12.

The new church at Macy, dedicated in 1943

The Reverend Robert Chaat, pastor of the Comanche Reformed Church in Lawton, Oklahoma, preached the dedicatory sermon, and the Macy choir of eighteen young people—about half of them Indians—sang an anthem. At the afternoon service Chaat baptized young David Laug, the first time an ordained Reformed Church American Indian pastor officiated at the baptism of the child of white missionaries. At the Sunday evening service—the third that day—the message was brought by the Reverend Gradus Aalberts of the Winnebago church, who also brought members of the choir with him. A roll call revealed that fourteen tribes of Indian people and eight nationalities of white people were represented.

The Second World War was underway, and forty-five stars hung on the church's service flag. Some families left the reservation for war work in Omaha and meat packing work in Sioux City, but Laug reported that the auditorium was nearly filled at each Sunday service.

Winnie Bouma Becomes Community Worker

In 1942 the work in Macy was enhanced by the arrival of Winnie Bouma, who had previously served for fourteen years in McKee, Kentucky, as a community worker. One of her duties was driving her Ford, "Polly," up and down the back roads, visiting people, getting acquainted, and inviting them to worship services, Sunday school, and evangelistic services. Her arrival was frequently heralded by the children

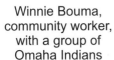

Winnie Bouma,
community worker,
with a group of
Omaha Indians

running into their homes and announcing, "Here comes the missionary lady." Polly also became a kind of free taxi service for reservation people who needed transportation to the store or to see relatives.

Bouma also taught Bible school and Sunday school at several locations. Indian girls were frequent visitors at her tiny house. "I found that they like to sing," she wrote, "so we often sing one chorus after another and many times I tell a Bible story....I keep the cookie jar filled for the little folks." Older girls also came to her home. "We talk and work together. We also sing together....I am able to point them to the higher values of life." Responses from older people came more slowly. "It has taken three years," she wrote in the article quoted above, "to become more closely connected with our Indian people. They are slow to respond. We are beginning to know a little of their personal experiences and feelings."[24]

Christian Education and Camp Meetings

By 1943 Sunday schools were being conducted at two locations, and daily vacation Bible schools were held at three locations—all attended by both Indian and white children. In addition to Macy, Sunday school was conducted at McCauley School, about six miles south of Macy, with an average attendance of twenty-five and with Bouma and one of the local white women as teachers. A year later Bouma also began conducting a Sunday school at an empty house rented for that purpose

24. Winnie H. Bouma, "After Three Years," *Church Herald*, Nov. 2, 1945, 12.

Children who attended vacation Bible school
in an empty house in Walthill

in Walthill. Vacation Bible schools were conducted in Macy (thirty-five students), in Walthill (twenty students), and at McCauley School (sixteen students). Teachers included Bouma, seminary students, and others. Meanwhile, the schedule of the church was very much like that of most white churches in the Midwest—a midweek prayer meeting, a monthly men's meeting, a weekly women's meeting, a weekly meeting of teenage girls, and a Saturday afternoon gathering of children.

As among the other ministries at Native American churches, summer "camp meetings" were an integral component of the work in Macy. These revival meetings, at which appeals were made for commitment and recommitment to Christ, were generally held for four days, with a guest speaker as the evangelist. The Reverend Raymond Meengs, pastor of the Central Reformed Church in Sioux Center, Iowa, brought the messages in 1942, and the response was so positive that he was invited to return in 1943. Each meeting was preceded by a feast of stew, Indian fry bread, sweet rolls, and coffee—the sweet rolls being a sure sign of the changing times.

Macy at Mid-Century

In 1944 George Laug accepted a call to plant a mission church in Casnovia, Michigan, and the Reverend Gradus Aalberts of nearby Winnebago, together with Winnie Bouma, carried on in Macy until a new pastor could be found. The board then called the Reverend Peter

Van Es, Jr., and his wife, Henrietta (usually known as Etta), to assume the work.

Peter and Etta Van Es

The Van Eses were among the elite group of people who might be called career missionaries among American Indians. Both Peter and Etta came originally from Orange City, Iowa, and were classmates at Hope College. Upon Peter's graduation from Western Theological Seminary in 1930 they accepted the appointment of the Women's Board to serve in Colony, Oklahoma. The Colony church closed two years later, when the government school closed and most of the Indians moved away; and the Van Eses went to Mescalero, New Mexico, where they served for twelve years. It was at their own request that they undertook the work in Macy in 1944. They were accompanied by Elizabeth Bayer, who had helped with household work and general mission activities in Mescalero.

'Tested to the Limit'

Just how well the work was going in Macy in the mid-1940s is not easy to determine. In the April 11, 1947, issue of the *Church Herald,* Etta wrote glowingly of increased attendance at Sunday school, young people's meetings, choir rehearsal, and women's meetings—although she said nothing about worship attendance. But in another article, printed in the next column of the same issue, her husband expressed quite a different sentiment:

> We could not honestly give too rosy a picture of Christian progress on this field, but we hold on because the future is as bright as the promises of God....We have every hope that some day we will have a strong Reformed church, composed of Indians and whites, here in Macy.[25]

The Van Eses's evaluation in November of the following year was even more tentative:

> There have been some results which are apparent, and many more that are of an intangible nature, which cannot be tabulated in statistical records, but are nonetheless real. Yet, if one were to

25. Peter Van Es, Jr., "Our Work Among the Omahas," *Church Herald,* April 11, 1947, 13.

look at this work in a hard-headed business way, he would very likely say, "Let's pull up stakes," or as one person did indeed say, "Let's give it back to the Presbyterians."

I am reminded of what the Rev. G. A. Watermulder wrote to us when he heard of our appointment to this field: "You are going to a place where your love for the Lord, and for the Indian people, will be tested to the limit." When I saw him for the last time on earth in June, 1946, I could tell him that this prediction was a true one. The confusion of religious ideas or concepts is simply baffling. False sects imported by white people, as well as their own variety, seem to these unevangelized Indians "just as good" and "just the same" as the eternal verities of God's Word, and reasoning about it does not penetrate to the soul.[26]

Once again the church building, less than two years old, was struck by fire. As before, the pastor's wife discovered the fire. It was on a Sunday morning, December 9, 1945, that Etta Van Es discovered flames near the chimney in the prayer meeting room. This time quick action by the fire department saved the building, and members of the church saved most of the furnishings from water damage. The congregation used the church basement for worship until the damage was repaired.

Economic Hardship Continues

Meanwhile, the economic plight of the Omahas was getting worse. An article in the *Sioux City Sunday Journal*, dated March 31, 1946, stated that the members of the Omaha Indian tribe "are striving determinedly to fit themselves into a world which seems to hold no place for them....The Omahas contributed more than two hundred men to the armed forces during the recent war, yet most of the homecoming veterans are unable to find employment at home."

There are no opportunities for employment except for farm work, said the article, but of the 1,700 members of the tribe, 1,100 have no land. In 1865 a large portion of the land had been sold to the Winnebagos as their reservation, and in 1881 Congress passed a law that allowed the Omahas to sell their allotments. Many of them had done so, to white farmers, and the land was lost forever to the tribe. The remaining parcels had been divided and subdivided by inheritance

---

26. Peter and Henrietta Van Es, "Progress at Our Macy Mission," *Church Herald*, Nov. 26, 1948, 10.

to the point of being worthless for income purposes, and other parcels were so hilly and heavily wooded that they couldn't be used for farming. The article went on to describe living conditions on the reservation:

> Excellent educational facilities are provided for the Indians, but few finish high school and still fewer attend college. To date, nobody has been able to strike the spark of incentive by proving to the Indian that he can better his lot by acquiring an extensive education.
>
> Living conditions are primitive, according to white man's standards. There are a few good roads and countless trails which wind through the hills to frame houses. Outside of the town of Macy, there is no electricity, no plumbing, and few of the items which we call modern conveniences.
>
> Field horses and heavy wagons provide most of the transportation....Macy, with its school, a government administration building, and three or four stores, is the focal point of all activities, but the Indians seldom go to town without a good reason. Even in town the average Omaha seems to be very much alone. There is little conversation and little laughter.
>
> Their isolated homes, usually situated on the fragment of land owned by some member of the family, are invariably poorer than those occupied by white farmers. They contain the essentials of life and little more.
>
> A cook stove doubles as a heater in winter, and most of the families burn wood. Most of the houses lack paint because paint...costs money, and money is not easily obtainable without employment or productive farm land.[27]

Peyote Problems

About this time, the missionaries publicized the use of peyote by the Omaha people as a major concern. "Our greatest problem," wrote Van Es shortly after his arrival in Macy, "is certainly the peyote problem. Every Saturday night there are peyote wakes, as many as three separate groups at a time. This place is saturated with the cult. Over 90 percent of the people here are involved."[28] Two years later Van Es again emphasized his concern:

27. Neil Miller, "Indian Life Is Still a Struggle," *Sioux City Sunday Journal*, Mar. 31, 1946, 1-2.
28. Peter Van Es, "First Days at Macy, Nebraska," *Church Herald*, Mar. 16, 1945, 12.

The peyote drug is taken amid much feasting, and night wears into morning, finding them listless, drugged, and sometimes fast asleep. What takes place at these meetings, a person has only to imagine. Drinking, gambling, immorality and other attendant vices also cast their shadow."[29]

A brochure, *Some Facts about the Omaha Indians*, produced by the Reformed Church around 1950, says, "The greatest single obstacle and deep-dyed evil of this tribe is the peyote cult."[30]

Whether or not peyote is, in fact, addictive is open to debate. Most medical sources say that it has not been proved to be harmful to body or mind. Its use, however, is central to the worship experience of the Native American Church—which in many tribal environments is a major competitor to the Christian faith.

Van Es also voiced concern about the inroads of other aggressive cults and sects, including the Mormons. On the positive side, the missionaries secured permission from parents to teach as many as two hundred children in weekday religious classes.

Winnie Bouma retired from active service in 1947 after five years in Macy. Also in 1947, in the fall, Leon Grant, a young Omaha, boarded a bus for Cook Christian Training School in Phoenix, Arizona. He had lost his right hand in a rodeo accident, had been visited by Van Es, and had made confession of faith and been baptized. Teenagers attending a youth conference at Lake Okoboji in Iowa had given a consecration offering sufficient to cover Grant's tuition. Grant graduated from Cook in 1951 and for several years directed the Phoenix Indian Center, a gathering place for Indian students in downtown Phoenix.

Summer Students in Macy

A significant aspect of the work in several American Indian churches, and very consistently in Macy, was the appointment of seminary students to serve for a summer. This arrangement provided valuable service to the mission at a minimal cost, planted the seeds of eventual financial support for Indian mission, and became a testing/ recruitment experience for students who might consider Indian ministry as their pastoral calling.

29. Peter Van Es, Jr., "Our Work Among the Omahas," *Church Herald*, April 11, 1947, 13.
30. Board of Domestic Missions, n.d.

Robert H. Schuller, later to find fame as minister of California's Crystal Cathedral and television preacher on *The Hour of Power*, spent the summer of 1947 in Macy after graduating from Hope College, an experience that he referred to briefly in his autobiography, *My Journey*. Several stories by summer students, as published in the *Church Herald*, reveal the initial impressions of young men who became immersed in a new culture, perhaps for the first time. John Hiemstra, who served in Macy during the summer of 1954, later became the Reformed Church's secretary for North American Ministries (1969-72). He reported, on the positive side, that he and his wife had been welcomed by the Indian people and had enjoyed the friendship of many fine Christians. But he also reported some "disappointing experiences":

> Too often work goes unappreciated and church functions are left with little support. Drinking, gambling, and idleness are paramount problems that tend to hold back the progress of the entire community—both materially and spiritually. A close Indian friend told us that the Indian youth are confused. In the past, the honorable and high traditions of the Indian yielded a desirable community and family life. Today many have forgotten the old ways and have not yet assimilated the new ways of the white man.[31]

Joseph Muyskens, who later served as the denomination's secretary for social ministries (1967-81), spent the summer of 1955 in Macy while a student at Western Theological Seminary. He observed, "The people are very poor. Their morals are not of the highest character. There is frequently more hate than love in their home life. As Christians, we have a message that will give these people hope for this life and for eternity, but the message must be presented in a form that they can understand."[32]

The Church Is Organized (1957) and a New Facility Built (1962)

Having spent twenty-one years of missionary service among Native Americans, Peter and Etta Van Es left Macy in 1952 for the Grace Reformed Church in Sonoma, California. The Reverend Harold

31. John and Norma Hiemstra, "A Summer at Macy," *Church Herald*, Nov. 19, 1954, 11.
32. Joseph Muyskens, "Your Mission at Macy—Its Witness for Christ," *Church Herald*, Dec. 15, 1955, 12.

Dykstra, who had just graduated from Western Theological Seminary, took over for a year; and then he and his wife, Dorothy, moved on to the Jicarilla Apache Reformed Church in Dulce, New Mexico. While the Dykstras were in Macy, a fire destroyed the government's community house adjacent to the mission property, and the church offered its basement for home economics classes and for serving hot lunches to children.

John and Hegla Lucius Begin Indian Ministry

The Reverend John and Helga Lucius arrived at the end of 1953. Helga Sawitzky had grown up in Canarsie, New York, where her father, Frederick, was pastor; and John was a native of Long Island City, New York. They met at Hope College, and after John graduated from New Brunswick Theological Seminary they had served the Prattsville Reformed Church and the Second Reformed Church of Astoria, both in New York.

For the Luciuses, it was the beginning of a thirty-one-year career of ministry among Native Americans. They stayed in Macy for four years. Then John served as pastor of the Jicarilla Apache Reformed Church in Dulce, New Mexico, from 1957 to 1961 and directed religious activities at the government's Phoenix Indian High School from 1961 until his retirement in 1984.

A major need at that time was a safe place for children and youth to gather socially. "We have absolutely nothing in our community for youngsters from the age of eight to eighteen," said the 1954 report of the Board of Domestic Missions. "The boys and girls wander up and down the streets at night looking for excitement or just plain fun. Most of our children have no home life."[33]

Lucius introduced a "teen canteen" in the basement of the church. Open on Friday evenings, its offerings were limited to ping pong, shuffleboard, three checkerboards, and a phonograph. The next year the tribal council donated a television set. The church then opened its doors for a "community night" on Wednesday evenings, and as many as a hundred people crowded into the basement each week to watch the new electronic wonder. A used clothing store was also opened, with items donated by Reformed congregations. On Mondays and Fridays as many as twenty people gathered on the parsonage lawn to catch a ride on the church van to the government hospital in

33. *Annual Report of the Board of Domestic Missions,* 1954, 28.

Winnebago. The missionaries were also frequently called on to provide emergency transportation, whether during the day or at three o'clock in the morning.

Cottage Meetings

"Cottage meetings" also emerged during this time as a primary vehicle for evangelism as well as spiritual growth. Summer student Joseph Muyskens described these meetings:

> These weekly meetings were conducted in different homes each week. The usual procedure was to call in a general area on Monday and to locate a home that would agree willingly to receive us for a prayer meeting. Then we would call on all neighbors and invite them too. The attendance was as high as thirty-two and as low as three, but attendance was not the most important factor. In fact, we felt our last and smallest meeting of the summer to be the most rewarding. Our impression of the cottage meetings is that they are the best means of evangelism for Macy.[34]

Two years later, summer seminarian Wilbur Daniels described Indian Christians who would "pour out their hearts to their Creator, often praying for as long as fifteen minutes or more, reaching a high state of emotion, often weeping, and pleading in their native tongue for the 'Great Spirit' to forgive them and deal with them in mercy."[35]

Edward and Eleanor Van Gent

Edward and Eleanor Van Gent joined the Macy mission in June of 1956. They had grown up in Otley and Leighton, Iowa, near Pella, and came to Macy immediately after graduating from Central College. Their assignment was typical of the "second couple" at most American Indian churches at the time: do maintenance work, sponsor the youth groups, and supervise the recreational program.

The Macy Church Is Organized, 1957

For twenty-three years the Reformed Church had conducted work in Macy as a mission, and year after year the annual reports of the

---

34. Muyskens, "Your Mission at Macy," 12.
35. Wilbur Daniels, "Macedonian Neighbors at Macy," *Church Herald*, Nov. 27, 1957, 13.

Edward and Eleanor Van Gent and family

Board of Domestic Missions spoke of the day when the church would be organized. In 1953 the board finally revealed the reason for the delay: "While it would be possible to organize immediately as a white church, there is not sufficient Indian leadership to proceed with the organization."[36]

Finally, on June 12, 1957, the worshiping community was organized as the "First Reformed Church of the Omaha Mission," with membership in the Classis of East Sioux, in the Particular Synod of Iowa. This was the year that all of the Indian churches were finally transferred from the Classis of New York to a synod and classis that was geographically close. The Winnebago Reformed Church, eight miles away, was assigned to the Classis of West Sioux, presumably to promote diversity in both classes.

The church name implied that the worshiping body, although now officially organized as an Reformed Church congregation, was still a component of the mission. The church was organized with fifty-three communicants in thirty-three families. Sunday school enrollment was listed as 250, which no doubt included students participating in the released time Bible study program held in cooperation with the local public school. The congregation's rules of order stipulated that the consistory must be made up of an equal number of Indians and non-Indians. Elected to serve on the first consistory were Henry Clay, Leonard Link, Frank Cayou, and Richard Link. The Indian members were Clay and Cayou.

36. *Annual Report of the Board of Domestic Missions*, 1953, 27.

A ladies sewing group gave profits to the church.

John and Maria Endert

John and Helga Lucius left Macy shortly after the church was organized to take up work in Dulce, New Mexico, and the Reverend Ira Hesselink, recently retired from a pastorate in Holland, Nebraska, served briefly as an interim. The new status of the congregation was recognized in 1958, when the congregation and the Board of Domestic Missions jointly extended a call to Johannes (John) Endert. Endert and his wife, Maria, had been born in the Netherlands, where John had been ordained in the Moravian Church. They had served as missionaries in Dutch Guiana for nine years before accepting a number of Reformed Church pastorates in New York, New Jersey, and Ontario.

In addition to the several programs for children and youth (youth meeting, teenage canteen, and Sunday school), Endert continued to participate in a released time program with the Macy Public School. Every Tuesday afternoon, the Enderts provided Bible instruction at the church for elementary children. The Macy church had two choirs at the time, a senior choir and an intermediate choir, with Maria Endert and Eleanor Van Gent as the directors. A brochure printed about this time included a photo of the senior choir, consisting of eight Indian women, singing at Endert's installation.

The Enderts' stay in Macy proved brief and unhappy, with Indian visitors being asked to arrive at the back door of the parsonage to protect the living room carpet. After two years, the Enderts moved to the Brockville Reformed Church (now Maitland Community Reformed Church) in Maitland, Ontario, where John died a year later at the age of fifty-eight.

Reuben and Bernice Ten Haken

The Enderts were followed by the Reverend Reuben and Bernice Ten Haken, who arrived in 1960. The Ten Hakens had previously been deeply involved in Indian ministry in Mescalero, New Mexico (1944-53), and then in an Indian relocation ministry in southern California (1957-60).

Apparently Ten Haken, like other pastors of American Indian congregations, felt the need not only to explain his ministry but also to defend it. In an undated speech to supporting churches, entitled "Reaping and Fainting," based on Galatians 6:9b ("we shall reap if we faint not"), and later printed in the *Church Herald*, Ten Haken had this to say:

> Those of us who work on the Indian field are often tested by the staggering statistics that come from our mushrooming extension churches. We cannot report bulging membership lists, impressive financial gains, nor spectacular leadership advances. What troubles us even more, down deep in our hearts, is knowing that we are trying to carry on in a classis environment where we are pretty much a little pea in a big pod with a lot of big peas. It is not the littleness in size that is disturbing. It is, rather, how do our larger sister churches see us as they throw the spotlight of "How are you doing?" on us. It is precisely at this point where the church in an Indian community finds itself a bit embarrassed and often misunderstood. She is judged by a set of standards that apply to the majority of churches in the classis. These are usually well-established churches with an above-average income and membership, a strong family structure, and a neatly organized program. They stand like the Rock of Gibraltar. The Corinthian problem of drunkenness at the Lord's Table would be unthinkable and cause for the severest discipline. Where the yardstick of proper church life is divided into thirty-seconds of an inch, for exact measurement, it is difficult for some to understand why churches in Indian communities act so irresponsibly and inconsistently at times. It surely must be taxing to the nerves of

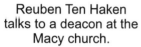

Reuben Ten Haken talks to a deacon at the Macy church.

the constitutional legalist to listen to the report of the missionary pastor's limping gait...

Words like *promote, drive, goals, percentages* have so far fallen rather flat on their faces where we live. In fact, they create suspicion. This is understandable. We are not far enough along to be pushed. Our people have been pressed from the outside all along. Change has been forced, a pressure tactic sort of approach....Our people will do better if allowed to let the Spirit dictate from within.[37]

Ten Haken went on to talk about the dynamics of white people and Indian people worshiping together. The Macy church, he said, had eight consistory members—four white and four Indian. The Indian men were sometimes reluctant to take hold because they did not feel at home with *Roberts Rules of Order*; and the white men hesitated to take the reins for fear they would interfere with Indian leadership development. Older Indian women were tested when they saw white women and girls sit in a posture that was considered in their culture to be immodest; and white women were tested when Indian women smoked and allowed their children to smoke. White men, he said, considered it proper to

37. Reuben Ten Haken, "Reaping and Fainting," typewritten ms., undated, 1-2; reprinted in slightly edited form as, "We Shall Reap If...." *Church Herald*, Nov. 8, 1963, 4-5, 21.

honor women with "ladies first," while Indian custom says a man must walk ahead of a woman to give her protection. "As a pastor in this kind of integrated fellowship," said Ten Haken, "I always stand somewhat amazed at how much the grace of God has conditioned our mutually proud spirits so that we not only tolerate each other, but actually defend each other."[38]

A New Sanctuary

Worship attendance during the Ten Haken years was taxing the church sanctuary, so plans were made to raise funds to expand the facilities, as well as to renovate the parsonage. An appeal by the Board of Domestic Missions netted $23,000, not quite enough, so construction was delayed until sufficient funds were made available through gifts and a loan from the denomination's Church Building Fund. A plan was devised to retain much of the original structure as a fellowship and educational area and to attach a new sanctuary facing the street.

The new cement block and wood building was dedicated August 31, 1962. Two of its living charter members—Maude Huff, a non-Indian, and Lucy Saunsouci, an Omaha—had been members of the Blackbird Presbyterian Church when the Reformed Church took over. Eight consistory members were pictured in the dedication brochure. The Indian consistory members were Frank Cayou, Sam Robinson, Albert Robinson, and Henry Clay. The non-Indian consistory members were Cecil Leinart, Kenneth Piere, David Dannon, and Willis Leinart. The brochure also pictured a Sunday school staff of twelve people, consisting of one Indian man, two white men, and nine white women. The piece also included a photo of a youth fellowship group of four girls, as well as two women's groups, both of which were integrated. Some two hundred children attended weekly Bible classes at the time, said the brochure. The church also sponsored a Boy Scout troop and operated a used clothing store. Shortly after the new building was dedicated, the Macy congregation hosted the Classis of East Sioux and the East Sioux Classical Women's Union.

Jurgens Succeed the Van Gents

The Van Gents left Macy in 1962 and moved eight miles down the road to Winnebago, where they served six more years. The Van Gents were succeeded by Lynn and Karen Jurgens, who both came from central Iowa and who served from 1962 to 1969. Lynn directed

38. Ibid, 3.

youth work and maintenance, and Karen led women's groups and did bookkeeping and secretarial work. Lynn also served as a deacon and elder in the church, sang in the choir, taught Sunday school, and led a Boy Scout troup. Lynn's parents, Lloyd and Frieda Jurgens, were houseparents in Winnebago during part of this time, 1966-67.

Active communicant membership held steady at about seventy during the Ten Haken years, with Sunday school and released time enrollment at about two hundred. An average of ten people made confession of faith each year, but with no appreciable increase in membership. About forty members were reported as being absent or inactive. The released time program was apparently discontinued in 1966, as Christian education enrollment dropped from 187 to 78. Reports of worship attendance were not required by the General Synod, but mission executive Albert Van Dyke reported that average attendance was fifty-two at the morning worship and that Sunday school attendance was forty at the time the Ten Hakens left. Among the faithful Omaha Christians at the time were Wilson Wolf, George Grant, and Betsy Wolf. Ministry challenges, in addition to the usual community concerns of alcoholism and family dysfunction, included intensified ministry by the Mormons and the Roman Catholic Church, to say nothing of the continuing popularity of the Native American Church.

The Ten Hakens left Macy in 1966, after spending six years there, and Reuben accepted a position as a hospital chaplain in Sheboygan Falls, Wisconsin. He worked in that capacity for ten years, served as stated supply for the Reformed Church in Hudson, Florida, for three years, and died in 1987 at the age of seventy-four. Bernice Ten Haken died in Sheboygan Falls in 2001 at the age of eighty-seven.

A Vignette of White/Indian Relations

Because the Reformed Church is the only Protestant church in town, many of the white farmers, business people, and teachers of the area have chosen to attend the church, a dynamic referred to earlier by Ten Haken in his defense of Indian ministry. Many of the white members have been willing to lead and to teach, and most Indians are by nature nonassertive and retiring. This has led to a dilemma faced by all the Indian congregations, but perhaps more pronounced in Macy than elsewhere: How does one balance the willing discipleship of white believers with the genuine but often nonassertive discipleship of Indian believers?

In the mid-sixties, with the civil rights movement gaining momentum and the Indian rights movement following suit, mission executives believed it was important to install Indian pastors in Indian churches. Beth Marcus, secretary of the Board of Domestic Missions, and Albert Van Dyke, director of Indian work for the board, considered the possibilities. Arrangements were made for the Reverend Jonah Washington, a Pima/Maricopa who was working as chaplain at the Chilocco Indian School in Chilocco, Oklahoma, to preach in Macy in the fall of 1967 as a potential pastoral candidate. Washington's subsequent report to Van Dyke presents a vignette on the delicate subject of race relations in a white/Indian congregation.

He had been graciously received by Indians and non-Indians alike, Washington wrote, but non-Indians had been more active in receiving him. More white people were at the service than Indians. Four consistory men and their families served a potluck dinner on Sunday, but no Indian consistory men or their families showed up. That evening, at an informal consistory meeting, all four non-Indians came, but only one Indian. The white consistory members denied that there was any ill feeling between the races, and if there was, they were unaware of it. The opinion of the Indians, said Washington, was quite different:

> Most of the Indian men I talked with felt that there was a division or tension within our mission work in regards to Indian and non-Indian relationship. As one of the men put it, "The whites would rather see us Indians pull out of the church. They would be glad to have it as their own." Another tribal leader said this prejudice of Indians and non-Indians is not just in the church but is widespread in the community and has been for many long years. He went on to say that this ill-feeling between the two races is a major problem there, and so far, no one, not even the missionaries, have been able to solve it.[39]

Lynn Jurgens reported to mission administer Van Dyke that Washington's sermon had been very academic, including references to Greek words, and that the interest of both pastor and congregation were minimal. Soon afterward, Washington accepted a call to the Jicarilla Apache Reformed Church in Dulce, New Mexico. No other pastor seemed interested in Macy, and the vacancy dragged on for three years. Attendance dropped off precipitously. Even the tribal council,

---

39. Letter from Jonah Washington to Albert Van Dyke, Nov. 13, 1967.

feeling abandoned by the denomination, threatened to revoke the lease on the church property.

While the church was without a pastor, newlyweds Vernon and Carla Sterk came to Macy as student interns from Western Theological Seminary. They spent the first six months of their internship in Chiapas, Mexico, and the next six months (1967) at the parsonage in Macy. The Sterks had a positive experience in Chiapas but a negative one in Macy, due to the mood of hopelessness, the great number of funerals due to alcoholism and violence, and even an assault on Carla Sterk in the church kitchen. After graduating, the Sterks were appointed as career missionaries to Chiapas.

Racial tensions, often denied or downplayed in Indian/white relations, again surfaced in 1969. Edward Cline, an elder in the Macy church and the Omaha tribal chairman, joined Gordon Beaver, who held similar positions in Winnebago, in writing an open letter to the Reformed Church in America, published in the *Church Herald*. [40] This letter was likely a contributing factor in the founding of the American Indian Council three years later.

Frank and Mary Patricia Love

In their three-year search for a pastor for Macy, Van Dyke and Marcus turned their attention to the Reverend Frank Love, the pastor in Mescalero. Love had been ordained by the Reformed Church and had served for a few years with the Reverend Robert Zap. In Mescalero, tensions ensued, Zap had left, and Love had been called to be the pastor, but things were not going well. Since Love was enrolled with the Omaha tribe, the possibilities at Macy looked more promising.

Love was born in Macy in 1933, the son of a French-Canadian father and an Omaha mother. He was raised by his grandparents and various foster parents and attended schools in several states. He joined the U.S. Army at age fourteen, signing a document that stated that he was seventeen. After his release from military service he roamed the country, often getting into trouble. Then in 1955, at age twenty-one, while in Phoenix, he was invited to attend a prayer meeting on the Pima reservation, and there he experienced what he called "a Christian revelation." He connected with the Reformed Church, which helped him attend Cook Christian Training School, Hope College, and

40. Dec. 29, 1969, 12.

Frank Love with children in the Head Start program in Macy

Western Theological Seminary, from which he graduated in 1965. He was ordained shortly thereafter.

Love's tenure in Macy included using volunteers to build Indian homes and serving as president of the school board, assisting in the successful effort to build a new school. He gained a reputation as being talented and visionary, but also often working without consultation and accountability. Church bills piled up, and the mission board eventually paid them in order to maintain the good reputation of the church.

After two years in Macy, Love left the pastoral ministry and began working with a series of Native American organizations, foundations, centers, and schools. Mary Patricia (Pat) Love died of cancer in 1997 at the age of sixty-six. As of this writing, Frank Love lives in the Seattle, Washington, area, is a member of the Classis of Cascades, and works part-time for a Methodist congregation.

William and Cathleen Vanden Berg

Again the Macy church experienced a considerable delay in acquiring pastoral care. Once again the pastor in nearby Winnebago, now the Reverend Wilbur De Cora, filled in as best he could. Robert Schut, a student at New Brunswick Theological Seminary, came to Macy for a summer assignment in 1972. The Schuts stayed for two years and later went on to serve a long pastorate (1984 to the present) at the Mescalero Reformed Church in New Mexico. While in Macy, the Schuts adopted their first Indian child, Patricia.

In 1973 the Macy consistory called the Reverend William Vanden Berg, then aged fifty-seven, and his wife, Cathleen. Although the Macy church had been organized in 1957, Vanden Berg was the first pastor to be called by the church independently of the mission board. Before coming to Macy, the Vanden Bergs had served several congregations in Iowa and Michigan. The Vanden Bergs' tenure in Macy lasted just three years and was generally unhappy. They left in 1976 for Valley Springs, South Dakota, their last pastorate before retirement. During the Vanden Berg years, the church reported membership statistics as high as 127 and as low as 66, with the number of absent/inactive members as high as 78 and as low as 19.

Steven and Kay Farmer

In 1976 the Macy congregation called its second pastor of Native American heritage, and this, too, turned out to be a short-lived relationship. The Reverend Steven Farmer, from the Rosebud Sioux Reservation in South Dakota, came from the Presbyterian Church and never transferred his membership to the Reformed Church. His ministry seemed to show great potential: as one of the white members said, "I could have followed him to the end of the earth." But there were allegations of an affair with a counselee of the congregation. He and his wife, Kay, were divorced, and Farmer left the church in 1978. Communicant membership dropped to the low forties during the Farmers' tenure, and membership never again reached fifty. Sunday school enrollment hovered between fifty and seventy.

1980 to the Present

Harvey and Angeline Calsbeek

After these several short, often struggling, pastorates, the Macy Church called the Reverend Harvey Calsbeek and his wife, Angeline, in 1978. The Calsbeeks had already served two American Indian congregations—in Mescalero, New Mexico (1954-62), and in Dulce, New Mexico (1962-66). They had then held three pastorates at white churches—Silver Creek, Minnesota; Yankton, South Dakota; and Willow Lake, South Dakota—before returning to Indian ministry in Macy.

Harvey Calsbeek meets with a tribal member at the parsonage.

Calsbeek had a reputation for patience and understanding. Those who were members during his tenure say things like, "He never gave up on people" and, "He was a pastor who listened." But acceptance does not come easily or quickly in an American Indian community. In prayer requests submitted for the Mission of the Month Prayer Calendar in 1981, the Calsbeeks wrote, "Rejoice with us that finally after three years there appears to be some acceptance in the community."

Nor did the Calsbeeks glamorize their task. In a 1981 *Church Herald* article Harvey said, "The events of the past days hardly seem romantic or rewarding. Answering doorbells for sweaty kids asking for a drink of water or for a basketball is hardly romantic. It can, in fact be annoying." He went on to say, "Seldom do we see earthshaking events, but we do see the Spirit of God touching the lives of some who hear the message of good news and respond in faith."[41]

In a letter to supporting congregations in December 1981, the Calsbeeks wrote that although they were pleased with the response of children, the response of adults was not encouraging. But a letter of February 1983 stated that attendance at worship had been increasing. "The strange fact," said the Calsbeeks, "is that the increase has come from people with whom we have not necessarily been working. This is a humble reminder that God's ways are not our ways."[42] A few years later

41. Harvey Calsbeek, "No Romance in Macy," *Church Herald*, Aug, 7, 1981, 12.
42. Letter from Harvey and Angeline Calsbeek to supporting churches, Feb. 1983.

Participants in an after-school program gather
on the steps of the Reformed church in Macy.

they wrote, "Often we wonder about the effectiveness of our ministry, but later we realize that God has been at work."[43]

Youth Trip to New York

Youth ministry in Macy has almost always involved participation in youth camps and conferences. These include the annual all-Indian youth camps and Rocky Mountain High, the major annual youth gathering of the Regional Synod of the Heartland, held in Estes Park, Colorado. But the Macy teens ventured farther afield in the summer of 1983 when they joined young people from the Winnebago church in a sixteen-day trip that took them all the way to New York. The trip itself was a remarkable achievement, bringing together in close proximity the two tribal groups that had a history of viewing each other warily.

During that same year another effort to improve relationships with the Winnebagos took place when the consistories of the two congregations held a retreat together, first in Winnebago and then at a motel in South Sioux City. Only one member—who was in the hospital at the time—did not attend. The church's former pastor, Reuben Ten Haken, was the speaker. Roger De Young was pastor of the Winnebago church at the time.

43. Letter from Harvey and Angeline Calsbeek to supporting churches, April 9, 1986.

Blackbird Bend Involvement

When the Blackbird Bend land dispute erupted in 1973, Calsbeek
and the Reformed Church in America took the side of the Omahas. As
part of their effort to reclaim some 2,900 acres of tribal land—land that
had been separated from the reservation by a radical change of course
by the Missouri River—the Omaha Tribal Council came to Calsbeek
and asked if the Reformed Church could be of assistance. Calsbeek put
the council in contact with Gregg Mast, the denomination's minister
of social witness, and Richard Vander Voet, mission secretary for the
Americas, as well as other denominational leaders and the American
Indian Council. The issue began to receive national attention,
including reports in the *City Gate*, the Reformed Church's social witness
newsletter.

In December of 1986, after many years of struggle in the courts,
Vander Voet wrote a letter to Daniel Inouye, chairman of the Senate
Select Committee on Indian Affairs, asking for justice in the case.
Among other things, Vander Voet wrote:

> Research by your staff in the history of this litigation will show a
> long history of legal maneuvers on the part of defendants to take
> away land originally granted to the Omaha Nation by treaty. It
> is clear from history that this land belonged to the Omaha Tribe
> and it can be proved through technical land study. An attempt is
> being made by the litigants to settle the manner without giving
> the Tribe the opportunity to prove the case.[44]

Eventually the tribe succeeded in regaining 2,200 of the 2,900
acres of disputed land, on which it built Casino Omaha.

Long-Term Volunteers

Over the years, several long-term (one year or longer) volunteers
have made their mark, not only in Macy, but elsewhere as well. Andrew
Hoolsema, a member of the Hope Reformed Church in Grand Rapids,
Michigan, served as a volunteer in Macy from 1983-84. Along with the
usual maintenance and youth work, he used his accounting skills to
help administer the alcoholism rehabilitation center. Hoolsema, who
later changed his name to Andrew Lee, served on the finance staff of the

44. Letter from Richard Vander Voet to Daniel Inouye, Dec. 26, 1986, Reformed
    Church Archives, New Brunswick, Neew Jersey.

Reformed Church in America from 1985 to 1992 and as treasurer of the denomination from 1992 to 1997. Later volunteers in Macy included Joan Lankamp, Carl and Jean Idema, and Douglas Leonard.

After nine years in Macy, and calling it "the challenge of our lives,"[45] the Calsbeeks retired in September 1987 and moved to Sibley, Iowa, Harvey's hometown. The next year they were called back to Dulce, New Mexico, for a one-year interim assignment following the resignation of the Reverend Russell Dykehouse. Of their thirty-five years of ministry, the Calsbeeks spent twenty-two with Native American people. Harvey Calsbeek died of a stroke after heart surgery May 25, 1996, at the age of seventy. At this writing, Angeline Calsbeek continues to live in Sibley and is an active member of her church and community.

Communicant membership during the Calsbeek years hovered consistently between forty and forty-three, and Sunday school enrollment ranged from fifty to seventy. The major difference from the previous pastorates was a significant drop in reported inactive members, from about seventy down to about twenty. As was the case with all the Indian churches, irrespective of pastoral leadership, members were seldom dropped from the church rolls; they simply disappeared from the records.

Thurman (Happy) Cook

A significant personage in Macy during the last two decades of the twentieth century was Thurman Cook, almost always known by his nickname, "Happy." A full-blooded Omaha, Cook had for most of his first forty years lived a life dominated by alcohol. Then, in 1978, he and his wife were rescued from a burning car he had driven into a bridge. Calsbeek, newly arrived at Macy, called on him in the hospital and invited him not only to come to church but also to do some work around the building. A volunteer crew from New York was working at the time, and they asked him to eat lunch with them. Impressed with their kindness and with the unrelenting friendship of Calsbeek despite his alcoholic relapses, Cook began to volunteer his services and to drive the church van as well as attend church.

Cook underwent alcohol rehabilitation treatment at a Christian center in Woodstock, Minnesota. During that time he faced other difficulties as well—the death of his mother, several heart attacks, a four-bypass surgery, and the loss of his job. After a period of recuperation,

45. Letter from Harvey Calsbeek to Frank and Pat Love, Feb. 19, 1983.

Thurman ("Happy")
Cook

Calsbeek urged him to help with youth work and the alcohol counseling program. "We are looking forward," wrote Calsbeek in 1981, "to mutual blessing in this relationship and all it could mean for the Lord's work amongst the Omaha Indian people here."[46] Calsbeek's hopeful reference to "all it could mean for the Lord's work" turned out to be prophetic, as Cook's ministry at Macy continued throughout the next three pastorates—that of the Reverends John Helmus, Christine Dyke, and Earl Smith.

Cook made the transition from volunteer to paid staff in 1986 when Calsbeek and the consistory selected him to work as a pastoral assistant, and the Reformed Church General Program Council allotted funds to pay his stipend and expenses. Cook, who often repeated the phrase, "We feel good about that," when talking about the ministry, participated in Alcohol Anonymous meetings (a long-standing program held at the church), made home and hospital visits, led worship services, translated hymns into the Omaha language, and did custodial work at the church. He was also active in tribal matters, serving on several committees.

Cook, who had considerable artistic talent, also designed a logo for the church. Inside a triangle, representing the Trinity, are a heart (Christ's love for us and our love for each other), a cross (Christ's

46. Missionary letter from Harvey and Angeline Calsbeek, March 1981.

sacrifice), a peace pipe (peace between cultures), eagle feathers (strength that comes through faith), and a tepee.

Cook was in many respects a traditionalist. Among other things, he taught the Omaha language at the local community college and frequently used it in his ministry. He referred to God as *Wako^{n}da*, and to Jesus as *Wako^{n}da Zinga*, God's Son. When he prayed in church he prayed first in his own language for the sake of the elderly Omaha members. "They get a sense that God is there if I pray my language with them," he said. "And it makes me feel good to communicate with God for them. I really respect my traditional values and what we are as a people. I can relate to my people because I am one of them."[47]

After having lived for fifteen years together in a common-law relationship, Cook and his wife, Alvina, were married in 1989 at a morning worship service at the Macy church, with pastor Helmus officiating.

In 1988 Cook took another step forward by enrolling in the TEE (Theological Education by Extension) program at Charles Cook Theological College in Tempe, Arizona. In January of 1991 he was awarded a Lay Leadership Certificate from the school, the first person in the U.S. to graduate from this program. After a long history of heart problems, Cook died of heart failure April 2, 1999, at the age of sixty-one.

John and Elaine Helmus

The parsonage in Macy was empty for only two weeks after the retirement of the Calsbeeks. The Reverend John Helmus accepted a call from the Macy consistory, and he and his wife, Elaine, were appointed as missionaries October 15, 1987. Helmus's ruddy complexion and broad face prompted a question from the very first person he met in Macy—"Are you an Indian?"

Helmus had been born in the Netherlands. He immigrated to the United States at the age of nineteen; settled in Grand Rapids, Michigan; and took high school courses at night. He attended four colleges—Northwestern, Calvin, Hope, and the University of Vancouver—and graduated from Western Theological Seminary in 1960. He met his future wife, Elaine Hesselink, at Northwestern College. The Helmuses began their ministry in Calgary, Alberta, and continued it at several churches in South Dakota and Iowa.

47. Video interview with John Grooters, April 1995.

John and Elaine Helmus

Helmus's contributions in Macy included the introduction of the Children and Worship program, based on the book, *Young Children and Worship*, by Sonja Stewart and Jerome Berryman. In this approach to religious education, the teacher and the children sit in a circle on the floor, and the teacher moves unpainted wooden figures to help tell the Bible story and asks "wondering questions." Helmus believed this style of teaching to be more friendly to the circle-dominated Indian culture (emphasized by Black Elk) than sitting on chairs in a straight line and listening to a lecture. The Helmuses also began a soup kitchen in the space that had been used previously as a clothing store. They reported that an average of more than one hundred people—including adults and children—stopped in at the parsonage each month.

This was not a good time in the life of the tribe. One historian stated, "In 1990 the tribe's economic development plan unsentimentally reported that 'Family violence, child abuse, teenage suicide, and sexual abuse are increasing,' and noted that between 1984 and 1987 the Omaha's life expectancy actually fell, from fifty-eight to forty-eight years, two-thirds the state average."[48]

---

48. Fergus M. Bordewich, *Killing the White Man's Indian: Reinventing Native Americans at the End of the Twentieth Century* (New York: Doubleday, 1996), 169.

Footsteps Volunteers

During the Helmuses' time in Macy, Reformed Church Women launched Footsteps, a volunteer program that sent groups of women to various mission sites in the United States and elsewhere. Among these groups was an eleven-woman delegation that came to Macy in July 1988 from the New Hackensack Reformed Church in Wappingers Falls, New York. The group brought more than three thousand children's books they had secured from publishing houses, churches, libraries, schools, and bookstores. In Macy they indexed the books, painted bookcases, and set up a library of 2,765 books at the church. They contributed the remaining books to the Day Care Center in nearby Winnebago.

The occasion was not a one-way event. The evenings were spent in storytelling with Thurman Cook and with an introduction to "handgames," a traditional Indian pastime. Handgames, which are usually sponsored by a family in honor of a special occasion such as a birthday, consist of guessing contests between two teams who hide stones from each other in their hands. The Macy church also sent women to the Triennial Assemblies of Reformed Church Women, held every three years in various places around the country. In 1989, for instance, the church sent five women to the Triennial in Holland, Michigan.

Reported membership during the Helmus years (1987-92) slid gradually from thirty-eight to thirty, while the number of inactive members remained about fifteen. Sunday school enrollment dropped from seventy to about fifty. Reports of worship attendance were first required in 1988, and reported attendance hovered between forty and fifty for the next four years.

Christine Dyke, the First Woman Pastor

In 1993 the Macy church made history by installing the Reverend Christine Dyke, the first woman to be pastor of a Reformed Church Native American congregation. Dyke grew up in the Bethel Reformed Church in Harvey, Illinois, and graduated from Illinois Wesleyan University (with a B.S. in nursing) and New Brunswick Theological Seminary. It was, in several ways, a most unlikely match. Dyke was a young unmarried woman who had served her only previous assignment in the inner city—as an associate pastor at the Middle Collegiate Church in New York. "My first seven months have been a time of great discovery and great adjustment," she wrote in a letter of March 1994. "I catch

Christine Dyke

myself saving quarters for the bus, or forgetting that a subway does not run a few blocks from my home."[49]

Dyke came with a commitment to be culturally sensitive, and soon after she arrived she facilitated—by vote of the congregation—a name change for the church. Instead of the First Reformed Church of the Omaha Mission (people had asked, "Is there a second?"), the church was now called the Umo^{n}ho^n Reformed Church, after the name of the Omaha people in their own language. (The "^{n}" stands for an unpronounced nasal sound.)

The Macy church received some denominational attention in December 1994 when its pastor and several members provided Advent devotionals for the *Church Herald*. The authors were Dyke; Thurman Cook; Mary Jean Leinart, a member of the greater consistory; and Viola Walker, a deacon.

In other aspects of her ministry, Dyke added arts and crafts to the weekday children's program, revived the women's quilting

49. Letter from Christine Dyke to supporting churches, March 1994.

Christmas program in 1995

activities, and began to get involved in such community issues as public education. She and the Reverend David Crump, pastor in nearby Winnebago, spent ten days in El Salvador as observers in the election process there.

Culture shock proved to be a two-way street. Some of the older Indian women, who wore long billowing dresses, considered Dyke's skirts too short, and some members of the congregation found her social ideas too liberal.

On May 21, 1994, at a ceremony conducted at the Macy church, Dyke married Shelby Gragg, a graphics designer from New York City. At the end of February 1995, she and her new husband moved back to New York, where she served two churches in Brooklyn: Greenpoint (1996-2000) and Bay Ridge United (2000-). The couple later divorced. Communicant membership continued to slip during Dyke's two years at Macy, from thirty-one to twenty-five, although only an average of six people were listed as inactive. Worship attendance also showed a moderate decline, finishing at about thirty-five. Sunday school enrollment continued to hover in the mid-forties.

Earl and Sarah Smith

The parsonage in Macy was not vacant long. Dyke's resignation was effective March 1, 1995, and the Reverend Earl and Sarah Smith

Earl and Sarah Smith

moved in October 1. Folks in Macy had asked ex-Netherlander John Helmus if he was an Indian, but they had no clue that Earl Smith, with his reddish hair, hazel eyes, and light skin, was three-fourths Oneida, originally from Green Bay, Wisconsin.

The Smiths met in Minneapolis, Minnesota, where Earl was studying for a career in broadcasting and where Sarah, from Rock Valley, Iowa, was a lab technician. Through the influence of the Reverend George Muyskens, pastor of the Peace Reformed Church in Eagan, Minnesota, Earl made a Christian commitment. He studied for two years at New Brunswick Theological Seminary, served for two years as lay pastor at the Comanche Reformed Church in Lawton, Oklahoma, then went to Western Theological Seminary, from which he graduated in 1981. Before arriving in Macy, the Smiths served the Reformed Church in McKee, Kentucky, and two churches in London and Wainfleet, Ontario.

Rudy Seahmer

Rudy (Butch) Seahmer, a Comanche, came to the Umo^{n}ho^n Reformed Church in the summer of 1999 as a summer intern after graduating from Cook College and Theological School with an associate in arts degree. Seahmer, a member of the Comache Reformed Church in Lawton, Oklahoma, had planned to enroll in a seminary in the fall, but instead stayed on at Macy for two years. There his duties included youth ministries, working with Alcoholics Anonymous, preaching in the absence of the pastor, conducting Bible studies, and maintaining the property. Seahmer left in 2001 to do youth work in Nevada.

Present Ministry

As of this writing, the usual church programs continue in Macy. Smith conducts Bible studies at the local nursing home and jail. The church holds vacation Bible school each summer, and volunteer work groups continue to make trips to the Omaha reservation. The old-time camp meetings are a thing of the past, although a series of outdoor revival meetings were held in the summer of 2001, with Seahmer and Smith doing the speaking. Over the years, Christmas boxes have become fewer and fewer, but a few churches still send cash gifts. Cross-cultural visits in 2002 included five women from the Cherokee Nation in North Carolina and six Korean college students from Maryland.

Communicant membership now hovers in the twenties instead of the thirties, which is reflected in worship attendance. A few non-Indian families continue their active membership. The Sunday school has floundered, suffering from a lack of teachers. One of the church's faithful white members, Gerry Piere, retired in 2004 for health reasons after teaching the preschool class for more than fifty years. Another long-time white member, Cecil Leinart, died in 2004.

As in other Indian ministries, the church van has been an integral part of the ministry, and the Reformed Church's Mission Services division periodically launches a campaign for a new one. The van, often driven by the pastor, the pastor's wife, or a pastoral assistant, picks up children, youth, and adults for such events as Sunday school, youth group, midweek children's programs, and various women's and senior citizen's events.

Relationships with Northwestern College and Colton Congregation

The church in Macy has had a long relationship with Northwestern College in Orange City, Iowa, sixty-five miles to the northeast, as students have come to help with the Wednesday afternoon children's club and other activities. With the retirement of the Northwestern professor who sparked the program, Keith Hoskins, that relationship has come to an end.

The longest cross-cultural relationship of any two congregations in the Reformed Church in America is likely that of the First Reformed Church in Colton, South Dakota, and the Reformed church in Macy, Nebraska. It began in the summer of 1979 under the ministry of Robert Schut, then the pastor at Colton, and has continued ever since. Each summer, volunteers from the Colton congregation, and often from other Colton churches as well, conduct a vacation Bible school in Macy, with attendance ranging from eighty to one hundred. One young woman from Colton, Shelli Rentschler, began coming to Macy at the age of sixteen. Now in her thirties, she still comes to help every summer.

The Umo^{n}ho^n Reformed Church, the most recent of the six American Indian congregations, continues to struggle in a very small community where poverty is rampant and where the Native American Church is unusually strong. Yet the church's impact on its community, together with its cross-cultural, two-way learning experiences, continue to shape a legacy that far outweighs its statistical reports.

CHAPTER 10

The American Indian Council and the Native American Indian Ministries Council

When in June of 1969 James Forman, a black activist, occupied the Reformed Church in America offices at 475 Riverside Drive in New York City, he could not have known what he was setting in motion. His action initiated a series of events that eventually led not only to the founding of the Black Council (1971) but also the American Indian Council (1972), the Hispanic Council (1974), and eventually the Council for Pacific and Asian American Ministries (1980).

The Birth of the American Indian Council, 1972

Forman's "Black Manifesto" made angry demands, among other things, for millions of dollars and the creation of four publishing houses. The 1969 General Synod responded by allocating $100,000 in undesignated funds for use by the African-American members of the Reformed Church in America, a grant that led two years later to the formation of the Black Council. But this was an era not only of black power but also of red power, and the large unrestricted financial grant to one minority group did not sit well with American Indian leaders. Edward Cline, tribal chair of the Omahas in Macy, Nebraska; and Gordon Beaver, tribal chair of the Winnebagos in Winnebago, Nebraska—both of them also elders in their respective congregations—wrote a stinging "open letter" to the Reformed Church in America, which was published in the December 26, 1969, issue of the *Church Herald*.

The letter, entitled, "Is a Show of Red Power Next?" asked, "Is this the only way the church will listen to the requests of minority groups?" Citing such grievances as the long pastoral vacancy in Macy and the reduction of funds for Winnebago, the two men wrote, "Too long have we been silent and allowed great white fathers and mothers to determine our future and destiny. All we ask is that we be treated as human beings rather than puppets dangling on a string....If you want 'Red Power,' we can furnish it."[1]

Several leaders of the American Indian congregations met in 1970 to discuss the possible formation of what was called at that time an Indian Caucus. This fact was included in the 1971 report of the General Program Council, which in an obvious reference to the black civil rights movement said, "American Indian communities too are discovering that 'empowerment' can often be achieved only if a spirit of cooperation prevails among exploited peoples." Implying that the spirit of these meetings was not always sweetness and light, the General Program Council said that it "is interested in keeping the lines of communication open with our Indian brothers, and to accept the creative tensions which may be involved in such encounters."[2] The synod's review committee affirmed the "principle of participation by all peoples" but felt it necessary "to raise a question about continuing the formation of specific ethnic groups and what kind of explicit representation in the GPC should be achieved. We do not have an answer."[3]

The General Program Council appointed the Reverend Russell Redeker, secretary for church planning and development, to assist, and the Reverend John Hiemstra, mission administrator, gave additional help. The group met in February 1972, and by spring was ready to hold its organizational meeting. On April 6, 1972, representatives of all six of the American Indian congregations, as well as their pastors, met on the campus of Cook Christian Training School in Tempe, Arizona.

At this organizational meeting, the American Indian Council elected Leeds Soatikee, of Apache, Oklahoma, as its chairman. Soatikee, a Pima originally from Phoenix, Arizona, had been instrumental in keeping the Apache church alive for the many years while it had no full-time pastor. Elected vice-chair was the Reverend Jonah Washington, pastor of the Dulce congregation. The Reverend Wilbur De Cora,

1. Gordon C. Beaver and Edward L. Cline, "Is a Show of 'Red Power' Next? An Open Letter to the Reformed Church in America," *Church Herald*, Dec. 26, 1969, 12.
2. *Minutes of the General Synod*, 1971, 65.
3. Ibid., 76.

pastor in Winnebago, was elected secretary-treasurer; and the Reverend Robert Chaat, pastor of the Comanche church, was elected to chair the committee to draw up a constitution.

Leeds Soatikee's Personal Struggle

For Soatikee, participation in the founding of the Indian Caucus was a personal struggle. The first gatherings were far too militant for his taste, and he feared that the organization could become a seedbed for agitation rather than a center for positive spiritual growth. After the first meeting his wife said, "I'm not going there any more." Leeds shared her misgivings, but he ventured the opinion that their views ought to be represented. Some members, for instance, had argued that since the Indian churches were scattered among several classes of large non-Indian congregations, the Indian churches had little voice and should be gathered into their own classis. Others, like Soatikee and Chaat, argued that their classis had treated them with respect, and that Indians should not separate themselves from their non-Indian brothers and sisters.

Soatikee continued to express his hesitancy even after being elected to the chair. At the fall meeting following the group's organization in 1972, he offered to step down if the organization had trouble with his viewpoint. The idea of an American Indian Council, he said, struck a "discordant note somewhere in my system," and he expressed apprehension about any action that might "disrupt mine or my people's harmonious relationship with our God." He urged his fellow members to look forward rather than backward:

> We must have an organization that is free of grudges of past wrongs...knowing that injustice cannot be undone by this generation....To look backward is to stumble, so we must look ahead for a brighter tomorrow.

Soatikee called on lay people to take a more prominent role and asked clergy to assume the role of consultant or advisor. "Should you disagree with me," he concluded, "it is your prerogative to find another to replace me as chairman."[4]

Apparently the council as a whole had no problem with Soatikee's views, because at the next meeting, held April 26-29, 1973, at the

4. Leeds Soatikee, typewritten ms. of address to the American Indian Council, Nov. 30, 1972.

Apache Reformed Church, the council formally elected him chair. The council elected Betsy Wolfe of Macy as vice-chair, Mildred Cleghorn of Apache as recording secretary and treasurer, and Dorcie Kazhe of Mescalero as corresponding secretary. Wolfe and Cleghorn were also elected to represent the American Indian Council as delegates to the denomination-wide General Program Council. (Actually, only one delegate was allowed, and Cleghorn served as an at-large delegate for two terms, 1973-79, and later as a delegate representing the American Indian Council, 1985-91.) At the advice of Redeker, who continued as the staff advisor, the council identified fourteen goals. These fell roughly into categories to be studied by five committees: Communication, Evangelism, Functions, Education, and Christian Action.

The Council's Concerns as Seen in its Reports to the General Synod

A significant event took place at the council's meeting in October 1973, held at the Winnebago Reformed Church: the conferring of an honorary Doctor of Divinity degree on the Reverend Robert Chaat, long-time pastor of the Comanche Reformed Church in Lawton, Oklahoma, by Northwestern College. Participants in the festivities included Lars Granberg, president of the college, several RCA staff members, and local pastors.

Present for the first time at the 1974 council meeting was the Reverend Harold "Shorty" Brown, newly named secretary for parish life and American Indian ministries. The council's report to the General Synod the following year expressed thanks for Brown's appointment, stating that he has proven to be "stable and courageous far in excess of his physical stature," and describing him as "a true friend and an understanding advisor."[5] When Brown resigned in 1979 to assume a new church start in Federal Way, Washington, the council said, "Shorty has won our love, respect, trust, and confidence in knowing that the RCA is truly dedicated to its work with the American Indian."[6]

As time went on, several items reappeared in nearly every report of the American Indian Council, sometimes nearly word for word:

1. Emphasis on leadership development, almost exclusively mentioning the summer leadership conferences held for the most part at Ghost Ranch, a Presbyterian conference center in New Mexico. The leaders were primarily professors from Western, Calvin, and

5. *Minutes of the General Synod,* 1975, 72.
6. *Minutes of the General Synod,* 1979, 86.

All-Indian youth camp, 1998,
at the Winnebago Reformed church

Dubuque seminaries. The American Indian Council also encouraged its congregations to use teaching materials and other resources developed by Cook Christian Training School.

2. The continual need for American Indian pastors, of which there were none in the Reformed Church after 1975, and the fact that no Indian students in either college or seminary were specifically training for the ministry. It is important to have Indian pastors, said the council, because "Native American church leaders adjust more readily to the cultural needs of the people" and have "a better likelihood of establishing rapport with Indian people and winning their confidence."[7]

3. The annual all-Indian summer youth camps, held on a rotating schedule at the six American Indian churches, staffed by pastors and youth leaders of the Indian churches. The camps were revived in 1992 after having been held sporadically before that time.

4. Reasons why Indian youth have trouble attaining an education beyond high school: financial needs, inadequate academic preparation, and cultural differences.

7. *Minutes of the General Synod,* 1984, 86. Actually, two mixed-blood Indian pastors were serving in the Reformed Church at that time—the Reverend Nickolas Miles in Bloomington, New York, and the Reverend Earl Smith in Kentucky, Canada, and later in Macy, Nebraska.

Officers of the American Indian Council in 1982 and 1983.
Left to right: Leeds Soatikee, vice-chairman, Dorothy Tomah,
secretary, Kenneth Mallory, chairman, Mildred Cleghorn,
treasurer, and Richard Vander Voet, mission administrator

5. American Indian interns and lay leaders, usually unnamed,
serving Indian congregations.

6. Church members serving as tribal leaders and as delegates
to denominational boards, especially the General Program Council.
Frequent mention was made of Mildred Cleghorn in Apache and Wade
Miller in Macy. In later years, mention was made that some leaders
were giving top priority to tribal leadership rather than to church
leadership.

7. The ongoing need for self-determination, also called self-
development, which was defined as "training in skills and processes
which will help Native Americans to make their own decisions regarding
the most effective way of reaching their people and bringing them into
the fellowship of Christ."[8] The council further clarified the concept by
saying, "The greatest need is for confidence, a positive image, and self-
determination."[9]

Soatikee need not have worried about the council being excessively
militant. Conspicuously absent from its reports were references
to justice and civil rights issues or to current concerns such as the

8. *Minutes of the General Synod,* 1985, 209.
9. *Minutes of the General Synod,* 1986, 87.

Blackbird Bend lawsuits of the Omaha tribe in northeastern Nebraska. An exception came in 1982, when the council expressed concerns about President Reagan's deep cuts in the social and welfare programs of American Indians, citing, "Eighty percent of the jobs and opportunities on reservations are in one way or another federally related."[10] In 1986 the General Synod passed a bland resolution regarding the possible government breaking of treaties—but that motion came from the floor of synod rather than from the American Indian Council. In 1993 the council presented to the General Synod a recommendation "to encourage members of the Reformed Church in America to support the elimination of names of sports teams that are derogatory to Native American peoples." The motion was approved.[11] The Advisory Committee for Christian Action strengthened the recommendation with an additional recommendation that the Office of Social Witness provide materials on the subject for Reformed Church congregations.

After the resignation of Brown in 1979, the responsibility for liaison with the American Indian Council fell to the Reverend Richard Vander Voet, mission secretary for the Americas. Three years later, the Reverend Herman Luben, secretary for Christian discipleship, took over while Vander Voet continued his other responsibilities for North American mission work.

Staff Leadership

Until 1983, the American Indian Council had functioned without a staff person, relying instead on elected officers for leadership. In 1983 the council named the Reverend Roe Lewis of Phoenix, Arizona, as its executive, a one-fourth-time position. Lewis, born into a Christian family of the Pima-Papago tribe, had been named after the legendary Walter Roe, pioneer missionary in Oklahoma. Lewis had graduated from San Francisco Theological Seminary in San Anselmo, California, had served as a pastor with the Presbyterian Church U.S.A., and at age seventy was still teaching part-time at Cook Christian Training School in Tempe, Arizona.

In 1985 the American Indian Council, in its thirteenth year of existence, submitted its first recommendation to the General Synod—that the synod ask the denomination's seminaries to become members of the Native American Theological Association. The recommendation

10. *Minutes of the General Synod,* 1982, 84.
11. *Minutes of the General Synod,* 1993, 112.

Roe Lewis

was adopted, but the association went out of business three years later. In 1986 Lewis acted as a resource person for a group of eighteen non-Indians who took a tour of the Native American mission sites. The Reverend Wendell Karsen, who organized and led the tour, reported on the trip in an article, "The Dawn of a New Day," in the September 5, 1986 issue of the *Church Herald*.

In June 1988, several representatives of the American Indian community traveled to the Bronx, New York, to participate in the Reformed Church Rainbow Festival, held in conjunction with that year's General Synod. At that time the Office of Promotion and Communication produced a slide program, *Moving Toward Self-Reliance*, an overview of the Reformed Church's American Indian ministries, later reproduced in video format. In 1990 the council fine-tuned its goals, listing four:

1. Church leadership development (ordained pastors).
2. Leadership training for church officers and church members.
3. Involvement in the denomination and its judicatories.
4. Self-determination.

Kenneth Mallory

Roe Lewis died September 21, 1990, at the age of seventy-seven, following two brain surgeries. He had served for seven years as executive for the council. The following year Kenneth Mallory, an elder at the Winnebago Reformed Church, was hired for the part-time position of executive secretary. Mallory had spent many years as a child at the children's home in Winnebago, had served several terms as chair of the American Indian Council, and was the first (and only) member of the Reformed Church to be named as the council's executive.

In 1990 the Reformed Church initiated a series of responses to the upcoming 500th anniversary of Columbus's arrival in the western hemisphere. One may have expected the American Indian Council to be proactive and even strident, but this was not the case. It was, in fact, the Hispanic Council that submitted, on behalf of the four ethnic/racial councils, a resolution to the 1990 General Synod that the synod "proclaim 1992 as a year of reflection and repentance, standing in solidarity with the peoples of the Americas who have suffered the onslaught of colonialism, neocolonialism, and cultural imperialism; call to the church to confess its complicity in this suffering...and plan the 1992 synod festival around the theme of reflection and repentance."[12]

---

12. *Minutes of the General Synod,* 1990, 123.

The following year the American Indian Council made it clear
that its participation in the upcoming observance would emphasize
the positive:

> Let us understand the history, but let us seek understanding
> which enables us to live more fully as sisters and brothers today
> and tomorrow. Let us reflect on the past that we might understand
> our common history. Let us repent and seek reconciliation today,
> and as sisters and brothers seek openness and understanding of
> one another, and let us walk together in the future.[13]

In 1992, the year of the Columbus Quincentenary, the council
held its annual meeting in June in conjunction with the General Synod
meeting in Albany, New York. Ironically, the council failed to submit
a report to the General Synod that year. Also in 1992, the American
Indian Council elected its first woman to the chair, Tonia Keller of
Winnebago.

In 1994 the American Indian Council enlarged its scope
by accepting into membership the interdenominational urban
congregations in Omaha and Lincoln, Nebraska, of which the Reverend
Reaves Nahwooks was pastor. The Reformed Church, especially the
pastors and lay leaders in Macy and Winnebago, had helped establish
these congregations in the late 1980s.

Kenneth Mallory resigned his position in 1996, citing increased
leadership responsibilities with his tribe and stating that the council
was now ready for a new phase of its history.

One Hundredth Anniversary Celebration

At its annual meeting in June 1997, the General Synod of the
Reformed Church in America observed the one hundredth anniversary
of the Reformed Church's mission work among Native Americans.[14]
The various American Indian congregations set up displays adjacent
to the meeting hall on the Milwaukee campus of the University of
Wisconsin, and the synod set aside an evening for the observance. Nola
Aalberts, the Reformed Church staff person assigned to American
Indian ministries, introduced the program. This included the

13. *Minutes of the General Synod*, 1991, 113.
14. Actually, the celebration was two years late, the work having begun in 1895
    when the Woman's Executive Committee of Domestic Missions sent the
    Reverend Frank Hall Wright to Oklahoma.

Raymond Nauni, Jr., of the Comanche Reformed church,
addressing the 1997 General Synod

introduction of former missionaries, a tribute to Mildred Cleghorn of
Apache, a presentation to Kenneth Mallory, and greetings from all six
Native American congregations. Raymond Nauni, Jr., of the Comanche
church, addressed the synod on behalf of the council. Nauni quoted
extensively from an 1867 speech by a Comanche chief, describing how
their people had lost their land and their lives to the white settlers and
the government. Nauni then gave a brief history of Reformed Church
mission work among Indian peoples and concluded with a word of
appreciation to the denomination:

> We thank the Reformed Church in America for leading us to God
> through examples, words, deeds, love, and tolerance. Although we
> are in various stages of growth in the Native American churches,
> we know we are all one in the Spirit and all striving for the same
> goal—to follow the Jesus Road and be with one Lord and God in
> heaven.[15]

15. Raymond Nauni, typewritten ms., delivered to the General Synod of the
Reformed Church in America, Milwaukee, Wisconsin, June 17, 1997.

Transition and Uncertainty

During the closing years of the twentieth century, the American Indian Council was becoming more and more frustrated with the difficulty of defining its function and with its inability to implement positive change. Each year's minutes were very much like those of the year before.

The council's emphasis on recruiting Native American pastors was clearly not going anywhere. Members of Indian churches showed little interest in being appointed to the committees, councils, and agencies of the Reformed Church. Most of the conversations at council meetings centered on how to strengthen the ministry of local congregations. So the American Indian Council approached the General Synod Council and asked for help in redefining its function and perhaps restructuring the council itself. To oversee the transition, the American Indian Council employed the Reverend Reaves Nahwooks on a one-year contract (later extended by six months) as interim executive. Nahwooks, a Comanche-Kiowa, had recently retired as pastor of the Omaha and Lincoln urban ministries. Nahwooks began his assignment in November 1996.

The Reverend Kenneth Bradsell, director of policy, planning, and administration services, was appointed staff advisor. The council, with Bradsell's help, wrote a new *Constitution and Bylaws*, which was approved by the 1998 General Synod. The council changed its name to the Native American Indian Ministries Council, thus incorporating the more contemporary "Native American" while retaining the traditional "American Indian" and at the same time avoiding identification with the Native American Church. Instead of the unwieldy seventeen to twenty-three members, the new council has eight members—one from each of the six Native American churches and two pastors serving as nonvoting members.

The new constitution begins with this vision statement:

> The vision of the Native American Indian Ministries Council is to embrace and live in the spirit of our Lord, utilizing all our gifts for one another. The Native American Indian Ministries Council seeks to work with other cultures in North America and the world, giving testimony to God's grace and God's activity among us, and the making, teaching, and sustaining of disciples throughout the earth.[16]

16. *Minutes of the General Synod,* 1998, 300.

The Constitution goes on to say that the council "proclaims the gospel of Christ and seeks to empower RCA Native American ministries" and "seeks to strengthen the discipleship, fellowship, leadership, and stewardship of congregations, ministries, and individuals."[17] The following year the council summarized its organizational changes by saying that the former structure "had primary purposes of advocacy and ordained leadership development," and the new one is "a smaller structure whose primary focus is on mission, discipleship, and lay leadership development."[18]

Nahwook's term as interim executive concluded in September 1998. A new executive had not yet been hired, and leadership was needed, so the General Synod Council hired the Reverend George Montanari, pastor of the Apache church, as interim associate, under contract with Policy, Planning, and Administration Services. The General Synod Council also appointed a Native American Indian Ministries Council task force to study the needs of the congregations and to aid in the search for a new executive. The task force consisted of one member from each of the six Indian congregations, three members of the General Synod Council, and two pastors of the RCA's Indian congregations. Two candidates for the executive position were interviewed, but neither was interested in accepting a one-fourth-time position, and the General Synod Council was not interested in increasing the position to half time.

Needing Native American expertise, the task force contracted with the Reverend Stanley Jim, regional director of the Classis of Red Mesa for Christian Reformed Home Missions. Jim's assignment was to visit the six Indian congregations to determine their strengths and weaknesses. But Jim never completed his task and never submitted a report, so his services were terminated.

Montanari's term as interim associate expired in 2000 amid a fair amount of disagreement about the role of white versus Native American leadership in setting goals and vision for the reconstituted council. One view was that white leaders could and should do a better job of developing indigenous leaders within a council structure. The opposing view was that indigenous leadership and vision for Native American Indian ministries could and should develop at the initiative of the congregations.

17. Ibid.
18. *Minutes of the General Synod*, 1999, 81.

In the fall of 2002 the task force decided it was unable to complete the task as assigned. In response, the General Synod Council requested the General Synod Office, the Office for Ministry Services, and the Mission Services staff to "work cooperatively with RCA Native American Indian congregations to develop and implement plans for equipping the consistories and other church leaders of the RCA's Native American Indian congregations"[19] and that these offices work with the congregations to convene annual leadership training events.

The 2003 General Synod also passed a recommendation urging the General Synod Council to "explore possibilities for working with Comanche Reformed Church in Lawton, Oklahoma, in developing a new model for a ministry with the RCA's Native American Indian congregations."[20]

As of this writing, the Native American Indian Ministries Council is dormant, with no officers or meetings, and the annual leadership conferences and Indian youth camps have been suspended. The council has requested that its budget be used for leadership development and training in local congregations. The denominational mission staff states that it is ready to help with training events and programs at the initiative of local congregations.

19. *Minutes of the General Synod*, 2003, 111.
20. Ibid., 112.

Conclusion

A Ministry of Hope

It can be argued that, with the possible exception of mission work in the Middle East and Japan, the Reformed Church's ministry effort among Native Americans has been among its most difficult. The Indian culture of nonassertiveness, sharing, and cooperation run counter to the capitalistic culture of competition and accumulation. The goals of self-sufficiency and self-determination are largely unachieved. The image of Christianity as the white man's religion is still very much a reality. The long history of the dominant culture's injustice, greed, and paternalism still casts a pall over efforts to proclaim the gospel.

The intensity of the work, the investment of personnel, and the continuing financial costs, as compared to the statistically modest returns in terms of church membership and worship attendance, have prompted questions. Why do the pastors and other mission workers continue their labors? Why do the mission agencies and executives of the Reformed Church continue their involvement? Why do the congregations of the denomination continue to send volunteers and financial support?

One incident that took place in Winnebago in 1987 gives a partial answer. In that year, at the request of the tribal chair, a representative of Americans for Indian Opportunity, Georgetown University, conducted a nine-family pilot survey of Winnebago, with special consideration to the three most common killers in Indian communities—alcohol, diabetes, and suicide. Only one family in the survey was affiliated with

457

the Reformed Church. The person who made the survey paid a visit to Bernice Tegeler and told her some of the its findings. "All nine families," related Tegeler, "had made a similar statement—that amidst continual changes and hardships, the most stabilizing force in the community has been the Reformed Church."[1] One can only speculate about how many other congregations this can be said.

Whatever have been the shortcomings of its mission work among Native Americans, the Reformed Church in America has maintained it steadily and faithfully for more than a hundred years. When the Women's Board of Domestic Missions sent a missionary to Oklahoma, funded by mission teas, it took an extraordinary step of faith. While other Christian groups have given up and gone away, the Reformed Church has weathered storms of opposition and long dry spells of indifference. Despite lapses of understanding, the church's concern for the social, spiritual, and material welfare of the Indian people has been genuine, and its presence has been a consistent, dependable, compassionate, and steadying factor in American Indian communities. Despite the confusion of culture and faith, the first and foremost goal of Reformed Church mission work has been the proclamation of the good news of Jesus Christ. Reformed congregations have long maintained generous and steady financial support for the work. Those directly involved—pastors, spouses, and other mission workers—have displayed extraordinary courage, resiliency, and patience.

In the course of interviews with the pastors of American Indian congregations, a word that surfaces again and again is "hope." The Reverend Bill De Boer, pastor of the Jicarilla Apache Reformed Church in Dulce, New Mexico, summarized it this way: "Indian communities often have a very low level of hope. The gospel is the only source of hope that a lot of these people have—the only source of empowerment for their personal lives."[2] Into a society battered by centuries of abuse by the dominant culture, by alcohol, by poverty, by disillusionment, and by despair, the Reformed Church in America continues to bring—in word and action—a message of faith, hope, and love. The "Jesus Road," after all, is the only one that can lead to a new dawn of hope for the indigenous peoples of our hemisphere.

1. Bernice Tegeler, missionary letter, Advent 1987.
2. Video interview with Bill and Peggy De Boer by John Grooters of RCA Productions, 1995.

Pastors, Workers, Administrators, and Other Personnel of Native American Ministries

Native American Pastors Ordained by the Reformed Church in America

The Rev. Robert Chaat (Comanche)
Born: Robert Chahtinneyackque, Lawton, Oklahoma, September 6, 1900
Education:
    National Bible Institute, Philadelphia, 1922
    Cook Christian Training School, graduated 1924
Ordination: Classis of New York, 1934
Pastorate: Comanche Reformed Church, Lawton, Oklahoma: assistant, 1924-30; pastor, 1930-69; moderator, 1969-71
Died: October 7, 1992, Lawton, Oklahoma

The Rev. Wendell Chino (Apache)
Born: Mescalero, New Mexico, December 27, 1923
Education:
    Central College, 1945-46
    Cook Christian Training School, graduated 1948
    Western Theological Seminary, graduated 1951
Ordination: Classis of New York, 1951
Pastorate: Mescalero Reformed Church, Mescalero, New Mexico, 1951-55
Demitted: 1972
Other:
    Mescalero Tribal Chairperson, 1955-98
    President, National Congress of American Indians, two terms
Died: November 4, 1998, Santa Monica, California

The Rev. Wilbur De Cora (Winnebago)
Born: Winnebago, Nebraska, April 28, 1915
Education:
    Cook Christian Training School, 1953-54
    New Brunswick Theological Seminary, 1957-58
Ordination: Classis of West Sioux, 1958
Pastorates:
    Mescalero Reformed Church, Mescalero, New Mexico, assistant, 1955-57
    Winnebago Reformed Church, Winnebago, Nebraska, 1958-62
        (resigned, 1962; reordained 1970)
    Winnebago Reformed Church, 1970-75
Died: November 3, 1975, Winnebago, Nebraska

The Rev. Frank Love (Omaha)
Born: Arkansas City, Kansas, December 14, 1933
Education:
    Cook Christian Training School, 1958
    Hope College, graduated 1961
    Western Theological Seminary, graduated 1965
Ordination: Classis of California, 1965
Pastorates:
    Mescalero Reformed Church, Mescalero, New Mexico, 1965-68 (assistant)
    and 1968-69 (pastor)
    First Reformed Church of the Omaha Mission, Macy, Nebraska, 1969-71
Other:
    Staff positions with several American Indian agencies, 1971ff

The Rev. James Ottipoby (Comanche)
Born: October 26, 1900, Lawton, Oklahoma
Education:
    Central College, 1921-22
    Hope College, graduated 1925
    Western Theological Seminary, 1925-26
Ordination: Classis of New York, 1938
Pastorates:
    Winnebago Reformed Church, Winnebago, Nebraska, assistant, 1938-40
    Mescalero Reformed Church, Mescalero, New Mexico, assistant, 1940-43
Other:
    Military Chaplain, 1943-46
Dismissed: Presbyterian Church, 1946
Died: October 5, 1960, Albuquerque, New Mexico

The Rev. Jonah Washington (Pima)

Born: Mesa, Arizona, January 4, 1916
Education:
    New Mexico Highlands University, 1939-40
    Austin Presbyterian Seminary, graduated 1958
Ordination: Classis of West Central, 1958
Pastorates:
    Mescalero Reformed Church, Mescalero, New Mexico, assistant, 1946-51
    Apache Reformed Church, Apache, Oklahoma, 1958-59
    Jicarilla Apache Reformed Church, Dulce, New Mexico, 1968-72
Other:
    Director of the Religion Education Program, Chilocco Indian School,
    Chilocco, Oklahoma, 1959-68.
Died: 1987 Laveen, Arizona

Pastors and Mission Workers at Indian Mission Sites

(Note: Because many records are incomplete and sometimes contradictory, these lists are likely to contain inaccuracies and omissions.)

Reformed Church Mission and the Columbian Memorial Church, Colony, Oklahoma

Pastors:

The Rev. Frank Hall Wright, 1895-1922 (d.)

The Rev. Walter, 1897-13 (d.) and Mary Roe, 1897-1913

The Rev. Arthur Brokaw, (assoc.) 1904-05 (d.)

The Rev. L. L. Legters, (assoc.) 1906-07

The Rev. Richard and Ella Mae Harper, (assoc.)1907-09

The Rev. William and Mrs. Wauchop

The Rev. John Baxter (assoc.), 1910-13

The Rev. Henry and Mrs. Vruwink, 1913-17

The Rev. John Leighton and Betty Lou Read, 1917-23

The Rev. Peter and Henrietta Van Es, Jr., 1930-32

Mission Workers:

Wauton (interpreter), 1899
William Little Chief (interpreter), 1899
Mary Jensen, 1900
Mary Stewart, 1900
Reese and Mrs. Kincaide, 1904-32
Miss Ritter, 1904-12
Joel Littlebird, 1904
Ella Bolts, 1904
Johanna Meengs, 1906-10, 1919-27
Leah Kleman, 1906-07
William Fletcher, 1910-12
Miss Wilcox, 1911
Anna Berkenpas, 1911-12
Mr. and Mrs. Pikkart, 1913-14
Frank Hamilton (interpreter), 1914-20
Miss Felton, 1921
Charles and Mrs. Eggers, 1924
Charrles Sore Thumb (interpreter) 1927-29
Marie DeKeyser, 1928-30
Mrs. Al Van Brakle, 1929
Minnie Van Zoeren, 1929

Apache Mission at Fort Sill and the Apache Reformed Church, Apache, Oklahoma

Pastors:

The Rev. Frank Hall Wright and the Rev. Walter and Mary Roe helped with the Apache and Comanche missions (1899-1906) while serving in Colony, Oklahoma.

Mission Workers:

Maud Adkisson, 1899-1906
Miss Mosely, 1899
Anna Baty, 1900
Mary McMillan, 1900-06
Mary Ewing, 1901-13
Kate Hawkins, 1901-02
Jane Hawkins, 1903
Dr. George and Mrs. Baker, 1903
Miss Weddle, 1904

Miss Apsley, 1905-08
Miss Markley, 1904-13
J. P. and Laura McClurken, 1904
Hendrina Hospers, 1905-13
William Pulis, 1905-08
The Rev. C. H. Spaan, 1905-06
Roberta Ashley, 1905-08
Mary Moore, 1906-07
Joan Saunders, 1906-08

The Rev. L. L. and Maud (Adkisson) Clover Mahan, 1907-14
Legters, 1906-10 (served the Anna Heersma, 1908-1912
Comanche and Apache Martha Prince, 1909-1913
congregations) Anna Voss, 1909-13
James Kawaykla (interpreter), 1909-10
Hattie Hospers, 1909-11
Jennie Pikkart, 1912-13
The Rev. Henry Sluyter, 1911-13 William Pulis, 1908
(served the Comanche and
Apache congregations)
Church served 1914-58 part-time
by pastors of the Comanche
Reformed Church, the Revs.
James Dykema (1913-14), Harold Johns, 1956
Richard Harper (1915-23), John John Padocony, 1957
Read (1923-31) and Robert Chaat
(1931-58, 1960-62)
The Rev. Jonah and Edith
Washington, 1958-59
The Rev. Andy and Marjorie Ray and Jayne Hendricksma, 1968-69
Kamphuis, 1962-85 (Andy Wayne and Elizabeth Buteyn, 1970-71
ordained 1970) Aiko and Mrs. Jager, 1970-71
(many students during summers,
1974-87)
Linda Doane, summers 1974-82
Linda Rotman, 1975-82
The Rev. Carl and Kathy Gearhart, Darrell Dalman, 1987-90
1985-90 Steven and Cathleen Boint, 1988-89
John and Sylvia Peshlakai, 1989-90
The Rev. George and Mary Ann Bruce and Melanie Hole, 1991-92
Montanari, 1990-2002 Ellis and Theda Jefferson, 1992-94
The Rev. Janine Dekker (assoc.), Jill Floyd, 1999-2000
1999-2004 Herman and Joyce Van Galen, 2002

Comanche Mission and the
Comanche Reformed Church, Lawton, Oklahoma

Pastors:

The Rev. Frank Hall Wright and the Rev. Walter and Mary Roe helped with the Comanche and Apache missions 1899-1906 while serving at Colony, Oklahoma.

Leonard (L.L.) and Maud (Adkisson) Legters (Comanche and Apache congregations), 1906-10.

The Rev. Henry Sluyter (Comanche and Apache congregations), 1910-13)

The Rev. James Dykema, 1913-14

The Rev. Richard and Ella Mae Harper, 1915-23

The Rev. John Leighton and Betty Lou Read, 1923-31

The Rev. Robert and Elsie Chaat, 1931-69

John Pahdocony (interim), 1971-72

The Rev. Herman and Joyce Van Galen, 1973-78

Earl Smith (student pastor), 1978-80

The Rev. Gerald and Dorothy Dykstra, 1981-86

Robert Chaat, Jr., (interim), 1987-89

The Rev. Robert Graham (interim), 1989-93

The Rev. Charles and Judy Spencer (part-time contract), 1994-

Mission Workers:

(From 1895 to 1913 the mission teachers and community workers among the Chiricahua Apaches at Fort Sill also spent time evangelizing and teaching the Comanches who had settled nearby. See the Apache list of mission workers.)

Mescalero Mission and the
Mescalero Reformed Church, Mescalero, New Mexico

Pastors:

The Rev. E. B. and Mrs. Fincher, 1907-10

The Rev. Richard and Ella Mae Harper, 1910-15

The Rev. and Mrs. James Dykema, 1915-16

The Rev. James and Katherine Arthur, 1914-19 (White Tail)

The Rev. and Mrs. Norman Curtis, 1916-18

Mission Workers:

Solon Sombrero (interpreter), 1908-33

Martha Prince, 1913-14
Hendrina Hospers, 1913-14
Lucille Owens, 1914-15

Uncas Noche (interpreter), 1915-42
Edna Barncastle, 1916

The Rev. Nathan and Melissa
Overman, 1918-30

The Rev. and Mrs. John Mixon,
1930-32

The Rev. Peter and Henrietta Van Es,
Jr., 1932-44
The Rev. James and Lucille Ottipoby
(assist.), 1940-43
The Rev. Reuben and Bernice Ten
Haken, 1944-53

The Rev. Wendell and Patricia
Chino, 1951-55
The Rev. Harvey and Angeline
Calsbeek, 1954-62

The Rev. Robert and Joyce Zap,
1962-67
The Rev. Frank and Patricia Love,
1965-68
The Rev. Thomas and Mrs. Beech,
1970-74
The Rev. Roger and Adilee Bruggink,
1974-80
The Rev. Clarence and Helen Van
Heukelom, 1981-84

The Rev. Robert and Linda Schut,
1984-

The Rev. Herman and Joyce Van
Galen, 1996-99 (assist.)

Jennie Dubbink, 1917-24
Eugene Chihuahua (interpreter),
Melissa Hughes, 1920
Bessie Wood, summers of 1926, 27,
29
Nellie Ensing, summers of 1926, 27,
29
Robert and Elsie Chaat, 1929
Walter Scott (interpreter), 1932-53
Mary Broomhall, 1936-39

Elizabeth Bayer, 1941-45

Bernice Tegeler, 1944-51
Jonah and Edit Washington, 1946-
51, 54

Wilbur and Lupita De Cora, 1955-57
Earl and Mrs. Crum, 1955-57
Beverly Smits, 1957
Herman and Joyce Van Galen, 1957-68

Terry and Rachel Meekma, 1982-83
Harry and Judy Willemstyn, 1983-84
Stan and Cheryl Deelstra, 1985
Luke and Chris Schouten, 1985-86
Wayne Peterman, 1986-87
John and Elizabeth Maynard, 1988-89
Keith and Linda Burton, 1991-94
Bethany Graves, 1999-02
Bethany Buege, 2002-03
Janice Merino, 2004-

Jicarilla Apache Mission and the
Jicarilla Apache Reformed Church, Dulce, New Mexico

Pastors:
The Rev. J. Denton and Mary
Simms, 1914-36

Mission Workers:
Hendrina Hospers, 1914-1946
Regis Allentoyah (interpreter), 1915-16
Lacy and Mrs. Simms, 1919

Edna Van De Vrede, 1920-54
Kate Velier, 1921
Edna Regan, 1921
Henrietta Dulmes, 1921-22
Eugene and Mrs. Simms, 1921-25
Elizabeth Conners, 1922
Uncas (interpreter), 1922-23
Bertha Van Eldik, 1923
Anna Bach, 1923-26
Hendrena Webenga, 1923-26
Mary Gramleck, 1924
Nella Rylaarsdam, 1924-26
Jennnie Brinkman, 1924-26
Hattie Brinkman, 1924-27
Edward and Mrs. Duerksen, 1925
Hazel Sailda, 1925-29
Helen Dick, 1925-26
Alfred Velarde (interpreter), 1925-27
Garfield Veldarde (interpreter), dates
    uncertain
Henry Ladd "Buster" Vicenti
    (interpreter), dates uncertain
J. Theodora Alam, 1927
Tena Zandstra, 1927
Lillian Talk, 1927
Dena Nettings, 1927
Mrs. Alva Alvers, 1927
Naomi Ruyvalid, 1927
Ruth Norden, 1927-33
Albert and Marguerite Rymes, 1928-40
Tito Sisneros (interpreter), dates
    uncertain
Anna Lifferdink, 1928
Effie Baker, 1928-29
Minnie Roskins, 1929-30
Ruth Bird, 1929
Anna Boyenga, 1929
Marie Van Vuren, 1929-59
Ignacio Martinez (interpreter), 1929
William and Mrs. Clark, 1929
Luella Van't Kerkhoff, 1930-32
Jeanette Decker, 1930-33
Rachel Kolenbrander, 1930-34

Bernadine Vinkemuler, 1932-33
Minnie Richert, 1932-33
Bertha Bruining, 1933-34
James Lynch, 1934
Irene Boyaard, 1934-36
Caroline Ammerman, 1935-36
Katheryn Buteyn, 1935-36
Bessie Engelenhoven, 1935
Wilma Van Ommen, 1936-44

The Rev. John and Nina Keuning,
   1936-44

Dorothy Vermeer, 1935
Bernice Vedder, 1936-41
Gertrude Van Roekel, 1937-59
Alice Hesselink, 1937
Jay Pruis, 1937
Matilda Van Roekel, 1937-40
Harold and Henrietta Kraai, 1938-
   42, 1944-48
Robert Ladd Vicente, 1939
Theodore Bennick, 1942

The Rev. Herbert and Alberta Gee,
   1945-52

Jeanette Vander Ploeg, 1947-49
James and Inez Hassall, 1948-59
Murril Boskreil, 1951
Kay Mulder, 1952

The Rev. Harold and Dorothy
   Dykstra, 1953-56

Adrian Boombaars, 1954
Derwin and Edith Hesselink, 1956-61

The Rev. John and Helga Lucius,
   1957-61

William and Marion Hocking, 1961-68
Stuart and Joan Schouten, 1961-71

The Rev. Robert Robinson (interim),
   1961-62
The Rev. Harvey and Angeline
   Calsbeek, 1962-66
The Rev. Calvin and Janet Hays,
   1967-68

Robert and Dorothea Kampman,
   1967-77

The Rev. Jonah and Harriet
   Washington, 1968-72
The Rev. Russell and Genevieve
   Dykehouse, 1973-88

Derwin and Edith Hesselink, 1973-88
Robert and Bonnie Vander Schaaf,
   1982-85

The Rev. Harvey and Angeline
   Calsbeek, 1988

Jerry Jansma (Putting People in
   Mission volunteer), 1992

The Rev. John and Phyllis Bandt,
   1989-94

Duane and Carol Peterson, 1993-96

The Rev. William and Peggy De Boer,
   1994-

Ina Ramon Montoya, 1998-

Winnebago Mission and the
Winnebago Reformed Church, Winnebago, Nebraska

Pastors:

The Rev. Gustavus Adolf
Watermulder, 1908-42
Fanny (Verbeck) Watermulder,
1908-10
Hattie (Hospers) Watermulder,
1912-42

Mission Workers:

William and Mrs. De Bruyn, 1910-14

Nellie Van Zimmerman, 1910-13
Jean Baptiste (interpreter), 1910-12
Mr. Harris, 1912-?
Miss Muilenburg, 1912-?\?
Henry De Cora (interpreter), 1912-?
Frank Beaver (interpreter), 1913-14,
    1925-26
James and Katherine Arthur, 1913-14
Henry Thomas (interpreter), 1913-16
Grover Mallory (interpreter), 1915-
    17, 1919-20
Margaret Bradley, 1915-16
Harrison Tebo (interpreter), 1916
Margaret Van Donsellaer, 1917-20
Bertha DeJong, 1917-25
Bessie Veenschoten, 1917-20, 1922-26
Emeline Reed, 1918-26
Anna Van Der Werff, 1918-26
Antoinette DeLange, 1918
Lois Oldermeyer, 1918
George Smith (interpreter), 1918, 1925
Fanny Semeyn, 1919-21
Nellie Semeyn, 1919-21
The Rev. Robert and Mrs. McElwie,
    1919-20
Priscilla Harmelink, 1919-21
Gertrude Van Atterloo, 1920
Marquerite Craig, 1921
Ella Reardon, 1921
Elizabeth Bayer, 1922
Ruth Anderson, 1922-24
Dena Habink, 1923-24
Josephine Suydam, 1923-30
Mrs. John Alan, 1923-24
Marie DeKeyser, 1924-37
Louise Grether, 1924
Forest Alan, 1925
Anna Elenbaas, 1926, 1928-29, 1932-
    33, 1937
Hattie Venema, 1926-28

	Helen De Cora, 1926-28
	Levi Dupuis (interpreter), 1926-28
	Leonard Alam, 1926
	Martha Buxum, 1927
	Claudia Jensen, 1927
	Gertrude Bjerks, 1927
	Mollie Doran, 1928
	Henrietta Beyers, 1928
	Benjamin Horn (interpreter), 1928
	Henrietta (Kots) Kraai, 1929
	Elsie Johnson, 1929-33
The Rev. John and Mrs. Mixon (assist.) 1930	Miss J. Bobeldyke, 1930
The Rev. Timothy and Genevieve Cramer (assist.), 1930-32	Helen DeJong, 1930-33
	Marie Strover, 1931-35
	Alice Mallory, 1934-42
	Mrs. D. Leap, 1934-38, 1940
	Will Hunter, 1934
	Martha Timmerman, 1935-36
	Lucy Hunter, 1936
	Mr. and Mrs. Kennedy, 1936-42
	Edward Hatchett (interpreter), 1936
	Rose Lewis, 1936
	Ida Hoseth 1939-44
The Rev. James and Lucille Ottipoby (assist.), 1938-40	W. D. Carter, 1939
	Agnes Overold, 1939-42
	Janet Huizenga, 1946-57
	Suzan Leynse, 1947-51
The Rev. Gradus and Auriel Aalberts, 1942-58	Miss Rave, 1947, 1949
	Charles and Helen Whitebear, 1947
	Rachel Hiniman, 1947
	Bernice Tegeler, 1951-90
	Bernice Roos, 1950-51, 1954
	Margaret Meyer, 1951
	Betty DeRyde, 1952
	Janet Van Der Woude, 1952
	Alice Porter, 1953-61
	Edna Den Hartog, 1954
	Ben Walker, 1956-59
	Alvina Walker, 1956-59
	Clara Hardin, 1957-61
The Rev. Wilbur and Lupita De Cora, 1958-62	Andy and Marjorie Kamphuis, 1957-61
	Dorothy Kroontje, 1959
	Helen Zigmund, 1959
	Janet Maxam, 1962-66
	Harold and Mary Farmer, 1962-66
	Durand and Beatrice Gray, 1962-66

The Rev. Gradus and Auriel
Aalberts, 1964-70 (d.)

The Rev. Wilbur and Lupita
De Cora, 1970-75 (d.)
The Rev. Dirk and Linda Kramer,
1976-79
The Rev. Roger and Janet De Young,
1980-86
The Rev. David and Nancy Crump,
1987-94
The Rev. Darrell and Dawn Dalman,
1994-

Edward and Eleanor Van Gent,
1962-66
Arthur and Ann Sieplinga, 1966-72,
1979
Lloyd and Frieda Jurgens, 1967-68
Judy Kloostra, 1968
Everett Howaard, 1969
Matthew and Katie Boley, 1971

The Omaha Mission and the
Umonhon Reformed Church, Macy, Nebraska

Pastors
The Rev. George and Mildred Laug,
1934-43
The Rev. Peter and Henrietta Van Es,
Jr., 1944-52
The Rev. Harold and Dorothy
Dykstra, 1952-53
The Rev. John and Helga Lucius,
1953-57
The Rev. Ira and Mrs. Hesselink
(interim), 1957-58
The Rev. John and Maria Endert,
1958-60
The Rev. Reuben and Bernice
Ten Haken, 1960-66
The Rev. Frank and Patricia Love,
1969-71
The Rev. William and Cathleen
Vanden Berg, 1973-76
The Rev. Steven and Kay Farmer,
1976-78
The Rev. Harvey and Angeline
Calsbeek, 1978-87
The Rev. John and Elaine Helmus,
1987-92

The Rev. Christine Dyke, 1993-95
The Rev. Earl and Sarah Smith,
1995-

Mission Workers
Winnie Bouma, 1942-47

Elizabeth Boyer, 1945

Mary Huff, 1948-49
Wendell Chino, 1951
Edward and Eleanor Van Gent,
1956-62

Lynn and Karen Jurgens, 1962-69

Robert and Linda Schut, 1972-74

Andrew Hoolsema, 1983-84
Joan Lankamp, 1984-85
Thurman Cook, 1986-99 (d.)
Douglas Leonard, 1991-92 (AIM),
1992-93
Carl and Jean Idema, various times
Rudy (Butch) Seahmer, 1999-2001

Supervising Boards of Reformed Church Mission Work in North America

Woman's Executive Committee of Domestic Missions, 1883-96
Women's Executive Committee of the Board of Domestic Missions, 1896-1909
Women's Board of Domestic Missions, 1909-51
Board of Domestic Missions, 1951-60
Board of North American Missions, 1960-68
World Mission Division of the General Program Council, 1968-93
Mission Services of the General Synod Council, 1993-

Administrators of American Indian Ministries

The Rev. Walter Roe, part-time superintendent of Indian missions, 1905-1913
The Rev. G. A. Watermulder, part-time "advisory and consultative services," 1914-42
Beth Marcus, executive secretary of the Board of Domestic/North American Missions, 1953-68
The Rev. Albert Van Dyke, director of Indian work for the Board of North American Missions, 1967-70
The Rev. John Hiemstra, secretary for North American ministries, 1969-72
The Rev. Harold "Shorty" Brown, area secretary for American Indian ministries (with other responsibilities), 1972-79
The Rev. Richard Vander Voet, secretary for the Americas, 1980-92
The Rev. Robert Terwilliger, supervisor of Native American Indian mission churches (with other responsibilities), 1993-1996
Nola Aalberts, supervisor of Native American Indian ministries (with other responsibilities), 1996-2001
The Rev. Roger De Young, supervisor of Native American Indian ministries (with other responsibilities), 2001-

Executives of the American Indian Council

The Rev. Roe Lewis, 1983-90 (d)
Kenneth Malory, 1991-96
The Rev. Reaves Nahwooks (contract), 1996-98

Executive Committees of the American Indian Council and the Native American Indian Ministries Council

(As reported to the General Synod in the years indicated)

Pre-organization Meeting Officers (1972):
Leeds Soatikee, chair
The Rev. Jonah Washington, vice-chair
The Rev. Wilbur De Cora, secretary-treasurer
The Rev. Robert Chaat, chair of Constitution Committee

1973, 1974:
    Leeds Soatikee, chair
    Betsy Wolfe, vice-chair
    Mildred Cleghorn, recording secretary
    Dorcie Kazhe, corresponding secretary

1975, 1976, 1977 (entire council listed):

Leonard Atole	Wade Miller
Anna Baltazan	Rose Nauni
Mildred Cleghorn	Alice Porter
Geneva Ewing	Leeds Soatikee
Berle Kanseah	Dorothy Tomah
Dorcie Kazhe	Betsy Wolfe

1978:

Leonard Atole	Wade Miller
Anna Baltazan	Rose Nauni
Geneve Ewing	Leeds Soatikee
Berle Kanseah	Dorothy Tomah
Dorcie Kazhe	Betsy Wolfe
Kenneth Mallory, chair	

1979, 1980, 1981:
    Kenneth Mallory, chair
    Betsy Wolfe, vice-chair
    Dorothy Tomah, secretary
    Mildred Cleghorn, treasurer

1982, 1983:
    Kenneth Mallory, chair
    Leeds Soatikee, vice-chair
    Dorothy Tomah, secretary
    Mildred Cleghorn, treasurer

1984, 1985:
    Kenneth Mallory, chair
    Leeds Soatikee, secretary
    Dorothy Tomah, secretary
    Mildred Cleghorn, treasurer
    The Rev. Robert Chaat

1986:
    Kenneth Mallory, chair
    Dorothy Tomah, secretary
    Mildred Cleghorn, treasurer
    Tonia Keller
    Norman Nauni, Jr.

1987, 1988, 1989:
Kenneth Mallory, chair
Dorothy Tomah, secretary
Mildred Cleghorn, treasurer
Tonia Keller
The Rev. Robert Chaat

1990:
Kenneth Mallory, chair
The Rev. Robert Chaat
Mildred Cleghorn
Tonia Keller
Norman Nauni, Jr.
Dorothy Tomah

1991:
George Klinekole, chair
Wanda Lewis
Kenneth Mallory
Judy Manwell
Norman Nauni, Jr.

1992, 1993:
Tonia Keller, chair
Thurman Cook
Wanda Lewis
Judy Manwell

1994:
Tonia Keller, chair
Thurman Cook
Tommy Johnson, treasurer
Judy Manwell

1995, 1996:
Thurman Cook, chair
Tonia Keller
Lynette Kanseah
Katherine Lovejoy

1997:
Raymond Nauni, Jr., chair
Tonia Keller
Lynette Kanseah
Katherine Lovejoy

1998:
Raymond Nauni, Jr. chair
Regina Brannock
Lynette Kanseah

1999:
Carl Buurma, chair
Ina Ramon, secretary

2000:
Esa Attocknie, vice-chair
Carl Buurma
Tonia Keller
Bernice Mast
Charlie Poafpbitty
Ina Ramon, secretary

2001, 2002, 2003:
Esa Attocknie, chair
Nancy Gillis
Ina Montoya, secretary
Marvin Yuzos, vice-chair

Native Americans Serving Denominational Agencies

General Program Council:

Mildred Cleghorn
 At-Large, 1973-76
 Representing the American Indian Council, 1976-79
Wilma Phone
 At-large, 1974-77
Dorothy Tomah
 Representing the American Indian Council, 1980-82, 1982-85
Mildred Cleghorn
 Representing the American Indian Council, 1985-88, 1988-91
Tonia Keller
 Representing the American Indian Council, 1991-94, 1994-96
Arvilla Craig
 At-Large, 1993-96
Regina Brannock
 At-Large, 1996-99, 1999-2002
Esa Attocknie
 Representing the Native American Indian Ministries Council, 2000-2003

Editorial Council of the Church Herald:
Mary Polanco, 1985-88, 1988-91 (second term on Executive Committee)
 Representing the Synod of the West/Far West

Women's Ministries Restructure Conference
   Regina Brannock, 1999

Missionary Pastors and Educators with Ten or More Years of Service (as of 2005)

Total Years Name, Place, Dates

38   The Rev. Robert and Elsie Chaat, Comanche, 1931-69

38   The Rev. G. A. Watermulder, Winnebago, 1908-42; Cook School, 1942- 46 (d). [wives Fanny, 1908-10 (d), and Hattie, 1912-42]

30   The Rev. John and Helga Lucius, Macy, 1953-57; Dulce, 1957-61; Cook School, 1961-83

28   The Rev. Gradus and Auriel Aalberts, Winnebago, 1942-58; Minneapolis, 1958-64; Winnebago, 1964-70 (d)

27   The Rev. Frank Hall and Addie Wright, itinerant evangelist, 1895-1922 (d)

23   The Rev. Andy and Marjorie Kamphuis, Apache, 1962-85

22   J. Denton and Mary Simms, Dulce, 1914-36

22   The Rev. Harvey and Angeline Calsbeek, Mescalero, 1954-62; Dulce, 1962-66; Macy, 1978-87; Dulce, 1988

22   The Rev. Peter and Henrietta Van Es, Colony, 1930-32; Mescalero, 1932-44; Macy, 1944-52

21 (cont.) The Rev. Robert and Linda Schut, Mescalero, 1984-present

20   The Rev. Harry and Luella Van't Kerkhoff, Cook School, 1949-69

18   The Rev. Reuben and Bernice Ten Haken, Mescalero, 1944-53, Macy, 1960-55; Los Angeles, 1957-60

16   The Rev. Walter and Mary Roe, Colony, 1897-1913 (d)

16   The Rev. Richard and Ella Mae Harper, Colony, 1907-09; Mescalero, 1910-15; Comanche, 1915-23

15   The Rev. Russell and Genevieve Dykehouse, Dulce, 1973-88

14   The Rev. Jonah and Harriet Washington, Apache, 1958-59; Dulce, 1968-72; Chilocco School, 1959-68

14   The Rev. John Leighton and Betty Lou Read, Colony, 1917-23, 1923-31

12   The Rev. George and Mary Ann Montanari, Apache, 1990-2002

11 (cont.) The Rev. William and Peggy DeBoer, Dulce, 1994-present

11 (cont.) The Rev. Charles and Judy Spencer, Comanche, 1994-present (part-time)

11 (cont.) The Rev. Darrell and Dawn (1994-2003) Dalman, Winnebago, 1994-present

Mission Workers with Ten or More Years of Service (as of 2005)

Years	Names, Places, Dates
46	Bernice Tegeler, Mescalero, 1944-51; Winnebago, 1951-90
41	Hendrina Hospers, Apache, 1905-13; Mescalero, 1013-14; Dulce, 1914-46
34	Edna Van DeVrede, Dulce, 1920-55
30	Marie Van Vuren, Dulce, 1929-59
28	Reese and Mrs. Kincade, Colony, 1904-32
27	Uncas Noche, Mescalero (interpreter), 1915-42
22	Gertrude Van Roekel, Dulce, 1937-59
20	William and Marion Hocking, Dulce, 1961-68; Cook School, 1968-81
19	Walter Scott, Mescalero (interpreter, 1932-53)
14	Johanna Meengs, Colony, 1906-10, 1919-27
13	Marie DeKeyser, Winnebago, 1924-37
13	Thurman Cook, Macy, 1986-99 (d)
12	Mary Ewing, Apache, 1901-13
12	Albert and Marguerite Rymes, Dulce, 1928-40
11	James and Inez Hassall, Dulce, 1948-59
11	Janet Huizenga, Winnebago, 1946-57
11	Bill and Peggy DeBoer, Cook School, 1971-82
11	Herman and Joyce Van Galen, Mescalero, 1957-68
10	Stuart and Joan Schouten, Dulce, 1961-71
10	Robert and Dorthea Kampman, Dulce, 1967-77
10	Edward and Eleanor Van Gent, Macy, 1956-62; Winnebago, 1962-66
10	Derwin and Edith Hesselink, Dulce, 1956-61, 1978-83

Partial List of New Brunswick (NBTS) and Western Theological Seminary (WTS) Students Who Served Summer Assignments in Native American Congregations

Umo^{n}ho^n Reformed Church, Macy, Nebraska
Robert H. Schuller, WTS, 1947
John Hiemstra, NBTS, 1954
Joseph Muyskens, WTS, 1955
Donald Baird, NBTS, 1956
Wilbur Daniels, WTS, 1957
Roger Leonard, NBTS, 1958
Ervin Roorda, WTS, 1959
Wayne Joosse, WTS, 1963
Vernon Sterk, WTS, 1966
Robert Schut, NBTS, 1972

Winnebago Reformed Church, Winnebago, Nebraska
Joseph Sizoo, NBTS, 1909
John Van Strien, NBTS, 1914
Joshua Hogenboom, WTS, 1927
Alvin Neevel, WTS, 1929
Gradus C. Aalberts, WTS, 1938
James Vos, WTS, 1946
Wilbur Brandi, NBTS, 1947, 1948
John Mongin, NBTS, 1956, 1957
Arthur Hielkema, WTS, 1958
Brenda Snowball, Dubuque TS, 2000, 2001

Mescalero Reformed Church, Mescalero, New Mexico
David Laman (also at Dulce), WTS, 1937
Harvey Calsbeek, WTS, 1952
Wilmer Vermeer, WTS, 1958
Corstain and Bethany DeVos, WTS, 2003

Jicarilla Apache Reformed Church, Dulce, New Mexico
John G. Gebhard, Jr., NBTS, 1919
David Laman (also at Mescalero), WTS, 1937
Arnold Van Lummel, WTS, 1944
John Janssen, WTS, 1946
Ray Rewerts, WTS, 1949
Donald Lam, WTS, 1950
Norman Van Hoekelom, WTS, 1951
James Dunham, NBTS, 1952
Henry Stegenga, WTS, 1958
William Cameron, NBTS, 1958
Norman Swier, WTS, 1976
Jeffrey Neevel, WTS, 1991

Comanche Reformed Church, Lawton, Oklahoma
Bradley Folensbee, Princeton Seminary, 1916
John Kempers, WTS, 1923

Index

Note: Most individual churches are listed under their location

The Historical Series
of the
Reformed Church in America
Books in print, William B. Eerdmans, publisher

Dorothy F. Van Ess
Pioneers in the Arab World

James W. Van Hoeven, editor
Piety and Patriotism

Mildred W. Schuppert
Digest and Index of the Minutes of General Synod, 1958-1977

Mildred W. Schuppert
Digest and Index of the Minutes of General Synod, 1906-1957

Gerald F. De Jong
From Strength to Strength

D. Ivan Dykstra
"B. D."

John W. Beardslee III, editor
Vision From the Hill

Howard G. Hageman
Two Centuries Plus

Marvin D. Hoff
Structures for Mission

James I. Cook, editor
The Church Speaks: Papers of the Commission on Theology of the Reformed Church in America, 1959-1984

James W. Van Hoeven, editor
Word and World

Gerrit J. tenZythoff
Sources of Secession: The Netherlands Hervormde Kerk on the Eve of the Dutch Immigration to the Midwest

Gordon J. Van Wylen
Vision for a Christian College

Jack D. Klunder and Russell L. Gasero, editors
Servant Gladly

Jeanette Boersma
Grace in the Gulf

Arie R. Brouwer
Ecumenical Testimony

Gerald F. De Jong
The Reformed Church in China, 1842-1951

Russell L. Gasero
Historical Directory of the Reformed Church in America, 1628-1992

Daniel J. Meeter
Meeting Each Other in Doctrine, Liturgy, and Government

Allan J. Janssen
Gathered at Albany

Elton J. Bruins
The Americanization of a Congregation, 2nd ed., by Elton J. Bruins (1995)

Gregg A. Mast
In Remembrance and Hope: The Ministry and Vision of Howard G. Hageman

Janny Venema, translator & editor
Deacons' Accounts, 1652-1674, First Dutch Reformed Church of Beverwyck/ Albany

Morrill F. Swart
The Call of Africa

Lewis R. Scudder III
The Arabian Mission's Story: In Search of Abraham's Other Son

Renée S. House and John W. Coakley, editors
Patterns and Portraits: Women in the History of the Reformed Church in America

Elton J. Bruins & Robert P. Swierenga
Family Quarrels in the Dutch Reformed Churches in the Nineteenth Century

Allan J. Janssen
Constitutional Theology: Notes on the Book of Church Order of the Reformed Church In America

Gregg A. Mast, editor
Raising the Dead: Sermons of Howard G. Hageman

James Hart Brumm, editor
Equipping the Saints: The Synod of New York, 1800-2000

Joel R. Beeke, editor
Forerunner of the Great Awakening

Russell L. Gasero
Historical Directory of the Reformed Church in America, 1628-2000

Eugene Heideman
From Mission to Church: The Reformed Church in America in India

Harry Boonstra
Our School: Calvin College and the Christian Reformed Church

James I. Cook, editor
The Church Speaks, Vol. 2: *Papers of the Commission on Theology of the Reformed Church in America, 1985-2000*

John W. Coakley
Concord Makes Strength

Robert P. Swierenga
Dutch Chicago: A History of the Hollanders in the Windy City

Paul L. Armerding
Doctors for the Kingdom, The Work of the American Mission Hospitals in the Kingdom of Saudi Arabia

Donald J. Bruggink & Kim N. Baker
By Grace Alone, Stories of the Reformed Church in America

June Potter Durkee
Travels of an American Girl

Mary L. Kansfield
Letters to Hazel, Ministry Within the Women's Board of Foreign Missions of the Reformed Church in America

Johan Stellingwerf, Robert P. Swierenga, ed.
Iowa Letters, Dutch Immigrants on the American Frontier

Robert P. Swierenga
Elim: A Chicago Christian School and Life-Training Center for the Disabled